AF600563

THE CATHOLIC UNIVERSITY OF AMERICA
CANON LAW STUDIES
No. 141

THE PRINCIPLES OF AUTHENTIC INTERPRETATION IN CANON 17 OF THE CODE OF CANON LAW

A Commentary

A DISSERTATION

Submitted to the Faculty of Canon Law of the Catholic University of America in Partial Fulfillment of the Requirements for the Degree of

DOCTOR IN CANON LAW

BY

JOHN ROGG SCHMIDT, A.B., J.C.L.
Priest of the Diocese of Amarillo

THE CATHOLIC UNIVERSITY OF AMERICA PRESS

WASHINGTON, D. C.

1941

Nihil Obstat:

EDUARDUS ROELKER, S.T.D., J.C.D.

Censor Deputatus.

Imprimatur:

FRANCISCUS J. POKLUDA

Vicarius Capitularis Amarillensis 31 Maii, 1941.

Copyright 1941, by

THE CATHOLIC UNIVERSITY OF AMERICA PRESS

Printed by

THE RIVERSIDE PRESS, OF ATHENS, PENNA.

TO

MY MOTHER AND FATHER

TABLE OF CONTENTS

CHAPTER IV.

CHAPTER V.

CHAPTER VI.

CHAPTER VII.

CHAPTER VIII.

INTRODUCTION

The purpose of this study is to present in the form of a commentary to canon 17 of the Code of Canon Law the application of the principles of authentic interpretation contained in that canon. In order to execute this purpose these principles were first traced chronologically, in order to ascertain their historical sequence and coherence. The result was submitted in partial fulfillment of the requirements for the degree of licentiate in Canon Law. This plan still appears in part especially in Chapter II of the present study and also in other portions thereof. The findings represented in this general scheme were converted into the present commentary, to which more material was added from the same and connected sources. The study proceeds, after a brief introductory article on Justinian Law, upon the general order of canon 17.

Omitted from the present work is a substantial investigation into the notion of interpretation during the period of the Roman Republic. Only the bibliography has been retained. Likewise, the results of previous research into the question of authentic interpretation by judicial sentence and rescript, being more or less of a purely historical character, have been considerably reduced in this presentation. The sources were very carefully investigated and followed in whatever direction they led, and their doctrines are here rendered as they appeared to the writer.

The notion of authentic interpretation presents a compound idea; on the one hand that of "authentic", and on the other that of "interpretation". The study as such will not begin with a definition. The meaning of authentic interpretation is presented to the reader as the writer found it. However, before entering upon a detailed investigation of this question, it seems useful to introduce in a general way the ideas which will be dealt with in one or other section of this study.

Etymologically, the term *interpretari,* to interpret, is a compound word regarding the component parts of which there does not seem to be agreement among the scholars. Yet in its strict meaning *interpretari* signifies to act the part of an intermediary, to explain, expound.[1] Thus Cicero speaks of augurs and astrologers as interpreting the phenomena of nature as portents of future happenings.[2] He says also, "Fuisse in civitate nostra viros qui id [ius civile] interpretari populo et responsitare soliti sint", referring to the Roman lawyers.[3]

A survey of Roman law reveals a quadruple division of interpretation: legislative,[4] judicial,[5] customary,[6] and doctrinal.[7] The glossators of the *Decretum* of Gratian (+before 1160) and of the Decretals and earlier decretalists also set forth these four species of interpretation.[8] Later decretalists and commentators also recognize the four-fold division. Suarez (+1617) admits only a threefold partition, wherein he allocates the interpretation of the judge to the category of customary interpretation.[9]

The doctrine of this quadruple division of interpretation is set down by the glossator to *"Ad haec"*, a law in the Gregorian Decretals.[10] Legislative interpretation, which is

---

1 Forcellini, *Lexicon Totius Latinitatis,* (Patavii, 1864), s. v. Interpres, *Interpretari.*

2 *De Divinatione,* (Lipsiae, 1905), I, 6.

3 *De Legibus,* (Lipsiae, 1905), I, 4, 14.

4 C. (1, 14) 1; 12; D. (1, 4) 1.

5 *Glossa,* D. (1, 3) 37.

6 D. (1, 3) 37; 38.

7 C. (12, 15).

8 Cf. Henricus Boich, Commentary to c. 31, X, *de sententia excommunicationis,* V, 39; Abbas Panormitanus, Commentary to c. 1, *de postulatione praelatorum,* I, 5; *Summae Sylvestrinae,* (Venetiis, 1601), s. v. *Interpretatio.*

9 *De Legibus,* (Parisiis, 1856), VI, cap. 1, 1.

10 *Glossa* ad v. *Interpretatus,* c. 1, X, *de postulatione praelatorum,* I, 5.

that of the "princeps", the head of a perfect society, is called "generalis et necessaria". Interpretation by custom is also "generalis et necessaria", but is not committed to writing, which is a requirement in legislative interpretation. By legistive is here meant statutory. That of the judge is termed "non generalis, sed necessaria" and must also appear in writing, since it is represented in the judicial sentence, which must be in writing. Finally there is the interpretation of the doctor, which in the scale of immediate legislative value is secondary; it is styled "nec generalis, nec necessaria, nec redigenda in scriptis". However, the interpretation of the legal expert does have great influence in the forming of law.

In presenting the commentary the writer has advisedly made frequent verbal quotations in order to permit the reader to review the material which has been used in this study. This statement is true especially of the material taken from the editions of the primary legal sources which contain the glossaries and from the folio editions of the old commentators on civil and canon law.

In the use of commentators on pre-Code legislation those principally have been employed in the text who reflect the juristic thought of their era. Though it would, indeed, be very useful to introduce the reader by way of footnote to each eminent jurist whose teaching is proposed, the writer begs leave to confine his remarks to an appreciation of the *Glossa Ordinaria,* or simply, *Glossa,* which represents the marginal annotations to the laws in the *Corpus Iuris Canonici* and the *Corpus Iuris Civilis.*

Accordingly, Reiffenstuel (+1703) declares, citing Bartolus a Saxoferrato (+1357), a civilist, Baldus de Ubaldis (+1400), a civilist and decretalist, Felinus Sandaeus (+1503), a decretalist, Iason de Mayno (+circa 1507), a civilist, all eminent jurists, that the authority of the Gloss in the *Corpus Iuris Canonici* is greater than that of any author, so that in causes of great moment one may not depart from its teaching. Hence, he closes, the opinion of the Gloss has been called the idol of advocates. Its interpretation, however, is not authentic.[11] Regarding the *Glossa* of the *Corpus Iuris Civilis,* which was compiled by the great romanist, Accursius (+1260), "For over a half century," says Sherman, "the 'Great Gloss' of Accursius obtained an authority greater than the Roman texts themselves".[12]

The writer wishes to take this opportunity to express his most sincere and hearty thanks to His Excellency, the Most Reverend Robert E. Lucey, S. T. D., LL. D., Archbishop of San Antonio, former Bishop of Amarillo, Texas, to His Eminence, Dennis Cardinal Dougherty, Archbishop of Philadelphia, to His Excellency, the Most Reverend Joseph M. Corrigan, S. T. D., LL. D., Litt. D., D. S. Sc., Titular Bishop of Bilta, Rector Magnificus, and the Faculty of the School of Canon Law of the Catholic University of America, to the Very Reverend Newton T. Miller, J. C. D., of the Archdiocese of Philadelphia and Chancellor of the Diocese of Amarillo, and to all others who have so kindly aided the author in his studies in the field of Canon Law.

[11] *Ius Canonicum Universum,* (ed. novissima, 1831-1833), *Prooemium,* nn. 146-147.

[12] *Roman Law in the Modern World,* (2 ed., New York: Baker, Voorhis & Co., 1924), I, sec. 213; "Seinen grossen Ruf und Einfluss aber verdankt Accursius keiner eigenen Schrift, sondern der grossen Sammlung von Glossen seiner Vorganger und Zeitgenossen, welche unter dem Namen *Glossa* schlechthin, oder auch *Glossa Ordinaria,* bekannt ist."—Savigny, *Geschichte des Romischen Rechts im Mittelalter,* (Heidelberg, 1829), V, 252-253.

CHAPTER I.

Notion of Authentic Interpretation in Roman (Justinian) Law.

Introduction.

This chapter will treat the notion of authentic interpretation in Justinian law. It has been found necessary and convenient to present the doctrine of canonists and civilists, as it were in parallel, in dealing with this subject in Canon law, because these jurists share in common both their primary legal sources, legislative enactments, as well as the doctrines of their predecessors in either field of Roman and Canon law. This chapter, however, will offer, rather by way of introduction a brief conspectus of the chief legislative enactments in Roman law which bear out the notion of authentic interpretation. The burden of this subject will be dealt with in the remaining portions of this study. The legal enactments introduced here will recur time and again in the several chapters to follow to illustrate some point of law.

ARTICLE I. *The Lex "Inter Aequitatem".*

In the Codex of Justinian in the law *"Inter aequitatem"* is enunciated the principle that when a question is to be settled by the rules of law and equity, the emperor alone can decide by rendering the proper interpretation.[1] This passage is to be understood that when there arises a doubt as to whether a legal provision is equitable recourse must be had to the emperor.[2] In this law *interpretatio* is used in the sense of correction, whereby the rigor of the law is mitigated by the benign influence of equity. The glossator gives an example of the corrective influence of equity upon *ius strictum* in a law of the Digest *"Qui operas"*,[3] a case where unwritten equity modifies the strict written law.[4] This enactment of the Digest of Justinian states concerning itself that its provision was restricted by humane interpretation.[5]

Equity, a marginal gloss explains, is a perfect squaring or harmonization whereby laws are interpreted, corrected, supplemented, and distinguished; every law that is good and equitable is a result of its influence.[6] Thus the application of equity to the written law is called interpretation and is a function proper only to the head of the State. Its effect is described as general and necessary, and its provision must be committed to writing.[7]

Evidently "generalis" means that such interpretation is

---

1 "Inter aequitatem iusque interpositam interpretationem nobis solis et oportet et licet inspicere."—C. (1, 14) 1.

2 "Cum dubium sit an ius scriptum et strictum sit aequum, et si non est, quis faciat ius super ea aequitate? Respondet Imperator, nobis solis licet inspicere."—*Glossa* ad v. *Inter aequitatem,* C. (1, 14) 1.

3 D. (38, 17) 1, 6.

4 "Et pone casum in iure scripto et stricto et aequitate non scripta ut . . . ff. ad Tertyl., lex 1. par., qui operas."—*Glossa* ad v. *Et ius,* C. (1, 14) 1.

5 This matter will again be taken upon in a later chapter concerning *interpretatio restrictiva.*

6 "Porro aequitas nihil aliud est, quam perfecta quadratio, quae leges et omne scriptum dictumque interpretatur, emendat, supplet, distinguit, ex qua ius manat, quod aequum et bonum dicitur."—*Glossa marginalis,* C. (1, 14) 1. This statement will be found important relative to the authentic interpretation of canon 17, § 3, of the Code of Canon Law.

7 ". . . quaedam est interpretatio generalis et necessaria et in scriptis redigenda: et ista soli Imperatori competit."—*Glossa* ad v. *Solis,* C. (1, 14) 1.

binding upon all subjects, because it is distinguished from judicial interpretation, which is "necessaria tantum" and applicable only to a single cause.[8] One is then to conclude that the *interpretatio* which is proper only to the emperor is the interpretation which is universal in its effect. An interesting marginal annotation to the present law points out the probability that the principle of authentic interpretation recited in *"Inter alia"*, a law in the Decretals of Gregory IX, which will be treated later, derives its origin from this law.[9]

ARTICLE II. *The Lex "Leges Sacratissimae"*.

The concept of *interpretatio* just described in the previous article is not the only notion of interpretation revealed in the Justinian Code. In the law *"Leges sacratissimae"* [10] it is provided that if the law is fraught with obscurity, recourse must be had to the emperor for an interpretation. Evidently, *interpretatio* in this place signifies the exposition, clarification, of a doubtful text. This act of the head of the State is distinguished in the context of the same law from an imperial act which applies clemency to the rigor of the law by opportune correction.[11] It is noteworthy that the doubt envisioned by this enactment is objective doubt, one of the criteria of

---

[8] "Necessaria tantum, ut iudicis in una causa."—*Glossa* ad v. *Et ius*, C. (1, 14) 1.

[9] "Concordat l. inter alia, ante med., ibi, ut igitur prodiit [*sic*] interpretatio quoque procedat. Quae verba (ulli dubium) sunt ex hac lege sumpta." —*Glossa marginalis,* C. (1, 14) 1.

[10] C. (1, 14) 9.

[11] "Si quid vero in isdem legibus latum fortassis obscurius fuerit, oportet id imperatoria interpretatione patefieri duritiamque legum nostrae humanitati incongruam emendari."—C. (1, 14) 9. Both kinds of interpretation could operate simultaneously.

which is the disagreement of experts in the legal profession.[12] The double function of *interpretatio* is recognized by Brunnemann, who observes that when the wording of the law is obscure or when it comes into conflict with equity, the "princeps" must be petitioned to issue an explanation of its provision.[13]

ARTICLE III. *The Lex "Cum de Novo".*

When there is a doubt of law, there are two sources of authentic interpretation. This principle is enunciated in the law *"Cum de novo"*,[14] which contemplates a doubt arising from a new law the meaning of which has not been determined by custom.[15] This law prescribes that the decision *(suggestio)* of the judge and the imperial pronouncement are binding. The former has the force of law as between the litigants; the latter, issuing from the founder of the law, obtains as general law.[16] It will be noticed that this law implicitly sets down a third source of authentic interpretation,

---

[12] "Et idem ubicumque est dissensio doctorum."—*Glossa* ad v. *Obscurius,* C. (1, 14) 9.

[13] *Commentarius in Codicem Iustinianeum,* (Coloniae, Allobrogum, 1771), Lib. I, Tit. XIV, *De Legibus, constit., et Edictis, L. Leges Sacratissimae,* 9, n. 7.

[14] "Cum de novo iure, quod inveterato usu non adhuc stabilitum est, dubitatio emergat, necessaria est tam suggestio iudicantis quam sententiae principalis auctoritas."—C. (1, 14) 11.

[15] "Si vero super lege, si quidem certo modo per consuetudinem est intellecta, eius intellectui stabitur."—*Glossa* ad v. *Cum de novo,* C. (1, 14) 11.

[16] "Dubitatio super nova lege noviter emergens debet dirimi per interpretationem conditoris. h. d. Non intelligas quod non possit dirimi per iudicem causa inter litgantes, sed inter universos debet dirimi per conditorem. h. d. Et tunc habet vim legis generalis. h. d. lex seq. Bal."—*Superscriptio,* ad *Cum de novo,* C. (1, 14) 11.

custom *(inveterato usu)*. By positive law custom is a source of authentic interpretation.[17]

ARTICLE IV. *The Lex "Si Imperialis"*.

The principle of authentic interpretation is laid down in the law *"Si Imperialis"* of the Justinian Code, a law which is cited in the glosses and commentaries of the Decretals as a parallel passage with the law *"Inter alia"* of decretal law for the establishment and explanation of this principle. This law at the same time outlines the avenues through which interpretation proceeds from the "princeps". If the emperor has in a judicial procedure pronounced sentence in a given case, this decision is a precedent which binds all judges in similar cases.[18] This law in its various aspects will be met with from time to time in the course of the present study.

The head of the State by pronouncing sentence shows how a certain law is to be understood and applied,—". . . quis tantae superbiae fastidio tumidus est, ut regalem sensum contemnat . . ."; his interpretation of the law becomes a piece

---

[17] "Minime sunt mutanda, quae interpretationem certam semper habuerunt."—D. (1, 3) 23; "Si de interpretatione legis quaeratur, in primis inspiciendum est, quo iure civitas retro in eiusmodi casibus usa fuisset: optima enim est legum interpres consuetudo."—D. (1, 3) 37; "Nam imperator noster Severus rescripsit in ambiguitatibus quae ex legibus proficiscuntur consuetudinem aut rerum perpetuo similiter iudicatarum auctoritatem vim legis optinere debere."—D. (1, 3) 38.

[18] "Si imperialis maiestas causam cognitionaliter examinaverit et partibus cominus constitutis sententiam dixerit, omnes omnino iudices, qui sub nostro, imperio sunt, sciant hoc esse legem non solum illi causae, pro qua producta est, sed omnibus similibus."—C. (1, 14) 12, pr.

of universal legislation.[19] This enactment establishes a privilege accorded only to the imperial judicial sentence; inferior judges are enjoined not to follow without previous examination any responses or, with the exception of imperial sentence, judicial precedent. They are to have the courage of their own convictions in accord with truth, law, and justice.[20] Even here there is recognized a clear exception as noted in the gloss to the present law, attributed to Accursius (+1260); namely, where a series of decisions has created a custom, according to the laws of the Digest *"Si de interpretatione"* and *"Nam imperator"*, mentioned above.[21] Thus in case of doubt the opinions of men of great authority are to be followed for the reason that they have proved to be sound. One of the chief reasons for the law of the Code under consideration seems to be to obviate the practice of blindly following existing opinions and previous judicial decisions.[22] The custom enters,

---

[19] *Casus*: "Si causa ventilata est coram principe: et ab eo definita: dicitur quod illa sententia est lex communis etiam ad similia . . ."—C. (1, 14) 17 [12].

[20] "Nemo iudex vel arbiter existimet neque consultationes, quas non rite iudicatas esse putaverit sequendum . . . (non enim, si quid non bene dirimatur, hoc et in aliorum iudicum vitium extendi oportet, cum non exemplis, sed legibus iudicandum est), nec si cognitionales sint amplissimae praefecturae vel alicuius maximi magistratus prolatae sententiae: sed omnes iudices nostros veritatem et legum et iustitiae sequi vestigia sancimus."—C. (7, 45) 13.

[21] "Nisi sint tot sententiae ut consuetudinem inducant: et tunc magis dicor sequi consuetudinem, quam sententiam . . . lex, si de interpretatione, et lex nam imperator. Accur."

[22] "Deinde nota erroneas sententias non sequendas ne in pectoribus iudicum extendatur vitium et error, si autem exempla essent bona: quia bonos parerent fructus in dubio sequenda sunt: ut sunt exempla magnae auctoritatis virorum, ut Labeonis: ut dixit tex., Inst. de codici (§ 1) [J. (2, 25) pr.,—an interesting case where the opinion of jurists became law], et lex apud, ff. de manu. vin., [D. (40, 2) 1;—rather, *"An apud", ibid.,* lex 5 (?)—where in the case of doubt the practice of a teacher became a received legal precedent]."—Baldi Ubaldi Perusini, *Commentaria in XI Codicis Libros,* (Venetiis, 1572), [ad] C. (7, 45) 13, [The works of commentators on Roman Law will be cited in full when they are introduced; thereafter their works will be cited by the name of the author and the word *Commentaria* together with the place; the title and law will be added as it appears in the commentary after

as Baldus de Ubaldis (+1400) observes, by tacit consent of the people, the existence of which consent becomes a matter of presumption over a long period of time and usage.[23] Precedents, aside from becoming obligatory by reason of judicial custom as such, may dictate the course of a decision because the law in question is considered doubtful but nevertheless has been understood under a definite construction as evidenced by a limited number of previous decisions.[24] As indicated previously, this rule is sanctioned by a law of the Digest.[25]

The judicial decisions of the emperor are truly a source of authentic interpretation of law. Extra-judicial pronouncements have a like effect. This fact is set down in virtue of the positive enactment of the present law, *"Si Imperialis"*.[26] Evidently the power of the head of the Roman State in this regard had been questioned in the past; Justinian emphatically corrects this error.[27] His language is challenging—let

---

the manner of the following example, which has reference to the present passage of *Baldus de Ubaldis.*]: (Titulus: *De sent. et interlo. om. ind..* Lex XIII, *Nemo*), n. 1.

23 "Et haec vera sunt quando talia sunt deducta in notitiam populi et in hoc populus tacite consentit, qui consensus praesumitur ex temporis diuturnitate et actuum solennitate, quia non fuerunt revocati: ut ff., de reg. iur., lex, nemo, §, temporales."—*op. cit.*, n. 2.

24 "Nisi tot essent res iudicatae, ex quibus consuetudo colligi possit, nam et haec iuris species est. Vel nisi ius esset dubium, quod exemplis declarari posset, nam exempla tantum declarant ius dubium."—Iohannis Brunnemanni, *Commentarius in Codicem Iustinianeum,* Lib. VII, Tit. *De Sentent. et Interloc., etc., L. Nemo Iudex,* n. 4.

25 D. (1, 3) 38.

26 "Definimus autem omnem imperatoris legum interpretationem sive in precibus sive in iudiciis sive alio quocumque modo factam ratam et indubitatam haberi."—C. (1, 14) 12, 3.

27 "Cum igitur et hoc in veteribus legibus invenimus dubitatum si imperialis sensus legem interpretatus est, an oportet huiusmodi regiam interpretationem obtinere, eorum quidem vanam scrupulositatem tam risimus quam corrigendam esse censuimus."—*Ibid.*, fr. 2.

none dare to contemn the dictates of the imperial mind,—". . . quis tantae superbiae fastidio tumidus est ut regalem sensum contemnat . . ." More absolute and forceful words could hardly have been used. Furthermore, the head of the Roman State alone enjoys the exercise of this prerogative because he alone can establish a law.[28] In other words, the power of authentic interpretation demands or presupposes the faculty to establish law, the power to command obedience under the terms of the interpretation rendered.[29] Baldus de Ubaldis expresses this thought clearly when he announces the principle: "Eius est interpretari cuius est condere", the principle of authentic interpretation. He observes in this context that certain lawmakers being removed from office can no longer issue an interpretation because they cannot establish law.[30] Certainly, this author does not mean to say that these persons no longer knew the meaning of their law; rather, they had lost the power to command, which power is of the essence of lawmaking.

As previously observed, this faculty of interpreting authentically does not come into operation only when a law is to be amended, but also, when a doubt in the law demands solution, as the terminology of *"Si Imperialis"* points out. This doubt may arise in litigation: ". . . si dubitatio in litibus oriatur . . . ambiguitates iudicum, quas ex legibus oriri evenit . . ." Or it may appear on any other occasion: "Vel quis legum aenigmata solvere et omnibus aperire . . ." The glossator understands the exercise of this function under the same contingency, a doubt of law.[31]

---

28 "Si enim in praesenti leges condere soli imperatori concessum est, et leges interpretari solum dignum imperio esse oportet."—Ibid., fr. 3.

29 "Vel quis legum aenigmata solvere et omnibus aperire idoneus esse videbitur nisi is, cui soli legis latorem esse concessum est?"—*Ibid.*, fr. 4.

30 Baldi Ubaldi Perusini, *Commentaria in Digestum,* (Venetiis, 1572), D. (1, 4) 1 (Titulus: *De Constitutionibus Principum,* Lex I, *Quod Principi*), n. 19.

31 "Secundo quaerebatur, an princeps possit legem dubiam interpretari?

Besides the imperial tribunal as an agency of interpretation, there is the response of the emperor to petition *(preces)* or, as the present constitution reads, any other medium employed by the emperor to the same end *(alio quocumque modo)*. Here arises the question whether an imperial rescript emanating as an interpretation in a particular case becomes *ipso facto* an adjunct of common law, an extra-judicial, binding precedent for similar cases. The wording of the law, "*Si Imperialis*" does not seem necessarily to answer this question in the affirmative. The phrase "sive in precibus . . . sive alio quocumque modo", mentioned in the context quoted above, does not force one to conclude, considering even the entire constitution, that the rescript initiates general law. The glossator is silent on this point. As will be shown in the chapter on rescripts, Bartolus a Saxoferrato (+1357) denies such force to particular imperial rescript. The commentary of Baldus de Ubaldis to this law regarding the present question seems ambiguous. He declares that the "sententia" of the head of the State which is declaratory of a doubtful law has the force of a general statute, a result which is peculiar to the act of the "princeps". However, he seems to be discussing the judicial sentence.[32] Generally speaking, the term "sententia" does not mean exclusively a judicial sentence; it also signifies an extra-judicial pronouncement.

Quam dubitationem removet dicens: cum et legem possit condere de novo, quare alia[s] recurretur ad eum pro his et aliis dubiis, si eius interpretatio non valeret?"—*Glossa* ad *Casus,* C. (1, 14) 17 [12].

32 "Et nota primo quod quando sententia Principis venit ad declarandum aliquod dubium iuris, quod talis sententia facit ius quo ad omnes: quia non solum habet vim sententiae, sed etiam habet vim generalis statuti et ecce unum speciale in sententia Principis. Et est aliud speciale: quia Princpes non tenetur servare ordinem iudiciorum in procedendo . . . Debet tamen pars citari, alias non valet sententia Principis et potest opponi de nullitate."—*Commentaria,* C. (1, 14) 12 (Titulus: *De legibus et constitut.,* Lex XII, *Si imperialis*), nn. 1-2.

ARTICLE V. *The Lex "Quod Principi"*.

Concerning the juridic scope of the imperial rescript, there is the law *"Quod Principi"* of the Digest, which seems to be clearer on this issue: Whatsoever the emperor has decreed by letter under his signature is law. Does it represent *general* law? So it would seem, because, as this law states, together with other methods of issuing imperial decrees a matter expedited in this fashion falls under the term "constitutio".[33] According to the description given in this law, "constitutio" ordinarily has the force of a general statute. It is personal only when it represents a grant of the imperial majesty elicited in virtue of personal merit or an extraordinary gesture on the part of the emperor, or when he inflicts a particular penalty.[34] The logical conclusion derived from this wording of the law would seem to be that an imperial letter given in reply to a doubt of law *(dubium iuris)* presented in an individual case and not possessing the criteria of a personal matter would have the force of a general statute for a similar eventuality. As commentary to the present law: "Quod principi placuit, legis habet vigorem: . . .", Bartolus declares that the will of the supreme rulers expressed with a mind to establish law has the force of a general statute unless it has respect to determined persons, in which case the disposition cannot serve as a precedent.[35] This jurist demands an "animus ius condendi", which stipulation directly implies, for example, that in a particular response there must appear the

---

[33] "Quodcumque igitur imperator per epistulam et subscriptionem statuit vel cognoscens decrevit vel de plano interlocutus est vel edicto praecepit legem esse constat. Haec sunt quas vulgo constitutiones appellamus."—D. (1, 4) 1, 1.

[34] D. (1, 4) 1, 2.

[35] "Principum placita animo ius condendi facta, habent vim legis generalis: nisi sint facta ad certas personas, quia tunc personas non egrediuntur." —Bartoli a Saxoferrato, *In Digestum Commentaria*, (Venetiis, 1590) D. (1, 4) 1 (Titulus: *De constitutionib. Princip.*, Lex I, *Quod principi*).

will to establish a legal precedent. This thought appears in the works of jurists, canonists and civilists, who wrote long after Bartolus. Behind this demand seems to lie the concept of the necessity of promulgating as a law the reply made by the "princeps" in a particular case. Just how this "animus ius condendi" is to be manifested Bartolus does not seem to say.[36]

The demand for publication of the settlement of a particular case in order that it have the force of general law is marked in the commentary of Paulus de Castro (+1441). He suggests that this publication be effected by directing the decision, even a judicial decision, to the "universitas" (the community at large).[37] It is common knowledge that this procedure was one method of promulgating law. Alexander Tartagnus (+1472), on the other hand, makes special note of the fact that Angelus de Ubaldis (+1412) declares as general law for similar cases the sentence or epistle of the "princeps", as in keeping with the principle laid down in the constitutions *"Quod principi"* and *"Si Imperialis"*, a legal force which is denied to inferior legislators. Alexander Tartagnus embraces this opinion; this prerogative is peculiar to the position of the head of the State, according to the law *"Si Imperialis"*. It is to be noted that according to his terminology

[36] It must be noted here that the jurisprudence concerning the juridic scope of the imperial rescript could easily have changed between A. D. 529-534 (period of Justinian's codification) and the time of Bartolus (fourteenth century), just as it changed in the jurisprudence of the later decretalists, as appears in the second portion of the last chapter of this study.

[37] "Et nota quod tunc epistolae principis et sententiae diffinitivae vel interlocutoriae faciunt ius quo ad omnes licet fuerint directae ad singulares personas, quando ab ipso principe traduntur universitati [omnimode?], ut contigit in Codice in quo fuerunt redactae epistolae principum et in Decretalibus. Et sic sunt inclusae in volumine iuris communis, alias secus: quia faciunt ius singulare . . ."—Pauli Castrensis, *In Digestum Patavinae Praelectiones,* (Lugduni, 1553), D. (1, 4) 1 (Titulus: *De Constitutionibus,* Lex I, *Quod principi*), n. 5.

"sententia principis" includes the "epistola principis". Thus he seems to include a particular rescript as having the force of general law under the terms of that constitution *(Si Imperialis)*.[38] It will be noticed that Alexander Tartagnus cites a case where Angelus de Ubaldis reverses his view on the present question. Iason de Mayno (+circa 1507) is clear in stating that the rescript under discussion is general law to the effect that it can be cited in a similar case. In passing he mentions the doctrine of Paulus de Castro. Strangely enough, he cites Angelus de Ubaldis to confirm his stand in the very place which Alexander Tartagnus cites as stating the former's reversal of opinion.[39] The reversal of Angelus de Ubaldis seems to have been made in view of a particular situation.[40] Iason accounts for the situation by observing that

[38] "In gl. in vers derogare oportet, in fin. hanc gl. iuncto tex., reputat signanter notandum Ange [lus] hic ad hoc videlicet quod licet sententia lata a principe, vel eius epistola habeat vim legis etiam in aliis causis, lex 1, de consti. princ. et lex fi. C. de legi. tamen secus in sententia alterius inferioris quantumcunque habentis potestatem legis condendae. Contrarium tamen tenuit Ange., in lege, item veniunt § caeterum, ff. de peti. haere. [D. (5, 3) 20, 12—*De haereditatis petitione.*] Sed istud quod hic ponit magis placet per istam gl., et quia speciale est in sententia principis, ut d. lege fi."—Alexandri Tartagni Imolensis, *In Digestum Commentaria,* (Venetiis, 1570), D. (2, 12) 1 (Titulus: *De Feriis,* Lex I), nn. 23-24.

[39] "Adde quod eodem modo epistola transmissa per Principem . . . qui habet potestatem legis condendae, habet vim legis et potest in simili allegari pro lege. Ita notat Ange., in l. item veniunt, § caeterum, per illum tex., ff. de pe. hr. Et ibi dicit Ang., quod ista quondam vigebat tunc de facto in civitate Taruisii . . ."—Iasonis Mayni Mediolanensis, *In Digestum Commentaria,* (Venetiis, 1589), D. (12, 1) 27 (Titulus *De rebus cred., Si cert. pet.,* [lex] *Civitas*), n. 7.

[40] In favor of the general legal effect of rescripts Felinus Sandaeus (+1503), a decretalist, cites "Ang [elus de Ubaldis] in lege 1, ff. de feriis propter gloss., ibi, quod incipit, Imo derogatur", and Alexander Tartagnus, who holds the same opinion "post alios quicquid dixerit idem Angel loquens de epistola ducis Venetorum in l. item veniunt, § caeterum, ff. de peti. haere. Quem etiam reprobat Alexander . . . [The duke of Venice may have enjoyed the power of a "princeps", or this fact may have been called into question]: . . respondet [Alexander] ad d. § caeterum quod loquitur in habente potestatem principis".—*Commentaria Felini Sandaei Ferrariensis in V. Libros Decre-*

the rescript of the Pope or emperor is law generally, a matter peculiar to their official positions or to any other prince over whom there is no superior power (referring, undoubtedly, to the independent city-states); that the same prerogative may exist by privilege or custom, as in the case of the Venetians.[41]

The foregoing considerations have importance in understanding more fully the jurisprudence concerning rescripts. What must be discussed further on this point is more appropriately studied in the chapter on rescripts.

---

talium, (Venetiis, 1570), lib. I, tit. III, *Rubrica,* n. 1. [The works of commentators of the Decretals who follow the arrangement of the earlier decretalists will be cited in full when they are introduced; thereafter their works will be cited by the name of the author and the word *Commentaria* together with the book, title, chapter, of the Decretals to which their comment (the columnar number will be added, as in the citation above) refers.]

41 " . . . quod verum est, quod Papa vel Imperator rescribendo vel epistolam transmittendo dicitur legem condere quia talis epistola habetur pro lege. Istud solum habet locum in Papa vel Imperatore, vel alio Principe qui non recognoscit superiorem; vel privilegio vel consuetudine, ut sunt Veneti . . ."—*Commentaria,* D. (12, 1) 27 (Titulus: *De rebus cred. Si cert. pet.,* [lex] *Civitas*), n. 7.

CHAPTER II.

Notion of Authentic Interpretation in Canon Law.

"Leges Authentice Interpretatur Legislator Eiusve Successor"

Introduction of Canon 17, §1.

It will become apparent in the course of this chapter that the introductory observations of chapter one are important as a background for understanding the jurisprudence concerning the principle of authentic interpretation, which is directly implied in canon 17, §1, of the Code of Canon Law.

The first part of paragraph one of canon 17, declares that the legislator or his successor authentically interprets laws. The laws which are considered in this study are human positive ecclesiastical enactments. These enactments are written, *leges,* not custom. There is no intention to discuss the prerogative of infallibility, which the Sovereign Pontiff as the direct successor of St. Peter enjoys exclusively in the interpretation of divine law, either positive or natural,[1] which therefore certainly cannot be delegated, since it is a prerogative of the Pope and peculiar to his exalted office.[2]

---

[1] Koeniger, *Katholisches Kirchenrecht,* (Freiburg i. Breisgau: Herder & Co., 1926), p. 87.

[2] Cf. Haring, *Grundzuge des Katholischen Kirchenrechts,* (3te Auflage,

It will be noted that according to the explicit language of canon 17, no distinction is made between the actual founder of the law and his successor. Both have equal jurisdiction to interpret law. This statement implies immediately that to interpret authentically it is not necessary to know the personal mind or intent of the original legislator [3] in order, for instance, to render a declarative authentic interpretation envisioned in the second paragraph of this canon. By the same token, a delegate can authentically interpret laws. This last question will be taken up in the following chapter.

The rule of interpretation set down in the present canon holds likewise for inferior legislators, because its language is general. Therefore, e. g., the residential Bishop [4] can delegate [5] his faculty of authentic interpretation. The present norm is not confined to the canons of the Code, because the rule reads *"leges"*, not *canones*. Hence Diocesan statutes or, in general, any body of particular ecclesiastical law as distinguished from the *ius commune* of the Code is comprised under its provisions. All these matters will be dealt with in discussing the principle of authentic interpretation which unfolds in the progress of the succeeding articles. The principle itself is, of course, nothing new. Consequently, canon 17, §1, receives its interpretation from pre-Code jurisprudence.[6]

Graz: Verlag von Ulrich Mosers Buchhandlung, J. Meyerhoff, 1924), Erster Teil, 72.

3 Reiffenstuel, *Ius Canonicum Universum,* (Venetiis, 1735), lib. I, tit. II, n. 382.

4 Cf. can. 362.

5 Cf. can. 199.

6 Cf. can. 6, 2°.

ARTICLE I. *Authentic Interpretation by the Supreme Legislator.*

Pope Pelagius I, (+559) writes to a certain Valerian that in matters of doubt a particular synod may not be convened in judgment concerning the dispositions of a general synod, but that such matters must be referred to the Apostolic See.[7] In other words, the seat of authority in the matter of interpretation is with the author of the law.

---

[7] "Sed nec licuit aliquando nec licebit particularem synodum ad diiudicandam generalem synodum congregari. Sed quotiens aliqua de universali synodo aliquibus dubitatio nascitur, ad recipiendam de eo quod non intelligunt rationem . . . ad apostolicas sedes . . . conveniant."—Migne, J. P., *Patrologiae Cursus Completus* (cited *MPL*), LXIX, (Lutetiae Parisiorum, 1865), col. 413: Jaffe, *Regesta Romanorum Pontificum ab condita Ecclesia ad annum post Christum natum MCXCVIII,* (Berolini, 1851), p. 84, n. 634. This declaration recalls the thoughts contained in the spurious "letter of Pope Marcellus": "Simul idem constituerunt [i. e., according to apostolic tradition] ut nulla synodus fieret praeter eiusdem sedis [apostolicae] auctoritatem."—*Epist. Prima Marcelli Papae ad Eppos Antiochenae Provinciae,—MPL,* VII, (Parisiis: Vrayet, 1844), col. 1091. The document is spurious: "Barbarismi frequentes epistolae artificem produnt: versionis Hieronymae (cum libet) sequacem: Innocentii, Leonis, Hilarii, Gregorii, Adriani I, Acacii sententiarum exscriptorem pluribus saeculis Marcello posteriorem".—Blondellus, *Pseudo-Isidorus et Turrianus Vapulantes,* (Genevae, 1628), p. 397, who quotes the entire text of this document. Cf. Jaffe, *Regesta Pontificum Romanorum,* p. 927. Nevertheless, granting that the letter is spurious there is value attached to this document as will appear. Its clauses, falsely attributed to Pope Marcellus (+308): ". . . ut malefacta corrigantur atque bona sectentur, *et patrum nostrorum exempla et statuta imitentur*" (italics inserted), reveal a distinct reference to law and ecclesiastical discipline, concerning which the Holy See is the judge: ". . . ad quam [sedem Petri] cuncta maiora ecclesiastica negotia . . . iussa sunt referri, ut ab ea regulariter disponantur, a qua sumpsere principia". Together with the last clause the document reveals the idea of juridic personality in the See of Rome (there are frequent references to the "See" of Peter): "Eius [Petri] sedes primitus apud vos [i. e., Antiochi] fuit, quae postea . . . Romam translata est, cui . . . hodierna praesedimus [i. e., Marcellus] die". This See of Peter gives the final decision in matters of ecclesiastical discipline: ". . . . Episcoporum iudicia et summarum causarum negotia, sive *cuncta dubia, apostolicae sedis auctoritate sunt agenda et finienda*" (italics inserted). From the citations given above it is certain that this writing is of

The decree of Pope Pelagius is reported in substance in the chapter title of the *Collectio Canonica* of St. Anselm, Bishop of Lucca (+1086),[8] and is contained verbatim in the *Decretum* of St. Ives, Bishop of Chartres (+1116).[9]

Gratian (+circa 1160) received this decree into his *Decretum*.[10] The commentary of the gloss to this citation in the *Decretum* is to the effect that it is the prerogative of the Pope

---

Pseudo-Isidorian origin. Cf. Cicognani, *Canon Law,* Discussing Blondel's collection of the Pseudo-Isidorian Decretals (2 ed., authorized English version, Philadelphia: The Dolphin Press, 1935), p. 243. However, the Pseudo-Isidorian Collection (composed between 845-852—Cicognani, *op. cit.,* p. 244) reveals principles of ecclesiastical government already extant. For, as Cicognani (*op. cit.,* p. 247) declares, with full approval quoting Coviello [in *Manuale di Diritto Ecclesiastico,* published by V. Del Giudice, (Rome, 1922), Vol. I, p. 34.], " 'It is finally established that this collection introduced no new legislation but merely gave a new formulation to legislation already existing in practice in the Church's life. In short Pseudo-Isidore wished to give the authority of law to that which was already accepted in fact'. It is sufficient to note that if novelties had been introduced, the collection would not have been so readily accepted; objections would have arisen, and the fraud would have been easily detected". "Substantially", says Cicognani (*loc. cit*), "all its enactments were already in existence." Considering the words of Blondel quoted above, this fact seems to be born out regarding this particular document. From the present disquisition this study wishes to derive a principle of jurisprudence, that of authentic interpretation, in the words; ". . . cuncta maiora ecclesiastica negotia . . . iussa sunt referri, ut ab ea [sede Petri] regulariter disponantur, a qua sumpsere principia"; and: ". . . et summarum causarum negotia, sive cuncta dubia, apostolicae sedis auctoritate sunt agenda et finienda". For, granted that these ideas were extant at the time of their publication, it necessarily follows that, tradition as a witness, the See of Rome was the juridic arbiter, hence the authentic interpreter, of ecclesiastical legislation, because it was the author of ecclesiastical discipline (a qua sumpsere principia).

8 "Et quotiens de universali synodo dubitetur, ab apostolica sede veritas requiratur."—*De Custodia Aquileiensis et Mediolanensis Episcopi,—MPL,* CXLIX, (Lutetiae Parisiorum, 1853), col. 532.

9 *MPL,* CLXI, (Lutetiae Parisiorum, 1855), cap. 239, col. 315.

10 C. 4, D. XVII.

alone to interpret the statutes of a general council.[11] The gloss also gives an opinion to the contrary; namely, that the interpretation can be effected by all the Bishops or by the more prudent number, "a saniori parte", who were present at the council. The reason adduced by the gloss for this stand is the principle that interpretation must issue from the "judge" who established the law.[12] The principle is rooted in tradition, as appears from what has been said. It is also clear that its application in the second opinion is incorrectly made.[13]

The exclusive right of the legislator to interpret his law is enunciated in a dictum of Gratian.[14] The gloss to this passage reads: "Nam unde ius prodiit, ab eo interpretatio requiritur". It falls short of expressing the juridic authority contained in the dictum of Gratian.

Innocent III (+1216) in the law of the Decretals of Gregory IX, *"Inter alia"*, responding to the teachers of the Decretals at Bologna, wishes to allay any further dispute relative to his previous reply to the Archbishop of Gran concerning the constitution of his predecessor, Gregory VII, *"Quoniam multos"*.[15] The Pope appeals to the principle that interpretation issues whence comes the law.[16] It will be noted that authentic interpretation is directly implied in the words of

---

[11] "Videtur hic quod ad solum Papam spectat interpretari statuta universalis concilii."

[12] "Quia ab eo iudice prodire debet interpretatio, qui ius statuit."

[13] Henricus Boich (+1350), a decretalist, seems to be of the opinion that the Pope alone without the major portion of the Bishops present thereat can not interpret the acts of general council. (Also erroneous.) He attributes to Ioannes Andreas (+1348) the prior opinion, cited above from the gloss to the *Decretum* of Gratian.—*In quinque Decretalium Libros Commentaria,* (Venetiis, 1576), lib. V, tit. XXXIX, cap. *Sicut nobis.*

[14] ". . . ille solus habet ius interpretandi canones, qui habet potestatem condendi eos."—c. 30, C. XI, q. 1.

[15] C. 103, C. XI, q. 3.

[16] ". . . ut igitur, unde ius prodiit, interpretatio quoque procedat, ambiguitatem huiusmodi taliter duximus absolvendum."—c. 31, X, *de sententia excommunicationis,* V, 39.

the Pontiff, because his purpose is to dispel further doubt among the doctors. In his message there is another element—that a successor is interpreting a constitution of his predecessor, a matter which will be considered later. The gloss to the word "interpretatio" in the letter of Innocent III repeats the same principle: "Ad quem pertinet iuris constitutio ad ipsum pertinet interpretatio." By way of reference the gloss recalls the dictum of Gratian[17] and the law of Justinian "*Si Imperialis*".[18]

Felinus Sandaeus (+1503) in his comment to this law of Innocent III observes that interpretation rendered by the legislator is the explanation of the law, and that his interpretation is universal in scope, meaning that such interpretation is legally valid for all subjects.[19] This commentator distinguishes the interpretation of the lawgiver from that of a judge or a doctor; the interpretation of the former he calls universal, that of the latter, particular.[20]

Gregory IX (+1241) makes reply[21] to a question of doubt concerning a constitution which he had issued to the church of St. Mary Major at Rome. He declares *(declaramus)* that his decree has respect only to the future, not to the past. The gloss to the word "*declaramus*" states that this term is aptly employed, because none other could declare or interpret the constitution, and it bases this statement on the prin-

---

17 C. 30, C. XI, q. 1.

18 C. (1, 14) 12.

19 "Nota ibi 'ut igitur' quod ad eum spectat declaratio iuris qui ipsum condidit . . . Hoc limita verum de interpretatione universali."—*Commentaria*, lib. V, tit. XXXIX, cap. XXXI, Inter alia, n. 1.

20 ". . . sed de particulari secus, quia iudex vel doctor poterit interpretari legem in causa vertente coram eo."—*Ibid.*

21 C. 13, X, *de constitutionibus*, I, 2.

ciple under discussion.[22] This comment certainly does not mean to say that the question at issue is not open to doctoral interpretation, since nothing in the constitution itself [23] forbids such interpretation. It must mean that none other than the author of the law can *authentically,* authoritatively, interpret its content, because the commentator makes reference to the *"Inter alia"* of Innocent III,[24] the place in the *Decretum* of Gratian, cited in the foregoing,[25] and the parallel texts bearing on this subject in the Code of Justinian,[26] where the emperor declares that his interpretation has the force of law. Cardinal Hostiensis (Henricus de Segusio, +1271) in his commentary to the words of Innocent says: "Eius enim est interpretari cuius est condere".[27] He cites the dictum of Gratian and makes reference to his commentary to the reply of Gregory IX in the law *"Quoniam constitutio",*[28] both of which have been mentioned previously as bearing out this principle of interpretation.

Boniface VIII (+1303), wishing to remove all doubt with respect to a previous constitution which he had issued, introduces his explanation thereof by applying this maxim of law.[29] He makes it clear to the addressees that his words

---

22 "Bene dicit declaramus, quia nullus alius posset eam declarare sive interpretari, quia ad eum pertinet interpretatio ad quem pertinet constituere. Infra de sent. excom. c. inter § ut igitur, et 11, q. 1, c. sicut, § ex h. omnibus, et C. de leg. lex 1. et ult."

23 C. 15, X, *de maioritate et obedientia,* I, 33.

24 C. 31, X, *de sententia excommunicationis,* V, 39.

25 C. 30, C. XI, q. 1.

26 C. (1, 14) 1; 12.

27 *In Decretalium Commentaria,* (Venetiis, 1581), lib. V, tit. XXXIX, cap. XXXI, *Inter alia.*

28 *Commentaria,* lib. I, tit. II, cap. XIII, *Quoniam constitutio,* where concerning the word *"declaramus"* Hostiensis says: "Quia ad nos spectat interpretatio ex quo et ipsam constitutionem condimus, dic ut inf., de sent. excom. Inter alia". This last by way of parallel reference.

29 ". . . ut, unde praefatae constitutionis revocatoria processit editio, interpretatio eius quoque procedat."—c. 8, *de concessione praebendae et ecclesiae non vacantis,* III, 7, in VIo.

have the sanction of law: "praesenti declarandum duximus sanctione".[30] Consequently, his interpretation has legal force. Ioannes Andreas (+1348), the author of the gloss relative to the rule under discussion, without further comment simply refers to the same passage of Gratian, to the "*Inter alia*" of Innocent III, and to Justinian's law "*Si Imperialis*". It would seem that at his time the principle needed no further elucidation.[31] One or all of the three places just mentioned are practically always referred to as parallel passages in commentaries of the Decretals on authentic interpretation. Finally, Panormitanus (Nicolaus de Tudeschis, +1435), known also as Abbas Siculus, in his annotations to "*Inter alia*" carries forward this maxim of law. He also points out that the interpretation of the author of the law is general; that it holds good for everyone,[32] whereas the interpretation of a judge has reference only to the case before him.[33]

In substance, therefore, however the principle may have been enunciated before the rise of jurisprudence at Bologna, —the question of terminology matters little—the principle that law must be interpreted by its author is rooted in the tradition of the Church.

In closing for the present the discussion concerning this fundamental principle or axiom of law, it will suffice to say

---

30 *Ibid.*

31 Ioannes Andreas is the milestone marking the close of the classical period of Canon Law, during which a more profound knowledge of the principles of law and the scientific interpretation of the Decretals had been achieved.—Cf. Van Hove, *Commentarium Lovaniense in Codicem Iuris Canonici, I, Prolegomena,* (Mechliniae-Romae: H. Dessain, 1928), n. 272.

32 "Nota 1, ex textu quod ad eum spectat interpretatio, qui ius edidit, et intellige in interpretatione generali, ut faciat fidem quo ad omnes."—*Omnia Quae Extant Commentaria in Decretales,* (Venetiis, 1588), lib. V. tit. XXXIX, cap. XXXI, *Inter alia.*

33 ". . . nam quilibet iudex, seu doctor potest ius interpretari, sed interpretatio iudicis non facit fidem, nisi quod ad causam vertentem coram se."—*Ibid.*

that it is frequently referred to by the glossators of the *Corpus Iuris Canonici.*[34]

ARTICLE II. *Authentic Interpretation by the Successor.*

The same principle is applied by the glossators and commentators where a successor interprets the enactment of his predecessor; the interpretation is intended as final and binding and is accepted as such.

It has been shown how the *"Inter alia"* of Innocent III is cited as a leading case to establish the juridic principle that authentic interpretation proceeds from the legislator and from him alone. In order to set forth this doctrine incontestably, reference should be made again to the *"Quoniam constitutio"* of Gregory IX.[35] In passing, it will be noted that Gregory IX (1227-1241) succeeded Innocent III (+1216) after the lapse of about a decade. To the *"declaramus"* of Gregory IX the commentator of this decretal recites the familiar principle of authentic interpretation after having stated that it is within the exclusive power of the Pope to declare or interpret his constitution, ". . . quia nullus alius posset eam declarare sive interpretari," precisely because of this principle. In corroboration of his stand he cites, among the other prominent instances,[36] the *"Inter alia"* of Innocent III. Now this last document, addressed to the Doctors of Bologna, which is frequently used to show that it is the office of the legislator *(qui ius condidit, edidit)*, authentically to interpret his law, actually represents a case where the successor undertakes to

---

[34] Other places in glossaries: c. 12, X, *de iudiciis,* II, 1; c. 23, X, *de verborum significatione,* V, 40; C. 31, X, *de verborum significatione,* V, 40; C. 1, *de verborum significatione,* 14, in Extravag.

[35] C. 13, X, *de constitutionibus,* I, 2.

[36] C. 30, C. XI, q. 1; C. (1, 14) 1; 12.

interpret the law of his predecessor.[37] In other words, in citing *"Inter alia"* the individual person of the legislator is set aside in the mind of the glossators and commentators of the Decretals; the office alone is considered. These commentators do not expressly set forth this juridic phenomenon, but it is immediately implied by an analysis of their citations, and thus their mode of approach in annotating the acts of the "princeps" embraces our idea of juridic personality. As a matter of fact, they apply this principle alike to the act of the author of the law or to his successor.

The pertinent text of the *"Inter alia"* of Innocent III reads: "Ut igitur, unde ius prodiit interpretatio quoque procedat, ambiguitatem huiusmodi taliter duximus absolvendam".[38] The original law issued from Gregory VII, a predecessor of Innocent III who declares that thence should come the interpretation, and yet at the same time, he, the successor, proceeds to give the interpretation which is to have legal standing. That the enactment which he is clarifying originally proceeded from Gregory VII is evident from the present text of Innocent III. In short, Pope Innocent takes the stand that the law and its interpretation *de iure* proceed from the same source, even though from different persons. This procedure means nothing more or less than that it was understood in the world of Canon Law that law and its interpretation issued from the same office regardless of the individuals vested with that office. Hence if the dictum of Innocent III is placed beside that of Boniface VIII (+1303),[39] it will

---

[37] It is a review of *"Quoniam multos"* of Gregory VII (+1085), c. 103, C. XI, q. 3.

[38] C. 31, X, *de sententia excommunicationis,* V. 39: "Wherefore, in order that interpretation may also proceed whence issued the law, we have in mind to solve this difference of opinion—[there was a dispute regarding the law]—in the following manner."

[39] "Quoniam ex constitutione nostra . . . multae dubitationes insurgunt, ut, unde praefatae constitutionis revocatoriae processit editio, interpretatio

appear that both Pontiffs are using the same principle of interpretation. The former employs it with regard to the law of his predecessor; the latter, in view of his own legislation. And Ioannes Andreas, who is the author of the gloss to the present decretal in the *Liber Sextus* of Boniface VIII, finds apparently no difficulty in declaring by way of reference that the same principle is to be found in the *"Inter alia"*.[40]

Accordingly, one finds in a reply of Innocent III to the Bishop of Saragossa that the Pope defines the word *"novale"* (fallow land) in a papal indult issued by his predecessors.[41] The commentator's gloss accepts this answer as the meaning of *"novale"* in canon law as regards tithing.[42] Thus, the Pope by interpretation sets forth the law of his predecessors. It will be noticed that the decision in this case is taken as the definition of the meaning of *"novale"* in Canon law as such.

The same Pontiff decides a controversy concerning two privileges granted by his predecessors, Popes Paschal and Calixtus. Innocent hears the witnesses and examines the tenor of the privileges. He distinguishes several interpretations in the privilege of Pope Paschal and chooses the one which renders a clearer meaning.[43] It may be pointed out here that the legislator does not have to proceed in this manner, after the fashion of doctrinal interpretation. This fact will appear in

---

quoque procedat . . ."—c. 8, *de concessione praebendae et ecclesiae non vacantis,* III, 7, in VIo.

40 *Glossa* ad v. *Procedat,* c. 8, *de concessione praebendae et ecclesiae non vacantis,* III, 7, in VIo. In fact, in this place he reviews all the chief places which exemplify the use of this principle: "11. q. 1 c. sicut, § ex his, de sen. excomm. inter alia, § ut igitur. C. de leg. l. ult . . . et de postu. c. 1. Io. An.".

41 "Nos igitur inquisitioni tuae respondemus quod eam credimus praedecessorum nostrorum intentionem fuisse . . ."—c. 21, X, *de verborum significatione,* V, 40. Here the Pope sets aside the definition given in civil law.

42 "Secundum canones dicitur novale ager de novo ad cultum redactus . . . quantum ad ius decimarum."—*Glossae* ad *Casus* et ad v. *De novo, loc. cit.*

43 ". . . hic autem sensus rectior videtur."—c. 25, X, *de verborum significatione,* V, 40.

the following example. However, in the present case, the Pope gives his reason for his choice; namely, that a privilege, being a private law, should as such not be obscure or misleading, but certain and manifest,[44] an essential characteristic of every law. In the case of the privilege granted by Pope Calixtus, Innocent declares that the text is clear.[45] The Pope then renders his decision,[46] which is based on the interpretation of the privileges, as appears from the text of the Pope's pronouncement. That is to say, the Pontiff determines the mind of the grantors as manifested by their texts; he does so with the authority of law. He has rendered an authentic interpretation. But the point here is that it was not necessary for him to proceed to his interpretation by the method of a textual exegesis of the documents before him. The following example offers a striking contrast.

Innocent III writes to the Bishop of Paris that he is aware of the need of an explanation of a clause contained in ancient canons [47] and in his own decretal.[48] There were both variant interpretations extant issued by his predecessors and apparently a divergence of opinion generally regarding the matter.[49] The Pontiff then proceeds to set down exactly what is to be held on that particular point. The glossator recognizes

---

[44] ". . . cum privilegium sit lex privata, et lex non debeat esse obscura vel captiosa sed certa et manifesta."—*Ibid.*

[45] ". . . maxime cum supradictus C. Papa . . . verbis aequioribus usus, determinationem illam prorsus amoverit, ut ambiguitas tolleretur . . ."—c. 25, X, *de verborum significatione,* V. 40.

[46] ". . . his igitur diligenter auditis . . . adiudicavimus . . ."—*Ibid.*

[47] The "antiqui canones" are: c. 18, C. XI, q. 1, "*Si quis sacerdotum*", recited as from the Epist. II of Pope Pius; c. 8, C. III, q. 4, "*Clericus*", recited as from the Epist. II, cap. 8, of Pope Stephan.

[48] "Novimus expedire ut verbum illud quod in antiquis canonibus et in nostro decreto . . . apertius exponamus."—c. 27, X, *de verborum significatione*, V, 40.

[49] "Cum enim quidam antecessorum nostrorum super hoc consulti diversa responderint, et quorumdam sit opinio a pluribus approbata . . ."—*Ibid.*

the legal import of the interpretation.[50] Thus with his interpretation the Pope cuts through all former pronouncements of his predecessors and existing opinions. The present case typifies the positive element in the texture of human law, which in this instance operates by the agency of authentic interpretation. The interpreter approaches his problem from the standpoint of a legislator rather than by way of an exegetical and scientific examination of the legal text, as did the same pope in the case of the two privileges mentioned above; in both cases, of course, the decision stands as law. Hence it is not necessary for the authentic interpreter to know the mind of the original legislator in order to render an interpretation.[51] He simply proclaims how the law is to be understood. Consequently, as clearly shown in the present instance, for the practical purposes of interpretation, which for him in effect amount to the administration of the ecclesiastical body politic, Pope Innocent, in keeping with his principle, identifies himself with the legal personality of his predecessors. One can hardly say that Hostiensis, Panormitanus, Felinus Sandaeus, in their annotations to the *"Inter alia"* of Innocent III failed to see that Innocent III was actually not the author of the law which he is interpreting by means of his law *"Inter alia"*. In their commentaries to this law they repeat as it were in concert with Innocent III the principle of authentic interpretation, which in the text of this law implicitly identifies the authentic interpreter with the author of the law. Ioannes Andreas in his commentary to the decretal of Boniface VIII [52] refers to the *"Inter alia"* as containing the same prin-

50 "Licet sit a pluribus approbata [opinio] tamen stabimus ei quod papa hic dicit."—*Glossa* ad v. *A pluribus, loc. cit.*

51 Reiffenstuel, lib. I, tit. II, n. 382.

52 Cf. *Glossa* ad c. 8, *de concessione praebendae et ecclesiae non vacantis*, III, 7, in VIo. In this decretal this Pope interprets one of his own previous constitutions; yet Ioannes Andreas here implicitly indicates that this principle is operative as well in the interpretive law of Innocent III as in the present decretal of Boniface VIII.

ciple. In effect therefore these jurists identify *de iure* the person of the lawgiver with that of the interpreter.[53] Further, the doctrine of the juridic identity of the lawgiver with the successor is the explicit teaching of the gloss relative to the Bull *"Rex Pacificus"* of Gregory IX.

In the Bull *"Rex Pacificus"* of Gregory IX, 5 September, 1234, which forms the introduction to the Gregorian Decretals, the Pope mentions the various operations which brought this collection of former laws into being. He writes that he has added his own constitutions and decretals, whereby certain matters which were doubtful in the legislation of the past are interpreted.[54] The *Casus* of the glossator of this document calls attention to the fact that persons do not have authority to command their peers. Nevertheless, the commentator adds, a successor in office has the authority to correct and interpret the statute of his predecessor.[55] The reason that a successor has such authority is also given in the present commentary; namely, that the successor is considered the same person as his predecessor.[56] This statement reveals beyond question

---

[53] Thus, in effect, Honorius III (+1227) identifies himself with the tribunal of his predecessor, Innocent III, inasmuch as he reviews and interprets a definitive sentence of the latter concerning the term "tempus motae litis": "Nos igitur considerata eadem sententia quam Innocentius Papa praedecessor noster . . . promulgavit . . . quod in praefato capitulo dicitur de tempore motae litis, interpretamur esse referendum ad tempus quo litis contestatio facta fuit." —c. 30, X, *de verborum significatione,* V, 40. That the decision is final, and therefore authentic, is apparent from the remark of the glossator, who, in a matter-of-fact observation, simply declares that the "tempus motae litis" must be understood as referring to the joinder of issue.

[54] ". . . adiicientes constitutiones nostras et decretales epistolas per quas nonnulla quae in prioribus erant dubia declarantur . . ."—*Decretalium D. Gregorii Papae IX Compilatio, Prooemium.*

[55] "Nota quod licet par in parem non habeat imperium, tamen successor statutum antecessoris corrigere potest et declarare, et sic nota quod per posteriora priora declarantur."

[56] "Potest ergo Dominus Papa derogare constitutionibus praedecessorum suorum non obstante quod par in parem non habet imperium . . . Et est ratio,

that the idea of juridic personality is clearly understood in its practical import.

This same concept is contained in the *regula iuris* of Boniface VIII (+1303), which states in effect that a successor in office must exercise the same juridic status as his predecessor.[57] The glossary comment to this rule in the *Liber Sextus* proposes cases of property rights and sets forth that by fiction of law the heir is deemed the same person as the deceased. The present discussion, however, represents an issue concerning jurisdiction. Ioannes Andreas (+1348) also, except for a few remarks, confines his commentary to the discussion of property rights. However, at the beginning of his comments he renders the word "eo iure" (that juridic status) with the term "ea sede" (that seat). His rendition means "authority of government", as appears from his application of the rule elsewhere, to which he refers the reader.[58] In that tract the powers of the cathedral chapter during the vacancy of the episcopal office are under consideration. The chapter may perform certain acts of government which are proper to the permanent incumbent. It administers spiritual and temporal affairs; it pronounces judgment upon heretics; appoints inquisitors concerning heresy; confirms elections; institutes those who are presented for appointment, etc. Certain acts it may not perform; the validity of others is doubtful. The point is that this jurist understands the rule of law as applicable to succession in jurisdiction, not only to succession in material rights and duties. In other words, the permanent

---

quia eadem persona censetur eo cui succedit . . ."—*Glossa* ad v. *Resecatis, Decretalium D. Gregorii Papae IX Compilatio, Prooemium.*

[57] "Is, qui in ius succedit alterius, eo iure, quo ille, uti debebit."—Reg. 46, R. J., in VIo. This rule of law has its counterpart among the *regulae iuris* in the Digest.—D. (50, 17) 177.

[58] ". . . eo iure, an ea sede, vide quod dixi de maioritate et obedientia, cap. primum."—Ioannis Andreae Bononiensis, *In Sextum Decretalium Librum Novella Commentaria,* (Venetiis, 1581), *De regulis iuris,* Regula XLVI—*Is qui in ius.*

incumbent in any rank of jurisdiction *must (debebit)*, under the wording of this rule of law—which is itself a law—employ the same powers as his predecessor. That the power is attached to the office and not to the individual person is clear from the term "sede" as it is applied by Ioannes Andreas.

Accordingly, Pope John XXII (+1334) undertakes to interpret the interpretations of his predecessors concerning the Rule of the Friars Minor.[59] In this act of jurisdiction the Pope is using his power to safeguard from malinterpretation the declarations of his predecessors. The action of the Pontiff is accepted without question as authoritative. The glossator adds that every rule of religion correctly set down proceeds, at least by approbation, from the Supreme Pontiff; he is therefore the authority to which recourse must be had for an authentic interpretation. Here also is applicable the basic principle of interpretation—the author has exclusively the right to interpret his law.[60] As a matter of fact, John XXII neither brought into being the Rule of the Friars Minor nor was he the first to issue declarations concerning it. Yet for all the purposes of law and the administration thereof, he is considered the founder of that religious observance. Moreover, the present procedure is considered not at all incongruous or even uncommon, as the commentator observes; even those

[59] "Quorundam exigit caecae scrupulositatis ambiguum . . . ut nos post praedecessorum nostrorum . . . Romanorum Pontificum super intellectu et observantia regulae ordinis fratrum Minorum declarationes salubriter editas . . . nostras Domino favente indubias ipsorum praedecessorum declarationibus declarationes adiungamus . . . ne perperam paucorum . . . inscitia recta ipsarum declarationum verba convertens in devium, illaque suis eis profecto contraria accommodans sensibus . . . praefato ordini . . . unionem scindens, si valeat, reddatur."—c. 1, *de verborum significatione*, XIV, in Extravag.

[60] "Ex hoc collige Papam declarationem super regula religionis posse facere; cum enim omnis regula rite dictata ab ipso saltem per approbationem processerit . . . ad illum potest et debet spectare declaratio ad quem pertinuit editio . . . C. de leg. lex ult . . . extra de sent. excomm., Inter alia, 11, q, 1, § ex his omnibus."—*Glossa* ad v. *Declarationes, loc. cit.*

matters which had been omitted by a predecessor are very frequently supplemented and put into practice subsequently, an act which is therefore considered as demanding greater authority than that which is requisite for interpretation.[61]

All ecclesiatical institutes, as the gloss points out by reference to the *Decretum* of Gratian, depend for their existence upon the authority of the Chair of Peter.[62] Hence Sixtus V (+1590) calls the Roman Pontiff the founder of the sacred canons, using this concept as the basis, so to speak, for the power of rendering an authoritative and final interpretation to a certain constitution issued by himself.[63] Accordingly, Clement VIII (+1605) forbids religious superiors under penalty of invalidity and perpetual deprivation of rank and office to interpret or relax in any way the decrees of the Council of Trent or the provisions which were published on the occasion of his decree.[64]

The power of authentic interpretation, then, rests solely with the public ecclesiastical authority as such, whereby laws are administered. Which power is not considered individualis-

---

[61] Hoc non incongruum nec insolitum existit; cum et omissum per antecessorem per successorem suppleri et induci frequentissime sit repertum."—*Glossa* ad v. *Adiungamus*, c. 1, *de verborum significatione*, XIV, in Extravag.

[62] "Quis nesciat aut non advertat, id quod a principe Apostolorum Petro Romanae Ecclesiae traditum est, ac nunc usque custoditur, ab omnibus debere servari? Nec superinduci aut introduci aliquid quod aut auctoritatem non habeat; aut aliunde accipere videatur exemplum?"—c. 11, D. XI. The present quotation is an excerpt from the first letter of Innocent I, (+417) *ad Decentium*, Episcopum Eugubinum.—Jaffe, *Regesta Romanorum Pontificum*, p. 25, n. 108.

[63] "Ad Romanum spectat Pontificem, sacrorum canonum conditorem, quae per eum sancita sunt, ita suae declarationis arbitrio dilucida reddere, ut inde nemini possit dubitationis scrupulus exoriri . . . Nos, ad tollendam omnem amibiguitatis occasionem . . . praesentem nostram perpetuo valituram declarationis constitutionem duximus promulgandam."—*Bullarium Diplomatum et Privilegiorum Ss. Romanorum Pontificum Taurinensis editio*, (Neapoli, 1883), VIII, CXII, nn. 1-3.

[64] Clemens VIII, decr. "*Nullus omnino*", 25 iul. 1599, § 8.—Fontes n. 187. The present decree was issued to the Order of Servites.

tic and subjective, so that the question of authentic interpretation would depend upon the individual mind, or intellect, of the original lawgiver. Such is not the case. The authority of interpretation is not coupled with the intellectual content of the law as in the mind of the lawgiver, but rather with the power to establish *(condere)* a law; thus the dictum, "Eius est interpretari cuius est condere".

The present thought is clearly expressed by Philippus Decius (+1536), citing Baldus de Ubaldis (+1400) and Angelus de Ubaldis (+1412). Interpretation is at times understood in the sense of correction (of the law). Accordingly, the authentic interpretation of invalid statutes enacted by inferiors, which have been confirmed by the Sovereign Pontiff, is reserved to the latter. The reason is that they cannot be abrogated by the inferiors in question. And, this canonist continues, the subsequent interpretation which the Pope will give is to be received regardless of whether or not his intent was such from the beginning, i. e., when he confirmed the statute. Decius is here dealing with the question of declarative interpretation of a doubtful law.[65] Authentic interpretation in this concept is coupled with dominion over the substance of the law. The point at issue here is that it depends in no way upon the sense content which reposed in the mind and will of the original legislator. In fact, if such were not the case, the faculty to interpret authentically could not be delegated. Authentic interpretation is an implement of government for public welfare operating by means of positive law.

---

65 "Nam interpretatio quandoque pro correctione accipitur, . . . Et hac ratione statuta invalida, confirmata a summo pontifice, quia ab inferioribus tolli non possunt, a summo pontifice interpretari debent, ut notat Baldus et Angelus . . . Et quando ad papam recurritur, ut dictum est, declarationi et interpretationi eius omnino standum est, dato quod haec sua intentio a principio non fuisset . . . quasi illud quod declaratur a principio dictum fuisset . . ."—Philippi Decii Mediolanensis, *In Decretales Commentaria*, (Lugduni, 1576), lib. II, tit. I, cap. *Cum venissent*, nn. 9-11.

The continuity of the doctrine just outlined has been challenged. Felinus Sandaeus and Philippus Decius are quoted as expressly holding a contrary view.[66] Accordingly, it is said that jurists, canonists and civilists, of the 15th and 16th centuries held that authentic interpretation could be rendered only by the author of the law, personally, because he alone could know his own mind.[67]

Authentic interpretation is such interpretation which has the force of law; it is an adjunct of positive legislation. Regarding this divergent doctrine, an attempt will here be made to examine the sources and present them to the reader.

Felinus Sandaeus (+1503) declares that the power of interpretation adheres to the person and does not pass unto another.[68] This dictum has an immediate context which will, together with the texts to which he makes reference, be examined in order to establish what Felinus Sandaeus means when he states: "Potestas interpretandi cohaeret personae". Prior to this statement Sandaeus cites a passage from the *Liber Sextus,* concerning which he says that regarding the validity of a papal dispensation the Pope alone can take cognizance of the matter.[69] In the original text of the *Liber Sextus* to which Sandaeus refers Gregory X (+1276) prescribes that in case of doubt concerning the validity *(sufficientia)* of a dispensation recourse must be had to the Apostolic See, to which it appertains to render a decision.[70] The gloss to the

---

[66] Cf. Orio Giacchi, *Formazione e Sviluppo della Dottrina della Interpretazione Autentica in Diritto Canonico,* (Milano: Società Editrice "Vita e Pensiero"), p. 34, sq.

[67] "Essi vengono cosi a considerare la interpretazione autentica sopratutto come la interpretazione di una manifestazione di volontà, ad opera della stessa persona che ha compiuto tale manifestazione."—*op. cit.*, p. 35.

[68] "Potestas interpretandi cohaeret personae adeo quod non transit in alium."—*Commentaria,* lib. II, tit. I, cap. *Cum venissent,* n. 2.

[69] ". . . est textus quod si dubitetur de validitate dispensationis papae solus papa hoc cognoscit."—*Ibid.*

[70] "Si vero de dispensationis exhibitae sufficientia dubitetur super hoc

word *"aestimare"* in this decretal of Pope Gregory says that it is the office of the Holy See *(eius)* to interpret, citing Gratian, *"Inter alia"*, and Justinian, where the principle of authentic interpretation is recited.[71] Whether or not the term "solus Papa" which Felinus uses, and "sedes apostolica", the term that appears in the passage to which Felinus refers, are identical in the mind of Felinus, so that according to his supposed doctrine the "potestas interpretandi [legem]" must be conceived exclusively as a personal prerogative and not as attaching to the "sedes apostolica", i. e., to the office, does in no wise appear from Felinus' present text. There is nothing in the Pope's decretal or the gloss which confines authentic interpretation to the individual person of the lawgiver. Felinus goes on to cite the chapter of Boniface VIII (+1303), which contains the well known principle of authentic interpretation.[72] Thirdly, he draws upon the text of Angelus de Ubaldis (+1412) as stating that papal letters which interpret the intention of the Pope must be received even though it (the intention) never existed, because the Pontiff's testimony concerning his mind does not admit of proof to the contrary.[73]

Angelus de Ubaldis says that to the Pope's interpretation of a dispensation which he has given must be applied the general principle that the matter of interpretation belongs to the author. Though the dispensation contains no ambiguity, he continues, nevertheless, because the Pope in his letter attests

---

erit ad sedem apostolicam recurrendum, cuius est aestimare quem modum sui beneficii esse velit."—c. 3, *de officio ordinarii,* I, 16, in VIo.

71 "Eius enim [sedis] est interpretari, et c. 11, q. 1, c. clericum, § ex his; de sent. exc., Inter alia, C. de leg., lex ult."

72 C. 1, *de concessione praebendae et ecclesiae non vacantis,* III, 7, in VIo.

73 "Et vide Angelum, Consilium 273 [274] . . . ubi dicit quod statur litteris papae interpretantibus intentionem suam et si illa nunquam fuit quia cum attestatur de animo suo non admittitur probatio in contrarium."—*Commentarium,* lib. II, tit. I, cap. *Cum venissent,* n. 2.

his intention and will, one must receive his assertion; his intention is known to himself and God alone.[74] In confirmation hereof Angelus de Ubaldis cites the gloss of Ioannes Andreas to the word *"relinquatur"* in a law of the Decretals of Boniface VIII, giving examples from the Digest,[75] where the rightful authority to declare and interpret an ambiguous intent so adheres to the author thereof that it is not transmitted to an heir.[76] The gloss, attributed to Ioannes Andreas, is a comment to the word *"relinquatur"* found in a paragraph of Boniface VIII, which paragraph leaves *(relinquatur)* it to the conscience *(conscientiae)* of the delegate judge to decide whether he needs an assessor.[77] The examples from the Digest will be considered later. A gloss to *"conscientiae"* states that conscience is the knowledge of one's own heart.[78] The gloss to *"relinquatur"* reads that since this matter is left to conscience, God alone and none other knows and is judge. Angelus de Ubaldis concludes that the assertion of the Pontiff must be believed regarding those things which depend on a matter which he did or on his intention; that though on a thousand occasions it was never his intention, nevertheless no one can gainsay him.[79] Thus far, from the examples cited and from the

---

74 "Unde standum est ei [papae] in d. cap. pro hoc illud generale est eius interpretari cuius est condere. Sive dicamus dictam gratiosam dispensationem nullam ambiguitatem continere; quod verum puto. Tamen quia papa attestatur in literis de sua intentione quod voluit . . . standum est assertioni suae quoniam eius intentio sibi soli et Deo nota est." *Consilia D. Angeli de Ubaldis*, (Lugduni, 1571), Consilium 274, n. 1.

75 D. (6, 1) 5; (45, 1) 83.

76 ". . . in glossa Ioan. An. in c. Statutum, § insuper, in verbo relinquatur, de rescriptis, lib. VI, de rei ven., l. Pomponius scribit si frumentum, et de verb. oblig., l. inter stipulantem, § 1., ubi ius et potestas declarandi et interpretandi ambiguam intentionem adeo personae proferentis cohaeret quod ad haeredem non transit."—*Ibid.*

77 C. 11, *de rescriptis*, I, 3, in VIo.

78 "Conscientia est cognitio sui ipsius cordis."

79 ". . . quod omnino sit credendum assertioni pontificis in his quae a suo facto aut a sua intentione dependent . . . Et licet millies haec sua tunc non fuerit intentio, tamen nemo dicere potest oppositum. . ."—*Ibid.*

words of Angelus de Ubaldis one learns that the right to interpret or declare one's own internal intention or mind does not pass to another. This statement will be admitted by everyone. It is not said that the right to declare or interpret a *law* does not pass to a successor. It is in this preliminary context that Felinus Sandaeus sets forth his dictum: "Potestas interpretandi cohaeret personae adeo quod non transit in alium".

Felinus Sandaeus states furthermore that such is the dictum of Pope Innocent IV (Sinibaldus Fliscus, +1254; an eminent canonist), where a controversy as to the actual intent of a testator is settled,[80] and points to the gloss to the word *"appareat"* and the gloss to *"actori"*, found in the Digest as quoted above by Angelus de Ubaldis, as examples.[81] The text in which occurs the word *"appareat"* states that if it does not appear *(nec appareat)* regarding which of several slaves named Erotes judicial action was filed, the judgment is null.[82] The rubric which introduces this passage is set down by Bartolus (+1357) and declares: "Incertitudinem rei impedit condemnationem fieri"; judgment is not possible when the matter is uncertain. The gloss to "appareat" recites that it does not appear to the judge or defendant; that the explanation of the plaintiff must be accepted; but that in this case the plaintiff is deceased and thus cannot furnish the necessary explana-

---

80 "Hoc est dictum Innocentii in c. finali de successionibus ab intestato [c. 3, X, *de successionibus ab intestato,* III, 27]."—*Commentaria,* lib. II, tit. I, cap. *Cum venissent,* n. 2. This law has to do with the mental status (mental sanity) of a testator (archipresbyter) when making his last will in favor of a monastery; ". . . quod nisi praefatus Episcopus legitime probaverit saepedictum archipresbyterum suae mentis compotem non fuisse cum ultimam voluntatem expressit . . . perpetuum ei silentium imponatur." The issue is squarely one of fact; did the testator intend to bequeath his goods to the monastery?

81 D. (6, 1) 5; (45, 1) 83.

82 "Si plures sint eiusdem nominis servi, puta plures Erotes, nec appareat de quo actum sit, Pomponius dicit nullam fieri condemnationem."—D. (6, 1) 5, 5.

tion.[83] A marginal note adds that the declaration or interpretation of an obscure bill of plaint does not pass to the heir, citing Baldus de Ubaldis (+1400) and the parallel case of Innocent IV mentioned above. The second example regarding the gloss to *"actori"* is similar and will be dealt with below in connection with a citation from Bartolus. Considering what has been outlined, one is forced to conclude only that a man must be a mind reader in order to declare or interpret with certainty the thoughts of another regarding that which he has said or done. Thus it is, Sandaeus goes on, whether it be concerning the enactment of a law or any other matter, that the procurator cannot without a special mandate interpret the bill of plaint produced by his principle.[84] In confirmation of this statement he cites Baldus.[85]

A bill of complaint is the petition for the administration of justice upon the allegation of facts to be demonstrated in legal procedure. Baldus, citing Innocent IV, confirms this statement of Felinus; but he also adds that the law interprets, and points to an example from the Digest,[86] with the explanation that the citation in the Digest has to do with a doubt concerning law *(dubium iuris)*, that is, concerning the meaning of the word spoken, whereas here there is a doubt concerning fact. The present discussion therefore concerns a doubt of fact.[87] In the context of the place to which Sandaeus

[83] Appareat . . . iudici vel reo. Sed quomodo potest non apparere, cum semper stemus dicto actoris in [D. (45, 1) 83] quae est contra. Sol. [utio] dic actorem hic decessisse . . ."

[84] *Commentaria,* lib. II, tit. I, cap. *Cum venissent,* n. 2.

[85] "Ita dicit . . . Baldus in d. l. idem Pomponius, [D. (6, 1) 5]."—*Ibid.*

[86] "Si quis intentione ambigua vel oratione usus est, id quod utilius ei est accipiendum est."—D. (5, 1) 66.

[87] "Item notat Innocentius, extra de success. ab intestato, c. cum dilectus, quod est notabile. Sed videtur quod lex interpretetur, ut l. si quis inter commune ambigua [intentione ambigua] de iudiciis, sed ibi erat dubium iuris, idest, significationis verbi prolati hic erat dubium facti."—*Commentaria,* D. (6, 1) 5 (Titulus: *de rei vendicatione*; Additio Baldi, § *Idem Pomponius*), n. 1.

makes reference in Baldus the latter says that uncertainty vitiates the bill of plaint and the procedure; that the interpretation or declaration of an obscure bill does not devolve upon the heir;[88] he then speaks about the procurator, as mentioned above. He points out that the heir cannot interpret a doubtful clause laid down by the testator; that it is not for him to judge (since *facta* [facts] are outside the mind, they are not transmitted to the heir) whether someone by testament has been given his liberty.[89] It is in this context that Baldus raises the objection that the law *(lex)* acts as an interpreter *(sed videtur quod lex interpretetur)*. He answers that it does so when there is doubt concerning law *(dubium iuris)*; however, that he is at present discussing a doubt concerning a fact *(dubium facti)*. It seems that Baldus means to say that a man's internal thought is known only to himself. This thought he calls a fact.

After citing Baldus, Felinus Sandaeus says that in like manner a successor in office cannot interpret the sentence (Or thought? He uses the word *sententia*.) of his predecessor; again he calls upon Baldus.[90] Baldus de Ubaldis assents to this statement, but only after having set up a dialectic contradiction,[91] which is so common with the glossators and commentators. He asks the question whether a judge can interpret

[88] "Incertitudo vitiat libellum et processum causae . . . nec transit interpretatio vel declaratio libelli obscuri ad haeredem."—*Ibid.*

[89] "Nota quod haeres non potest interpretari verbum dubium a testatore prolatum iudicio cuius non est quia facta sunt extra animum non transeunt ad haeredem si quis testamento liber esse iussus fuerit."—*Ibid,* (Additio Baldi), n. 1.

[90] "Item successor in officio non potest interpretari sententiam praedecessoris . . . Et idem vult Baldus in 1. ii, C. de senten ex pericul. recitand. [C. (7, 44) 2]."—*Commentaria,* lib. II, tit. I, cap. *Cum venissent,* n. 3.

[91] By this term, used here and hereinafter, is meant the apparent contradiction, or antithesis, between one law and a second, which glossators in their annotations and commentators set up as a method of explaining a law under discussion more clearly.

the sentence of his predecessor and answers in the affirmative, because the magistracy is one and the same.[92] Without further explanation Baldus points to the text in the Digest,[93] which he calls a paragraph concerning the mind (articulus de ammo [animo]), and which he says seems to indicate the contrary. At this point Sandaeus goes on to explain what he means by his rule: "Potestas interpretandi cohaeret personae". Namely, a successor in office cannot interpret the sentence (thought?) of his predecessor from the vantage ground of the internal will of the latter.[94] He gives an example. A judge has decreed the amputation of a hand without specifying the left or the right. A successor, heir or any other is unable to know which hand the judge had in mind.[95] However, he concludes, citing Bartolus (+1357), that every successor can render an interpretation upon the basis of probable conjectures.[96]

It is clear that Sandaeus is here speaking about authentic interpretation. The sentence of a judge is law for the parties in the case. The judge alone can authentically interpret his own sentence from out of his own mind *(ex mera voluntate)*, as it were. Can the successor of the judge do the same upon the grounds of probable conjectures? Does Sandaeus here

---

[92] "Sed nunquid hoc potest facere [iudicis sententiam interpretari] successor eius. Et videtur quod sic, quia unus est magistratus. Contra videtur, quia est articulus de animo."—*Commentaria*, C. (7, 44) 2 (Titulus: *de senten. ex brevi, reci.*, Lex II, *Hac lege*), n. 7. N. B. The text of Venice, 1572, reads: "articulus de ammo, arg. ff., de rei ven. 1. idem Pomponius, § fin.". Considering what has been said, "animo" seems to be the correct rendering.

[93] D. (6, 1) 5, 5: "Si plures sint eiusdem nominis servi, puta plures Erotes, nec appareat de quo actum sit, Pomponius dicit nullam fieri condemnationem."

[94] "Intellige in interpretatione quae fit ex mera voluntate."—*Commentaria*, lib. II, tit. I, cap. *Cum venissent*, n. 3.

[95] "Puta si iudex condemnavit aliquem in una manu et non dixit de sinistra vel dextra, successor vel heres vel alii non poterunt interpretari."—*Ibid.*

[96] "Sed ubi agitur de interpretatione ex verisimilibus coniecturis hanc facere potest quilibet successor. Ita Bartolus in l. inter stipulantem, § 1, ibi omnia enim, etc., ff. de verb. oblig. [D. (45, 1) 83]."—*Ibid.*

deny that a successor can do so? There is no expression of denial in his text. His words with respect to a successor reminds one of the doctrine of Suarez (1548-1617), who, it seems, is also a witness to sixteenth century juristic thought. This jurist teaches that a person can with greater certainty explain the intention which he had when he established his law, because he alone knows for certain; a successor can only venture a conjecture. Nevertheless, a successor can interpret the meaning in which the law is to be received and observed, and thus his interpretation is called authentic.[97] Does Felinus Sandaeus (who cites the "*Inter alia*", mark, as the principle of authentic interpretation) confine interpretation which has the force of law to the possibility of knowing directly a man's mind?

In the context of the passage of Bartolus, referred to by Sandaeus in the foregoing, the former by way of antithesis cites the place in the Digest,[98] which has been discussed previously, together with the gloss accompanying the word "*actori*" in the text which he is now treating.[99] This text reads that a *stipulatio* is not created unless there is a meeting of the minds regarding the same object; that in the event of a suit it must be established what the plaintiff had in mind, and that his word must be accepted.[100] Bartolus points out that

---

97 ". . . successor vero solum potest illam [voluntatem] coniectare. Nihilominus tamen potest successor interpretari sensum in quo lex recipienda est et observanda, et hoc modo dicitur haec authentica interpretatio."—*De Legibus*, VI, cap. 1, n. 2.

98 D. (6, 1) 5, 5: "Si plures sint eiusdem nominis servi, puta plures Erotes, nec appareat de quo actum sit, Pomponius dicit nullam fieri condemnationem."

99 ". . . opponitur quod iudicium sit omnino nullum [in D. (6, 1) 5, 5]. Videte singularem glossam hic in verbum actori . . ."—*Commentaria*, D. (45, 1) 83 (Titulus: *de verborum oblig.*, l. *inter stipulantem*, § 1, *Si Stichum Stipulatus*), n. 2.

100 "Si Stichum stipulatus de alio sentiam, tu de alio, nihil actum erit . . .

the gloss to *"actori"* (plaintiff) supposes that the plaintiff is alive and is willing to declare his mind; that the situation would be otherwise (no judgment would issue—the gloss recites) if the complainant were not alive to declare his intent.[101] The situation is clear: if the plaintiff is deceased, he cannot express his mind, and the court will not pass upon the case. And thus, Bartolus explains, this right of declaring *(istud ius declarandi)* does not devolve upon the heir, according to this gloss, and he adds that the matter under discussion concerns the declaration of intent as to what the plaintiff really had in mind.[102]

Bartolus concludes his entire discussion of this matter with the remark that all that he has said in the foregoing concerning the fact that something cannot be declared by a successor (of a judge), or similar persons, must be understood when the declaration proceeds from the internal intent *(ex mera voluntate)*, but that a declaration can issue from a successor upon probable conjectures.[103] Therefore, if a successor of a judge (or persons in similar official capacity, as Bartolus seems to point out) can interpret the sentence of his predecessor, it follows necessarily that this interpretation is law for the parties to the suit. Consequently there is present authentic interpretation by a successor. It is clear from his cita-

in iudiciis . . . magis est, ut is petitus videatur de quo actor sensit . . . et ideo actori potius credendum est."—D. (45, 1) 83, 1.

101 ". . . ibi dicit [glossa] . . . quod hic actor vivebat . . . declarare volebat, secus si non viveret . . ."—*Commentaria*, D. (45, 1) 83 (Titulus: *de verborum oblig*, l. *inter stipulantem*, § 1, *Si Stichum Stipulatus*), n. 2. The *glossa* ad v. *Actori* reads: "Actori . . . viventi et declarare volenti [credendum] . . . alias nulla fieret ei condemnatio."—D. (45, 1) 83, 1.

102 ". . . et sic istud ius declarandi non transit ad haeredem secundum istam gl . . . sed hic loquitur de declaratione voluntatis, quidnam de certo sensit."—*Ibid*, n. 3.

103 "Omnia enim quae supra dixi non posse declarari per successorem [iudicis successorem], vel similes, intelligo quando declaratio consistit ex mera voluntate, secus in declaratione quae fit per verisimilia."—*Ibid*, n. 3.

tion of Bartolus that Felinus Sandaeus holds this opinion as a conclusion.

Felinus Sandaeus calls upon Baldus to prove that a successor in office cannot interpret the sentence of his predecessor *(Idem vult Baldus)*. It has been shown that Baldus at first disagrees with him, but is in accord with regard to interpretation which proceeds from the mind *(ex mera voluntate)*. On the other hand, it has also been shown that Sandaeus holds that a successor can interpret on the basis of conjecture. Briefly, they both agree on either point. A text of Baldus in his commentary on the Code of Justinian represents clearly the two avenues of approach to declarative authentic interpretation, conjectural and psychological, as it were, and states that the former is sufficient for the purposes of authentic interpretation. According to his doctrine, the authentic interpretation of a law or of a canon appertains to the author thereof, but is not to be restricted to his person but to his office. Thus the emperor of his time can interpret a law enacted by Justinian, because he holds the same office.[104] In this immediate context Baldus refers to his treatment of a paragraph in the Digest,[105] pointing out that in that treatise he deals with interpretation which is restricted to the person, a matter, he says, which is different *(alia materia)* from the present subject.[106] In that commentary, it will be recalled,

---

104 "Ultimo nota quod interpretatio legis vel canonis pertinet ad conditorem, sed hoc dictum non est restringendum ad personam, sed ad officium. Nam Imperator qui est nunc potest interpretari legem Iustiniani quia gerit illud officium."—*Commentaria,* C. (1, 14) 11 [12] (Titulus: *de legibus et constitutionibus,* lex XI, *Si Imperialis*), n. 3.

105 D. (6, 1) 5, 5. This place in Baldus is referred to by Felinus to confirm that a procurator cannot interpret, as indicated previously.

106 "Sed in alia materia interpretatio restringitur ad personam ut ff., de rei ven., l. Idem Pomponius scribit si frumentum, § finali et ibi nota. [i. e., *Commentaria,* D. (6, 1) 5, 5 (Titulus: *de rei vendicatione;* Additio Baldi, § Idem Pomponius)]."—*Commentaria,* C. (1, 14) 11 [12] (Titulus: *de legibus et constitutionibus,* lex XI, *Si Imperialis*), n. 3.

Baldus declares that he is speaking about a doubt concerning fact *(dubium facti)*, not about a doubt concerning the signification of a word *(dubium iuris)*; elsewhere,[107] as indicated above, he had referred to said paragraph as the paragraph regarding the mind *(articulus de animo)*.[108]

What has been quoted in the previous pages represents practically the complete exposition given by Felinus Sandaeus in the place cited concerning interpretation by a successor.

Briefly, considering the passages examined in the foregoing, Felinus Sandaeus seems to teach that while a successor in office cannot reach into the interior mentality of his predecessor and thus interpret his enactment *(ex mera voluntate)* he can interpret on the basis of probable conjectures. There is nothing in his teaching in the place examined (and which is cited by the opposite opinion to support its view) to warrant the statement that Felinus Sandaeus confines authentic interpretation to the possibility of knowing the interior mind of the original lawgiver. If such were the doctrine of Felinus, he could not possibly call upon Baldus de Ubaldis *(Idem vult Baldus)* to confirm his view. Nor could he invoke the authority of Bartolus.

Finally, it must be remembered that Suarez also reflects the doctrine of approximately these times. If the teaching of the sixteenth century jurists were such as represented by the opposite opinion, the silence of Suarez to report this fact is, to say the least, most striking. For in his teaching on authentic interpretation this jurist never fails to refer to the teaching of his predecessors in the field of law. It seems that he would not have failed to mention this phenomenal departure from the classical jurisprudence and the period immediately following. Philippus Decius is also cited as having broken

---

[107] *Commentaria,* C. (7, 44) 2 (Titulus: *de senten. ex brevi. reci.,* lex II, *Hac lege*), n. 7.

[108] Viz., D. (6, 1) 5, 5.

with the juristic teaching of the past inasmuch as he is said to hold the same supposed view as Felinus Sandaeus. The passage in which this teaching is said to occur will now be investigated.

Philippus Decius (+circa 1536-1537) sets down practically the same statements as Felinus Sandaeus. The faculty of interpreting adheres to the person and does not devolve upon the heir; he cites passages which have already been noted. The successor in office cannot interpret the statute or the sentence of his predecessor. Decius solves the whole matter by indicating that Alexander Tartagnus (+1477) has written at length on the subject.[109] It is therefore necessary to consult Tartagnus. The solution will be presented as briefly as possible.

Alexander Tartagnus agrees with the statement of Decius, referring to the commentary of Bartolus to the Digest [110] and of Baldus de Ubaldis to the Code [111] and also adds that Bartolus, and Baldus and Angelus maintain the contrary upon reasons set down by Bartolus in the places to which Tartagnus refers his reader.[112] The contrary opinion of Baldus is stated

---

109 "Et etiam notandum quod facultas interpretandi personae cohaeret et non transit ad haeredem . . . Et successor in officio non potest interpretari—statutum vel sententiam praedecessoris . . . Et de his late scribit Alex., in dicta lege inter stipulantem, § 1."—*Commentaria*, lib. II, tit. I, cap. *Cum venissent*, nn. 24-26. In this place the present author cities the gloss to D. (6, 1) 5, 5; also, c. 3, X, *de successionibus ab intestato*, III, 27, which texts have already been explained above.

110 Commentary of Bartolus to D. (45, 1) 83, Cf. page 39.

111 Commentary of Baldus de Ubaldis to C. (7, 44) 2. Cf. page 37.

112 "Et ex hoc etiam infert Bartolus hic nota quod successor in officio non potest declarare ambiguam sententiam in sui praedecessoris. Idem tenuit Angelus in l. ex facto, in prin., supra de vulg. et pupil. [D. (28, 6) 43]. Et Baldus in l. iii [ii] C. de sent. ex brevi. reci. [C. (7, 44) 2]. Contrarium tenuit ipsemet Bartolus in l. ab. executore in prin., infra de app., [D. (49, 1) 4], et in l. terminato C. de fru. et lit expen. [C. (4, 51) 3], et Baldus in l. fi. C. de leg. [C. (1, 14) 12], et Angelus hic per rationes quas vide per

in Baldus' annotations to a law of the Code of Justinian,[113] mentioned above. The reasons adduced by Bartolus will now be examined.

Bartolus, establishing a dialectic contradiction, denies the power of a successor in the office of judge to interpret an obscure sentence of his predecessor, reciting the laws of the Digest,[114] where the power is denied to the heir. To the contrary he adduces as an example the power of the principal to interpret the sentence of the delegated judge. His reason is that the jurisdiction, tribunal, judgment, and judge are one and the same in the person of the principal and delegate. The right of interpretation is not proper to the former as to a private individual, but as to the judge. On the other hand, the heir and the deceased are not truly the same person, but only by fiction. It will be noted that according to this authority the union effected between delegant and delegated by the agency of jurisdiction is much more than a fiction; it is a reality in the domain of juridic authority. In this manner Bartolus solves the problem.[115] The second place in Bartolus, referred to by Alexander Tartagnus, very aptly takes up where Bar-

---

Bartolum in dict. leg. locis."—Alexandri Tartagni Imolensis, *In Digestum Commentaria,* (Venetiis, 1570), D. (45, 1) 83, 1 (Titulus: *de verb. oblig.,* [lex] *Inter stipulantem, § Si Stichum*).

113 C. (1, 14) 12; the words of Baldus are quoted above.

114 D. (6, 1) 5, 5; (45, 1) 83, which have been dealt with in the foregoing.

115 "Quaero utrum unus iudex possit interpretari sententiam praedecessoris sui? Videtur quod non, sicut haeres non potest interpretari libellum defuncti, ut nota [here this author cites D. (6, 1) 5, 5; (45, 1) 83, 1] In contrarium videtur . . . scilicet quod delegatus interpretatur sententiam delegati sui. Et istud puto verum, quia accipiendo iudicem pro iurisdictione, seu pro ipso tribunali, vere idem est iudicium, et idem iudex, l. proponebatur, supra de iud. [D. (5, 1) 76]. Nec enim ius interpretandi sibi competit ut privato, sed ut iudici. Haeres vero et defunctus non est eadem persona vere, sed ficte. Et ex hoc apparet solutio ad quaestionem . . ."—*Commentaria,* D. (49, 1) 4 (Titulus: *de appellationibus et relationibus,* Lex IV, *ab executore*), n. 9.

tolus concludes in the text just cited,[116] by repeating the example of the interpreting of a judicial sentence regarding court costs, where the judge reserves to himself to determine the amount. Can the successor interpret under this provision? He can. Bartolus points to the reason given in the Digest—the judges are the same as their predecessors.[117] He advances again the objection that the declaration of the will *(declaratio voluntaria)* does not pass to the heir. Bartolus gives no quarter, and answers with the insight of a great jurist. The declaration (of the sentence) is reserved only as to the judge, not as to a private person, the reason being precisely that the same judicial dignity obtains. In the instance of an heir it is reserved not as to a judge but as to a private individual. In fact, since the disposition in the present matter has respect only to the office, the distinction between person and office is not even applicable.[118] Thus Bartolus rules out entirely the question of the *declaratio voluntatis* (interpretation of the internal intent) of a private person in the interpretation of law. If the judge, jurisdiction, tribunal, judgment, are the same—and these are the same in the mind of Bartolus—it seems that the necessary conclusion is that there remains only

---

116 ". . . taxare expensas est declarare et interpretari suam sententiam." —*loc. cit.*

117 D. (5, 1) 76—as a ship is the same though every piece thereof is replaced in repair; as the person remains the same in spite of the process of metabolism.

118 "Quaero quid si iudex dicat condemnamus in expensis reservata nobis taxatione. Quaero an poterit taxare successor eius. Dico quo sic, arg. [here he cites D. (5, 1) 76]. Sed contra hoc facit [here he cites D. (6, 1) 5, 5] ubi dicit quod declaratio voluntaria non transit ad haeredem, ut [here he cites D. (45, 1) 83, 1] quod ibi nota . . . Sol. [utio] haec declaratio reservatur iudici non ut privatae personae, ideo reservatur, scilicet, quia idem iudex et eadem dignitas, ut [D. (5, 1) 76]. Ibi vero non ut iudici, sed ut privatae personae . . . quando dispositio praecedit super aliqua re . . . si non potest haberi respectus nisi ad officium tantum, tunc illa distinctio non habet locum." —Bartoli a Saxoferrato, *In Codicem Iustiniani Commentaria,* (Venetiis, 1585), C. (7, 51) 3 (Titulus: *de fruct. et litium expensis.* Lex III, *Terminato*), n. 6.

the will of the court to be interpreted, a will which endures with the passing of the individual incumbents of the judiciary.

In the present investigation it has been shown that this concept of authentic interpretation of a successor in office passed into Alexander Tartagnus (+1477) and from him to Philippus Decius (+1536-37). The fact that Decius leaves the matter to Tartagnus for explanation seems to indicate that in his time the validity of such interpretation was not questioned.

In the foregoing it was noted that Tartagnus established a dialectic contradiction. In conclusion his concordance thereof will be considered.

The opinions may be brought into harmony, he declares, according to Angelus and Ioannes ab Imola (+1436) and Raphael Fulgosius (+1427)—note, all fifteenth century jurists—to the effect that one has in mind either interpretation which proceeds from probable conjectures and documents *(ex actis)*, then the latter opinion obtains, because such interpretation is permitted to any judge, or, interpretation which proceeds from internal intent *(ex mera voluntate)*, which does not pass to a successor or heir. This concordance, he closes, is certainly in accord with the mind of Bartolus in his commentary to this law of the Digest.[119] Thus Felinus Sandaeus

---

[119] D. (45, 1) 83. "Potes opiniones concordare secundum Angelum et Imola in dicta lege executore [D. (49, 1) 4] et Raphael et Imola hic quod aut loquimur de interpretatione ex verisimilibus coniecturis et ex actis facienda et tunc procedit secunda opinio, quia talis interpretatio cuicumque iudici committitur . . . aut de interpretatione quae fit ex mera voluntate . . . cum pendeat ex voluntate iudicis non transit ad successorem, sicut nec ad haeredem . . . Et certe haec conclusio est de mente ipsius Bartoli hic ad finem"—*Commentaria*, D. (45, 1) 83, 1 (Titulus: *de verb. oblig.*, [lex] *Inter stipulantem*, § *Si Stichum*). See the text above from Bartolus, which begins, "*Omnia enim*", p. 40. A similar concordance is found in Bartolus, *Commentaria* C. (7, 51) 3 (Titulus: *de fruct. et litium expensis*, Lex III, *Terminato*); a third, also in Bartolus, *Commentaria*, D. (45, 1) 83 (Titulus: *de verborum oblig.*, Lex LXXXIII, *Inter stipulantem*, § *Si Stichum stipulatus*). Both concordances are

and Philippus Decius are simply stating a well known dialectic contradiction. A resume of their opinions is opportunely found in the concordance just outlined.

Suarez (+1617) gave express recognition to the enduring juristic personality concerning the interpretation of law. He declares, citing the *"Inter alia"* of Innocent III (+1216) [120] as an example, that the interpretation emanates from the same see *(eamdem sedem)*, the same power, regardless of the individual person of the predecessor or successor.[121] There simply is no evidence of change between Ioannes Andreas (+1348), Bartolus a Saxoferrato (+1357) and the time of Suarez. The same idea is briefly set down by Cardinal Tuschus (+1620), a contemporary of Suarez.[122] Nor has there appeared any evidence of a change since that time.[123]

---

noted by a commentator later than Alexander Tartagnus (+1477), because he is mentioned in the concordances.

[120] Cf. c. 31, X, *de sententia excommunicationis,* V, 39.

[121] "Est autem advertendum non tantum eamdem personam posse hoc modo legem suam interpretari, sed etiam eamdem sedem, ut ita dicam, seu successorem in eadem potestate, ut clare probatur in dicto cap. Inter alia. Et ratio est, quia lex non procedit a persona nisi ut habente potestatem, et lex semper pendet ab eadem potestate, in quacumque persona sit; ergo qui in eadem potestate succedit semper potest praedecessorum leges interpretari."—*De Legibus,* VI, cap. 1, n. 2.

[122] "Interpretatio literarum Apostolicarum et privilegiorum ab Apostolica Sede concessorum spectat ad Papam et Sedem ad quos est recurrendum."—*Practicae Conclusiones Iuris in omni foro frequentiores Dominici Tuschi,* (Lugduni, 1634), IV, Concl. 329.

[123] Cf. Reiffenstuel, lib. I, tit. II, n. 382; Michiels, *Normae Generales Iuris Canonici,* (Lublin: Universitas Catholica, 1929), I, 391.

ARTICLE III. *Authentic Interpretation by an Inferior Legislator.*

A. *General Principle.*

According to the law of the Decretals *"Ex parte"*, a Cardinal Legate of the Holy See had enacted a constitution concerning temporalities left by legacy. His successor restated the same law. A dispute arose, and the case was referred to Honorius III (+1227). It appears that both legates had given similar interpretations to the enactment. Honorius III reviews their interpretations and confirms them. The point under consideration at present is the fact that the legate was a legislator in the province of his jurisdiction, and that the same principle of law enunciated heretofore applies to an inferior legislator. Such is the clear doctrine of the gloss. Whoever can make a law (in his own right) can interpret that law authentically.[124]

B. *The Residential Bishop.*

The Bishop of the Diocese is the authentic interpreter of his synodal decrees. This principle is explicitly stated in canon 17, §1. His interpretation stands juridically on a par

---

124 "Ex hoc patet quod legatus potest facere constitutionem in sua provincia."—*Glossa* ad v. *Legatus,* c. 31, X, *de verborum significatione,* V, 40; "Sic ergo legatus interpretatur suam constitutionem; ille enim potest interpretari, qui ius constituit, C. de legi. lex ult., et supra tit. prox. Inter alia."—*Glossa* ad v. *Interpretatione, ibid.*

with his law.[125] In other words, having the force of law, it is authentic, it is *law*.

The residential Bishop is the sole legislator in the diocesan synod.[126] and outside the synod.[127] Therefore he alone can authentically interpret the diocesan statutes. To interpret authentically means to declare authoritatively in what meaning a law shall juridically be taken.[128] To execute this interpretation a legislative faculty is required. For, as Santi says, only the legislator or his successor can impose a law, speaking of the nature of authentic interpretation.[129] Hence the Vicar General, since he does not possess legislative power, cannot authentically interpret synodal or extra-synodal decrees. On the other hand, the Vicar Capitular or, as he is also called, the Administrator of the Diocese, can authentically interpret diocesan legislation, because he has the ordinary jurisdiction of the Bishop; he has the faculty to issue legisla-

---

125 "Authentica namque interpretatio quae manat ab Episcopis, qui Synodorum auctores sunt, tanti profecto est, quanti sunt ipsa decreta."—Leo XIII, const. "*Romanos Pontifices*", 8 maii 1881.—*Fontes*, n. 582, § 13.

126 Can. 362.

127 Cf. Coronata, *Institutiones Iuris Canonici*, I, (2. ed., Taurini: Ex Officina Libraria Marietti, 1939), n. 414, nota 1; Van Hove, *Commentarium Lovaniense in Codicem Iuris Canonici*, II, *De Legibus Ecclesiasticis*, (Mechliniae-Romae; H. Dessain, 1930), n. 243; Jone, *Gesetzbuch des kanonischen Rechtes*, (Paderborn: Ferdinand Schoningh, 1939), I, 295. Synodal decrees do not differ essentially from extra-synodal legislation.—Chelodi, *Ius de Personis*, (Tridenti: Libr. Edit. Tridentum, 1922), n 240.

128 "Interpretatio necessaria seu authentica generatim est illa cui necessario est acquiescendum et vim legis obtinet."—Reiffenstuel, lib. I, tit. II, n. 359, ". . . nam Princeps declarando authentice aliquam legem non tam declarat intentionem personalem imprimis Conditoris, quam sensum, in quo lex deinceps recipi et observari debeat."—Reiffenstuel, lib. I, tit. II, n. 382.

129 "Tertii generis interpretatio est ea quae dicitur authentica . . . verum enim legis sensum exhibet. Authenticam hanc interpretationem proponit legislator aut eius successor: nemo enim alius potest legem imponere."—*Praelectiones Iuris Canonici*, (Ratisbonae, 1886), lib. I, tit. II, n. 39.

tion.[130] There is nothing in law which denies this faculty to the Vicar Capitular.[131]

It is quite apparent that individual Bishops cannot authentically interpret decrees of provincial and plenary councils. The reason is that their single legislative jurisdiction does not extend to these enactments.[132] This statement is to be understood in the sense of canon 17, §2; that is, they have no power to issue authentic interpretations *per modum legis.* [133] By the same token, then, a Bishop could not, it seems, authoritatively by way of rescript render an interpretation of the law of a plenary or provincial council considered in the abstract. On the other hand, the Bishop can authentically interpret this legislation by judicial sentence.[134]

From the interpretation of the Diocesan statutes an appeal can be taken to the Holy See *in devolutivo* if the interpretation involves only a matter of diocesan statute; namely, where the interpretation does not at the same time conflict

---

[130] Cann. 435, 335.

[131] But note: "Sede vacante nihil innovetur."—can. 436.

[132] Cf. can. 335, § 1. With the permission of the Holy See the provincial council could give to the Metropolitan, to be used either alone or with the counsel or consent of the suffragans, the faculty to interpret authentically its decrees.—Maroto, *Institutiones Iuris Canonici,* (3. ed., Romae: Apud Commentarium pro Religiosis, 1921), n. 237, e.

[133] Van Hove, *De Legibus Ecclesiasticis,* n. 243, who in the present place denies that the Metropolitan or the Bishops either in conference (coetus episcoporum) or singly can authentically interpret the decrees of these councils "per norman generalem". The legislative power of the individual Bishops does not extend to these laws, which cannot, therefore, be called their enactments as individuals.—Michiels, *Normae Generales, Iuris Canonici,* (Lublin: Universitas Catholica, 1929), I, 397, nota 1.

[134] Cf. can. 1570, § 1; Van Hove, *De Legibus Ecclesiasticis,* n. 243, nota 4: ". . . quia ipsorum curae est commissa potestas applicandi leges in iudicio." Hence the *Officialis* (cf. can. 1573, § 2) can render a decision regarding provincial and plenary legislation. There does not seem to be in law a faculty whereby the Bishop could interpret this legislation by means of the rescript of canon 17, § 3.

with the rights of personages who are exempt from episcopal jurisdiction. In the latter case, the appeal is *in suspensivo*.[135]

C. *Other Ecclesiastical Superiors.*

For the sake of completeness this number has been injected. It deals with the power of authentic interpretation of religious superiors. There is no question here about any power of authentic interpretation of law properly so called in religious organizations of women; only clerics can possess jurisdiction,[136] and hence enjoy the legislative faculty requisite for authentic interpretation of law.

This number closes with Van Hove's remark that authentic interpretation in religious organizations takes place according to their respective statutes.[137]

---

[135] Van Hove, *De Legibus Ecclesiasticis*, n. 243, in fine: cf. Chapter III, Art. V, C; cf. can. 1601; *AAS*, XV (1923), 296-302; XVI (1924), 251.

[136] Can. 118. Only men (not women) are subjects of sacred orders.—cann. 968, 950.

[137] *De Legibus Ecclesiasticis*, n. 243, in fine.

CHAPTER III.

Power of Authentic Interpretation Committed to Inferiors.

"Leges Authentice Interpretatur . . . Is cui Potestas Interpretandi Fuerit ab Eisdem Commissa."

Introduction.

The power of authentic interpretation vests in him to whom this power has been committed by the legislator or by his successor.[1]

This third member envisioned by canon 17, §1, is recognized by the present organization of ecclesiastical government in the permanent institution known as the Pontifical Commission for the Authentic Interpretation of the Canons of the Code of Canon Law, created by Benedict XV in his Motu proprio, *"Cum iuris canonici"*, 15 September, 1917.[2] The act by which this Commission is brought into being, as in the case of any other of similar nature, involves the principle enunciated in the rule of law: "Potest quis per alium, quod potest facere per se ipsum".[3] Acts performed under such dele-

[1] Can. 17, § 1.

[2] *Acta Apostolicae Sedis* (*AAS*), IX (1917), 483-484.

[3] Reg. 68, R. J., in VIo. The principle is applicable to juridic acts and the exercise of jurisdiction—Cf. Reiffenstuel, *Tractatus de Regulis Iuris,* (Romae, 1834), Regula LXVIII, nn. 2, 7; *Glossa* ad Reg. LXVIII, R. J. in VIo, nn. 60-70.

gation are juridically valid: "Qui facit per alium, est perinde ac si faciat per se ipsum".[4] The reasons which prompted this most provident act of the Supreme Pontiff are founded in the history of ecclesiastical legislation and its administration. In order, therefore, to understand the importance of the Pontifical Commission as also the scope of its jurisdiction, it is necessary first to present its historical antecedents and then to outline in greater detail the function of this Commission by considering the provisions of the Motu proprio *"Cum iuris canonici"*.

ARTICLE I. *The Period of the "Immensa Aeterni Dei".*

As Pope Benedict XV himself indicates in his Motu proprio, the commission given by the Supreme Pontiff authentically to interpret law was exemplified in the establishment of the S. Congregation of the Council for interpreting the decrees of the Council of Trent, which closed its sessions in the early part of December, 1563.

Pius IV (+1565) had forbidden to any one under threat of severe penalties the editing of commentaries of any kind concerning the decrees of the Tridentine Council, in order to preserve intact these enactments and to prevent confusion regarding legal questions which would arise in view of the decrees.[5] He reserved to himself their interpretation if doubt should arise concerning them.[6] In order to effect the execution of his constitutions and ordinances with respect to the offices

[4] Reg. 72, R. J. in VIo; cf. Reiffenstuel, *Tractatus de Regulis Iuris*, Regula LXXII, nn. 2-3.

[5] Bulla, *"Benedictus Deus"*, 26 ian. 1564.—*Canones et Decreta S. Oecum. Conc. Trident.*, (Taurini, 1913), 285-286.

[6] *Ibid.*

and tribunals of the Holy See, as well as of the decrees of the Council of Trent, the same Pontiff appointed a committee of eight Cardinals. In the event of doubt or difficulty the matter in question was to be referred to him.[7]

Finally in virtue of the Constitution *"Immensa Aeterni Dei"*, January 22, 1587, the Congregation of the Council for the execution and interpretation of the decrees of the Council of Trent was established by Pope Sixtus V (+1590). The competence of this body of Cardinals concerned the reformation of morals and discipline, including judiciary matters, inasmuch as these affairs have respect to the decrees of the Council. The Congregation was therefore vested with the power to interpret law in case of doubt; however, it did not have the faculty to render extensive or restrictive interpretation.[8] It was also stipulated that this faculty shall be exercised upon consultation with the Supreme Pontiff, who, as he himself points out, alone had the authority to interpret the provisions created in general council.[9] This congregation was at once vested with executive power and the faculty to interpret. Fagnanus (+1678) is of the firm opinion that, in view of the constitution just mentioned, this body enjoyed the faculty of rendering any authentic interpretation, which, being properly signed and sealed, even in a particular case, had the force of general law, as if issuing from the Supreme Pon-

---

[7] Motu proprio, *"Alias nos"*, 2 aug. 1564.—*Bullarium Diplom. et Privileg. Ss. Rom. Pont. Taurin. Ed.*, (Neapoli, 1882), VII, XCIX, 300.

[8] Gonzalez-Tellez, *Commentaria Perpetua Decretalium,* (Lugduni, 1715), I, *Prooemium*, n. 57. However, Lega (*De Iudiciis Ecclesiasticis,* [Romae, 1898], II, n. 161) declares that this Congregation was vested with such power.

[9] *Prooem*: ". . . cum ad singularem Romani Pontificis auctoritatem spectet generalia concilia . . . interpretari . . . n. 1. Eorum quidem decretorum . . . cardinalibus vero praefectis interpretationi et executioni concilii Tridentini, si quando in his quae de morum reformatione, disciplina ac moderatione et ecclesiasticis iudiciis aliisque huiusmodi statuta sunt, dubietas aut difficultas emerserint, interpretandi facultatem nobis tamen consultis impartimur."—*Bull. Rom. Taur.*, (Neapoli, 1883), VIII, CXVII, 991.

tiff; that in fact such had been the declaration of the Congregation itself.[10] The question is raised and discussed with considerable disagreement whether the decisions of this Congregation had always the force of general law.[11]

Cappello concludes as the correct juristic teaching that these decisions had the force of law—he means general law—when they interpreted the disciplinary decrees of the Tridentine Council, provided that they appeared in authentic form and were rendered upon consultation with the Supreme Pontiff. This opinion is well in accord with that of Fagnanus. Wernz states that, while the Congregations were vested with wide faculties to interpret the law and to put it into execution, not all their interpretations, not even those of the S. Congregations of Rites and of the Council, much less those of the other Congregations, are to be taken indiscriminately as universal law.[12]

Of the other congregations brief mention may here be made of the S. Congregation of Bishops and Regulars.[13] According to Fagnanus this Congregation had the faculty of

---

10 *Commentaria Super Quinque Libros Decretalium,* (Romae, 1661), lib. II, tit. I, cap. *Cum venissent,* n. 17. The same view is held by Schmalzgrueber, *Ius Ecclesiasticum Universum,* (Romae, 1843-1845), lib. I, tit. II, n. 45. Gonzalez (I, *Prooemium,* n. 57), citing a number of canonists for each opinion, declares that some regarded all declarations of the S. C. Conc. as general law; that others held them only as doctrinal. He subscribes to the opinion that under certain conditions; namely, that: a) upon consultation with the Sovereign Pontiff; b) under seal, and signature of the prefect and secretary; c) after promulgation; d) it having been established that they are authentic; e) the Congregation did not exceed its competence of merely solving a doubt of law, without extending or restricting the law, the declarations in a particular case issued by the Congregation are general law.

11 Cf. Cappello, *De Curia Romana,* (Romae, 1911), I, 41.

12 *Ius Decretalium,* (2. ed., Romae, 1905), n. 130, citing D'Annibale, *Summula Theologiae Moralis,* I, P. I, n. 184, nota 5.

13 Cf. Bizzari, *Collectanea in Usum S. C. Episcoporum et Regularium,* (Romae, 1885), *Prologus,* p. XI.

giving responses which were binding generally in similar cases. Consequently the response in a given case would constitute a precedent.[14] Thus, to the time of the *"Sapienti Consilio"* of Pius X it was a moot question as to what extent responses in a particular case constitute general law. By way of a general statement it is taught that the decisions emanating from the Roman Congregations, from the time of the *"Immensa Aeterni Dei"* until the appearance of the *"Sapienti Consilio"* (1908), when given in a particular case were binding only for the question at issue.[15]

ARTICLE II. *The Period of the "Sapienti Consilio".*

With the issuance of the papal constitution *"Sapienti Consilio"* of Pius X, June 29, 1908,[16] whereby the affairs of ecclesiastical government were re-allocated to the various congregations, tribunals, and offices of the Roman Curia, the former preeminence of the S. Congregation of the Council ceased. It no longer enjoyed the exclusive power of executing and interpreting authentically the decrees of the Council of Trent, as described in the foregoing. The jurisdiction of authentic interpretation both as to the decrees of this Council as well as to other ecclesiastical laws was distributed among the various Congregations according to the respective competence of each with regard to ecclesiastical matters committed to its jurisdiction. The rendering of such interpretation was subject to the approval of the Roman Pontiff.[17] Cappello

---

[14] *Commentaria,* lib. II, tit. I, cap. *Cum venissent,* n. 18.

[15] Cappello, *De Curia Romana,* I, 40.

[16] *Fontes,* n. 682.

[17] "An post ordinationem Romanae Curiae a Pio PP. X statutam, Sacrae Congregationi Concilii adhuc competat exclusiva facultas authentice interpretandi omnia Concilii Tridentini decreta, quae ad morum reformationem, disciplinam aliaque huiusmodi pertinent, Summo Pontifice consulto; [Resp.]

denies as unwarranted by the *"Sapienti Consilio"* that the decrees or declarations *(decreta aut declarationes)* of the S. Congregations of the Council, of Rites, and of the Propagation of the Faith under this present re-organization, save for a special concession from the Supreme Pontiff, had the force of general law.[18]

The tribunals of the Sacred Roman Rota and the Supreme Signatura Apostolica did not receive the faculty of authentically interpreting ecclesiastical legislation with general legislative effect. It is explicitly set down that their judicial pronouncements decree law only as between the parties to the cause.[19] The question of the general legislative effect of a response given in a particular case will again be taken up in the chapter dealing with rescripts.

ARTICLE III. *The Period of the Motu Proprio "Cum Iuris Canonici".*

The very core of the Motu proprio *"Cum iuris canonici"* of Benedict XV, issued September 15, 1917,[20] is the word *stabilitas*—the stability of the Code of Canon Law, promulgated April 19, 1917.[21] It is in behalf of the permanence of

Negative. An facultas authentice interpretandi Concilii Tridentini decreta, aliasque leges ecclesiasticas vi Constitutionis *Sapienti Consilio* sit singulis Sacris Congregationibus commissa secundum propriam cuiusque competentiam, salva Romani Pontificis approbatione; [Resp.] Affirmative."—*Fontes,* n. 2079.

18 *De Curia Romana,* I, 42.

19 "An eadem potestas competat sacris tribunalibus Romanae Rotae et Signaturae Apostolicae; [Resp.] Negative. An iisdem sacris tribunalibus competat saltem facultas decreta Concilii Tridentini aliasque leges ecclesiasticas interpretandi iuridice in casibus particularibus, ita nempe ut ius faciant inter partes in causa. [Resp.] Affirmative.—*Fontes,* n. 2079.

20 AAS, IX (1917), 483-484 (Abbreviated *Mpr*)

21 AAS, IX (1917), § II, 6-8.

this body of law that the Motu proprio is written. The *Decretum Gratiani* characterizes as ridiculous and detestable the departure from the traditions of the fathers.[22] Indeed, change in the law is detrimental to the common good, unless such change is not only for the better but is imperative by reason of evident necessity or very great utility unto the commonwealth.[23] Thus the Code of Canon Law itself professes to retain for the most part the existing law, to which it adds opportune changes.[24] It is with the watchword of stability in behalf of the new body of law that the Sovereign Pontiff set to work the machinery of ecclesiastical government.

Benedict XV points out in his Motu proprio two factors which jeopardize this stability in the law, the dubious opinions and conjectures of private interpreters and the hasty accumulation of new legislation. To obviate the first of these dangers the Motu proprio establishes an organ of government known as the Pontificial Commission for the authentic interpretation of the Code. The second danger is met by the prohibition forbidding the Sacred Congregations to issue new law except in the case of serious necessity in the universal Church. At the same time the Motu proprio defines in a general way the offices of the Sacred Congregations, which shall ordinarily be executive in character, and the juridic relations between the Commission and the Congregations. Thus there is established a means of clear and uniform interpretation of the Code on the one hand and on the other the provision is made to safeguard as long as possible its contents from change.[25]

The function of the Pontifical Commission is firmly es-

[22] C. 5, D. XII.

[23] St. Thomas, *Summa Theologica,* (14 ed., Paris, 1885), I, IIae, qu. 97, Art. 2

[24] Can. 6. Cf. De Becker, "De Recta Methodo Interpretandi Codicem," *Ephemerides Theologicae Lovanienses (ETL),* II, (1925), 246.

[25] Hilling, "Zur Promulgation des Codex iuris canonici," *Arkiv fur Katholisches Kirchenrecht* (*AKKR*), XIIC (1918), 82.

tablished on a scientific basis. Besides its own members it has at its command a body of learned consultors, both its own and those of the various Congregations, and it is obliged to confer with the executive departments in all serious matters. Thus while there is a diversity of competence, there is in the authentic interpretation a merging of theory and practice.[26]

Since the Motu proprio effects a change in the *"Sapienti Consilio"* of Pius X regarding the competence of authentic interpretation, it is essential to examine its provisions more closely. It is hardly necessary to mention that the Motu proprio is law; that it represents permanent institutions.[27]

ARTICLE IV. *The Pontifical Commission for Authentic Interpretation.*

Briefly, the Pontifical Commission for the authentic interpretation of the Code of Canon Law consists of a committee of Cardinals, one of their number being the president, assisted by a body of consultors.[28]

The idea, as Benedict XV indicates, of instituting a body of Cardinals for the present purpose is nothing new. We have but to recall the establishment of a committee for the authentic interpretation of the disciplinary decrees of the Council of Trent, the S. Congregation of the Council. A marked dif-

---

26 Hilling, "Gesetzgeberische Tatigkeit Benedikts XV seit der Promulgation des CIC," *AKKR*, CIII (1923), 9.

27 ". . . certa scientia atque matura deliberatione Nostra, haec quae infra scripta sunt statuimus."—*Mpr*, pr; ". . . ea omnia et singula uti decreta sunt, ita rata et firma esse et manere volumus ac iubemus; contrariis non obstantibus quibuslibet."—*Mpr*, in fine.

28 For further particulars see the second document inserted at the beginning of the Code. Regarding the personnel of the Commission see Brems in *Jus Pontificium*, XVI (1936), 86-91; cf. also *Annuario Pontificio*.

ference between the Congregation of the Council and the Pontifical Commission lies in the fact that the Motu Proprio demands no approbation of the Sovereign Pontiff incident to its decisions.[29]

The action of a Cardinal in the capacity of a plenipotentiary of the Pope in the matter of authentic interpretation dates back at least to the early part of the twelfth century.[30] The papal legate in that instance is vested with the jurisdiction as even to extend the terms of a papal mandate beyond the tenor of the wording, namely, to render an extensive interpretation to the terms of an interdict, as appears from the text of the law *"Ad haec"* and the description of Cardinal Hostiensis (+1271).[31]

A. *Office of the Pontifical Commission.*

According to the terms of the Motu proprio a Commission of Cardinals is constituted, which Commission alone shall have the faculty to interpret authentically the canons of the Code.[32] In other words this Committee alone has the jurisdic-

29 Besides the *Mpr* no documents, commonly known as *Normae,* outlining the procedure of the Pontifical Commission have been made public. Cf. also Brems in *Jus Pontificium,* XV (1935), 162.

30 C. 1, X, *de postulatione praelatorum,* I, 5.

31 "Interpretatus scilicet ex plenitudine legationis, vel de speciali mandato vel vice nostra et nos ratificamus . . . Scripsit autem hic expresse dominus noster quod et si ex vi verborum positorum in literis apostolicis hoc facere nequisset, quia tamen generalis legatus erat, ratum debet esse, quod fecit authoritate legationis, ut sic in dubio potius valeat res quam pereat . . . Item in hoc casu interpretatio legati, papae est, et causam papae agebat utiliter, unde debet esse ratum . . . Nec mirum si interpretatio sua tenuit, nam et quilibet iudex de causa, de qua agitur coram eo interpretatur legem . . ." *Commentaria,* lib. I, tit. V, cap. primum, n. 22.

32 " . . . Consilium seu Commissionem, uti vocant, constituimus, cui uni ius erit Codicis authentice interpretandi."—*Mpr,* I; cf. Hilling in *AKKR,* CVIII (1928), 393-394.

tion to decree in what sense a canon or a part of a canon must be understood. Until this time the several S. Congregations enjoyed this power relative to the laws under their competence.[33] Now these Congregations are excluded from this office inasmuch as their existing power of interpreting authentically the ecclesiastical law of the Code is withdrawn.[34] It must be noted that this enactment is not in conflict with canon 245, which provides for the temporary appointment of a Committee of Cardinals to decide the conflicts of competence in the Roman Curia.[35]

On the other hand the Commission does not have executive power; this is placed into the hands of the S. Congregations.[36] It is not its office to apply the law to concrete cases, but rather to pronounced authentically upon the meaning of the law in a general and abstract manner.[37] In other words a line of division runs between the permanent institutions of the Pontifical Commission and the S. Congregations, between the interpretative and executive functions of government. Thus one danger militating against the stability of the Code is obviated.

---

[33] Cf. *Fontes*, nn. 682, 2079, quoted above; cf. also Michiels, *Normae Generales Iuris Canonici,* (Lublin, Polonia: Universitas Catholica, 1929) I, 394-395.

[34] Hilling, "Gesetzgeberische Tatigkeit Benedikts XV seit der Promulgation des CIC," *AKKR,* CIII (1923), 9; Brems, "De Interpretatione Authentica CIC per Pontificiam Commissionem," *Ius Pontificium* (*IP*), XVI (1936), 92-93; Boudinhon, "La Commission pour L'Interpretation Officielle du Code," *Le Canoniste Contemporain* (*LeCC*) XL (1917), 397.

[35] Hilling, *AKKR,* CIII (1923,) 9. An example of such procedure is in *AAS,* XI (1919), 251. In fact, the Pontifical Commission was recently appointed according to can. 245, to decide points of law as to the extent of the competence of the S. Congregation of the Discipline of the Sacraments in causes regarding the nullity of matrimony, concerning which competence a controversy had arisen.—Cf. *AAS,* XXXII (1940), 317-318.

[36] *Mpr,* II.

[37] Boudinhon, *LeCC,* XL (1917), 397-398.

B. *Object of the Competence of the Pontifical Commission.*

The Motu proprio declares that the Commission shall be engaged with the authentic interpretation of the Code; no other laws are placed under its jurisdiction.

The Code is called the *fons unicus* of the disciplinary laws of the universal Latin Church.[38] This statement must be understood of *ius scriptum;*[39] nor does the Code, generally speaking, intend to legislate in liturgical matters.[40] Therefore, liturgical law is outside the competence of the Pontifical Commission. Whatever of disciplinary law is contained in the Code either explicitly or implicitly[41] falls within its competence, including canons on liturgical matter.[42] Therefore the authentic interpretation of liturgical law outside the Code remains within the competence of the S. Congregation of Rites.[43]

The Pontifical Commission in a plenary session held December 9, 1917, determined that it would give a reply to doubts proposed only by Ordinaries and major Superiors of orders and religious congregations, etc., not by private individuals except by the medium of their proper Ordinary.[44]

---

[38] S. Congreg. de Seminariis et de Studiorum Universitatibus *"Cum novum iuris canonici,"* 7 aug. 1917—AAS. IX (1917), 439; Van Hove, *De Legibus Ecclesiasticis,* n. 69; Stutz, *Zeitschrift der Savigny-Stiftung für Rechtsgeschichte,* (*ZST*), Kanonistische Abteilung, VII (1917), XI-XII; Chelodi, *Ius de Personis,* (Tridenti: Libr. Edit. Tridentum, 1922), nn. 58-59; Cann. 1, 6, nn. 1, 5, 6. Disciplinary law is that which is neither dogmatic nor divine positive or natural law. Cf. Chelodi, *Ius de Personis,* n. 62, b.

[39] Can. 5.

[40] Can. 2.

[41] Can. 6; cf. Van Hove, *De Legibus Ecclesiasticis,* nn. 64-65.

[42] *Mpr.* I.

[43] Can. 253; *Fontes,* nn. 5938, 5971, 683, 2097.

[44] *AAS,* X (1918), 77. According to Maroto there is no doubt that the superiors general and provincial of religious organizations of women are included (can. 490). He suggests, however, that they act through their Ordinary,

Shortly after the appointment of the Pontifical Commission the President of this body received the faculty of replying to doubts of minor importance or of little difficulty without consulting the Commission.[45]

C. *Nature of the Jurisdiction of the Pontifical Commission.*

It is said that the Commission has no legislative power,[46] because this power is given to the Congregations according to the Motu proprio,[47] or because legislative power is reserved exclusively to the Roman Pontiff.[48] Others declare either implicitly that the Commission has legislative power [49] or ex-

---

the papal legate, the Cardinal Protector, or their procurator general (can. 570). The same may be said regarding societies living in common without vows (cann. 673, 675).—"Adnotationes" (ad *Motum proprium "Cum iuris canonici"*), *Commentarium pro Religious* (*CpR*), I (1920), 35-37.

45 *AAS,* XI (1919), 480. Cardinal Gasparri, the first president of the Commission, was the recipient of this faculty as a personal privilege; it was withdrawn after his death.—Cf. Brems in *IP,* XVI (1936), 103, nota 7; Van Hove, *Prolegomena,* (Mechliniae-Romae: H. Dessain, 1928), 346, nota 1. These responses are authentic and constitute general law if published in *AAS.*—Van Hove, *loc. cit;* Maroto, "Adnotationes" (ad *Mpr "Cum iuris canonici"*) *CpR,* I (1920), 38.

46 Van Hove, *De Legibus Ecclesiasticis,* n. 243, who also denies that the Sacred Congregations have legislative power. Cf. Van Hove, *Prolegomena,* n. 63.

47 Maroto, "Adnotationes" (ad *Mpr, "Cum iuris canonici"*), CpR, I (1920), 39. Who is cited and followed by Michiels, *Normae Generales,* I, 393, 396.

48 Beste, *Introductio in Codicem,* (Collegeville: St. John's Abbey Press, 1938), pp. 35, 78.

49 Toso, *Commentaria Minora ad Codicem Iuris Canonici,* (Tiferni Tiberini: ex offic. typogr. Viciana, 1921), I, 47: "Et primum docet [i. e. legislator] authenticam interpretationem sive immediate sive mediate nonnisi ab auctore legis manare posse; . . . Et revera, legum authentica interpretatio tum fieri dicitur cum ita fit, ut ab ea nemini eximere se liceat . . . Hic apertissime patet huiusmodi interpretationem fieri non posse nisi ab eo qui legem tulit . . . vel a constituto ab eo interprete . . ."

plicitly on the basis, it seems, of the principle of authentic interpretation: "Eius est interpretari cuius est condere",[50] or without a given reason.[51] Finally, authentic interpretation is considered as truly pertaining to legislative power, to approach very closely to this power, so that the delegate participates therein, but is not to be identified with it.[52] This opinion rests upon the concept of legislation.

It seems that the Pontifical Commission clearly fulfills the function of a legislator. The function of the Commission is legislative:

A) From the concept of legislator.

What makes a legislator to be a legislator?—It is of the essence of law to command or prohibit in a manner that the command or prohibition shall be obligatory or binding, so that it shall become the rule of action.[53] The legal obligation is induced by the constriction, shall one say, or the binding of the mind of the prospective subjects of the law to the terms of the legal proposition. The mind of the subject is the only point of contact between superior and subject.[54] A legislator

---

[50] ". . . je voudrais l' [i. e. l'interpretation] appeler legislative; elle ne peut avoir pour auteur que le legislateur ou qui agit par son ordre et son autorité."—Boudinhon, *LeCC*, XL (1917), 397.

[51] Cicognani, *Canon Law*, (2. ed., authorized English transl., Philadelphia: Dolphin Press, 1935), pp. 76, 434; "Adnotatio", *IP*, VI (1926), 82.

[52] Brems, "De Interpretatione Authentica CIC per Pont. Commissionem," *IP*, XVI (1936), 86, 100.

[53] ". . . ad legem pertinet praecipere et prohibere . . . Respondeo dicendum quod lex quaedam regula est et mensura actuum secundum quam duciter aliquis ad agendum, vel ab agendo retrahitur: dicitur enim lex a ligando, quia obligat ad agendum . . ."—S. Thomas, *Summa Theologica*, I, IIae, qu. 90, art. I, in corp.

[54] "Nullus ligatur per praeceptum nisi mediante scientia illius praecepti." —St. Thomas, *De Veritate*, Quaest. 17, art. 3. Cf. also St. Thomas, *Summa Theologica*, I, IIae, qu. 90, art. IV, in corp.

alone can issue a precept to his subjects in this manner; and he is a legislator only because he has power to do so.[55] Now the authentic interpreter manages exactly this function in pronouncing his interpretation of the law. He not only declares what is the meaning of the law, but he binds the intellects of his subjects to understand the law in this meaning and in no other. He performs the function of editing positive legislation.

B) From the concept: "Eius est interpretari cuius est condere".

It has been shown that the principle: "Eius est interpretari cuius est condere", resounds through the ages of jurisprudence, both civil and canonical, as the principle of authentic interpretation: to him pertains the office of authentic interpreter who has the prerogative of establishing law. Every manual of canon law recites the cases of Innocent III and Boniface VIII. There is no question that therein the subject of authentic interpretation is under discussion. In the recitation of this principle in the classical cases mentioned, there is no question of constituting a materially new law; the principle is applied to an operation upon existing legislation. To perform such operation there is sought out not any interpreter, but one who has legislative power. In the vernacular he is called an authentic interpreter. According to the principle the office of interpreter is identified with that of legislator, inasmuch as the interpreter is formally the agent of the legislator. Hence Schmier (+1728) explicitly applies the principle of authentic interpretation enunciated in the *"Inter alia"* of Innocent III as well to the interpretive function of the S. Congregation of the Council, the delegate of the Supreme Pon-

55 St. Thomas, *Summa Theologica,* I, IIae, qu. 90, art. III, ad secundum.

tiff, as to the interpretive act of the legislator himself, his successor, or superior.[56] And Suarez (+1617) identifies the act of authentic interpretation with that of legislating, where he compares the former with the force of legal custom as a medium of authentic interpretation, as appears from his context. Interpretation is authentic because it has the force of law.[57] Consequently Ottaviani says very correctly that the declaration of controverted law *(iuris controversi)* issued to the community ". . . est actus potestatis legiferae".[58]

In fact, a close examination of this principle of authentic interpretation will reveal that to interpret authentically *(interpretari)* demands a legislative faculty *(condere)*, so that he alone can interpret authentically who is able to found a law, i. e., to lay down authoritatively a rule of action. Thus Baldus de Ubaldis (+1400), announcing this dictum of jurisprudence, observes that certain lawmakers being removed from office can no longer issue an interpretation because they cannot establish law.[59] Namely, they had lost the power to command, as Bartolus (+1357) declares, which power of *imperium* is of the essence of lawmaking.[60] Hence authentic interpretation postulates legislative jurisdiction.

---

[56] "Non tamen Legislatori soli, qui Legem tulit, potestas competit authentice Legem interpretandi, sed etiam Successori in officio vel Superiori vel cui Legislator specialiter indulsit facultatem interpretandi, veluti Cardinalibus data est licentia Concilium Trident. interpretandi. Textus in d. cap. inter alia 31. de sent. excommunic. Unde ius prodiit interpretatio quoque procedat."—*Jurisprudentia Canonico-Civilis seu Ius Canonicum Universum,* (Venetiis, 1754), I, *Tractatus Praeambulus,* cap. III, § 1, 4, n. 29.

[57] "Sicut ergo diximus supra, interpretationem lege factam esse authenticam ex efficacia legis, quae potest illam stabilire; ita dicendum est de consuetudine quando ad illum gradum pervenit ut vim legis obtineat."—*De Legibus,* VII, cap. 17, n. 3.

[58] *Institutiones Iuris Publici Ecclesiastici,* (2. ed., Typis Polyglottis Vaticanis, 1935), I, n. 46, nota 56.

[59] "Ergo statutarii remoti ab officio: non possunt interpretari: quia nec condere . . ."—*Commentaria,* D. (1, 4) 1 (Titulus: *De constitutionibus principum,* Lex I, *Quod principi*), n. 19.

[60] "Veritas est secundum omnes quod . . . cum illi sapientes statutarii sint

No one will contend that the Cardinal legate, mentioned at the beginning of this article, described by Hostiensis is a legislator in the ordinary acceptation of the term; he certainly is in a definite juridic sense. The principle does not pretend to say that the interpreter must be able to establish materially new law. It does demand that he have power over the existing law. A legislative faculty must be present whether the interpretation is extensive, restrictive, explicative, or even declarative if it is to be authentic. Because such an interpretation alone can pronounce and command how the law shall be understood and accepted. Every legislator is an interpreter: "Plus semper in se continet quod est minus";[61] but not necessarily vice versa. Namely, the authentic interpreter "fully discharges the office of legislator",[62] though extensively, in the sense of establishing materially new law he may not have full legislative power. Such power the Commission does not have.[63] It has power over the existing law of the Code.

Canon 17 sanctions this principle. It declares in effect that authentic interpretation is the faculty to oblige collectively or singly under the meaning of the law as interpreted.[64] It states that this faculty is exercised by the legislator, his successor and the one to whom the faculty may be committed.[65]

Those who deny legislative power to the Commission state explicitly that the legislator renders authentic interpre-

---

functi officio suo, nec amplius habent Imperium, et sic non habent ius interpretandi . . ."—*Commentaria,* D. (1, 1) 9 (Titulus: *De iustitia et iure,* Lex IX, *Omnes populi*), n. 56.

61 Reg. 35, R. J., in VIo.

62 Cicognani, *Canon Law,* p. 434.

63 Compare *Mpr,* I with *Mpr,* II and III.

64 Can. 17, §§ 2 and 3.

65 Can. 17, § 1.

tation, implying that such interpretation is law, because from him the law derives its obligatory force;[66] they identify the office of legislator and interpreter, the latter constituting one person with the lawgiver.[67] *A pari,* the Commission must have legislative power. Finally Suarez characterizes authentic interpretation as a legislative faculty.[68] To exist it must have all the properties of positive law;[69] consequently it must proceed from one who has legislative power.

c) From the principle "Lex dubia, lex nulla".

The Code adopts the principle: "Lex dubia non obligat".[70] Juridically and for all practical purposes a doubtful law does not exist, because the essence of the law is its binding power. The Code treats the interpretation of a doubtful law like a new law. It must be promulgated; it is not instituted as a law until promulgation takes place and enjoys a *vacatio legis.*[71] Certainly the Commission can solve a *dubium iuris.* The same may be said of restrictive and extensive interpretation.[72] This statement has reference to the scope of the competence of the Commission, which will be treated in the following paragraphs. As to the present matter, upon the

66 Michiels, *Normae Generales,* I, 390.

67 Van Hove, *De Legibus Ecclesiasticis,* n. 243; cf. also Toso, *Commentaria Minora,* I, 47.

68 "Authenticam voco quae fit auctaritate illius qui potest legem condere. . . . certum est . . . hanc vero fieri non posses nisi . . . ab ipsomet legislatore . . . potest ergo cum auctoritate legis ab eo fieri, non vero ab inferiori qui legem ferendi non habet potestatem, vel non talem ut cadat in actum superioris."—*De Legibus,* VI, cap. 1, n. 2.

69 "Ut ergo authentica sit interpretatio, oportet ut habeat omnes legis humanae conditiones, atque adeo ut sit iusta, procedens a legitima potestate, sufficienter promulgata, etc."—*Ibid,* n. 3.

70 Can. 15; cf. Van Hove, *De Legibus Ecclesiasticis,* nn. 229-230.

71 Cann. 17, § 2; 8; 9.

72 Cf. Van Hove, *De Legibus Ecclesiasticis,* n. 243.

basis of what has been said the writer chooses to call the power of the Commission a truly legislative faculty; it makes law.

D. *Scope of the Competence of the Pontifical Commission.*

It is admitted generally that the Commission can render authoritatively an interpretation of an objectively doubtful law *(dubium iuris)*. Nor is there question as to its power regarding merely declarative interpretation. From what has been said in the foregoing sections and especially from what is to follow in the present, these points will be considered as demonstrated. As will be shown, historically interpretation in its proper sense has been considered as referring to the solution of objective doubt. This approach to the present question is not the burden of the discussion here; rather the legal definition of canon 17 is to be considered.

All authors are not in accord that the competence of the Commission embraces restrictive-extensive interpretation. The question here is whether under the terms of the Motu proprio §1 the Commission can render such interpretations of the canons of the Code. To what extent does this body have power over the law?

Some authors deny that the Commission can render restrictive-extensive interpretations, its power being "mere interpretativa, nullo modo legislativa".[73] Others simply declare

[73] Michiels, *Normae Generales*, I, 393-394. His reason is that the power of making new laws rests with the S. Congregations according to the *Mpr*. Restrictive and extensive interpretation, being only *abusive* interpretations, are new laws. Since the Commission cannot make new law, it cannot render such interpretations. Under this contention he is seemingly obliged to take refuge in defining his terms: "vere extensiva vel restrictiva"—which is denied to the

that the Commission has no more than the power of giving explicative interpretation, i. e., to solve the question of objective doubt; no reason is given by them.[74] On the other hand a second group claims that the Commission can interpret law restrictively and extensively[75] because it functions as a legislator,[76] or because the faculty which the Commission enjoys must be understood under the terms of can. 17, § 2, and because a doubtful law, being no law, is juridically equivalent to extension and restriction according to the same canon considered together with can. 15.[77]

The issue has this practical aspect, which also Cappello points out.[78] Namely, canonists have discussed and will continue to discuss whether or not an interpretation is explicative, extensive, or restrictive.[79] If furthermore, the scope of the competence of the Commission is brought seriously into

---

Commission—is that interpretation "quae non tantum ultra vel infra propriam verborum significationem sed ultra vel infra significationem a legislatore intentam protrahitur". (Like other subdivisions of authors concerning the present question, this division is merely arbitrary; it has no foundation in can. 17.) Now the limits of the "intentio legislatoris" are best known to the Commission. Thus in practice the Commission's interpretations are only explicative at most and must be obeyed. Maroto, ["Adnotationes" (ad *Mpr "Cum iuris canonici"*), CpR, I (1920), 39, and *Institutiones,* I, n. 239,] pursues the same line of argument and is cited by Michiels.

[74] Gasparri, *Tractatus Canonicus de Matrimonio,* (ed. nova ad mentem CIC, Typis Polyglottis Vaticanis, 1932), II, n. 1025; Woywod, "Recent Studies on the New Code," *The Homiletic Monthly and Pastoral Review* (*HPR*), XIX (1918-1919), 546-547.

[75] Vermeersch, "Adnotationes" (ad *Mpr "Cum iuris canonici"*), *Periodica,* IX (1921), 17; Beste, *Introductio in Codicem,* p. 78.

[76] Cicognani, *Canon Law,* p. 434.

[77] Van Hove, *De Legibus Ecclesiasticis,* n. 243; *idem, Prolegomena,* n. 370; Cappello, "Il Trattato sul Matrimonio," *La Civilta Cattolica (LaCC),* III (1933), 366. Cf. also Brems, "De Interpretatione Authentica CIC per Pont. Commissionem," *IP,* XVI (1936), 93-102.

[78] "Il Trattato sul Matrimonio," *LaCC,* III (1933), 366.

[79] Cf. e. g., *Apollinaris,* III (1930), 601-616, concerning the response on *ab acatholicis nati,* [*AAS,* XXI (1929), 573; XXII (1930), 195]; Brems, *IP,* XVI (1936), 98.

question, juridically the effect of a given response—it being debated whether such response is, say, extensive or only explicative—would be jeopardized under canon 15. Even *a priori* then, since the question is so fundamental, it would seem that the competence of the Commission under the Motu proprio should be beyond dispute. In this connection De Becker sounds a sober warning when he points out that a law vindicates unto itself a great presumption that it is clear.[80] Thus it will be necessary to attempt to determine from the Motu proprio and the Code whether or not the competence of the Commission embraces restrictive-extensive interpretation.

The Motu proprio simply declares in a general way that the Commission alone has the right to interpret the Code authentically.[81] Canon 17, § 1, declares that laws are authentically interpreted by one who is so delegated by the legislator or his successor. The Commission is an example of such delegation. The second paragraph of the same canon implicitly defines the scope of authentic interpretation; it can be merely declarative, explicative, restrictive, or extensive. Here the legislator gives a juridic definition, stating by law the scope of authentic interpretation; he sets down the species of such interpretation. The question is, do the words, "is cui potestas interpretandi fuerit ab eisdem commissa", embrace the species of interpretation outlined in the second paragraph. The legislator commands that ecclesiastical laws must be understood according to their signification considered in their text and context.[82] The term "interpretandi" in the first paragraph can be taken in a proper or extended meaning. But in its context,

---

[80] "Recordemur nos non esse legislatores sed modestos interpretes alicuius legis quae in suum favorem magnam habet praesumptionem claritatis . . ."—"De Recta Methodo Interpretandi Codicem," *ETL*, II (1925), 245.

[81] ". . . Consilium seu Commissionem, uti vocant, constituimus, cui uni ius erit Codicis authentice interpretandi . . ."—§I.

[82] Can. 18.

which is found in the second paragraph, the legislator shows clearly what he means by "interpretandi". It is an axiom in interpreting law that the meaning of the words may not be considered separately and apart, but according to the will of the one who utters them;[83] the intention must be preferred to the words.[84] Nor can one expect the legislator to repeat himself; the meaning is presumed to remain the same in the context unless the contrary is manifest.[85] Thus there is no reasonable doubt that, nothing having been stated by the principal to the contrary, the delegate of can. 17, § 1 will enjoy the power to interpret according to the definition in the second paragraph of the same canon.

Therefore the further question is whether the scope of interpretation as just outlined is to be understood in the terms of the appointment of the Pontifical Commission. Considered alone the clause, "cui uni ius erit Codicis authentice interpretandi",[86] can also refer to interpretation in a strict or extended sense. It is apparent from the present discussion that its meaning has been doubted. The legislator has laid down a method of solution. If the law is not clear from its text and context, parallel passages of the Code must be referred to.[87] A parallel passage is one whose text treats of the same matter; its use for purposes of interpretation is valid because the legislator commands it, and because the Canon law represents a harmony and continuity.[88] Evidently the Motu proprio (§ I) and canon 17 are parallel texts; the *Mpr* is a law whose par-

---

[83] ". . . non debet aliquis considerare verba sed voluntatem, cum non intentio verbis, sed verba intentioni debent deservire . . ."—c. 15, X. *de verborum significatione*, V, 40; c. 11, C. XXII, q. 5; c. 6, X, *de verb. signif.*, V, 40; D. (1, 3), 24.

[84] *Glossa* Ioannis Andreae, ad c. 1, X, *de iuramento calumniae*, II, 7, n. 10.

[85] "Non aliter a significatione verborum recedi oportet, quam cum manifestum est aliud sensisse testatorem."—D. (32, 69).

[86] *Mpr*, I.

[87] Can. 18.

[88] Van Hove, *De Legibus Ecclesiasticis*, n. 256.

allel passage is in the Code. In framing the Motu proprio the legislator cannot be presumed to have disturbed the provision of his previous law in canon 17 or to have restricted its meaning on this occasion. Since the legislator has not indicated that the faculty of interpretation given to the Pontifical Commission must be understood in the strict sense, the two laws must be reconciled.[89] Therefore the Motu proprio (§ I) must be understood according to the terminology of canon 17, § 1 and § 2. Accordingly the argument of those who deny restrictive-extensive interpretation to the Commission would rest on the gratuitous assumption, contrary to the existing juridic definition, that the faculty of interpretation must be understood in a strict sense. Moreover, it is also a clear fact in the history of jurisprudence, as will be shown, that restrictive-extensive interpretation has also been termed simply *interpretatio*.

Again, the denial of this faculty rests on the contention that the Commission is not a legislator under the Motu proprio; that the S. Congregations are so charged.[90] Granted for the present that such is the case, what is the measure of their power? It is to make new legislation. Restrictive-extensive interpretation is considered new legislation by those who hold the negative opinion. One may well ask into what category the solution of a doubtful law shall be put. Does the law distinguish between the "nova Decreta Generalia" of the Motu proprio (§ II) and restrictive-extensive interpretation?

The Motu proprio states the measure of new legislation. Namely, it will either be such that it contradicts the law of the Code, which it is designed to replace; or it will be *praeter Codicem* and will be added to the Code. The new law will then appear in the Code in the form of one or more canons. Such procedure shall take place only when serious necessity

---

89 Can. 23.

90 *Mpr*, II-III.

of the universal Church shall warrant it.[91] In other words, the S. Congregations have, presumably, under the Motu proprio a legislative power regarding laws which at the present time do not yet exist. And upon this premise it is contended that they, and not the Commission, can render restrictive-extensive interpretation upon the law of the Code. The Motu proprio is here speaking about materially and substantially new, future legislation. When the same Motu proprio speaks about authentic interpretation, it has reference explicitly to the existing law of the Code. Surely, it is a far cry between the initiation of new legislation and withdrawing the force of the law from one or several cases which fall under its proper wording or extending it to a number of instances beyond its proper wording. The latter is the function of restrictive-extensive interpretation. As to the argument that the Commission cannot render such interpretation one simply demurs—"Qui nimis probat, nihil probat", because the question of new legislation has nothing to do with the matter of authentic interpretation. Suarez declares it a not infrequent means necessary for the common good to extend or restrict the law; all of which falls within the power of the authentic interpreter.[92] And if there is not an authentic interpreter at hand to do so, private interpreters will. In the end no one will know what the law really means and whither it extends. This catastrophe is just what Benedict XV wishes to avoid. Thus from the purpose of the law there is derived an argument.[93]

History records similar dilemmas. Thus Justinian

---

[91] *Mpr,* II-III.

[92] "Unde etiam intelligitur frequenter contingere, ut haec interpretatio non sit nuda declaratio sensus prioris legis, sed mutatio etiam aliqua, vel addendo vel minuendo, quia totum hoc cadit sub potestatem eius cuius auctoritate fit talis interpretatio, et potest esse ad bonum commune necessarium. Unde . . . non est dubitandum de auctoritate et efficacia interpretationis . . ." —*De Legibus,* VI, cap. 1, n. 3.

[93] Cf. Can. 18.

(+565) forbade the composition of commentaries upon the law in order to forestall confusion.[94] Nicholas III (+1280) prohibited any except a merely grammatical, or declarative, interpretation upon his constitution *"Exiit qui seminat"*.[95] It was shown in the foregoing that Pius IV (+1565) outlawed under serious penalties the interpreting of the decrees of the Council of Trent; again the purpose is to avoid adulterations of the law and confusion. Nevertheless Paaserini (+1677) reports that in his time many controversies and divergent opinions are rampant among the doctors of the law concerning the existence and obligation of many laws, so that there is no certainty concerning them.[96] By the same token, in an effort to preserve the Code Benedict XV establishes the Pontifical Commission for its authentic interpretation. To deny that the Commission has the power of restrictive-extensive interpretation—and the Pope has not modified his terms by adjectival adjuncts—is to forget the vicissitudes of law in the course of legal history. Therefore the observation of Van Hove[97] is good; namely, that explicative, restrictive, and extensive interpretation "aequiparantur", for the reasons given in the foregoing. Thus the law of the Motu proprio regarding the Commission is one most favorable to the common good and must be widely interpreted. In conclusion, the opinion is submitted that there is no reasonable doubt that the Commission has the faculty of restrictive-extensive interpretation.

It is necessary at this point to review the provisions of the Motu proprio concerning the duties of the Sacred Congregations.

---

[94] D. *De Confirmatione Digestorum*, n. 21.

[95] C. 3, *de verborum significatione*, V, 12, in VIo.

[96] *Commentaria in Sextum Librum Decretalium*, (Venetiis, 1698), lib. I, cap. II, quaest. 1, art. 12, n. 244.

[97] *De Legibus Ecclesiasticis*, n. 243.

ARTICLE V. *The Competence of the Sacred Congregations for the Interpretation of Law.*

The duties of the S. Congregations with reference to the universal Latin Church as such are outlined in the Motu proprio *"Cum iuris canonici"*. In order to understand better the competence of the Pontifical Commission, it is necessary to examine that of the Congregations.

The Congregations are directed that for the future they are not to enact new legislation.[98] Their ordinary occupation in the matter of general decrees shall be: first, to manage the conscientious observance of the prescripts of the Code; second, to issue opportunely such Instructions which shall furnish both greater clarity to the laws of the Code and render them the more effectual.[99] It must be remembered that before the Motu proprio *"Cum iuris canonici"* each Congregation was the authentic interpreter of the law which bore upon matters within its respective competence. With the advent of the Code and *"Cum iuris canonici"* this relation to the general law was changed. The Congregations are now to issue decrees which are not new laws, and in so doing they are to fulfill a twofold duty in behalf of the Code.

It is clear from the text of the Motu proprio that Benedict XV uses the word *decreta* in a generic sense, under which term two specific activities are intended. In the time of the *"Sapienti Consilio"* the word *decretum* signified any acts that

---

[98] *Mpr.*, II. The term "nova Decreta Generalia" evidently refers to new general laws for the Latin Church, as appears from the *Mpr.*, II-III and can. 1. For a brief conspectus of the legislative faculty of the S. Congregations, cf. Wernz-Vidal, *Ius Canonicum,* (Romae: apud Aedes Universitatis Gregorianae, 1938), I, n. 209, nota 43.

[99] ". . . ordinarium igitur earum [i. e., Congregationum] munus in hoc genere [i. e., decretorum] erit tum curare ut Codicis praescripta religiose serventur, tum Instructiones, si res ferat, edere, quae iisdem Codicis praeceptis maiorem et lucem afferant et efficientiam pariant."—*Mpr.*, II.

issued in any manner from the Sacred Congregations.[100] Also under the Code legislation the term has various meanings.[101] However, aside from the several significations which the word may have, the question here to be determined is what juridic value each of these two species of general enactments has relative to the authentic interpretation of the law of the Code. From their nature and purpose one immediately concludes to their juridic value.

A. *Decreta*

". . . Ordinarium igitur earum munus in hoc genere erit tum curare ut Codicis praescripta religiose serventur."

The first of the ordinary duties of the Sacred Congregations is to take care that the laws of the Code are religiously observed. They are empowered to do so by the issuing of general *decreta*.

Canonists who wrote before the period of the *"Sapienti Consilio"* treat at great length concerning the decrees of the Roman Congregations, above all concerning those of the S. Congregation of the Council, as also those of the S. Congregations of the Inquisition, of Sacred Rites, of Bishops and Regulars, of the Propagation of the Faith. They are described as having legislative power, so that their decrees (which are said to take on the nature of a papal constitution), resolutions,

---

[100] Monin, *De Curia Romana*, (Lovanii, 1912), p. 215. The same is to be said of this term anterior to this time. Cf. Choupin, *Valeur des Decisions Doctrinales et Disciplinaires du Saint-Siege* (*Valeur des Decisions*), (Paris, 1907), p. 65.

[101] Van Hove, *De Legibus Ecclesiasticis*, n. 371.

and declarations (extensive, restrictive, declarative interpretations of law) concerning the law have universal legal force.[102] They speak about the decrees of the Roman dicasteries in terms of law, authentic interpretation and promulgation.[103] All these acts on the part of the Roman Curia are acts of administration of the ecclesiastical body politic in the name of the Sovereign Pontiff.

Under the re-organization of the Roman Curia by the *"Sapienti Consilio"* of Pius X, Monin describes the administrative power of the S. Congregations as that which has for its object the attainment of the social welfare by securing the observance of the law, by procuring the interest of the members of society, and by stimulating and aiding their activity. In order to accomplish this goal at times it is necessary to interpret the law authentically, an act which is proper exclusively to the legislator but can be committed to the administrator.[104] While the Roman Congregations are the organs of the Supreme Pontiff, and though their acts and decrees have the greatest authority and must be received and carried out by the faithful as coming from the head of the Church, they are not considered as having *per se* (no specific faculty having been granted by the Pope) the force of universal law.[105] The reason assigned by Cappello is that the Constitution *"Sapienti Consilio"* neither confirms the power to issue

---

102 Simor, "De Sacris Congregationibus et Illarum Auctoritate," *AKKR*, XI, (1864), 418-423. This question, of course, is disputed. Cf. Cappello, *De Curia Romana*, (Romae, 1911), I, 40-47.

103 Bouix, *Tractatus de Curia Romana*, (Parisiis, 1859), 295-494; Lega, *Praelectiones de Iudiciis Ecclesiasticis*, (Romae, 1898), II, nn. 282-297; Choupin, *Valeur des Decisions*, p. 65-67; Wernz, *Ius Decretalium*, I, nn. 144-147; cf. also Ojetti, *De Romana Curia*, (Romae, 1910), p. 11-12.

104 *De Curia Romana*, pp. 198-199, 216-218; Cappello, *De Curia Romana*, I, 48-49.

105 Cappello, *De Curia Romana*, I, 40-42; Monin, *De Curia Romana*, pp. 202, 216-218. The same is insinuated by Ojetti, *De Romana Curia*, p. 13.

such decrees nor renews it.[106] Here there is a manifest change of opinion regarding the decrees of the S. Congregations.[107] However, the fact still remains that the controversy as to whether or not a response in a particular instance—which is also called a *decretum*—has the force of universal law [108] was not juridically settled at this time, though from what has just been said, together with the authority of Wernz [109] it would seem apparent that at the turn of the last century the balance of juristic opinion taught what is legally defined in the Code.[110] This question was not solved by the *"Sapienti Consilio"*. Moreover, it is also a fact, as noted in the foregoing, that the S. Congregations were in this period competent to render authentic interpretation of the common law. This consideration together with the fact of the unsolved controversy just mentioned may explain why canonists after the *"Sapienti*

---

106 "Iamvero in praelaudata constitutione, neque confirmatur facultas decreta edendi vim legis habentia, neque e novo conceditur."—*De Curia Romana*, I, 42

107 Could the intense discussion on the universal legal value of a response given in a particular instance, and the apparent ascendancy of the affirmative side of the question from Fagnanus to Lega (cf. Wernz, *Ius Decretalium*, I, 146, IV, for a brief resume) in spite of the philosophic necessity of promulgation already propounded by St. Thomas (*Summa Theologica*, I, IIae, qu. 90, Art. IV. of which all authors are aware)—could this intense discussion have been at all possible if the popular persuasion (shall one say custom in the Church?) had not inclined to receive such declarations as universal law? Simor says (*AKKR*, XI (1864), 421): "Atque ex hac persuasione de legislativa potestate ac sublimi sacrarum Congregationum auctoritate explicari unice potest summa illa pietas et reverentia, qua decisiones earumdem a sinceris Ecclesiae filiis quovis tempore expetitae exceptaeque fuerunt . . . Sic Salmanticenses: 'Tales, inquiunt, declarationes maximi ponderis esse, magnamque habere auctoritatem et gravitatem, utpote a gravissimis viris, auctoritate summi Pastoris congregatis expensae: proindeque adhuc in sententia illorum, qui dicunt non habere vim legis, deserendae non sunt, nisi gravissima ratione et causa interveniente.' "

108 Cf. Monin, *De Curia Romana*, p. 219; Lega, *Praelectiones de Iudiciis Ecclesiasticis*, II, nn. 289-297; Bouix, *De Curia Romana*, p. 297-353.

109 *Ius Decretalium*, I, nn. 144-147.

110 Can. 17, §§ 2, 3.

Consilio" are reported to have conceded to the Congregations a power to legislate.[111] These canonists were, at least, not totally wrong. As a matter of fact, the Congregations had a legislative faculty because they were authentic interpreters. Accordingly, the situation seems clear. Besides the power of authentic interpretation the Congregations had executive power under the reform measures of Pius X. The concept of interpretation is not legally defined in these measures, so that there is no reason why authentic interpretation—be it extensive, restrictive, or even declarative of doubtful law—coupled as it is with executive power, both residing in the same agent, cannot in this period be conceived simply and without making further distinction as new legislation.[112] The general *decreta* of the Sacred Congregations were considered by canonists as practically equivalent to pontifical law.[113] It is therefore not surprising then that Benedict XV must explicitly allude to this state of things when he completely prohibits their proposing new legislation in the ordinary conduct of ecclesiastical affairs: "Sacrae Romanae Congregationes nova Decreta Generalia *iamnunc* ne ferant, nisi. . ."[114]

This idea that legislative and executive power coupled with that of authentic interpretation resided in the Sacred Congregations during the periods prior to the Motu proprio of 1917 forms a basis of comparison whereby their present

[111] "Quae canonistae, etiam post reformationem Pianam, de potestate legislativa S. C. disseruerunt, per hoc decretum (*Cum iuris canonici*), quod in re decisivum est, sunt antiquata."—Chelodi, *Ius de Personis,* n. 161, c, nota 2.

[112] It is true, decisions of the SS. CC., except under certain conditions, require the approval of the Sovereign Pontiff, and nothing of a serious and extraordinary nature can be entertained without first approaching him.—*Fontes,* n. 682, *in fine*. Nevertheless, the "legislative powers enjoyed by the Roman Congregations" are considered as having been "exercised rather freely" before the Motu proprio of 1917.—Kinane, "Recent 'Motu proprio' regarding the New Code of Canon Law,"—*The Irish Ecclesiastical Record* (*IER*), X (1917), 421.

[113] Chelodi, *Ius de Personis,* n. 161, c.

[114] *Mpr.,* II. Italics inserted.

status is more easily discernible. One arrives at the knowledge of this status, for the most part, by noting a process of subtraction of power from the Congregations.

The power of authentic interpretation of the general, common law of the Latin Church is withdrawn and reduced to certain definite limits.[115] The authority of issuing general decrees as regards the common disciplinary law is confined in subject matter to the existing discipline of the Code.[116] The S. Congregations can propose new legislation but they are not legislators of general, universal law. Actually the Sovereign Pontiff is the legislator.[117]

Accordingly, there is a most important residue remaining as the competence of the S. Congregations: ". . . curare ut Codicis praescripta religiose serventur". It is an executive faculty described by Monin as inherent in the power of the S. Congregations, though even at that time, under the "*Sapienti Consilio*", he denies that they have legislative power, but points out that their general administrative decrees may have an admixture of authentic interpretation, an element which is within the *potestas ordinaria* for the discharge of their duties.[118] This admixture of authentic interpretation in the general *decreta* is withdrawn by the Motu proprio. The Congregations remain, as they have always been, the immediate and supreme organs of the Roman Pontiff for the gov-

---

[115] *Mpr.*, I. Cf. Chelodi, *Ius de Personis*, n. 161, c.; Vermeersch, "Adnotationes" (ad *Mpr. "Cum iuris canonici"*),—Periodica, IX (1921), 17; Toso, *Commentaria Minora*, II, 50-51.

[116] *Mpr.*, II; Cann. 1, 2, 6.

[117] *Mpr.*, II-III; Cf. Chelodi, *Ius de Personis*, n. 161, c; Van Hove, *Prolegomena*, n. 63; Boudinhon, "La Commission pour L'Interprétation Officielle du Code,"—*LeCC*, XL (1917), 399; Sipos, *Enchiridion Iuris Canonici*, (Pecs: ex Typographia "Haladas" R. T., 1926), p. 191; Vermeersch, *Periodica*, IX (1921), 17-18; Toso, *Commentaria Minora*, II, 50-51; Jone, *Gesetzbuch des kanonischen* Rechts, (Paderborn: Ferdinand Schoningh, 1939), I, 239.

[118] *De Curia Romana*, pp. 198, 201-202, 216.

ernment of the Universal Church, according to the limitations just outlined. Thus the idea of *decreta* is not juridically the same since the time of the Motu proprio of 1917.

It is not the purpose of this study to explain in a detailed manner the notion of *decretum* and the nature of its obligation.[119] It will suffice for the present purpose to show from a positive approach that this enactment of public authority lies outside the pale of authentic interpretation.

An administrative decree is the act of the public authority, proceeding not from legislative or judicial power, but from executive power. It is the result of the deliberation of the public superior to put existing law into effect under a given set of circumstances.[120] As such it can issue from an authority which is not vested with legislative power.[121] However, the faculty must not be conceived as a mere application of the law. Law is ordinarily phrased in general terms. Thus its form demands more practical determinations and dispositions in view of the exigencies of time and circumstances in order to have the law produce its desired effect. To make these more specific enactments is the function of executive power, which, of its nature, embraces also a certain discretionary power, and to which is joined the element of command *(imperium)*.[122]

Certainly, it is not becoming to the dignity of law, which should possess the characteristic of perpetuity,[123] that its ex-

---

119 For literature on this topic, cf. Van Hove, *De Legibus Ecclesiasticis*, n. 368; Cicognani, *Canon Law*, (2, ed.), p. 85.

120 Van Hove, *Prolegomena*, n. 63; Maroto, *Institutiones*, n. 274.

121 Van Hove, *De Legibus Ecclesiasticis*, n. 368; Hergenröther, *Lehrbuch des Katolischen Kirchenrechts*, (2te Aufl., v. Dr. Jos. Holweck, Freiburg i. Breisgau, 1905), n. 624.

122 Ottaviani, *Ius Publicum Ecclesiasticum*, I, 120-121; Vermeersch-Creusen, *Epitome*, I, n. 132.

123 S. Thomas, *Summa Theologica*, I, IIae, quaest. 96, Art. I; *ibid.*, quaest. 97, Art. I, ad 2.

pression should be so flexible as to attend the proper conduct of the many minute affairs in a frequently changing society. Thus rather than conceive this power of applying the law by decree, indispensable as it is to the maintenance of a good social order, as a legislative function, it is held to be a *praeceptum communitati datum* and is a temporary measure. Its efficacy derives from the law itself.[124] Thus there is no question about its being of obligation; from the very nature of things there must be some prescribed uniformity of action in expediting the concrete problems of social life.

Of such kind is precisely one of the ordinary occupations assigned to the Roman Congregations—to place the law of the Code into effect.[125] Hergenröther declares that until his time little attention has been paid by canonical-juristic teaching to the difference between legislative and administrative power, though the points of difference are both manifold and important.[126] According to him the administrative decree is

---

124 Van Hove, *De Legibus Ecclesiasticis,* n. 368. Maroto (*Institutiones,* n. 275) would give this decree the character of perpetuity.

125 "Die Hauptaufgabe der Kongregationem bestecht nach der Herausgabe des Kodex in dem Erlass von Durchführungsanweisungen."—Haring, *Grundzüge des Katholischen Kirchenrechts,* I, 247; Coronata, *Institutiones Iuris Canonici,* I, (2. ed., Taurini: ex officina Marietti, 1939), n. 335, 2°; Cicognani, *Canon Law,* p. 85-86.

126 "Die kanonistische Doktrin hat bisher den Unterschied zwischen gesetzgebender und Verordnungsgewahlt wenig beachtet, obwohl derselbe immerhin ein mehrfacher und erheblicher ist."—*Lehrbuch des katolischen Kirchenrechts,* p. 488. This thought bears out the statements made in the brief survey of the nature of the *decreta* of the S. Congregations; namely, that practically up to the Motu proprio of 1917 they were thought of in terms of legislation and interpretation. Sagmüller (*Lehrbuch des katholischen Kirchenrechts,* [4te Aufl., Freiburg im Breisgau: B. Herder & Co., 1926], 1 Bd., zweiter Teil, 179) hesitates seriously in admitting to the sphere of Canon Law what he calls "Verordnungen oder Verfügungen" (ordinances or decrees)—which Hergenröther identifies with the administrative *decretum* of the Congregations—as being sharply distinguished from legislation. However, a close examination of *Mpr.,* II-III of Benedict XV seems certainly to reveal that the Pontiff makes a drastic distinction between legislation and the ordinary enact-

of temporary duration; it is a provisory measure calculated to regulate general, current, concrete conditions in accord with existing law and is not to counteract the law in any way.[127]

Such is the description here submitted of the decree of the Congregations under the Motu proprio. It does not have the character of law. And the juridic reason is that these bodies do not have the necessary legislative power. The statement that the decree is of a "temporary" nature is made by way of contradistinction to the character of perpetuity which resides in the law. In fact, its very origin is called forth by untoward conditions which spring up in spite of the existing law.[128]

The obligatory nature of the administrative decree is emphasized by authors to the extent that they say that a general decree binds *like* universal law *(per modum legis)*.[129] The decrees of the Congregations do not have legal force because the legislator intends that they do not have such force. The decrees rather contain the moral cogency to use the imme-

---

ments of the S. Congregations issued in the form of *decreta*. The distinction is not verbal; it is basically conceptual and has as its reason the integrity of the common law of the Code. Ojetti (*De Romana Curia*, pp. 11, 13) speaks of *ordinationes administrativae* as of the time before the *"Sapienti Consilio"*, but they are given only by special mandate of the Roman Pontiff and are universal law.

127 *Lehrbuch des Katolischen Kirchenrechts*, p. 487-490.

128 The relatively transitory nature of the decree is given explicit recognition by the Holy See itself concerning the employment of the *Consilium a Vigilantia* and the *Iuramentum anti-modernisticum*: "Praescriptiones praedictas, ob serpentes in praesenti modernisticos errores latas, natura quidem sua, temporarias esse ac transitorias, ideoque in Codicem Iuris Canonici referri non potuisse; aliunde tamen, cum virus Modernismi diffundi minime cessaverit, eas in pleno suo robore manere debere usquedum hac super re Apostolica Sedes aliter statuerit".—*AAS*, X (1918), 136.

129 Vermeersch-Creusen, *Epitome*, II, n. 360: he explains in his context that decrees do not have legal value; Cicognani, *Canon Law*, p. 85-86: et al. These authors are not contradicting themselves; they are simply employing a figure of speech, a simile.

diately practical means determined as such by legitimate public authority in order that the law may be adequately fulfilled.[130]

This distinctionn between decrees and law may seem at first glance as impractical. However, a cursory review of canons 22 and 23 will immediately reveal how important is the juridic distinction. If the decrees were to be considered as laws,[131] then these canons would be operative in relation to them. As a result the decrees would be considered by writers as authentic interpretations of anterior law "per modum legis exhibitae".[132] And in the last analysis there would be confusion among the authors: "incertis privatorum hominum [e. g., auctorum] de germano canonum sensu opinionibus et coniecturis" as to the status of the law, the very situation which Benedict XV wishes to eliminate. The law would be practically in the same condition as it was before its codification.

Since decrees do not have legal force, they do not require legal promulgation. They exert their force immediately upon notice from the legitimate public authority and are not bound to conform to the manner of promulgating law.[133]

Another conclusion from the premises stated above is that the *decretum* does not admit the principle: "lex dubia non obligat".[134] Therefore the decree is beyond the reach of

---

130 The function of the public authority is not only to legislate, but in a more specific manner to direct and govern. This operation is administrative.

131 This hypothesis is immediately eliminated by *Mpr.*, § II-III.

132 This statement is not extravagant, because there are authors who consider the *Instructiones* referred to in *Mpr.*, II as merely declarative authentic interpretations of the Code. Thus, Michiels, *Normae Generales*, I, 395, who seems to follow Maroto in "Adnotationes" (ad *Mpr.*, "*Cum iuris canonici*")—*CpR*, I (1920), 40.

133 Cf. Cann. 8, § 1, and 9.

134 Cf. Can. 15.

the one who is prone to find a *dubium iuris* in its wording. The decree must be fulfilled *meliori modo quo fieri potest* in favor of the law.[135] The situation would be entirely different if the decree were a product of authentic interpretation. This follows the norms of law.[136]

Decrees will, moreover, not authentically solve a doubt of law; namely, a question of law which is moot in the circle of experts. The reason is that the decree is the product of purely administrative jurisdiction. The former statement needs clarification to the following extent. Such an enactment of the Holy See may reveal the *mens legislatoris* or the *finis legis*. In which case it is the basis of doctrinal interpretation, which is admitted by the law.[137] In this contingency, however, the principles: "Mens legislatoris non est lex" and "finis legis non cadit sub lege",[138] must be borne in mind.[139]

Since the decree may possibly add something new *ultra legem*,[140] this addition may not be confused with extensive interpretation, to say nothing of the enactment of a new law. The reason is that the administrative power of the Congregations does not represent the legislator *as legislator* but only as administrator.[141]

---

[135] The rule of law: "In obscuris minimum est sequendum", does not seem to obtain in the present matter. Cf. *Glossa* ad Reg. 30, R. J. in VIo.

[136] Cf. Can. 17.

[137] Cf. Can. 18.

[138] Cf. Van Hove, *De Legibus Ecclesiasticis*, n. 260, explaining *finis legis*.

[139] As regards the *mens legislatoris* in particular, it is to be said that the *mens* which in no way is revealed in the law even after the issuance of the decree cannot be a norm for even doctrinal interpretation. Because what the legislator has in his mind and has in no way revealed in the law (and not first in the decree) is simply not to be brought into the law. If it appears first in the decree, it may be a sign of the turn in the jurisprudence of the Roman Curia and a presage of a possible authentic restrictive or extensive interpretation in the future.

[140] Cf. Ottaviani, *Ius Publicum Ecclesiasticum*, I, 120, 121; Van Hove, *De Legibus Ecclesiasticis*, n. 368; Monin, *De Curia Romana*, pp. 199-200.

[141] Therefore in no sense can one apply canons 22 and 23.

The fact that the decrees of the S. Congregations have the approbation of the Roman Pontiff,[142] does not *eo ipso* change their nature from administrative decrees to pontifical laws. This approbation is given *in forma communi* or *in forma specifica.* The confirmation accorded *in forma communi,* while it certainly adds greater weight and force to the contents of the enactment, leaves to the decree its original status—an administrative act of the respective Congregation.[143] By virtue of the second species of confirmation, *in forma specifica,*[144] the decree becomes the special act of the Roman Pontiff himself, whereby, as Lega declares, it proceeds from the plenitude of his power, being ratified after the manner of the definitions of an ecumenical council; it becomes a law, having the force of a papal constitution.[145]

The foregoing remarks have been set down to illustrate that both in origin—proceeding from administrative jurisdiction only—and in the course of their application the decrees of the Roman Congregations do not have respect to the field of authentic interpretation or legislation.

---

142 Cf. can. 244, § 2.

143 Cappello (*De Curia Romana,* I, 54) has set down clauses which indicate this manner of approbation: "Facto verbo cum SSmo"; "SSmus D. N. resolutionem Emorum Patrum approbavit et confirmavit"; "SSmus D. N. . . . Papa . . . audita relatione R. P. D. Secretarii eiusdem S. C. supra relatam Emorum Patrum declarationem ratam habere et confirmare dignatus est".

144 Expressed in formulas like the following: "Ex motu proprio"; "Ex scientia certa, de Apostolicae auctoritatis plenitudine declaramus, statuimus"; "Non obstante quacumque lege seu consuetudine in contrarium"; "Supplentes omnes iuris et facti defectus; etc."—Cappello, *loc. cit.*

145 Lega, *Praelectiones de Iudiciis Ecclesiasticis,* II, n. 285; Hergenröther, *Lehrbuch des Katolischen Kirchenrechts,* p. 488, note 2. The same obtains if the enactment is issued "ex speciali Pontificis commissione"—Monin, *De Curia Romana,* p. 216; Vermeersch-Cruesen, *Epitome,* II, n. 360; Wernz, *Ius Decretalium,* I, n. 115.

B. *Instructiones*

"... Instructiones, si res ferat, edere, quae iisdem Codicis praeceptis maiorem et lucem afferant et efficientiam pariant."

The second specific duty of the S. Congregations is to issue opportunely instructions which shall afford greater clarity to the precepts of the Code and make them more effective.

The legislator does not presume that his law is obscure;[146] one is supposed to know the law. Nevertheless the knowledge of the practical meaning, extent, and application of the law is oftentimes fraught with great difficulties, which require painstaking effort to surmount. Therefore Benedict XV has created in his Motu proprio an instrumentality to aid in overcoming these difficulties, charging the Congregations with the duty of issuing timely instructions on the law of the Code.

1. Nature and force of the *Instructio* before the Motu proprio *"Cum iuris canonici"*.

Hergenröther describes the instruction given by a S. Congregation in the same terms as the *decretum,* a "Verordnung" (ordinance), which has been outlined in the foregoing. It does not have the force of law. Therefore, as of the time before the *"Sapienti Consilio"* it was also an administrative measure of the Congregations, which are considered by this author as not having legislative power, the S. C. of the Council and of Sacred Rites excepted. Also, he expressly excludes the interpre-

---

[146] Can. 16, § 2; "Ignorantia facti non iuris excusat."—Reg. 13, R. J. in VIo.

tation of law as an element of the instruction.[147] As of the same period of time, Ojetti gives the same general description of what he calls administrative or executive ordinances *(ordinationes quaedam executoriae seu administrativae)*. However, he permits them to have the force of general law because they are issued only by special mandate of the Roman Pontiff.[148]

After the *"Sapienti Consilio"* these ordinances are considered as not having the character of law and are issued only in *forma communi*.[149] Accordingly they are described as proceding from a *potestas executiva seu oeconomica,* and they do not concern themselves with the interpretation of law, but with setting forth, in virtue of administrative and discretional powers, practical means for carrying out the law.[150]

The chief question at issue is clear; namely, that the instruction is a product of executive or administrative power. Whether or not the instruction at the same time emanates also from a legislative and interpretative faculty during this period is, as appears from what has been said, a controverted question.[151]

---

[147] *Lehrbuch des Katolischen Kirchenrechts, passim,* nn. 185, 622-623.

[148] *De Romana Curia,* pp. 13, 20.

[149] Ojetti, *De Curia Romana,* p. 13; Wernz (*Ius Decretalium,* [2. ed., 1905], I, n. 146, III) already asserts: "Instructiones quoque SS. CC. ne quaquam per se et indiscriminatim vim legum universalium et definitionum habent", but offers no further explanation.

[150] "Potestate executiva, seu oeconomica; qua potestate utuntur [S. Congregationes] praesertim in solvendis quaestionibus particularibus quae tamen de sensu legis non moveantur, sed circa dubium facti versantur. Item in condendis instructionibus aut decretis, et generalibus, quibus media practica proponuntur ad executionem legis, additis etiam forsan quibusdam novis praescriptionibus, quibus melius procuretur praedicta executio."—Monin, *De Curia Romana,* p. 199; ". . . facultates discretionales, quae dicuntur, ipsi [administratori] omnino necessariae, quum eius provisiones fundentur potius in rationibus facti quam in strictis rationibus iuris."—Ojetti, *De Romana Curia,* pp. 20-21.

[151] So much is certain. The clear separation between legislative, inter-

2. Nature of the *Instructio* under the Motu proprio *"Cum iuris canonici"*.

Benedict XV does not leave to conjecture the description of the *Instructio* which he has in mind in his Motu proprio:

> . . . Ordinarium igitur earum munus in hoc genere [decretorum generalium] erit . . . Instructiones, si res ferat, edere, quae iisdem Codicis praeceptis maiorem et lucem afferant et efficientiam pariant. Eiusmodi vero documenta sic conficiantur, ut non modo sint, sed appareant etiam quasi quaedam explanationes et complementa canonum, qui idcirco in documentorum contextu peropportune afferentur.

The instruction is to be issued opportunely; namely, if conditions warrant such action. This thought is apparent from the words "si res ferat". The *res* is therefore supposed as a state of affairs which is more or less general and of which the Holy See must take cognizance by explaining more clearly the content of the law inasmuch as it bears upon the matter to be regulated, thus affording the law, its content being more clearly understood, greater efficiency to meet the exigencies of the common good. A more or less general state of things is the supposition of the Motu proprio as justifying the issuance of instructions, because it speaks of *decreta generalia*.

The instruction is conceived by modern writers as containing the elements of an administrative decree. Thus, instructions are called "règlements d'administration publique", and are spoken of as positive executive measures.[152] This fact is revealed in the Motu proprio itself. While it renders a ma-

---

pretative, and administrative jurisdiction in the S. Congregations does not exist before the Motu proprio of 1917.—Cf. Monin, *De Curia Romana*, p. 201-202.

[152] Boudinhon, *LeCC*, XL (1917), 399; Vermeersch, *Periodica*, IX (1921), 19; Hilling, *AKKR*, CIII (1923), 9; *idem*, *AKKR*, CVIII (1928), 392-393.

terial description of the instruction, this instrument is not designed to be a purely doctrinal solution of the difficulties which confront the observance of the law in a given set of circumstances. The element of executive jurisdiction appears in the fact that the Motu proprio views the instruction from the standpoint of *decretum,* which, though it is described by Monin as any act which emanates from the S. Congregations, must nevertheless be considered as an authoritative regulation of ecclesiastical government. This thought corresponds exactly with the basic purpose of the S. Congregations, which are organs that act in the name of the Sovereign Pontiff ". . . per quae idem Romanus Pontifex negotia Ecclesiae universae expedire solet".[153] From this consideration it seems that the clause ". . . maiorem . . . efficientiam pariant" must be considered as designating more than a subsidiary function of the instruction whereby it merely paves the way for the law to exercise its effect. It contains also the element of authority found in an executive decree.

3. Authoritative force of the *Instructio.*

The matter here to be determined is whether the instruction described previously contains either the element of law or of authentic interpretation. To the exclusion for the present of the law of the Motu proprio contained in the first paragraph of that document concerning the exclusive competence of the Pontifical Commission, let the remaining portions of the document be considered, where, first of all, is described the nature and purpose of the instruction. The question then is whether, considering the nature and purpose of the instruction, this instrument is an apt medium of interpreting law in

---

[153] Can. 7.

its pure state, so to say, that is, in the abstract, taken alone and apart from the concrete situations which the instruction is calculated to remedy.

From a consideration of the two remaining portions of the Motu proprio it appears that the S. Congregations cannot issue materially new law. There remains therefore the further question as to whether in the instruction referred to in the Motu proprio (§ II) one may expect to find or even be expected to find the element of authentic interpretation of law as such. In other words, is there as it were an "interpretatio authentica per modum instructionis in re peculiari"? [154] The *res peculiaris* is here considered as a particular situation or state of things prevalent more or less generally, such as the instruction, considering the clear language of the Motu proprio (§ II), is expressly designated to regulate. Can this general instruction, whose nature and purpose is described by the Motu proprio, be an authentic interpretation of law as such issued "per modum legis", supposing that a S. Congregation had the power (which it has not) to interpret authentically the canons of the Code? It has been said that the S. Congregations have this power, and that it has been exercised; namely, that the S. Congregations have rendered authentic interpretations "mere declarativas" *per modum legis* through the medium of the instruction provided for in the Motu proprio.[155] This statement is in clear contradiction to the lan-

[154] This clause has been formulated merely to describe the question at issue.

[155] "Indubitanter quoque iis [i. e., S. Congregationibus] vindicanda est potestas dandi interpretationes generales seu per modum legis exhibitas, mere declarativas. Hoc resultat: tum ex aperta concessione iis in Motu proprio data; ibi enim dicitur quod 'ordinarium earum munus in hoc genere erit Instructiones si res ferat, edere, [etc., cf. Motu proprio, § II, quoted above in the text'] . . .; tum ex constanti earundem S. Congregationum praxi, quae, edito iam Codice, plures authenticas dederunt interpretationes canonum, quorum executio iisdem respective committitur."—Michiels, *Normae Generales,* I, 395; cf. etiam, Maroto, "Adnotationes" (ad *Mpr, "Cum iuris canonici"*),—*CpR,* I (1920), 40-41.

guage of the first paragraph of the Motu proprio. Moreover, it definitely smacks of pre-Code jurisprudence, when the Sacred Congregations, each in its own province after the "*Sapienti Consilio*" of 1908, were authentic interpreters of ecclesiastical law in general.[156] Yet the clear language of Wernz (+1914) already bears witness that the *Instructiones* of the S. Congregations could not *per se* and indiscriminately be accepted as vehicles of general law or of authentic definitions.[157]

The thesis is here proposed that the nature and purpose themselves to which the instruction is expressly dedicated by the Motu proprio renders that instrument inept as a vehicle of authentic interpretation of law as such.

It is clear from the wording of the Motu proprio (§ II), that the province of the S. Congregations is the administration, the execution of the general law of the Church. The administrator puts law into practice. He does not approach law, the abstract, only; he approaches at the same time a case, a concrete situation or state of things, which is a complex entity. Whether that case is conceived as a particular situation as between definite parties or as a generally prevalent condition of affairs in the commonwealth of the Church does not matter as far as the act of applying law is concerned, except that in the former instance the application is precise, because the circumstances in the issue are accurately defined.

Immediately the administrator is confronted not by one law but by several laws, because any one concrete situation is the subject not of one but of several laws governing at

---

[156] "An facultas authentice interpretandi Concilii Tridentini decreta aliasque leges ecclesiasticas vi Constitutionis *Sapienti Consilio* sit singulis Sacris Congregationibus commissa secundum propriam cuiusque competentiam, salva Romani Pontificis approbatione; [Resp.] Affirmative."—*Fontes*, n. 2079.

[157] "Instructiones quoque SS. CC. nequaquam per se et indiscriminatim vim legum universalium et definitionum habent."—*Ius Decretalium*, (Prati, 1913), I, n. 146, III.

once, time, person, place, status, etc. Here the administrator or executor of the law is dealing with the application of a logical system of law. The period of interpretation in the stage of application is a matter necessarily presupposed, because one cannot begin to regulate a concrete situation without an aggregate of clear laws. Moreover, the administrator must apprehend the facts as they are and understand or interpret them as well as possible, and as he sees them. This function never enters into the province of pure interpretation of law. In fact, the laws to be applied are, as it were, counterpoised upon the concrete situation in such a manner as to modify each other in that given particular case.[158]

Thus it will be seen that the approach of the administrator is entirely different from that of the interpreter. The interpreter, as formal agent of the legislator, proceeds by induction; the administrator, by synthesis. The latter makes his synthesis of the individual laws operative in a case in view of that particular case. The authentic interpreter, on the other hand, is not especially concerned with a particular situation. Such is the difference between interpretation and application of law. The administrator, in his formal capacity of executor of law, does not enunciate that a law means this or that in the abstract. His duty is to see that the laws respecting a particular exigency of society are properly carried out.

What approach does the Motu proprio prescribe for the S. Congregations? As mentioned previously, the instruction which they are charged to issue shall be contingent upon the exigencies of an aggregate of concrete circumstances extant generally in society at large; namely, "*si res ferat*". They approach a general case, a complex entity. Therefore the Congregations approach their task from the viewpoint of an administrator of law. Their operation is not directed to the gen-

---

[158] "Generi per speciem derogatur."—Reg. 34, R. J., in VIo.

eral concepts of law *in se* and apart and as an end. What there is of generality, and of their concern, is territorial, or is at least referable to the concrete. They are directed to universal propositions of law as modified in a general case. The "quaedam explanationes et complementa canonum" which they are to render in order to afford greater clarity and efficiency to the precepts of the Code are explanations on the application of the law to concrete facts, that is, explanations concerning how the laws are operative under given circumstances. This statement will be clarified in the following.

The Motu proprio in § II does not provide simply that explanations of the canons *in se,* that is, in the abstract, are to be issued. The text reads: ". . . quaedam explanationes et complementa canonum". It is clear that *explanationes* signifies explanation, clarification. The question is, what manner of clarification. The phrase *complementa canonum* cannot have reference to filling in lacunae in the law. This hypothesis postulates that the Congregations would be supplying, or have the power to supply, something new; they would be making new law if their action is supposed to have anything to do with authentic interpretation or legislation. Here the Motu proprio has in mind their ordinary duty, which does not, as the text itself clearly reveals, concern itself with anything new; whether that something new shall be classified in the species "law" or "interpretation" makes no difference. But "complementa canonum" can mean fulfillment or fulfilling of the existing law, and, by exclusion of the aforementioned hypothesis, such is all that the term can mean. Thus, the instructions of the Congregations are to be and appear as *certain explanations* of the fulfillment of the law.[159] In other

[159] It is here submitted that the Motu proprio (§ II) in the phrase "explanationes et complementa canonum" uses a usual turn in Latin style commonly known as the hendiadys, whereby two words (usually nouns) are employed to express one idea, one of which (in the present instance: *com-*

words, the Congregations have the office of explaining the application or function of law in a determined general state of affairs. This thought agrees exactly with the context of the Motu proprio (§ II), which envisions the exercise of jurisdiction in a concrete situation: *"si res ferat"*.

If the S. Congregations have, as asserted, rendered general authentic interpretations by the medium of the instruction, where in the Motu proprio (§ II) is this power granted? The fact that they have jurisdiction to execute law does not *eo ipso* give them power to interpret authentically. This statement is founded upon a fact of history, arranged by the supreme ecclesiastical legislator himself.

It will be remembered that in order to effect the execution of his constitutions and ordinances with respect to the offices and tribunals of the Holy See as also of the decrees of the Council of Trent, Pius IV had appointed a group of eight Cardinals. The comment of Fagnanus concerning this appointment is that at its inception this S. Congregation did not have the faculty to interpret but only to put into execution the decrees of the Council of Trent.[160] Subsequently, because doubt had arisen as to the validity of the responses, Pius V

---

plementa) performs an attributive function to the other (in the present insta *explanationes*) either in the capacity of attributive genitive (as in the present instance) or adjective. Thus, Kühner-Stegman, *Ausführliche Grammatik der Lateinischen Sprache*, (2. Aufl., 4 vols., Hannover, 1914), II, II, 26: "Diese eigentümliche Ausdrucksweise (i. e., *hendiadyoin*) besteht darin, dass zwei Wörter (besonders Substantive), von denen der Begriff des einen dem des anderen untergeordnet ist und daher entweder durch einen attributiven Genetiv oder ein attributives Adjektiv ausgedrückt werden sollte, in gleichem Kasus durch *et*, *que* und *atque* (ac) verbunden werden. Beide Wörter bezeichnen dieselbe Sache, beleuchten sie aber von verschiedenen Seiten, so dass sie sich gegenseitig zu einem Begriffe ergänzen und vervollständigen. Gewöhnlich geht der allgemeinere Begriff voran, der besondere wird explikativ hinzgefügt". *Complementa* is a qualification of *explanationes*.

160 "Itaque sacra Congregatio ab initio Tridentini Concilii decretis non interpretandis sed exequendis dumtaxat praefecta est . . ."—*Commentaria*, lib, I, tit. II, cap. *Quoniam*, n. 7.

permitted this Congregation to reply authentically in cases in which the law itself was deemed as clear; where there was doubt, the matter was to be referred directly to the Supreme Pontiff.[161]

Moreover, the second paragraph of the Motu proprio reads "*quaedam* explanationes et complementa canonum": *certain* or *some,* explanations on the application of the law.[162] The instruction does not presume to be *the* explanation of the application of the law in the given general case.[163] In other words, it does not presume to be the *law* on that general case; it is not, therefore, to the general community what the authentic interpretation "per modum rescripti in re peculiari" [164] is to the individual party or parties who receive such a rescript in answer to the presentation of the concrete, specific, case, and for whom the rescript "ius facit". Why? Because in the general case, or, the generally prevalent situation envisioned by the Motu proprio (§II) the Superior does not and cannot measure and classify the individual cases of each place in his domain which conspire in their totality to create the common situation which he wishes to regulate as well as possible by the instruction. It is not so with the case contemplated in canon 17, § 3. Here the facts presented are accurately appraised and the law is accurately applied. One cannot *ex natura rei* pronounce authoritative judgment upon a set of facts as being in agreement or disagreement with the law unless those facts are accurately examined and compared with the norm of law. Therefore the instruction does not pur-

---

161 Fagnanus, *ibid.*

162 Italics inserted.

163 "General" is here used in the sense of "territorially general". For it is just such a general situation, or case, of which the instruction, being of the genus *decretorum generalium*, is designed to take cognizance.

164 Cf. can. 17, § 3.

port to be this kind of judgment upon a general state of events.

To return to the original question as to whether the instruction can be an apt medium of authentic interpretation "per modum legis", the following conclusion is presented.

The *Instructio* provided by the Motu proprio (§II) speaks of laws, not in the abstract, but applicable to the concrete, the particular, because it supposes, as noted repeatedly, a concrete state of things; at the same time it supposes an application of an aggregate of laws. Hence the laws thus applied never mirror or reflect their general comprehension as they are individually and in the abstract. To know the law, which is an abstract proposition, only as operative in a given particular case even though a general case, does not guarantee a knowledge of the law *in se*. Therefore, the application of the law in a particular case, be that case general or specific, does not represent interpretation, not to say *authentic* interpretation, of the law as such, *in se,* because it does not represent the law in its generality. Therefore the *Instructio* provided by the Motu proprio, fulfilling strictly its nature and purposes, is not an apt medium of interpreting law as such. Nor was it, manifestly, ever intended to fulfill this office. That office belongs exclusively to the Pontifical Commission, as the Motu proprio most explicitly sets forth: ". . . Consilium seu Commissionem, uti vocant, constituimus, *cui uni* ius erit Codicis authentice interpretandi . . .".[165]

Hence Jone, speaking in connection with the solution of a marriage case and with reference to the authentic interpretation of canon 1099, §2, says correctly that the Congregation of the Holy Office does not have authority to render an authentic interpretation save for the solution of the particular

---

[165] *Mpr.*, I. (Italics inserted).

case,[166] which solution is manifestly referable to the provision of canon 17, §3. Hence the further conclusion is presented, that the instruction is not a medium of authentic interpretation in any manner; authentic interpretation is law.[167]

Therefore, the greater clarity of the law, which the instruction seeks to furnish is not in its authentic interpretation, but in its application of law in view of a given, more or less general, state of things: ". . . quae iisdem Codicis praeceptis maiorem et lucem afferant et efficientiam pariant".[168]

It is clear that the instruction issues from the supreme organs of government in the Church. This document has therefore great doctrinal value, and while it is not law,[169] because it is a vehicle neither of authentic interpretation nor of new law, it seeks to introduce a knowledge of the spirit of the law.[170]

---

166 "Eine authentische Erklärung aber wurde nicht gegeben und konnte auch nicht von dem Heiligen Offizium, sondern nur von der Interpretationskommission gegeben werden. Das Heilige Offizium aber hat offenbar die Antwort nicht an die Interpretationskommission weitergegeben, sondern sich damit begnügt, den einzelnen vorgelegten praktischen Fall su lösen."—"Die Verpflichtung der Form bei der Eheschliessung," *Theologisch-Praktische Quartalschrift*, LXXXII (1929), 782; an identical statement is made concerning the competence of the Holy Office by Hilling, "Kompetcnz des Hl. Offiziums in Ehesachen," *AKKR*, CVIII (1928), 548.

167 Can. 17.

168 The reader's attention would be called to the parallelism in expression and thought between this clause and: ". . . quaedam explanationes et complementa canonum . . ."

169 "Instructiones habent sane magnam auctoritatem sed leges non sunt et secundum ius esse debent."—Chelodi, *Ius de Personis*, n. 161, c; this author (*op. cit.*, n. 67, nota 2) asserts: "Quaenam autem exinde sit natura interpretationis, quae Instructionibus Congregationum (Mp. cit. ad II) suberit, clarum non est".

170 Jone, *Gesetzbuch des kan. Rechtes*, I, 239.

The instruction as such is called a simple declarative norm whose direction must be followed rather than its liberal observance fulfilled.[171] This remark is not one made at random, or because of the absence of a more precise concept of the instrument. The distinction between direction and literal observance has its beginnings, it seems, in the Holy Office. Pope Clement X commanded the secretary of the S. C. for the Propagation of the Faith to be advised that the resolutions of the Holy See in answer to proposed doubts should be transmitted by this Congregation to its missionaries and its other ministers after the manner of an instruction and not of a definition.[172] It is upon this distinction that seems to be based the present concept of the instruction. Modern authors [173] referring to this papal mandate have preserved this concept of the instruction. Wernz [174] points out that the resolutions (of the Holy Office and S. C. for the Propagation of the Faith) are commanded by Clement X to be sent as "simplices instructiones", not as "definitiones", whereby the mis-

---

[171] Vermeersch-Creusen, *Epitome,* I, n. 132.

[172] "Ssmus D. N. Clemens Papa X mandavit . . . notificari r. p. d. Secretario eiusdem sacrae Congr. quod, quotiescumque remittantur Missionariis vel aliis Ministris praedictae sac. Congregationis huiusmodi resolutiones, mittantur per modum instructionis, non autem definitionis."—*Iuris Pontificii de Propaganda Fide,* (Romae, 1904), I, Pars Secunda, CCCXXIX, I.

[173] Chelodi, *Ius de Personis,* n. 161, c; Van Hove, *Prolegomena,* n. 64; Vermeersch Creusen, *Epitome,* I, n. 132; Coronata, *Institutiones,* I, n. 335, 2°. Choupin, (*Valeur des Décisions Doctrinales et Disciplinaires du Saint-Siege,* 3. ed., Paris: Gabriel Beauchesne, 1928, pp. 96-97, 99-100) still speaks of the general decrees or acta of the S. Congregations in terms of general law and authentic interpretation: "Et d'une manière générale, les décrets [i. e., declarations, resolutions, decisions, responses ou decrets.—Dans l'usage ordinaire on emploie ces termes indistinctement.] édictés par les autres Congrégations [i. e., non ceux du Saint-Office] sont purement disciplinaires . . . Les décrets formellement universals, légitimement promulgués, ont force de loi dans toute l'Eglise; . . . Ils ne sont autres, en effet, que des actes du Saint-Siège, publics et solennels, par lequels l'authorité compétente interprète authentiquement une loi ancienne ou édicte une loi nouvelle".

[174] *Ius Decretalium*, I, n. 146, III, quoting *Collectanea* (Paris) *Const. S. Sed.* n. 5; cf. etiam Wernz-Vidal, *Ius Canonicum,* I, n. 211, III.

sionaries and other ministers ". . . in occurrentibus dubiis gubernari valeant et debeant". And he espouses this idea as conveying the general character of the instruction in his time. There is no doubt here that the instrument conveys an obligation. The response, under this concept of instruction, has no legal force, since it is not a definition. It has a moral force. The instruction is therefore conceived as an immediate means for the proper observance of the law. In this fashion is to be considered the instruction under the Motu proprio. If there is something unclear in the instrument, one does not raise the objection "lex dubia non obligat", because it is not a "lex". Nor is the instruction bound by the other norms of law concerning promulgation, *vacatio legis*, etc. As regards its interpretation in the face of doubt, it must rather be interpreted in such a manner, according to the adage, "ut res potius valeat quam pereat". In other words the law to which the instruction refers is to be favored. As mentioned in the discussion on the *decretum*, pontifical approbation *in forma communi* does not, as is recognized by everyone, change its intrinsic nature.[175] In particular, however, an instruction may have the general character of a decree. Thus the Instruction of the S. C. of the Sacraments of December 21, 1930, on the examination of candidates for sacred orders, is a document whose direction must be observed exactly by Ordinaries.[176] In general, it is correctly stated that the decisions of the S. Congregations, which are the pontifical departments of ecclesiastical government, are binding under obedience according to the tenor of their wording.[177]

---

175 Wernz, *Ius Decretalium*, I, n. 122; Toso, *Commentaria Minora* II, 47; Hilling, *AKKR*, CVIII (1928), 392-393; et al.

176 Cf. *AAS*, XXIII (1931), 120.

177 Müller, *Papst und Kurie*, (Gotha: Friedrich Andreas Perthes A.-G., 1921), p. 116.

In concluding this chapter the following general observations are presented to the reader.

The Motu proprio "*Cum iuris canonici*" is framed to present in definite general outline the avenues of ecclesiastical government.The document segregates a department for the authentic interpretation of the Code, granting to the Pontifical Commission appointed exclusive competence to do so. And this competence has reference to any species and mode of interpretation which is purely such. The Motu proprio does not grant to the Commission competence to apply the law. The S. Congregations are assigned to the very important task of issuing decrees and instructions in the domain of executive government. Benedict XV most wisely chose instruments which are not laws in order to place the law in operation. To make a law to enforce law is placing a hindrance to unimpaired progress in government, because a law must follow the norms of law as to its institution and interpretation. There is no legal provision that demands such procedure for the acts of the S. Congregations issued according to the Motu proprio (§ II). Benedict XV saw this situation clearly. He perceived, as all legal history demonstrates, that a law will receive scrutiny, analysis, treatment, discussion and debate. It will be interpreted and compared with previous law [178] in order to determine the extent of the old law and the new, until there is danger that no one will know what the law means.[179] Therefore he made the decision that the Church has sufficient law for a long time and purposed to use decrees and instructions, which are not laws, but which are not the less commands to fulfill the existing law as directed and as well as possible.

The form of the instruction or decree would be a fruitful field for scrutiny and debate, whether one consider it as law

178 Witness e. g., can. 22-23.

179 Cf. *Mpr.*, in prin.

or authentic interpretation. The thoughts are expressed at much greater length—as intended—than is the thought content of the canon. There is more detail and consequently more obvious material for debate, as contrasted with the little more than the *"affirmative"* and *"negative"* of the response from the Pontifical Commission, which does not lend itself easily to cleavage by a *dubium iuris*. With great ingenuity, therefore, Benedict XV chose means whose efficacy would not be touched by the *dubium iuris*, *vacatio legis*, etc. His will is that the acts of the S. Congregations issued under the Motu proprio (§ II) be not law or authentic interpretation but timely injunctions containing opportune directions for expediting efficiently the current problems and difficulties of the Church under the law of the Code, the most of which, being materially old law, has still to be studied, but according to the received sources and traditions.[180]

C. *Power of Authentic Interpretation*

It is necessary here, as complementary to what has been said in the previous sections of this article, to insist that the power of authentic interpretation which is denied to the S. Congregations has respect only to the canons of the Code of Canon Law. The S. Congregations are the immediate organs through which the Sovereign Pontiff expedites the affairs of the entire Church, hence in the aggregate or singly they are termed the Holy See.[181]

The S. Congregations have the administrative power to interpret authentically the canons of the Code in their appli-

[180] Cf. can. 6.

[181] Can. 7. Their competence is described severally in Lib. II, Caput IV. of the Code of Canon Law.

cation to particular cases according to the prescript of canon 17, § 3.[182] As will be shown in the chapter on judicial sentence and rescript, this authentic interpretation does not represent the interpretation of law in the abstract, rendering the comprehensive meaning of the law as such and apart from its application to a case surrounded as it is with its concrete circumstances whereby the law's application is made specific.[183]

It must also be remembered that there are many other ecclesiastical laws, e. g., a body of particular law, which are outside the Code. The power of the Pontifical Commission does not extend to these laws, inasmuch as the grant of the faculty of authentic interpretation given to this body has reference only to the canons of the Code, as the Motu proprio "*Cum iuris canonici*" clearly reveals.[184] Hence, e. g., the S. Congregation of the Council can authentically interpret Diocesan statutes. The seat of this power is to be found in canon 250, § 1 [185], which is a verbal restatement of a provision in the constitution *"Sapienti Consilio"*.[186] Hence the power of this S. Congregation is to be understood according to pre-Code legislation on this matter. In this particular there is the authentic response of the S. Consistorial Congregation, 11 February 1911, concerning the competence of the various Congregations in the interpretation of law.[187] This document recites among other things that each Congregation according to the matters allocated to its competence by the constitution aforementioned has power authentically to interpret all eccle-

---

[182] Blat, *Commentarium Textus Codicis Iuris Canonici,* (Romae: Ex Typographia Pontificia in Instituto Pii IX, 1921), I, 98.

[183] Cf. Jone, *Gesetzbuch des kanonischen Rechtes,* (Paderborn: Ferdinand Schöningh, 1939), I, 37.

[184] *AAS,* IX (1917), 483.

[185] Blat, *Commentarium,* (Romae: Libreria del Collegio "Angelico", 1921), II, 258.

[186] *Fontes,* n. 682, § I, 4.

[187] Cf. *AAS,* III (1911), 99-100.

siastical laws.[188] This provision is now circumscribed, of course, by the supervening Motu proprio "*Cum iuris canonici*" of Benedict XV, regarding the canons of the Code.[189]

That recourse to the Holy See from the authentic interpretation of the Diocesan statutes rendered by the residential Bishop is admissible is clear fundamental law of the Church, as Leo XIII (+1903) points out quoting Popes Gelasius I (+496) and Nicholas I (+867). This recourse is *in devolutivo*, meaning that in the interim the interpretation must be followed as well by religious in matters of purely Diocesan statute which affect them as by any other subject in the Diocese.[190]

---

188 "An, post ordinationem Romanae Curiae a Pio PP. X statutam . . . facultas authentice interpretandi Concilii Tridentini decreta aliasque leges ecclesiasticas vi Constitutionis *Sapienti Consilio* sit singulis Sacris Congregationibus commissa secundum propriam cuiusque competentiam, salva Romani Pontificis approbatione· [Resp.] Affirmative."—*Fontes*, n. 2079.

189 *AAS*, IX (1917,, 483. The same line of reasoning may be pursued on the basis of the Code of Canon Law, the constitution "*Sapienti Consilio*" and the authentic interpretation of 11 February 1911, mentioned above with respect to the several Congregations. Concerning the present matter, Sipos says of the Congregations: "Expediunt negotia et dirimunt controversias via administrativa. Praeterea exclusive cognoscunt de recursibus contra decreta Ordinariorum."—*Enchiridion Iuris Canonici*, (Pecs: Ex Typographia "Haladas R. T.", 1926), p. 191.

190 "Profecto dubitare non licet quin ab iis interpretationibus [scil., decretorum synodalium] ad Sedem Apostolicam provocatio sit; 'siquidem, Gelasio I et Nicolao I auctoribus, ad illam de qualibet mundi parte canones appellari voluerunt: ab illa autem nemo sit appellare permissus'. Quare . . . illud omnino est consequens, licere religiosis sodalibus . . . appellare a lege communi, scilicet *in devolutivo*, [nota 1] Benedict XIV, *de Synod. dioec.* lib. 13, cap. 5 § 2."—const. "*Romanos Pontifices*", 8 maii 1881,—*Fontes*, n. 582, § 13. Cf. Can. 1601. As regards a case of conflict with the rights of religious resulting from an interpretation of Diocesan law, the same document recites: ". . . quo vero ad interpretationem aliorum decretorum etiam *in suspensivo* . . . At vero ad reliqua decreta quod attinet, ea certe lata contra regulares vim rationemque legis amittunt: quare constat illos sic exemptionem a iurisdictione episcopali possidere uti ante possederint; donec Pontificis maximi auctoritate iudicetur, iure ne an secus cum iis actum sit. Hactenus de ex-

In passing it may be remarked that here is applicable the fundamental principle of authentic interpretation. For the Supreme Pontiff in virtue of his office and by divine right has supreme, plenary, and immediate jurisdiction over all the faithful as well in matters of faith and morals as in questions of ecclesiastical discipline.[191] Being therefore the superior of other ecclesiastical prelates in the field of jurisdiction, he can authentically interpret their laws. [192]

---

emptionis privilegio . . ."—*loc. cit.*, § 13-14. Thus Vermeersch-Creusen declare: "Sed ab inferioris interpretatione dabitur appellatio, sicut ab ipsa lege; ergo . . . in *suspensivo* tamen, si obiciantur laesiones iurium personarum exemptarum", referring to the document above of Leo XIII.—*Epitome Iuris Canonici*, I, n. 121; Cf. Can. 1601.

[191] Cann. 218-219.

[192] Concerning the authentic interpretation by a superior in jurisdiction, the doctrine of Suarez is to the point: "Unde etiam manifestum est, posse superiorem hoc modo legem inferioris interpretari, quia non est necesse, ut attingere certo possit personalem (ut ita dicam) sensum, et mentem eius quia hoc neque in successore est necessarium, sed satis est ut possit definire, ac statuere, quomodo talis lex accipienda sit . . . quod melius potest facere per iurisdictionem superiorem quam per aequalem, ut constat. Superiorem enim voco . . . in subordinatione et praelatione. Quomodo . . . iurisdictio Papae [est superior] iurisdictione Episcopi . . ."—*Tractatus de Legibus ac Deo Legislatore*, (Lugduni, 1609), VI, cap. 1, n. 2.

CHAPTER IV.

Aspects of General Authentic Interpretation.

Introduction.

The first paragraph of canon 17 deals with the source of authentic interpretation, and at the same time it indicates its nature, because authentic interpretation is attributed to the office of the legislator. The remaining portion of this canon treats directly concerning the force or effect of authentic interpretation.

The first clause of the second paragraph of canon 17 makes a statement which embraces in a general survey the law enunciated in the remainder of the paragraph: "Interpretatio authentica, per modum legis exhibita, eandem vim habet ac lex ipsa; . . ." The structure of the paragraph proceeds from the general to the particular. The clause sets down that authentic interpretation, the idea of which has been developed in the previous chapters, when it is published after the manner of law, has the same force as the law which it interprets; therefore in a general way it defines the force and scope of this kind of authentic interpretation, namely, general authentic interpretation.[1] This proposition includes the four species of general authentic interpretation, which in this study will be known respectively as: a) declarative or declaratory, b) restrictive, c) extensive, d) explicative or explanatory. The

[1] Other kinds of authentic interpretation are the subject of can. 17, § 3, and will be treated in a succeeding chapter.

fact that this introductory clause is intended to make a general statement in which all the four species partake is indicated by the conjunction "et" in the phrase "et si verba legis", and from the fact that conceptually all the four species share in its provision. Consequently, it is necessary to treat at the outset the general statement which introduces the second paragraph of canon 17, since both declarative interpretation and the other species are included in this enactment. The interpretation which is contemplated in canon 17, § 2, is not any authentic interpretation in general, but such as is given "per modum legis". The law of this canon sets down that the authentic interpretation which proceeds "per modum legis" has the force of law: ". . . eandem vim habet ac lex ipsa".

ARTICLE I. **Interpretatio Authentica.**

The word "authentica" must not be misunderstood. Authentic in the context does not mean that which is authenticated, as one commonly understands a document to be authenticated, that is, when it bears the marks of being genuine.[2] Canon 17 does not have to do with authentic documents in this sense, in the meaning of authenticated. Indeed, authentic interpretation is genuine in the sense that it expounds the sense in which the law must be understood.

In the present paragraph authentic signifies authoritative

---

[2] A document is authentic or genuine when it comes from the source from which it claims to emanate. The most erroneous and unauthoritative statement can be authenticated, can be shown to be genuine, though it is far from being authoritative. Authentic in this sense has usually to do with the external signs which a document bears. Thus Canon law speaks of documents "authentica forma exarata", "attestationes authenticae", of notarized instruments, etc. Cf. cann. 1813-1818; 1585; 1643-1645.

in a specific sense. Every interpretation which is authentic is authoritative, but not vice versa. An interpretation may be founded on authority of the greatest weight, when it comes from one who is a private expert in the law. Authentic interpretation under the terminology of canon 17, § 2, means interpretation which has the force of law: ". . . eandem vim habet ac lex ipsa". Such interpretation is law in its own right. This last statement will be clarified in the progress of this chapter.

ARTICLE II. **Per Modum Legis.**

Fagnanus (+1678) uses the term "per modum legis" in speaking about the manner in which authentic interpretation issues from the Holy See. As to the manner in which it proceeds, it is addressed either to the Church at large (which interpretation is then said to be given generally and "per modum legis"), or it is given as an answer to consultation in a particular case.[3] The concept contained in this phrase *(per modum legis)* is referable to the subjects to whom the authentic interpretation is directed. And as distinguished from interpretation in answer to a particular consultation it is to be considered as that interpretation which goes out to the entire Church. The same concept inheres in the clause "per modum legis exhibita" of the present canon. It is that interpretation which is issued in the fashion in which law is published, and law goes out to the general public.[4] Therefore this clause has reference to the *form* in which the authentic interpretation appears,[5] as is also apparent from the context in canon 17,

---

[3] ". . . interpretatio . . . facit ius quoad omnes etiamsi non generaliter et per modum legis, sed in aliquo speciali casu et ad consultationem alicuius edita fuerit."—*Commentaria*, lib. II, tit. I, cap. *Cum venissent*, n. 16.

[4] Coronata *Institutiones*, n. 23.

[5] Bareille, *Code du Droit Canonique*, (nouvelle ed., Montrejeau: Cardeillac-Soubiron, 1929), n. 11; Bernhardt, *Die Normae generales des CIC*,

§ 3: "Data autem per modum sententiae iudicialis aut rescripti in re peculiari".

ARTICLE III. **Exhibita.**

The authentic interpretation is said to be "exhibita", or, as Fagnanus states in the quotation given above, "edita fuerit"—published. The term "exhibita" is chosen advisedly, at least in a negative sense, in contradistinction to the idea of promulgation, which occurs in the same paragraph. The word "exhibita" has no special intrinsic juridic signification, in the sense that no particular meaning attaches to it, *per se,* other than that which may be found in the ordinary Latin lexicon. Not so with the terms "promulgatione" and "promulgari" in the same context.

Every law or interpretation which is "promulgata" is at the same time "exhibita"; but not vice versa. The idea of promulgation is one which has a precise juridic meaning in Canon law. Laws are instituted, that is, they formally become law, only when they are promulgated according to the law of the Code.[6] Accordingly, the Code gives a juridic meaning to the concept of promulgation by declaring the manner in which promulgation must take place; namely, by publication in the official bulletin of the Church known as the *Acta Apostolicae Sedis*, unless on particular occasions another means of promulgation is provided for. And moreover, except for particular circumstances, the law enjoys a *vacatio legis* for three months from the date of publication.[7] Therefore "exhibita"

(Marburg: [ ], 1927), p. 32; Mothon, *Institutions Canoniques,* (Paris: Desclee et Cie, 1922), I, art. 33; Toso, *Comment. Min.,* I, 45; Michiels, *Normae Generales,* I, 388-389.

[6] Can. 8, § 1.

[7] Cf. can. 9. In this canon the legislator institutes the use of the official

is placed in the present paragraph in contradistinction to the idea of promulgation. Thus in the case of declarative interpretation the law reads: "promulgatione non eget". This clause does not deny that the declarative authentic interpretation—which issues when the law is already clear and certain even without such interpretation—is to be published to the respective subjects in order to have the force of law. On the contrary, the interpretation must be published.

"Per modum legis exhibita" is a qualifying clause referable to the terms "interpretatio authentica", so that the present law reads: *Authentic interpretation when it is published in the form of law has the same force as the law itself.* The clause is restrictive, not explanatory. In other words, the clause does not mean to say that all authentic interpretation—the subject of discussion here is exclusively interpretation which is purely such and not at the same time the application of law—must appear "per modum legis". Implicitly it has reference to interpretation issued "per modum rescripti". This statement is clear from the following facts.

The Pontifical Commission drew up a resolution that it would respond only to the doubts proposed by Ordinaries and other higher ecclesiastical superiors, or by their intervention in the case of private individuals.[8] Therefore, the Pontifical Commission means to issue responses "per modum rescripti" [9], which will be interpretation of law purely in the abstract.[10]

---

bulletin established by Pius X as the means of legally promulgating acts of the Holy See. Cf. *Fontes*, n. 684.

[8] *AAS*, X (1917), 77.

[9] The present discussion has nothing to do with the rescript "in re peculiari" of can. 17, § 3. That rescript represents an authentic interpretation of law in its application to concrete circumstances and proceeds not only from interpretative but at the same time also from administrative jurisdiction.

[10] "Mais à la Commission il appartiendra exclusivement de dire le sens authentique de la loi, non pour les applications aux cas concrets, mais bien de manière abstraite et générale."—Boudinhon, *LeCC*, XL (1917), 397.

In fact, the Motu proprio (§I) does not grant to the Commission the power of executive jurisdiction to apply the law. Thus it is clear that these doubts are answered "per modum rescripti". For Gasparri says that the Commission received many petitions and gave many responses; that of these responses individual ones were published in the *Acta Apostolicae Sedis*.[11] The Cardinal does not say that each and every response given during the period of seventeen years appeared in this official bulletin. There is no law which directs that such procedure must obtain. Under pre-Code legislation there were certain decisions, especially those of the S. C. of the Council, which were known as interpretations formally particular but equivalently general.[12] The interpretations of the Pontifical Commission, given "per modum rescripti" are formally particular, but juridically they are not equivalently general. The law does not so direct; and this matter is purely a subject of positive law.[13]

The obvious conclusion in this discussion is that authentic interpretation in order to have the same force as the law itself, though it does not need promulgation, must nevertheless be published "per modum legis". A further reason is that it would be a substantial corruption of the legal text to delete the clause "per modum legis exhibita". On the other hand, if it is true that an authentic interpretation, a declarative interpretation, given "per modum rescripti", *per se* binds third

---

[11] "Multa . . . quaesita Pontificiae Commissioni . . . allata sunt, multaque pariter ab eadem reddita sunt responsa. Quum vero singula eiusmodi responsa per Acta Apostolicae Sedis edita . . . inveniantur . . ."—*Codicis Iuris Canonici Interpretationes seu Responsa,* (ed. Joseph Bruno, Typis Polyglottis Vaticanis, 1935), Praefatio, p. VI-VII.

[12] ". . . de decretis in casu peculiari datis, sed interpretationem legis dubiae et obscurae continentibus, quae proinde formaliter particularia aequivalenter universalia dicebantur . . ."—Chelodi, *Ius de Personis,* n. 67.

[13] The question of interpretation "per modum rescripti in re peculari" will be discussed in the chapter on rescripts.

parties, then the clause "per modum legis exhibita" seems to be useless in the context of the present law.

It may be noted here that when the response of the Pontifical Commission is published, the formula of the question as well as the answer constitutes an authentic proclamation. This remark seems certain by the very nature of the situation, because one cannot understand the answer unless one knows the question. And therefore the response must be understood in no other sense than that which is warranted by the terms of the question as authentically published. Question and answer conspire as law to establish a question of law.

ARTICLE IV. **Eandem Vim Habet ac Lex Ipsa.**

Every authentic interpretation published in the form of law has the same force as the law itself. This legal proposition occasions the following consideration.

As an effect shows the nature of its cause, so authentic interpretation, having the same force as the law itself, indicates clearly that it proceeds from legislative jurisdiction. And therefore only he who can establish law can authentically interpret. This clause of can. 17, §2, is simply an application of the principle of authentic interpretation discussed in the previous chapters and is here formulated into a statement of positive law. The power of legislating is itself of natural law.[14]

[14] ". . . est lex quaedam ab hominibus inventa, secundum quam in particulari disponuntur quae in lege naturae continentur . . . Unde Tullius dicit in sua Rhet. (De invent. lib. II, aliquant. ante fin.) quod, 'initium iuris est a natura profectum; deinde quaedam in consuetudinem ex utilitatis ratione venerunt; postea res a natura profectas et consuetudine probatas legum metus et religio sanxit.' "—S. Thomas, *Summa Theologica,* I, IIae, qu. 91, art. III, in corp.

Pure human law, however, is of its essence positive law. This is to say, the legislative power, from an aggregate of many ways of attaining the respective social ends, selects and posits by virtue of its power certain rules of action to accomplish the purposes of society.[15] This consideration eminently illustrates the meaning of jurisdiction; it is *ius-dicere,* to declare law. Authentic interpretation possesses the same inherent purpose and force as vests in the legislative power; it establishes positive law in questions of law. It is therefore a formal subsidiary function of legislation and partakes of the essence of this jurisdiction, legislative jurisdiction.

Suarez (+1617) declares that authentic interpretation must vest itself with the properties of all law; among other things, it must be promulgated.[16] What he requires for promulgation is difficult to say. The method of promulgating interpretation seems to have been rather indefinite in the time of Suarez, because he mentions that there is no positive legislation concerning it.[17]

Upon the head of efficient cause, general authentic interpretation proceeds from public authority in virtue of legislative power and consequently begets a universal obligation.[18] All those for whom the law is made are bound by the law, and they are obliged to the extent and in the manner prescribed by law.[19] Since general authentic interpretation has the selfsame force as the law which it interprets, all those who are bound by the law are also obliged to observe the

---

15 "Quod principi placuit, legis habet vigorem."—D. (1, 4)1.

16 *De Legibus,* VI, cap. I, n. 3

17 *De Legibus,* III, cap. XV, n. 17.

18 "Interpretatio est authentica . . . quae ab auctoritate publica procedit obligatorio modo; estque generalis, si potestate legislativa fiat et omnes obligat; . . ."—Coronata, *Institutiones,* I, n. 22. This author uses the condition, "si potestate legislativa fiat", in contradistinction to judicial and administrative jurisdiction, referring to can. 17, § 3.

19 Cann. 8-17; 21.

direction given in the interpretation of the law under the same conditions in which the law obliges. In passing, a correction must here be noted concerning declarative interpretation; namely, that it takes effect without legal promulgation, but not without general notice. General authentic interpretation is legally commensurate with the law to which it refers. Naturally, extensive or restrictive interpretation will effect a change according to the tenor of the interpretation. Briefly, these considerations make it clear that general authentic interpretation has the status of law. By the same token, general authentic interpretation, being law, is governed by the rules of interpretation common to law.[20]

The clause "eandem vim habet ac lex ipsa" cannot mean that the legal force of the interpretation is a power which is borrowed from, or—to describe the thought metaphorically—which flows over from the law into its interpretation. In other words, authentic interpretation is law in its own right.[21] The basis of this remark may be established by the following considerations.

In the case of declarative interpretation, though this interpretation adds nothing materially new, it certainly adds something formally new. It gives in effect an authentic paraphrase of the law in part or as a whole; or it declares authentically that a certain concept is already included in the legal text. Thereby it gives to the retroactivity of the interpretation a legal force, an effect which doctrinal interpretation does not possess, because doctrinal interpretation is known to all legal history as "non necessaria", not obligatory. Thus there

---

20 Cf. cann. 6; 18-19; 22-23; 2219, §§ 1 and 3.

21 "Sie [i. e. die authentische Auslegung] erhält Gesetzeskraft, wie das durch sie erklärte Gesetz."—Keller, *Die "Normae Generales" des Codex iuris canonici*, (Calw: A. Oelschläger'sche Buchdruckerei, 1923), p. 58: "Legis declarantis naturam induunt omnes interpretationes authenticae."—Santi, *Praelectiones Iuris Canonici*, (Romae, 1886), lib. I, tit. II, n. 20.

would seem to be present a causal connection between the formally new element of authentic interpretation and the fact that general notice must be given of even declarative interpretation *(per modum legis exhibita)* in order that it may have the force of law; because a formally new element has appeared in the field of law, a general notice of this fact must be issued.

Explanatory, extensive, or restrictive authentic interpretation appears *prima facie* to be law in its own right, because in each case there is present something materially new.

ARTICLE V. *Application to Particular Law.*

What has been said must be applied not only to law in the form of authentic interpretation which proceeds from the Holy See, but also to the authentic interpretation of particular law. The authentic interpretation of laws enacted in plenary and provincial councils, in Diocesan synods and outside of Diocesan synods must follow the precepts of canon 17. The same obtains for the authentic interpretation of particular law of personal communities, such namely, as are not formally confined to a particular territory. The constitutions and rules of religious orders and congregations are in this class of particular law; they are personal. However, in such communities there can also be territorial law, e. g., of a religious province.[22] In any case, the authentic interpretation follows the law: "accessorium sequitur principale".

The reason that particular law is included in canon 17 is that the legislator speaks of *"Leges"*, the first word of the canon, in connection with the rules of authentic interpre-

---

[22] Cf. Van Hove, *De Legibus Ecclesiasticis,* n. 208.

tation. He does not confine himself to *canones:* "ubi legislator non distinguit, neque nos distinguere debemus".

The particular aspects of general authentic interpretation relative to its force and the manner in which it is to be understood in relation to the law which it interprets will be treated in the discussions on the individual species of interpretation.

CHAPTER V.

Nature of Declaratory Authentic Interpretation.

The legislator postulates that when the authentic interpretation of a law is nothing more than declaratory, or, as this interpretation is frequently called, *mere declarativa,* the terminology of the law is already clear in itself, for this interpretation merely re-iterates possibly in clearer terms the meaning which is already present in the law. The true signification of the law could have been known by those subject to the law even prior to the issuance of the authentic interpretation. This thought is expressed in the clause: ". . . et si verba legis in se certa declaret tantum".[1] Therefore, the terms of a law are said to be certain in themselves when there can be no objective doubt concerning them,[2] and the doubt which surrounds the law is purely in the mind of the subjects,[3] being referable to ignorance or inadvertence, so that the interpretation is merely a rendition of the law in clearer terms.[4] Such is the exposition given by contemporary authors generally concerning the meaning of the words, "verba legis in se certa". In fact, the declarative interpretation is at most merely a paraphrase of the existing law; it states what is already, objectively, present in the law. As the Roman legislator declared, the interpretation does not upon its appearance

[1] Can. 17, § 2.

[2] Cicognani, *Commentarium ad Lib. I Codicis,* (Romae: ex Schola Typographica "Pio X", 1925), p. 120.

[3] Toso, *Commentaria Minora,* I, 45.

[4] Beste, *Introductio in Codicem,* p. 76-77.

decree anything, rather it points out what has been decreed.[5]

Briefly, the legislator expects that his subjects should have come to the same interpretation as that which is revealed in the declarative authentic interpretation. Therefore if, after the interpretation is published, the same conclusion is arrived at by analysis of the law, the interpretation is known as declarative. It does not become declarative when it is finally agreed upon that the law is in itself clear. The interpretation has been declarative from the time of its publication, and the law under the meaning stated in the interpretation has been clear from the time of its promulgation. This position taken by the law is merely a corollary of what has been said in the foregoing. For if all to whom the law is directed are obliged by the law, they have a cognate obligation to learn the law. Thus from the law *"Ut canonum"* that all must be guided by the law according to its meaning and authority,[6] Gonzalez (+1649) makes the logical deduction, quoting the third synod of Orleans, that no one shall be permitted to be ignorant of, and by dissimulation to transgress, the law.[7]

Since under the legislation of the Code a declarative authentic interpretation has retroactive effect, one may inquire as to when the legal terminology must be considered as in itself reasonably clear. Or conversely, when can there be reasonable certainty of an objectively doubtful text? Often such questions are asked and discussed at the appearance of an authentic interpretation of a given law, so that the interpretation is, so to say, challenged, or examined as to whether or

---

5 ". . . nihil nunc dat, sed datum significat"—D. (28, 1), 21, 1. This principle and its use will receive further discussion in a following chapter on authentic interpretation of doubtful law.

6 C. 1, X, *de constitutionibus*, I, 2.

7 "Nec ignorare quemquam, nec dissimulare, idest praetermittere [canonum statuta] permittitur. ' "—*Commentaria*, lib. I, tit. II, cap. Primum, n. 4.

not it merely conveys and indicates a meaning which is already signified and warranted by the legal text.

The point of departure taken throughout the following discussion is the publication of an authentic interpretation. Therefore the question here is as to when this interpretation must be considered as declaratory. The general answer is: when it does no more than explain what is already in the law. Such is the answer of the legislator, as implied in the words, "et si verba legis in se certa declaret tantum". Consequently in order to know whether or not an authentic interpretation is declaratory and nothing more, it is necessary to analyze the law interpreted and compare the findings with the interpretation to discover whether or not the meaning rendered by this interpretation is already warranted in the law. Since the law is a precept to be observed, the legislator expects a careful examination of his law even before the appearance of declarative authentic interpretation. He does not presume ignorance of the law ordinarily,[8] and such ignorance, generally speaking, does not excuse[9] either from the obligation of observing the law or from penalty for its transgression. As a positive measure co-extensive with the obligation of knowing the law the legislator of the Code has established authoritatively norms of doctrinal interpretation.[10]

It is here submitted that, *per se,* the obligation of knowing the law is co-extensive with the prescripts of canons 18 and 19, which treat on the rules of doctrinal interpretation. This statement is founded on the fact that the knowledge of the law is requisite as an immediate means of fulfilling its injunction, that the legislator there prescribes the means of knowing his law, and that these rules of doctrinal interpretation are obligatory. The lawgiver states that ecclesiastical

---

[8] Can. 16.

[9] Reg. 13, R. J., in VIo.

[10] Cann. 18-19.

laws must be understood *(intelligendae sunt*—can. 18) in the manner which he prescribes in this canon; the same may be said of canon 19. What is over and above the prescripts of these two canons does not come within the law of learning the prescripts of the law and consequently is not of obligation. Any doubt as to further obligation of investigating the meaning of the law is set aside by the principle: ". . . in re igitur dubia melius est verbis edicti servire . . .".[11] Namely, the legislator has not manifested his mind as to any further obligation; then no further obligation can be affirmed, as the glossator explains this principle.[12] Thus also the dictum: "Quod voluit expressit, quod noluit tacuit".

Since therefore declarative authentic interpretation postulates that the law is already certain and could have been known by the rules of interpretation prescribed by positive law, these rules may be used as criteria in judging whether or not a given authentic interpretation is nothing more than declarative.

Let the following contingency be supposed, as it is also posited by the clause of canon 17, at present under discussion. There appears an authentic interpretation published to the Church at large. It is desirable to determine whether this interpretation is merely declaratory of existing law; namely, whether it is an exposition in parallel with the meaning of the law as intended by the legislator and already to be found in the law from its very inception.[13]

---

[11] D. (14, 1) 20.

[12] ". . . in dubiis standum esse verbis legis. Dic secundum Bal. [dum?] . . . Nam si per aliam legem non esset interpretatum, staremus verbis . . . sed hic non apparet de mente legislatoris; et ideo inhaerendum est verbis."—*Glossa* ad v. *Edicti*, D. (14, 1) 20.

[13] Cf. Maroto, *Institutiones*, n. 235.

ARTICLE I. *Criteria of "verba legis in se certa".*

It must be said at the outset that the norms of canons 18 and 19 will not necessarily determine whether the interpretation is declaratory, just as they will not infallibly of themselves produce the correct interpretation at any time. They must be properly applied; the procedure is not a mechanical one.[14] The certainty which results from the use of these rules will depend on factors which are beyond the control of the legislator, who prescribed the rules. The power of grasping the weight of argument depends on individual intellectual acumen.[15] What is nevertheless clear in itself may appear to an individual or group to be uncertain.[16] Again, the certainty of the conclusion of one's research into the meaning of the law is directly dependent upon the certainty of the principles or premises from which the conclusion derives.[17] In short, though the legal rules are authoritatively set down and are intended to produce the true and clear interpretation with moral certainty, they may fail for want of proper application both as regards the rules as such as well as the subject matters to which they refer. They are, however, the determinants of the meaning of the law. It may be noted here that these determinants are to be applied to all ecclesiastical law, for canon 18 decrees: "Leges ecclesiasticae intelligendae sunt . . .". It does not confine itself to *canones.*

For the sake of clarity it is again mentioned that the following discussion is intended as an attempt to present the

---

[14] Cf. Van Hove, *De Legibus Ecclesiasticis,* n. 248.

[15] ". . . certitudo invenitur . . . Essentialiter quidem . . . in vi cognoscitiva."—S. Thomas, *Summa Theologica,* II, IIae, quaest. 18, Art. I, in corp.

[16] ". . . nihil prohibet id quod est certius secundum naturam esse quoad nos minus certum propter debilitatem intellectus nostri . . ."—*Summa Theologica,* I, quaest. I, Art. V, ad 1.

[17] ". . . certitudo cognitionis conclusionum procedit ex certitudine principiorum."—*Summa Theologica,* II, IIae, quaest. 5, Art. VIII, ad 3.

intrinsic meaning and method of declarative interpretation of a law or canon—regarding which an authentic interpretation is supposed as having issued—being illustrated with a view to determining whether the authentic interpretation is to be considered as declaratory of law which is already clear and certain. Since authentic interpretation is also of the genus "law", these rules at the same time indicate the manner of dealing with the text of this interpretation directly. The chief aspect, however, under which these rules are considered here is the determination of the material scope of the phrase, "verba legis in se certa"; namely, when is the legal terminology to be considered certain in itself? On the other hand, the present discussion may not enter upon a detailed commentary of canons 18 and 19; there are no pretensions made here to do so.

The rules of interpretation authorized by canon 18 [18] are those which are to be applied in doctrinal interpretation of law. They are intended as means of bringing to light the inherent clarity of the legal text, for a law enjoys an inherent presumptive claim to perspicuity. For because of the very fact that it is intended to be an obligatory norm, it must be clear.[19] Their primary purpose is to dispel ignorance and subjective doubt, not to discover a *dubium iuris*. In fact, a *dubium iuris* cannot be pronounced until these rules have been applied. For how can one say that a law is objectively doubtful until one has examined and analyzed its text? The real doubt of law is the terminus of the investigation, and its existence is posited only upon the results of research. This statement is made precisely to illustrate the fact that an authentic

---

[18] As to its subject matter, can. 19 is an adjunct of can. 18, for it deals with the modification of the proper signification in the terminology of certain species of laws.

[19] "Quoniam constitutio Apostolicae Sedis omnes adstringit et nihil debet obscurum vel ambiguum continere; . . ."—c. 13, X, *de constitutionibus*, I, 2.

interpretation cannot be pronounced declarative, explanatory, restrictive, or extensive until the law in question has been probed and the results have been, as it were, placed side by side, after the manner of physical measurement, with the content of the authentic interpretation, which itself in its turn bears analysis. And there is then a result, which may be a clarification. But there may be another result called a probable opinion, based on the investigation. In this latter case there is another, similarly another probable opinion. At all events, only at this point may the law be said to be objectively doubtful.

The supreme ruling purpose in the interpretation of law is to discover the mind or will of the legislator, or more precisely and correctly, the will of the law.[20]

A. *Secundum propriam verborum significationem in textu et contextu consideratam.*

The first rule in determining whether or not the legal terminology of a law is "in se certa"—and by contraposition whether the authentic interpretation is declarative—is obtained from the law which decrees that eccesiastical laws must be understood according to their proper signification as considered in the text and context.[21] Note that the rule is not a suggestion; it is a law—*intelligendae sunt.*

This rule directs first of all that the proper signification of the words must be taken as from the legal wording itself *(in textu)*. This statement considers the legal text or wording

[20] "Virtus enim legis consistit in substantia rationis . . . quia mens legis idem est quod anima et spiritus ipsius scripturae. Nam scriptura sine mente nihil est. Item per vivam rationem interpretamur scripturas."—Baldus de Ubaldis, *Commentaria,* lib. I, tit. II, cap. primum, *Canonum,* nn. 43-44.

[21] Can. 18.

as such,[22] so that substitutes for the legal wording in the form of synonyms can never be considered as constituting the legal text. Only the actual words of the law constitute its legal terminology. The same is to be said as regards the sequence of the words. Thus the Code was promulgated as having the force of law ". . . sic ut digestus est".[23] And it, in turn, prescribes that the legal wording of all ecclesiastical laws alone is the instrument which is to convey the proper signification of the words. These considerations are at once submitted as evidence of the fact that even a declarative authentic interpretation, which, in form or effect, is merely a paraphrase of the law, must be published. Again, it must be noted from the wording of this canon— ". . . in textu et contextu considerdatam"—that the text and context must be considered as constituting a unit; they must be considered together in order to produce the proper signification.

The present precept of the legislator is aptly illustrated by the dicta of Roman law relative to the interpretation of the terminology of testaments.[24] Accordingly, there is a law of the Digest which declares that the meaning of the words of a testament must be adhered to unless it is manifest that the testator intended otherwise.[25] That the proper signification is here intended is apparent from the gloss of Accursius (Francisco Accorso, +1260), which suggests that the signification which is of more frequent use *(magis usitata)* is to be

---

[22] Cf. Van Hove, *De Legibus Ecclesiasticis*, nn. 249, 251.

[23] Benedict XV, const. *"Providentissima Mater Ecclesia"*, 27 maii 1917, in fine.—Cf. first introductory document to the Code.

[24] These documents, in fact, have the force of law as against all the world, for a law in the Code of Justinian shows that the provision of a last will must be obeyed to the full extent: ". . . tunc enim voluntati testatoris per omnia oboediendum est".—C. (3, 33), 3.

[25] "Non aliter a significatione verborum recedi oportet, quam cum manifestum est aliud sensisse testatorem."—D. (32, 69); *item*, D. (30, 74), with gloss; fr. 73, with marginal gloss.

understood in the testament. Again, another gloss indicates that the words are to be taken on their face value, as they sound,[26] unless this meaning is to be abandoned by the authority of the testator.[27] Bartolus (+1357) sees in this law the rule that the proper signification must obtain in interpreting law, as distinguished from an improper meaning.[28] Cardinal Tuschus invokes the same law as a principle of jurisprudence to demonstrate that in the field of law words must be understood in their proper, true, and natural signification.[29] This statement of Tuschus must be understood as a general characterization of the concept of proper signification in writing or speech. The author also recognizes this fact, for, as will be shown in the following, there is the all-important juridic signification as clearly distinguishable from the significations known as the natural and the usual.[30] On the other hand, from what has been said it may be gathered that in the interpretation of law the use of the proper signification is basic. In fact, the legislator of the Code under the explicit terms of canon 18, seems to insist upon its use exclusively.[31] From this consideration it follows that in his authentic inter-

---

[26] *Glossa* sv. *Aliud:* "quam verba sonora videntur."

[27] *Glossa* sv. *Testatorem:* "Tunc enim receditur a significatione verborum."

[28] *Commentaria,* in D. (1, 1), 9 (tit. *de iustitia et iure*), n. 56-58.

[29] "Verba sunt interpretanda secundum propriam significationem . . . quando non praeiudicatur ordinariae iurisdictioni . . . quia non est recedendum a propria significatione verborum, l. non aliter, ff. de lega . . . quia verba semper debent intelligi proprie, vere, et naturaliter . . ."—*Practicae Conclusiones,* (Lugduni, 1634), VIII, Littera V, Concl. 91, nn. 1-6.

[30] The last mentioned of these, of course, can become juridic—"Consuetudo est optima legum interpres" (can. 29)—and as such it is a source of authentic interpretation.

[31] Thus Suarez declares that in interpreting laws in order to establish harmony between laws, though some departure from the proper signification is permissible, yet a certain proper signification, at least a meaning that has the sanction of juridic usage, must remain: ". . . ut tamen servetur aliqua proprietas verborum saltem secundum consuetudinem iuris".—*De Legibus,* VI, cap. 1, n. 18.

pretation the lawgiver himself will use only a proper signification. Secondly, it is also clear that this supervening authentic interpretation will itself have to be understood in the light of the context of the law interpreted. For these reasons a further brief consideration of proper signification and context is entertained in the following numbers.

1. A. PROPER SIGNIFICATION.

The question here arises as to what is the proper signification of a word.

Accordingly, in the law *"Labeo"* of the Digest there is a minute discussion on the proper meaning of the word *supellex*. The historical changes concerning the acceptation of this word are there pointed out. The signification of this term [32] does not enter into this discussion. Rather the principle whereby is determined the proper signification of a word, which is found in the present law, is most useful. For names, the law reads, must be understood, not according to the opinion of individuals, but according to the sanction of common usage.[33] Since language is the vehicle of man's intercourse in society, it is for society to determine the definite usage, which is subject to change,[34] so that, as Accursius points out, a

[32] Meaning: furniture, household furnishings. It is defined in a negative manner by the Digest: "Supellex est domesticum patris familias instrumentum quod neque argento aurove facto vel vesti adnumeretur."—D. (33, 10) 1.

[33] ". . . non enim ex opinionibus singulorum, sed ex communi usu nomina exaudiri debere."—D. (33, 10) 7, 2.

[34] ". . . unde versus,

'Multa renascentur quae iam cecidere, caduntque
Quae nunc sunt in honore vocabula, si volet usus,
Quem penes arbitrium est et vis et norma loquendi.' "

—*Glossa* ad v. *Mutatam*, D. (30, 10) 7, 1, (Horatius, *Ars poetica*, § 5.)

figurative meaning can also be reduced to common use.[35] Common usage or observance, whether particular or universal, antecedently, as it were, prepares the signification which is called proper and according to which a subsequent law will be framed, except, of course, for legal definition of the terms to the contrary. The present discussion does not have respect to the formation of legal custom concerning the meaning in which a law has come to be received, which custom has arisen subsequent to the institution of a certain law.

Though there is a certain latitude in the proper meaning of the terms of language within which there may be doubt, which doubt in turn can be solved by recourse to the intention of the author, if this can be ascertained *(stabitur testatoris voluntati)*,[36] at all events the use of language can never be considered as subject to the mere choice [37] of an individual. It must derive its function from current, social usage,[38] otherwise human intercourse is impossible, unless under special

---

[35] *Glossa* ad v. *Ex communi usu,* D. (33, 10) 7, 2.

[36] "(Sed de iis quidem de quibus dubitari potest) supellectilis potius an argenti, an vestis sint. Servius fatetur sententiam eius qui legaverit aspici oportere, in quam rationem ea solitus sit referre . . ."—D. (33, 10) 7 (with gloss): "Cum aliquis audit aliqua verba, considerare debet causam dicendi; et non ipsam significationem verborum tantum; quia verba deserviunt intentioni: et non intentio verbis: verba enim inventa sunt, ut per ea intentionem suam quis exprimat."—*Glossa* ad v. *Intelligentia,* c. 6, X, *de verborum significatione,* V, 40; "Non statim debemus intelligere ut verba prima facie sonare videntur: maxime ubi ambigua sunt, sed debemus recurrere ad intentionem loquentis . . ."—*Glossa* ad v. *Ex causis* (c. 6, X, de V. S., V, 40); "Hoc verum est cum constat de intellectu."—*Glossa* ad v. *Verba,* c. 11, C, XXII, q. 5; cf. Baldus de Ubaldis, *Commentaria,* lib. I, tit. II, cap. primum, *Canonum.*

[37] ". . . licet perperam inferre volebat Tubero quem quolibet verbo dicere quicquid vellet."—*Glossa* ad v. *Agitaverit,* D. (33, 10) 7.

[38] Accursius, (*Glossa* ad v. *Ex communi usu*): "Scilicet, proprio: aut figurato, nam figurativa significatio communis est et sic usitata potest appellari." "Ex hoc nota quod verba testamenti sunt possibiliter, non impossibiliter interpretanda."—Baldus de Ubaldis, *Commentaria,* C. (3, 33) 13.

circumstances a person has clearly defined his own terms, e. g., in a testament.[39]

The same basic point of departure, social usage, obtains as a principle of jurisprudence also in Decretal law, which fact the glossator of the law *"Labeo"* points out. And in the annotations to the law *"Nonnulli"* the gloss reciprocally refers to *"Labeo"* for confirmation in the use of this principle: ". . . nomina ex communi usu intelligenda sunt . . . ff. de supell. l. labeo".[40]

One arrives at the stage where the proper signification of a word is set down by the law itself; the meaning is then said to be fixed by the interpretation of law.[41] Thus the Code defines certain terms.[42] The present study does not permit a digression into these details. There is, however, a most important matter which must engage the attention of anyone who is dealing with the canons of the Code, as will appear from the following—certain prescripts of Canon 6.[43]

Among other matters, canon 6 treats the relation between the old law and the Code of Canon law, which took effect on May 19, 1918, relative to the proper signification of the terminology of certain portions of the new law. The law of the Code is for the most part a restatement of the

39 Cf. C. (3, 33) 13, 3.

40 *Glossa* ad v. *Dietas*, c. 28, X, *de rescriptis*, I, 3; cf. c. 7, X, *de sponsalibus et matrimoniis*, IV, 1; *Glossa* ad v. *Proposuit*, c. 7, X, *de sponsalibus et matrimoniis*, IV, 1, referring to D. (32, 69).

41 ". . . si ius in aliquo loco interpretatur vocabulum, illa dicitur propria sigificatio."—Tuschus, *Conclusiones Practicae*, VIII, Litt. V, Concl. 91, n. 28; Bartolus, *Commentaria*, D. (1, 1) 9 (Titulus: *De iustitia et iure*), n. 59.

42 For example, *clerici*, in can. 108, § 1; *sacra ordinatio*, can. 950; can. 488 contains a long series of definitions. The Code determines more complex ideas, such as that of an ecclesiastical trial, cann. 1552-1553.

43 Cf. Neuberger, *Canon 6 or The Relation of the Codex Iuris Canonici to Preceding Legislation*, (The Catholic University of America Canon Law Studies, N. 44, Washington, D. C.: Catholic University of America, 1927).

traditional discipline of the Church. Those parts of the Code which restate or are in agreement with the discipline which existed before the Code went into effect must be evaluated according to the interpretation which they enjoyed under the authority of the old law. They are therefore to receive the interpretation which is found in the works of the approved authors who wrote commentaries on the old law.[44]

This law of the Code is of great consequence. Regarding the subject matters of its provision, the old approved authors are most valuable for the study of present Canon law, for they reflect the true canonico-juristic spirit, which, according to the testimony of De Becker (+1936), is unfortunately often wanting in the works of more recent writers.[45] The former law and the authentic interpretations thereof as received and expounded in the doctrine of the approved authors are therefore an authoritative source for interpreting the former discipline found in the Code. In other words, this body of doctrine fixes definitely to a certain extent the proper signification of the legal terminology, referred to in canon 18, as regards the laws of the Code which restate the former discipline. The disposition of canon 6 does not mean that the subject matter of the former discipline cannot now receive extensive and restrictive authentic interpretation. There is nothing to hinder such procedure. The sources just men-

[44] Can. 6, nn. 2-3.

[45] "Ac, imprimis, prouti S. Congregatio de Seminariis pro Professoribus insinuat (*AAS,* IX (1917), 439), non negligat interpres, etsi non Professor, nostros classicos Doctores, maxime post Tridentinos familiares habere et ad eos frequenter recurrere; inter quos paucos tantum citabo: Pirhing, Reiffenstuel, Schmalzgrueber, Giraldi, Böckhn, et praesertim Benedictus XIV in suis immortalibus operibus: apud ipsos reperiet verum spiritum canonicum et iuridicum qui, infeliciter saepe deest in recentioribus."—Cf., *ETL,* II (1925) 245. The *probati auctores* are those whose doctrine has been highly esteemed in the Roman Curia for the solution of questions of law.—Cf. *Fontes,* n. 350 § 8; Wernz, *Ius Decretalium,* I, n. 70, nota 120; Wernz-Vidal, *Ius Canonicum,* I, n. 105, II, nota 33; Van Hove, *De Legibus Ecclesiasticis,* n. 59, 2.

tioned, however, are not sources of authentic but of doctrinal interpretation of great value.[46]

B. PARTICULAR USAGE.

The proper signification can become modified by the use which it receives in a particular region, which use will then prevail, as Bartolus points out, against the proper signification as such.[47] The "natural", so to say, or more generally accepted meaning becomes the "usual" in this or that territory. This consideration has practical bearing on the formulation and subsequent interpretation of particular, especially territorial, laws, e. g., Diocesan statutes. It is precisely this species of usage which is one of the exceptions envisioned in the principle of interpretation which directs that the proper signification must be adhered to:

Non aliter a significatione verborum recedi oportet,

---

[46] Neuberger, *Canon 6,* p. 71; Wernz-Vidal, *Ius Canonicum,* I, n. 195, I; Cicognani, *Commentarium ad Lib. I Codicis,* p. 39. Even the common opinion of the doctors does not rise to the dignity and force of authentic interpretation, as seems evident from the words of Benedict XIV (Prosper Lambertini, +1758, a canonist of great authority): "Nobis etenim persuasum manet, opiniones Doctorum communes non ita facile parvipendendas esse; . . ."—*Fontes,* n. 350, § 8. The great weight of their common teaching, however, appears from his words:

> Qui enim in actionibus, vel Iudiciis Ecclesiasticis, suo sensu, et non communi Iurisperitorum omnium duceretur, sine dubio, suo illum iudicio Ecclesia coerceret.—*Ibid.,*

quoting Melchior Cano, *Tractatus de Locis Theologicis,* lib. VIII, cap. 7. Therefore, while their common opinion will engender moral certitude, legally it may be characterized by the traditional term, *non necessaria.* Cf. etiam, Van Hove, *Prolegomena,* n. 51.

[47] "Et plus statur usui quam significationi vocis . . . Imo usui statur contra naturam vocis."—*Glossa* ad v. *Dietas,* c. 28, X, *de rescriptis,* I, 3; "Vel si communis usus loquendi aliter se haberet . . . Hic enim usus omni regulae, omnique constitutioni, in exaudiendis vel examinandis sermonibus derogat . . ." —Bartolus, *Commentaria,* D. (1, 1) 9 (Titulus: *De iustita et iure*), n. 58.

quam cum manifestum est aliud sensisse testatorem[48]

—the manifest divergent acceptation extant in a particular territory.[49] However, in doubt as to the supposed particular customary use of the terminology, that is, if this custom is itself doubtful, the first part of the principle must apply; the proper signification does not then yield to particular usage.

Hostiensis (+1271) admits into the jurisprudence of Decretal law the employment of the particular usage of a certain region as against the proper signification as such,[50] according to the principle: "Intelligentia dictorum ex causis est assumenda: . . .".[51]

Canon 18 of the Code reveals the application of the same rule when it reads: ". . . ad legis . . . circumstantias . . . est recurrendum". Consequently a particular law must be understood as it appears in its surroundings of time and place. And hence it is "in se certa" under such contingencies. The application of the present rule of canon 18 exemplifies well how the mind of the law may be detected from a source outside the law itself. It must be noted that in this case the meaning is not interpreted into the law; circumstances are here used to discover what is already present *(datum significat)*.

2. Context.

It is not sufficient to know the proper signification only in its immediate text; the context must also be considered at the same time. The wording of canon 18 points out this fact

---

48 D. (32, 69).

49 "Tunc enim receditur a significatione verborum . . . quando est talis regionis consuetudo."—*Glossa* ad v. *Testatorem,* D. (32, 69); *item,* D. (30, 50) 3.

50 *Commentaria,* lib. V, tit. XL, cap. VIII, ad v. *Propterea.*

51 C. 6, X, *de verborum significatione,* V, 40.

unmistakably, for the proper signification must be considered in the combined text and context.

Roman law deemed barbaric an attempt to expound the law after considering it only in part and not in its entirety:

> Incivile est nisi tota lege perspecta una aliqua particula eius proposita iudicare et respondere.[52]

The same concept is present as a principle of law in the law "*Propterea*" of the Decretals of Gregory IX:

> Propterea si prolixam epistolam ad interpretandum accipere fortasse contigerit, rogo non verbum ex verbo, sed sensum ex sensu transferre: quia dum proprietas verborum attenditur, sensus veritatis amittitur.[53]

The text and context together conspire to convey the proper meaning of the words and consequently, the intention of their author, because ideas are not shackled by words, but rather words are to be subservient to thought.[54] Thus the result of the examination of the context—which process takes precedence over any of those to be described in the remainder of canon 18—may be the immediate revelation of the mind of the legislator as contained in the law under investigation. The law is then clear and "in se certa". And there is immediately applicable the traditional principle enunciated by Reiffenstuel (+1703): "Verba clara non admittunt interpretationem neque voluntatis coniecturam".[55] In fact, according to the express terms of canon 18, further investigation is not permissible.

---

[52] D. (1, 3) 24.

[53] C. 8, X, *de verborum significatione,* V, 40.

[54] ". . . quia non sermoni res, sed rei est sermo subiectus."—c. 6, X, *de verborum significatione,* V, 40.

[55] *Ius Canonicum Universum,* lib. I, tit. II, n. 384.

3. Nomenclature.

At this juncture of the discussion on the implications of declarative authentic interpretation, or, on the criteria of this species of interpretation, it will be useful to know in what relation declarative interpretation as viewed by the old jurists stands with what is called declarative interpretation after the Code.

It seems that the method of interpretation sketched briefly in the foregoing contains in part as one element the concept of what authors in the past called *interpretatio translativa.*

Fagnanus (+1678) refers to an example in the Digest,[56] pointing out that in this sense the *Septuaginta Interpretes* and St. Jerome are interpreters.[57] Baldus de Ubaldis (+1400) renders the same idea with the term *interpretatio expositiva,*[58] which he does not distinguish from what is called generally *interpretatio declarativa* or *declaratio* and which, according to him, includes the explanation of doubtful law.[59] Further

---

[56] "Diversitas linguae non vitiat stipulationem dummodo contrahentes intelligant per se, vel per interpretes. Hoc dicit Bartolus."—*Superscriptio,* D. (45, 1) 5. This is a case of two parties contracting in different languages through an interpreter; the contract is valid if they understand each other's intent.

[57] *Commentaria,* lib. II, tit. I, cap. *Cum venissent,* n. 3.

[58] "Ad interpretem [i. e., privatum] autem non pertinet novum facere, sed exponere et explicare; . . . interpretationem expositivam recipiunt [i. e., statuta]."—*Commentaria,* lib. I, tit. II, cap. primum, *Canonum,* n. 39. Baldus means here the intelligent exposition of the legal text by a private individual as appears from the examples which he proposes.—cf. *op. cit.,* nn. 36-38.

[59] Cf. *op. cit.,* cap. XIII, *Quoniam,* n. 15. For the sake of orientation it will be remarked briefly here that this *interpretatio declarativa* is distinguished in adequate fashion only from extensive and restrictive interpretation by the old authors; not so from *interpretatio translativa,* whose line of demarcation from *declaratio* is either not clear or not present at all. Cf. Bartolus, *Commentaria,* D. (1, 1) 9 (Titulus: *de iustitia et iure*), nn. 53-56; *idem, op cit.,* in

on Fagnanus, upon the authority of Panormitanus (whom he cites as quoted below), places ***interpretatio translativa*** as a subdivision of *declaratio,* and he again quotes his former example from the Digest [60] as an illustration,[61] which interpretation in like manner he calls ***interpretatio linguarum,*** following Panormitanus, as distinguished from interpretation of a doubtful meaning or terminology (both, however, seem to be referred to by Panormitanus with the word "declarat").[62]

D. (49, 1) 4 (Titulus: *de appellationibus et relationibus*), n. 7; Baldus de Ubaldis, *Commentaria,* lib. I, tit. II, cap. primum, *Canonum,* nn. 36-53; *idem, op. cit.,* cap XIII, *Quoniam,* nn. 15-16; Panormitanus, *Commentaria* lib. I, tit. XXIX (de *officio et potestate iudicis delegati*), cap. *Super quaestionum,* n. 8; Fagnanus, *Commentaria,* lib. I, tit. II, cap. *Quoniam,* nn. 14-19; *idem, op cit.,* lib. II, tit. I, cap. *Cum venissent,* nn 3-8; Reiffenstuel, lib. I, tit. II, nn. 351-356, 365-371; Schmalzgrueber, lib. I, tit. II, n. 44. Briefly, this interpretation (*Declaratio*) includes the doubtful law, the meaning of which "legi iam inerat a principio", "ex eius visceribus trahitur", as Reiffenstuel says (n. 376), by the agency of this interpretation which "nihil novi facit". The jurisprudence of this interpretation is based on the oft cited law of the Digest "*Haeredes palam*" (D. 28, 1, 21, 1), a case which presents actual objective doubt. This matter will occur in more detail in the following chapter.

60 (Quoted above, D. (45, 1) 5).

61 *Commentaria,* lib. II, tit. I, cap. *Cum venissent,* n. 8.

62 ". . . . et dic clarius quod interpretatio est duplex. Quaedam consistit in interpretatione linguarum, sicut interpretamur eucharistiam, id est, bonam gratiam ab eo quod est bonum etc. Quaedam consistit in obscuritate sensus, seu dubietate verborum, ut quando quis interpretatur verba dubia alicuius constitutionis; et de ista dicimus quod est eius interpretari cuius est condere, ut in c. inter alia, de sententia excommunicationis. Verumtamen proprie ille qui interpretatur, non corrigit, sed declarat rem obscuram, et hoc stricto modo; sed largo modo dicitur corrigere . . . sed quoad sensum non corrigit; et sic intelligitur l. haeredes palam, ff. de test."—Panormitanus, *Commentaria,* lib. I., tit. XXIX, (*de officio et potestate iudicis delegati*) cap. *Super quaestionum,* n. 8. A general survey of the use of the term *interpretatio* in the old authors cited in the foregoing is as follows. *Interpretatio* is first of all the most generic term. *Declaratio* is opposed to restrictive and extensive interpretation. *Declaratio* or *interpretatio declarativa* has sub-species: *declaratio* of even a doubtful law and *interpretatio translativa* or *linguarum,* which two, however, seem more or less to merge as to their line of demarcation. Panormitanus and others call *declaratio* the *interpretatio proprie dicta* (see Wernz, *Ius Decretalium,* I, nn. 127-128); Reiffenstuel calls restrictive and extensive interpretation the *inter-*

The other member of this subdivision of *declaratio* is such interpretation which deals with obscurity and doubt in the terminology, says Fagnanus (citing Panormitanus); or certainly, Fagnanus continues, that which explains the words in their inner signification and essential implication (the *sensus* or *intellectus)* ". . . qui legi intrinsece et essentialiter inest".[63] This last remark is entirely applicable as the other element of the interpretation described thus far. For Fagnanus defines *declaratio* as interpretation, properly so called, in the words of Baldus de Ubaldis (+1400) and Sylvester Prierias (+1523) upon the authority of Bartolus (+1357) i. e.,—an exposition of the legal terminology.[64] There does not necessarily have to be present an objective doubt of law before the interpretation is called *declaratio* or *interpretatio declarativa,* or the *mera declaratio* of Reiffenstuel. Briefly, Reiffenstuel (+1703) has in effect the same doctrine as outlined from Fagnanus, the same example among others, and the same explanations.[65] It is in Wernz (+1914) that one finds a very close approach, it seems, to the *declaratio* as described

pretatio proprie dicta (lib. I, tit. II, n. 376; but see also n. 353). There are other details which need no specific mention here. The old authors seem to be the sources whence the divisions of interpretation have entered the works of present day writers, possibly through Reiffenstuel. He is rather prolix. The whole matter begets confusion. One is therefore not surprised to note that the legislator of the Code, for the purposes of authentic interpretation, has cut through all the divisions and definitions and has implicitly defined the four species of interpretation, without any further distinction and subdivision, in can. 17.

[63] "Et hanc [interpretationem] Iura et Sacri Canones appellant legis rationem, intellectum, sententiam, mentem, animam, vim, robur, spiritum . . ." —*Commentaria,* lib. II, tit. I, cap. *Cum venissent,* n. 8.

[64] "Praemittenda est tertio diffinitio interpretationis proprie sumptae quae secundum Bald. in prooem. Decretal, num. 95 est sermonum difficilium vel perplexorum exposito, vel secundum Sylvest. in ver. interpretatio, in princ. est unius verbi per aliud, vel unius sententiae per aliam declaratio: propterea tamen cum verba legis exponimus, legem non interpretamur, sed declaramus, ut scripsit Bartolus in dicta l. Gallus, § Etiamsi, num. 1. ff. de liber. et posthum."—*op. cit.,* nn. 6-7.

[65] *Ius Canonicum Universum,* lib. I, tit. II, n. 365-367.

in canon 17, §2, as being equivalent to the concept contained in the clause ". . . et si verba legis in se certa declaret tantum . . .",[66] though even Reiffenstuel, it seems, fain would incline in this direction.[67]

Withal the point considered here is that the interpretation described thus far has the elements of *interpretatio translativa* and *declarativa* as these are explained in the jurisprudence of the authors mentioned. The former species of interpretation, i. e. *translativa,* does not connote a slavish verbal rendition of a text, but an intelligent one, as appears from the texts cited in these authors. In fact, when the terminology of a law is clear, it will permit no more than an intelligent verbal paraphrase, as in the classical example in the law of the Digest "*Prospexit*".[68]

However, it must further be noted that the *mera declaratio* of e. g., Reiffenstuel is by no means equivalent to the concept in the clause of canon 17, §2, "verba legis in se certa declaret tantum . . .", which today is often called *mere declarativa.* In Reiffenstuel, in spite of his inclination noted above, and in the authors before him, as mentioned above, *mera declaratio* or its equivalent includes interpretation of a

---

[66] Cf. *Ius Decretalium,* (2. ed., Romae, 1905), n. 127.

[67] Witness the words: "Nec obstat, quod interpretatio legis iam inerat legi a principio, et una cum ipsa sufficienter censeatur esse promulgata . . . quae est mera legis declaratio . . . unde merito, *praesertim si sit clara et manifesta* (italics inserted), ulteriori publicatione non indiget."—*Ius Canonicum Universum,* lib. I, tit. II, n. 376.

[68] Its prescript is clear *prima facie,* admitting no doubt or question: ". . . quod quidem perquam durum est, sed ita lex scripta est".—D. (49, 9) 12; "Sic ergo nota stari verbis legis . . . Item ubi lex non distinguit nec nos, ut hic . . . Item nota quod non licet alicui verba legis offendere."—*Glossa* ad v. *Lex scripta est.* This thought is ably set forth by Geny, *Méthode d'Interprétation et Source en Droit Privé Positif,* (2. ed., Paris: Librarie Generale de Droit et de Jurisprudence, 1932), I, n. 14.

dubium iuris, its concept being based on the classical example quoted from the Digest, *"Haeredes palam"*.[69] On the contrary, the clause in canon 17, §2, taken in view of canons 18 and 19, which are the legal measure or demarcation of a law certain in itself, implies that there is no doubt of law. In other words, the *interpretatio declarativa* in the jurisprudence of the authors before the Code is not co-extensive with that which is defined in canon 17, §2 in the words: ". . . verba legis in se certa declaret tantum . . ." It extends beyond this concept, as it were, and includes all interpretation which is not restrictive or extensive.

With these remarks the other means of interpreting law, as enjoined by canon 18, will now be considered.

ARTICLE II. *Quae Si Dubia Et Obscura Manserit.*

Under the condition that there remains doubt as to the proper meaning of the legal terminology, canon 18 further enumerates other sources to which resort must be had in order to know the law. There is a dictum of Roman law which sets forth in a general way a threefold source of knowing the law: "Scire leges non est verba earum tenere, sed vim ac potestatem",[70] the words, the proper sense, and an authority which is considered external to the law itself, but from which the law receives its full and adequate meaning.[71] The last member of this group, the external authority, seems to be represented in the residue of the norms outlined in canon 18. The

[69] Cf., *Ius Canonicum Universum,* lib. I, tit. II, nn. 367, 376.

[70] D (1, 3) 16.

[71] "Item sensum proprium qui ibi est, qui dicitur vis. Item potestatem, quae est ut quandoque aliter sumantur dicta verba . . . tria attendes verba et vim idest proprium sensum et potestatem."—*Glossa* ad v. *Scire leges,* D. (1, 3) 16.

question here is: What is the legislator's intent as presumably signified in the proper meaning of the legal terminology, which intent is to be discovered by means of a source external to the law which is to be interpreted? In passing it may be noted that according to the norm here quoted from Roman law the proper signification seems to represent a basic consideration as a point of departure in investigating the meaning of the law.

The sources which are proposed in canon 18, for clarifying obscurity in the legal terminology are not only clues to the probable or doubtful intent of the law. On the contrary, if their purpose is fulfilled, the law must be declared *in se certa.*

A. 1. *Ad locos Codicis parallelos est recurrendum.*

Canon 18 directs as the first source of further interpretation in the case of remaining doubt that parallel passages of the Code, if such may be found, shall be considered.

The term parallel passages signifies such places in which the law deals with the same subject matter.[72] A legislator is presumed to fashion all his laws into a harmonious unity[73] and subsequently to interpret these laws in a manner consistent with the jurisprudence of his system, ". . . quia secundum ius loqui praesumitur".[74] Thus parallel passages may in a certain sense be considered a remote context.

---

[72] Cf. Cicognani, *Commentarium ad Librum I Codicis,* p. 128; Van Hove, *De Legibus Ecclesiasticis,* n. 256; Michiels, *Normae Generales,* I, 410.

[73] Cf. C. (1, 17) 2, 15; Bulla, *"Rex Pacificus",* 5 sept. 1234, *Prooemium, Decretalium D. Gregorii IX Compilatio,* with *Glossa* ad v. *Contrarietatem,* where the commentator remarks that contradictions in law constitute an illegality; c. 1, *de constitutionibus,* I, 2, in VIo, with the *Glossa.*

[74] Suarez, *De Legibus,* VI, cap. 1, n. 18; cf. cann. 22-23.

The prescript of canon 18 concerning parallel passages guarantees a valid inference—as to the meaning of the terminology in the canon to be interpreted—upon the basis of the same subject matter which is treated both in the canon in question and in another canon. The reason for this guarantee is the inherent consistency and harmony of law as to the disposition of subject matter, which is expected and presumed especially in a body of codified legislation.[75] These brief considerations at once suggest the following practical conclusions.

Since parallel passages have a direct relation to the law to be interpreted, it follows that the authentic interpretations and the character of these interpretations (declarative, restrictive, extensive, explanatory) which may have issued regarding the passages in question must be taken into account. Moreover, because the authentic interpretation in canon 17, §2 has the force and status of general law, also canons 22 and 23 will have to be remembered.

In passing it may also be pointed out that the same considerations must be extended to the textual references which occur so frequently in the canons of the Code.[76]

2. *Interpretation of particular law.*

There remains a definite item to be pointed out concerning the interpretation of particular law, since the rules of

---

[75] This thought is well expressed by Geny, *Méthode d'Interprétation et Source en Droit Privé Positif,* (2. ed., Paris: Librairie Generale de Droit et de Jurisprudence, 1932), I, n. 102.

[76] Jurists of the past made a great deal of passages related by way of reference as a medium of interpretation: "Paria enim sunt quid esse certum per se seu per relationem ad aliud ex quo in scriptura referente contineri dicitur quicquid continetur in scriptura ad quam fit relatio."—Parisius, *Tertia Pars Consiliorum,* (Venetiis, 1552), Cons. II, n. 54; cf. Tuschus, *Practicae Conclusiones,* V, Litt. M, Concl. 198, n. 21; VI, Litt. R, Concl. 129, nn. 2, 9.

canon 18 and 19 are made for the interpretation of particular law as well as for that of the Code.

It will be noted that when a given law to be interpreted remains doubtful, recourse must be had to parallel passages of the Code. In other words there is established by the law of canon 18 a juridic relation between the common law and the particular law. There is a definite feature of jurisprudence behind this ruling. This relation is described as operating after the manner of a textual reference—which is mentioned in the immediately previous discussion—a reference, as it were, from the particular law to parallel passages of the Code. The juridic effect is the incorporation of the common law into the body of particular law in a given instance;[77] the common law becomes part of the particular law. This union of the common and particular law takes place in the case of doubt, where the proper signification of the particular law (considered according to the meaning of its terms in the common usage of that particular territory) is supplied by the common law, in which case the interpretation from the common law is to be accepted and favored in preference to another interpretation which would set the two bodies of law at variance on the particular matter,[78] because of the fundamental principle of jurisprudence which dictates a harmony of laws.[79]

[77] ". . . quia quod dicitur statutum habet et recipit interpretationem passivam a iure communi, operatur per relationem ad ius commune perinde ac si ius commune esset insertum et incorporatum in statuto."—Tuschus, *Practicae Conclusiones,* VI, Litt. R, Concl. 129; Baldus de Ubaldis, *Commentaria,* lib. I, tit. II, cap. primum, *Canonum,* nn. 42, 49.

[78] "Praeterea verba statuti in dubio explicari debent, ut, quantum fieri potest, salva eorum proprietate et communi acceptione, a iure communi non recedatur, sed ut cum eodem consentiat . . . quia derogatio seu correctio iuris communis, cum sit favorabile vitanda est, si possit . . . ita quidem ut si statutum sit ecclesiasticum, interpretari illud oporteat, secundum ius commune canonicum, et stylum Curiae Romanae."—Pirhing, Lib. I, tit. II, n. CV.

[79] "Ubi enim aliquid a iure communi discrepari videtur, reducendum est ad ius commune si fieri potest, ne pereat, quia promptum est leges legibus

The logical conclusion or result, which has particular bearing on the present study, is that the particular law is subject to all the pertinent authentic interpretations incident to the respective precept in the common law.[80]

After the solution of the supposed doubt in the particular law on the basis of the common law, the particular law is not concomitantly with the common law also subject thereafter to supervening restrictive or extensive interpretations. This conclusion is reached in view of canon 22. It must be remembered, however, that this procedure represents doctrinal interpretation. The immediate authentic interpreter, e. g., the Bishop of the diocese, could legitimately supervene with his own interpretation, which would definitely operate according to the prescripts of canon 17, §2.[81]

B. *Ad legis finem ac circumstantias est recurrendum.*

The subject concerning the purpose or reason for the existence of the law represents a very complicated discussion,

---

concordare."—*Glossa* ad v. *Iuri communi,* c. 8, X, *de consuetudine,* I, 4; C. (3, 30).

[80] Cf. Baldus de Ubaldis, *Commentaria,* lib. I, tit. II, cap. primum, *Canonum,* n. 46.

[81] This last statement obtains except where, upon the strength of doctrinal interpretation in virtue of parallel passages (e. g., where in virtue of the text and context alone the particular law was open to several proper significations—which hypothesis does not yet constitute in effect a *dubium iuris*) a legal custom has arisen contrary to what would have been merely a declarative authentic interpretation. In this case the supervening authentic interpretation is not declarative; it must be extensive or restrictive. For it seems that the subsidiary sources outlined in canon 18 must be used not disjunctively, but together, i. e., parallel passages *and* the accompanying subsidiary sources. The wording of the canon would seem to second this opinion. Thus in the present example the doctrinal interpretation did supposedly not exhaust all the prescribed sources, but joined hands with the common law in virtue of parallel passages, upon which interpretation a legal custom arose.—Pirhing (lib. I, tit. II, n. CIV.) seems to join the subsidiary sources.

which cannot be taken up in this study. Yet this source of interpretation is mandatory and as such, a means of rendering a law *in se certa*. Regarding the present medium of interpreting law, it may be pointed out that there are certain seemingly contradictory axioms: "Ratio iuris non facit ius"; "Ratio legis est anima legis"; "Ubi deficit ratio legis, deficit lex ipsa".[82]

Ratio iuris non facit ius. The reason for the law is here considered as antecedent to the law; namely, that which moves the legislator to make the law. Thus, as Suarez points out: "Ratio legis non est textus legis". The same law may owe its existence to many motives, which may be widely differentiated either as motivating one and the same or different legislators who fashion the same law, just as other acts in daily life may have several motives. Consequently, the attempt to determine with certainty the meaning of a law upon the principle of motivation is a precarious matter.[83] On the other hand, the second axiom represents a different turn.

Ratio legis est anima legis. Baldus de Ubaldis declares that the *causa finalis* serves for the purposes of interpreting a law while a mere motivating cause cannot be used to this end.[84] In the former sense the *ratio legis* is the same as the *mens legis,* or the soul of the law.[85] Here, as appears from the text of the law of the Digest *"Si extraneus"*, which Baldus cites as an example,[86] the existence of the law is dependent

---

82 Cf. Van Hove, *De Legibus Ecclesiasticis,* n. 260.

83 Cf. Suarez, *De Legibus,* III, cap. 20, nn. 3-5; VI, cap. 1, nn. 19-20.

84 "Item de interpretatione sumpta a causa fin. habes ff. de condi. ob cau. [de condictione causa data causa non secuta] l. si extraneus, sed a causa impulsiva non sumitur interpretatio."—*Commentaria,* lib. I, tit. II, cap. primum, *Canonum,* n. 53.

85 Cf. Tuschus, *Practicae Conclusiones,* VI, Litt. R, Concl. 31-32.

86 "Si extraneus pro muliere dotem dedisset et pactus esset, ut, quoquo modo finitum esset matrimonium, dos ei redderetur . . ."—D. (12, 4) 6.

entirely upon the continuance of a one and only clear purpose. Thus the purpose is the entire be-all and end-all of the law, the soul of the law. And so the third principle is explained as a necessary corollary to the contrary: "Ubi deficit ratio legis, deficit lex ipsa". However, as Suarez observes, even if the purpose of the law is expressed in the law itself—an instance which rarely occurs—being a strong indication *(magnum indicium)* of the mind of the law even to the point of moral certitude, nevertheless, because the expressed purpose can be subject to doubt, other circumstances must be taken into account.[87] This thought is in conformity with the wording of canon 18, which seems to unite into one source the clause, ". . . ad legis finem *ac* circumstantias *et* (italics inserted) . . . est recurrendum", in order thereby to render the law *in se certa*.

Circumstances play an important part. In Diocese X there is a statute: Catholics, subjects of the Ordinary, who attempt marriage before a civil official within the confines of said Diocese, incur *ipso facto* excommunication reserved to the Ordinary. By reason of a large non-Catholic population there is a large number of mixed marriages. Not infrequently marriages are illegitimately contracted without the observance of the canonical form to the scandal of the faithful. The statute itself in the abstract can have two meanings in respect to its subject matter: a) the attempted marriage of two Catholics; b) the attempted marriage of a Catholic with a non-Catholic. If for no other reason, under the circumstances mentioned there is no doubt that the statute means any attempted marriage in which even one party is a Catholic, a subject of the Ordinary. The law is *in se certa*, and an authentic interpretation on this question, in view of the circumstances, would be declarative.[88]

---

[87] *De Legibus*, VI, cap. 1, n. 20.

[88] "Colligitur autem ea mens et voluntas . . . ex circumstantiis, praecipue

C. *Ad mentem legislatoris est recurrendum.*

Finally canon 18 prescribes as a means of learning the proper signification of the law that the intent of the legislator shall be sought. It is necessary to understand correctly which intent is here envisioned by the term *mens legislatoris*. There is the *mens legis,* which is in the law; and the *mens legislatoris,* which is outside the law. The latter is here meant.

There is the intent or *mens* which resides in the proper signification of the words themselves. This is the *mens legalis,* so that if the words themselves do not reveal or warrant the meaning obtained through the agency of the *mens legislatoris,* there is no law, even if it be known what the legislator intended to say but actually did not put this thought into the words.[89] A supposed *mens legalis* which is not contained in the words deserves no attention. Such is the common teaching of the doctors in the field of Canon law, as Maroto points out,[90] so that, as Coronata says, it is more correct to say that doctrinal interpretation is the investigation into the mind of the law.[91] In fact, this thought is contained in the wording of canon 18. Further, this absent *mens legalis,* so to say, can be conjectured, possibly with moral certainty;

---

vero ex fine et causa sive ratione motiva ob quam lex fertur"—Pirhing, lib. I, tit. II, n. CIV.

[89] "Et confirmatur: nam si legislator per verba legis suam mentem non declaret non constitueretur lex, nec oriretur obligatio etiamsi ex aliis coniecturis possemus aliquo modo voluntas legislatoris cognoscere . . . sed necesse est ut in ipsa lege sufficienter contineatur [i. e., voluntas legislatoris] . . ."—Suarez, *De Legibus,* VI, cap. 1, n. 13.

[90] *Institutiones,* n. 236; Michiels, *Normae Generales,* I, 432; Augustine, *A Commentary of Canon Law,* (2. ed., Herder Book Co.: St. Louis, 1918), I. 93, 97-98.

[91] *Institutiones,* (2. ed., Taurini: ex Officina Libraria Marietti, 1939), I, n. 22, nota 4.

but the result of such investigation does not animate the terminology and create law. This act can be performed only by an official pronouncement of the legislator or his properly constituted agent. Until this act is performed the law cannot be said to be *in se certa* under the terms of canons 17, § 2 and 18. This act will be an authentic interpretation, which is at least a solution of an objective doubt, and which makes operative a "law" which was ineffective. This absent *mens legalis* therefore is not the mind or intent which is commanded in canon 18 as a source of knowing the law.

Like the other sources enumerated in canon 18 and the rule of canon 19, the *mens* here undoubtedly represents a special and distinct norm of interpretation.[92] This means is external to the law itself which is to be interpreted. And like the other norms it does not create the meaning of the law; it indicates the meaning which is supposed as present in the legal terminology under its proper signification, and thus with the other subsidiary means it helps to render the law *in se certa.*

In connection with the present topic a word may be said relative to the proper signification. Michiels, citing Suarez and Reiffenstuel, suggests as being the mind of the legislator that a law must always be interpreted in such a manner that it does not become absurd, useless, or unjust, even if the legal terminology must be taken in an improper meaning, because "Mens legislatoris est, ut omnis lex ab ipso condita censeatur rationi et iustitiae consentanea".[93] Now Suarez and Reiffenstuel are not commenting on canon 18, which is a piece of

---

[92] Cf. Michiels, *Normae Generales,* I, 432-433. The question of where to find this mind of the legislator and of the indications leading to its discovery lies outside the scope of the present study; in this regard cf. *Glossa* ad v. *Amplexus,* C. (1, 14) 5; can. 16, § 2; Michiels, *Normae Generales,* I, 433-434; Van Hove, *De Legibus Ecclesiasticis,* n. 266; Coronata, *Institutiones,* I, n. 25.

[93] *Normae Generales,* I, 435.

positive legislation of the Code. Aside from the fact that canon 18 commands that the law is to be understood in its *proper* signification (and in no other), Michiels' remark creates a serious difficulty when one considers the phrase "verba legis in se certa" of canon 17, §2. It is true, "verba debent aliquid operari". But if Michiels' rule of "save the law at any cost" is correct, where is the limit to a law's being *in se certa?* Under this rule practically any law is *in se certa.* From the consideration of the *significatio propria* of canon 18 one would conclude that the legislator does not mean to have his law salvaged at any cost. In that canon the legislator seems to guarantee that his law is going to be understood in its proper signification. And by an *argumentum a contrario* one must conclude that legally the law is not to be taken in any other sense. And finally one concludes that if the law is to be *in se certa,* it is going to be so under its proper signification, otherwise it is not to be considered certain in itself.[94]

CONCLUSION.

As mentioned at the beginning of this discussion, in a general way the foregoing has sought to show the relation between canons 18-19 and canon 17, §2. More particularly, it has endeavored to point out for practical purposes the meaning of the phrase, "verba legis in se certa". Namely, a law is in itself certain under the terms of canon 17 when its meaning can be arrived at by the rules of canons 18 and 19. If after the application of these rules—whose operation in relation to authentic interpretation has been pointed out from time to time—the law is still dubious, there is present an objective doubt, a *dubium iuris;* the law is in itself doubtful,

94 And in this eventuality the norms of canon 20 will be operative.

so that the measure of certainty required in canon 17, §2 is to be sought in canons 18 and 19. In these canons, by reason of their inter-relation, the legislator has stabilized the idea of *declaratio* or *interpretatio declarativa,* which in the jurisprudence before the Code included the interpretation of a *dubium iuris* and extended all the way, as it were, from the interpretation of clear law to extensive or restrictive interpretation.[95] In other words, by defining what shall be considered *in se certa* the legislator cut through the field and extent of this *interpretatio declarativa,* and thereby at the same time, as Van Hove correctly points out,[96] he decided the question as to whether or not and when the interpretation of doubt needs promulgation. He has decided by positive law when there shall be subjective and when there shall be objective doubt. And therefore one has in the canons aforementioned a pragmatic definition at once of what is clear law and what is a *dubium iuris*. This manner of definition is adopted in this study.

Besides what is mentioned at the beginning of this discussion, the opinion here advanced (concerning the definition or measure of the *dubium iuris*) is based on the following reasoning. On the one hand, the law as such is presumed to be clear in itself. On the other, in the usual course of events the meaning of the law can be obtained by means of the rules set down in canons 18 and 19. These canons represent positive law, which seeks to rule concerning the ordinary exigencies of the social order and omits from its provisions those isolated eventualities which rarely occur,[97] so that by an *argumentum a contrario* the application of rules other than those implied in these canons and of other possible sources is not of obligation and does not contribute legally to render

---

[95] Cf. *Nomenclature,* p. 134.

[96] *De Legibus Ecclesiasticis,* n. 244.

[97] "Iura constitui opertet, ut dixit Theophrastus, in his, quae plerumque accidunt, non quae praeter expectationem."—D. (1, 3) 3; Nam quod semel vel bis factum est, praetereunt legislatores."—D. (1, 3) 6.

a law *in se certa*. These canons are therefore a measure whereby it can be decided to what species belongs a given authentic interpretation.

EXAMPLES.

The response of the Pontifical Commission concerning the clause *"ab acatholicis nati"* in canon 1099, §2, which was published in the *Acta Apostolicae Sedis* under date of September 2, 1929, occasioned doctrinal interpretation in the manner suggested at the beginning of the present discussion.[97a] It was maintained that this response was a solution of a doubt of law.[98] Others maintained that the response represented extensive interpretation.[99]

The response:

> D. An *ab acatholicis nati*, de quibus in canone 1099, §2, dicendi sint etiam nati ab alterutro parente acatholico, cautionibus quoque praestitis ad normam canonum 1061 et 1071.
>
> R. Affirmative.[100]

Considering this matter in retrospect, it may well be questioned whether, at the time of this reply, the pertinent law could be considered as containing a doubt of law. For Maroto points out that many *(plures)* authors did not touch the question or weigh it; that they had not subjected the matter to closer examination; that often no basis at all or a super-

97a Cf. Beginning of this chapter.

98 Cf. *Apollinaris*, III (1930), 601-616 (Maroto); *American Ecclesiastical Review* (cited *AER*), LXXXIII, (1930), 484-496 (Schaaf).

99 *Apollinaris*, III (1930), 615.

100 *AAS*, XXI (1929), 573.

ficial one *(obiter)* was adduced for the respective opinion;[101] that the more common doctrine maintained that both parents had to be non-Catholic in order that their offspring, the other conditions of law being fulfilled, could be considered exempt from the canonical form.[102] The present response, of course, favors the opposite view. Really, it seems that the *dubium iuris* or the status of an authentic interpretation can be maintained only after the question has been examined maturely.

Jone, who held this opposite view, among other arguments of a corroborative nature taken from passages of the Code to show that one non-Catholic parent would suffice to free the offspring from the obligation, placed a great deal of weight upon the principle, "Odia sunt restringenda".[103] For he argued that John Doe and James Roe can be considered *ab acatholicis nati* even though only their mothers were non-Catholic. He is entirely correct; they are just as much *ab acatholicis nati* as they are *a catholicis nati* in the proper signification of the words. And thus he might have applied the principle: "In obscuris minimum est sequendum". Or again: "Quotiens dubia interpretatio libertatis est, secundum libertatem respondendum erit".[104] These two principles are shaped more or less from the same last as "Odia sunt restringenda". And in the present circumstances one is prone to ask as to which side, the prospective nupturient on the one side, or the good of religion and the Catholic body politic on the other, is the bearer of the *odium*. And so this principle, which is surrounded by many exceptions,[105] begins to lose its force and its appeal to the assent.

The Code in canon 19 states: "Leges quae . . . liberum

---

[101] *Apollinaris*, III, (1930), 603, 616.

[102] *Apollinaris*, III (1930), 603.

[103] *Theologisch-Praktische Quartalschrift*, LXXXII (1929), 782-783.

[104] D. (50, 17) 20.

[105] Cf. Van Hove, *De Legibus Ecclesiasticis*, nn. 297-299.

iurium exercitium coarctant . . . strictae subsunt interpretationi", a principle which seems much more tangible and operative in the present circumstances. The exercise of the natural right to contract a valid marriage[106] is restricted by the law of canonical form.[107] Therefore the law of canon 1099 must be interpreted strictly, that is to say, the law demanding the canonical form of marriage, where there is a case of Catholic baptism with subsequent neglect of Catholic training from infancy, must be understood as restricted to the offspring of parents both of whom are Catholic.[108] The point here is that this interpretation of *ab acatholicis nati* could, it seems, have been established with the aid of canon 19 prior to the response of the Pontifical Commission, and that on the strength of the proper signification of *ab acatholicis nati* described in the foregoing and the application of canon 19 the law is *in se certa* and that the authentic interpretation should have been considered declarative and not explanatory. As a corroborative consideration for the use of the proper signification as described, there is the following—the principle of interpretation from the circumstances of the law. Conservatively speaking, marriage cases of children of mixed marriages where the provisions of canon 1099, §2, are verified

---

[106] "Impedimenta sunt stricte interpretanda. Lex namque statuens impedimentum est lex restrictiva iuris, cuicumque agniti, in can. 1035, ad matrimonium ineundum, adeoque dictae legi applicanda est dispositio can. 19."—De Smet, *Tractatus Theologico-Canonicus De Sponsalibus et Matrimonio*, (4. ed., inde a Codice altera, Brugis: Car. Beyaert, 1927), p. 412.

[107] Cf. Gasparri, *Tractatus Canonicus de Matrimonio*, (ed. nova ad mentem Codicis I. C., Typis Polyglottis Vaticanis, 1932), n. 201-204.

[108] Cf. also the response regarding apostates.—*AAS*, XXII (1930), 195. It may here be added that in this case of a restriction of the exercise of a natural right the principle of strict interpretation as proposed above from canon 19 prevails over a second principle in the same canon: "Leges quae . . . exceptionem a lege continent, strictae subsunt interpretationi", because the exercise of a natural right takes precedence over the application of the second principle.

are just as frequent as cases of children of parents both of whom are non-Catholic. In fact, it seems more correct to say that the provisions of this canon are of comparatively infrequent application in the latter instance. Indeed, with an eye to actual life, one is more inclined to think that the law meant to provide at least equally also for children of mixed marriages, baptized Catholic, but whose Catholic education has been neglected from their infancy.[109]

There is a second reply of the Pontifical Commission, concerning its authentic interpretation considered in the foregoing:

> D. Utrum interpretatio diei 20 iulii 1929 ad canonem 1099, §2 sit declarativa, an extensiva.
>
> R. Affirmative ad primam partem, negative ad secundam.[110]

Maroto sees in this response a confirmation of his stand that the former authentic interpretation was the solution of a *dubium iuris*. In other words, he understands the term *declarativa* in the sense in which it was accepted by jurists before the Code.[111]

In the foregoing it was shown: a) that the question and answer, the form in which the response of the Pontifical Commission appears when published, conspire as a unit to interpret a given law;[112] b) that the authentic interpretation has the status of law; c) that to interpret an authentic response the rules of interpretation prescribed by law must be fulfilled.[113]

---

[109] Maroto (*Apollinaris*, III (1930), 609-610) admits this point clearly.
[110] *AAS*, XXIII (1931), 388.
[111] Cf. *Apollinaris*, III (1930), 616; IV (1931), 383.
[112] Chap. IV, Art. III, in fine.
[113] *Ibid.*, Art. IV.

These rules are to be applied in the present instance. What does *declarativa* mean in this response? In other words, is this term referable to the clause of canon 17, §2: ". . . et si verba legis in se certa declaret tantum . . ." or to ". . . si legem . . . dubiam explicet"? *Declarativa* must be referable to one of these, for the agent of the legislator must be presumed to speak *secundum ius*. The present clauses of canon 17 must be considered as parallel passages to the response. There is, moreover, the context of the response, the phrase: ". . . an extensiva". Here, it seems, there remains no alternative but to adhere to the letter of the text upon the authority of the glossator of the law *"Ad audientiam"* of the Decretals.[114] Accordingly, if *extensiva* has reference to the clause ". . . si legem . . . extendat . . .", *declarativa* must refer to ". . . et si verba legis in se certa declaret tantum . . .".[115]

---

114 "Argumentum quod a forma verborum sine certa scientia non est recedendum."—*Glossa* ad v. *Intelligeremus,* c. 12, X, *de decimis,* III, 30.

115 The response of the Commission is so understood by Sartori, *Enchiridion Canonicum,* p. 253; Jone, *Gesetzbuch des kanonischen Rechtes,* (Paderborn: Ferdinand Schoningh, 1940), II, 320-321; Vermeersch-Creusen, *Epitome,* (5. ed., Mechliniae-Romae: H. Dessain, 1934), II, n. 407, 2, nota 2.

CHAPTER VI.

Effects of Declarative Authentic Interpretation.

ARTICLE I. *Promulgatione Non Eget.*

The first effect of a declarative authentic interpretation is described by canon 17, §2, in a negative manner. The interpretation does not need promulgation.

Promulgation is here taken in the technical sense of canon 9. This fact appears clearly from the context of canon 17, §2, where the legislator disposes concerning the other species of authentic interpretation, all of which, he declares, must be promulgated. Why? Because these interpretations are in effect new laws. A doubtful law is no law at all.[1] By the same token restrictive and extensive interpretation, as appears in the following chapter, adds something to the law or suppresses something therein so as to change substantially its disposition.

The fact that a declarative authentic interpretation does not need promulgation is a logical deduction from the fact that the law which is thereby interpreted has been clear in itself from the time of its promulgation; it is not promulgated a second time. The sense and measure in which a law is to be considered certain and clear in itself has already been explained.[2] This species of interpretation adds nothing, nor does

[1] Cf. can. 15.

[2] Cf. Chap. V, especially *Conclusion*.

it suppress anything in the law, it merely discovers *(declaret tantum)* what has been present from the beginning.[3]

One must distinguish the legal promulgation as contained in canon 9 from the publication which every authentic interpretation demands in order that it have the status of general law,[4] as Bernhardt also points out.[5] Therefore the declarative interpretation of the Pontifical Commission does not have to appear in the *Acta Apost. Sedis* in order to receive the status of law; publication to the Church at large made in any other way will suffice.[6]

ARTICLE II. *Valet Retrorsum.*

When the authentic interpretation is declarative, the law is understood and operates under the interpretation as if it had been explicitly present since the very time when the law first took its effect. Such is the meaning of the clause: "Interpretatio authentica . . . si verba legis in se certa declaret tantum . . . valet retrorsum . . .". This interpretation has retroactive effect. This fact is implicitly expressed by canon 17, §2, where it declares that this interpretation does not need promulgation. One concludes from this statement, with a view to canon 8, §1: "Leges instituuntur, cum promulgantur", that the law already embodied this interpretation or meaning when it was established by promulgation. There is also the further

[3] Cf. Chap. V.

[4] Cf. Chap. IV, Art. II and III.

[5] "Eine solche Kundbarmachung muss auch heute noch in allen Fällen stattfinden, wenn die rein erklärende authentische Interpretation Gesetz sein soll. Nur ist nicht die Publication in den AAS, die nach der Regel des can. 9 erforderlich ist, nötig."—*Die Normae generales des Codex iuris canonici,* (Marburg: [ ], 1927), p. 32.

[6] Coronata, *Institutiones,* I, n. 23.

consideration that, according to canon 17, the authentic interpretation has the same force as the law itself which it interprets. Now if the declarative interpretation has this force of the law itself and at the same time needs no promulgation—meaning, in the terms of canon 8, §1, that the law is already instituted under the terms of the declarative interpretation—the interpretation must operate as from the beginning when the law took effect. Therefore in the instances of invalidating laws and those which declare personal incapacity *(leges irritantes et inhabilitantes)*,[7] the declarative interpretation states in effect that juridically the acts performed under such circumstances are simply null and void from the beginning. Quite logically therefore in the case of declarative interpretation there is no *vacatio legis*.[8]

The doctrine concerning the retroactive effect of declarative authentic interpretation is one of long standing in the jurisprudence of Roman (Justinian) and Canon law. An example of its application is afforded in the following case.

A. *Example of the retroactivity of declarative authentic interpretation.*

The Archbishop of Braga reported a custom of his province whereby clerics permit themselves to be struck with the fist thirty or forty times, more or less, in satisfaction for some offence which they had given. The question is whether or not the one who thus struck a cleric falls under the *ipso facto* excommunication which sanctions the *privilegium canonis*.[9] Innocent III (+1216) replies, pointing out that the law in

---

[7] Cf. cann. 11, 16, § 1.

[8] Cf. can. 9.

[9] "Unde nos humiliter consulebas, utrum huiusmodi percussores in canonem incidant sententiae promulgatae."—c. 36, X, *de sententia excommunicationis*, V, 39.

question operates in favor of the clerical state and adds that thenceforward, if the cleric freely submits to this punishment, both parties should be excommunicated. This response presents a complex law. It is declarative, first of all, of the *privilegium canonis,*[10] which in the present case was erroneously taken to be a personal prerogative, which the subject could waive at will. The Pope replies with a contrary interpretation to the effect that by the laying of hands upon the cleric violence is not committed upon his person, but that nevertheless the injury done to the clerical state is forbidden by the law. The privilege exists chiefly to protect the dignity of this state.[11]

According to Hostiensis (+1271) this interpretation appears to be retroactive; this canonist discusses the question as to whether the one who inflicted the blows is excommunicated. He holds that the excommunication upon the layman has been incurred, and in confirmation of his opinion he makes reference to another law of the Decretals of Gregory IX, *"Tua nos"*.[12] This law, a response of Clement III (+1191), recites that those who rashly lay hands upon clerics are to be sent to the Holy See for absolution.[13] In his com-

---

[10] "Si quis suadente diabolo huius sacrilegii reatum incurrerit, quod in clericum vel monachum violentas manus iniecerit, anathematis vinculo subiaceat."—c. 29, C. XVII, q. 4.

[11] "Nos . . . respondemus quod huiusmodi manus iniectio, etsi non violenta, tamen iniuriosa videtur, quum ille canon non tam in favorem clerici ordinati quam in favorem ordinis clericalis fuerit promulgatus."—*Ibid.*

[12] "Sed numquid talis verberator est excommunicatus? Huic quaestioni respondere non videtur expresse. Tu tamen dicas quod excommunicatus est . . . Et innuunt verba praecedentia, ibi, 'iniuriosa' et ibi, 'non tam in favorem' . . . argumentum tua nos [c. 19, eodem titulo]. Laicum autem non est necesse excommunicare cum iam sit excommunicatus."—*Commentaria,* lib. V, tit. XXXIX, cap XXXVI, n. 11.

[13] Fraternitati tuae taliter respondemus quod . . . qui in clericos temerarias manus iniiciunt . . . pro absolutionis beneficio ad Apostolicam Sedem sunt mittendi."—c. 19, X, *de sententia excommunicationis,* V, 39.

mentary to this law Hostiensis declares that the law does not confine itself to punishing only violence: "Quaedam manus dicuntur temerariae etsi non violentae." Thus the commentator seems to argue—and this reasoning illustrates the point at issue, the retroactivity of the interpretation—that by such rash procedure, which is already included in the law, the penalty was incurred. The gloss to the response of Innocent III seems to hold the same opinion.[14] Also, the minute commentary of Panormitanus (+1435) concerning this reply of Pope Innocent is more clearly in favor of this stand—the reply is retroactive, the layman has already incurred the penalty of excommunication.[15] Thus, to use the implications of canon 17, §2, in view of the material furnished by this case, the *privilegium canonis* should have been understood, concerning its prohibition and penalty as regards the person who inflicted the physical retribution, under the terms of the reply and its accompanying commentaries even before the reply was issued. If for no other reason, the law could have been known under this interpretation by reason of the purpose for which the privilege was established, as the gloss quoted above seems to insinuate.

Secondly, it may also be noted that besides a declarative interpretation the reply contains a piece of new legislation in that a cleric incurs excommunication *ferendae sententiae* if in the future he should submit to such treatment.[16] This portion of the reply is, of course, not retroactive, as is clear from

---

[14] "Non videtur responderi ad quaestionem quae fuit an huiusmodi percussores incidant in canonem. Sed dic quod bene sunt excommunicati, quia iniuriosas et temerarias manus iniiciunt et satis innuitur, dum dicit, tam in favorem clerici quam ordinis . . ."—*Glossa* ad v. *Prohibeas attentari.*

[15] *Commentaria,* lib. V, tit. XXXIX, cap. XXXVI, nn. 1-7.

[16] "Unde sequitur quod tales sunt excommunicati, et si qui clericus post huiusmodi prohibitionem sponte se subiecerit excommunicetur . . . Quod clericus sponte patiens verbera non est excommunicatus ipso facto sed excommunicandus."—Panormitanus, *Commentaria,* lib. V, tit. XXXIX, cap. XXXVI, nn. 1-7.

the commentary of Panormitanus; it has respect only to the future.

B. *The principle of retroactivity of declarative authentic interpretation.*

The foregoing example presents merely one illustration of the retroactivity of declarative authentic interpretation. The existing law was found to be, in terms of canon 17, §2, *in se certa.* The principle, itself, or the basic reasoning, from which flows the retroactive effects of this interpretation will now be presented together with the practical results which are attendant upon the principle.

The last law, "*Quoniam*", of the title "*De Constitutionibus*" in the Decretals of Gregory IX, lays down the rule that laws have to do with future events; they do not have respect to the affairs of the past unless they expressly take cognizance of them.[17] This rule is repeated in the Code of Canon Law in canon 10. Since authentic interpretation has the status of law and follows the rules according to which laws are operative, the exception set down in this canon, ". . . nisi nominatim de praeteritis caveatur", has definite bearing upon the question of the retroactivity of declarative authentic inter-

[17] C. 13, X, *de constitutionibus,* I, 2. This law has to do principally with a constitution which enacts a new law. However, even here Hostiensis notes an exception: "Haec regula quod constitutio nova respicit tantum futura non praeterita . . . nisi concordet cum iure antiquo per quod id praecipitur."—*Commentaria,* lib. I, tit. II, cap. 13. Again, Baldus de Ubaldis cites Iacobus de Belvisio (+1335) to the effect that a new law is retroactive if according to its mind it cannot be extended into the future.—*Commentaria,* C. (1, 14) 7 (Titulus: *de legibus et constitut.*), n. 4. These remarks may well be noted in view of can. 23, and may be of use in the interpretation of existing law in view of later enactments.

pretation, as will appear immediately. For the principal exception to this rule, according to the commentaries of the decretalists on the law *"Quoniam"* is the law which is declaratory of passed legislation, which exception, in terms of the Code, is found in declarative authentic interpretation.

The law *"Quoniam"* is from the hand of Gregory IX, an answer to the question whether or not his previous constitution has reference to the past. The Pope declares in his reply, *"Quoniam"*, that the previous constitution is to be interpreted for matters in the future. Ioannes Andreas sets forth a commentary to the word *"declaramus"* in the reply. He accepts the meaning of this word as an apparent indication that the law, or constitution, to which *"Quoniam"* has reference should have been understood under the terms of the interpretation (conveyed in *"Quoniam"*) even before this was edited:

> Per quod patet quod prius lex sic debuit intelligi . . . Sed constitutio modo declaret quod fuit ambiguum.[18]

Another expression of this principle is set down in the law *"Sicut Nobis"* in the *Liber Sextus* with its gloss, which is attributed to Ioannes Andreas,[19] where the same glossator in his context appropriately points out that the same rule is also verified when a successor in office interprets the law of his predecessor.[20]

Thus Ioannes Andreas indicates the principle of retroactivity in declarative authentic interpretation. The constitution of the Pope merely declares what is already present. It will be noticed, of course, that this jurist applies the principle even in the case of a doubtful law. But such was the juris-

---

18 *Novella Commentaria,* lib. I, tit. II, cap. *Quoniam,* n. 10. Cf. etiam *Glossa* ad v. *De caetero, Clementis Papae Quinti,* Prooemium; Felinus Sandaeus, *Commentaria,* lib. I, tit. II, cap. 13, n. 4.

19 *Glossa* ad v. *Respondemus,* c. 5, *de verborum significatione,* V, 12, in VIo.

20 Cf. c. 2, *de verborum significatione,* V, 12, in VIo.

prüdence of the civilists and canonists of the past, according to the lengthy discussion of Fagnanus.[21] However, the great disparity between the jurisprudence of the past and that of the Code is simply the question of subject matter to which the principle of retroactivity is applicable. The point to be noted in the present discussion is that the Code retains the same principle together with the practical consequences incident thereto and to be described herein, but confines it to a law which is *in se certa* and does not apply it to a *dubium iuris* as was the case in the jurisprudence of the past.[22]

Accordingly, a declarative interpretation simply discovers what is already present in the anterior law and is therefore retroactive.[23] The interpreting agent does not constitute a new rule of action; the source of obligation derives rather from the existing law than from the interpreting law.[24] Thus it supposes the law as already existing and already having

---

21 *Commentaria,* lib. I, tit. II, cap. *Quoniam,* nn. 14-45. It will be sufficient here to quote the text of Paulus de Castro (+1441) from his commentary on the law of the Digest *"Haeredes palam"*, upon the authority of Ioannes Andreas: "Declaratio autem illius verbi obscuri potest fieri post litis contestationem quia non facit esse novum libellum . . . Item nota ex hoc quod declaratio trahitur retro ad tempus dispositionis factae. H. d. Io. An . . . et ex hoc multa sequuntur, scil., quod nova l. declarativa veteris trahitur ad praeterita negotia . . . Quod hodie declaratur tanquam tunc fuisset dictum . . . quasi hoc declaratur a principio fuisse dictum . . . et hoc intellige de propria declaratione quae consistit circa aliquod verbum dubium. Sed interdum consistit circa id quod non erat dubium de iure. Et tunc declaratio habet vim novae dispositionis . . ."—*Patavinae Praelectiones,* D. (28, 1) 21 (Titulus: *De testamentis,* § *Siquid.*), nn. 3-4.

22 Cf. Chapter V, Art. I, *Nomenclature* and Art. II, *Conclusion.* (See Table of Contents.)

23 Baldus de Ubaldis, *Commentaria,* C. (1, 14) 5 (Titulus: *de legibus et constit.*), n. 2.

24 "Fallit secundo regula huius decretalis in constitutione declaratoria iuris antiqui, ut trahatur ad praeterita secundum omnes hic . . . quia declarando nihil de novo inducit, lex 'Haeredes palam' . . . et potius ligat constitutio antiqua quam nova declaratoria . . ."—Felinus Sandaeus, *Commentaria,* lib. I, tit. II, cap. 13, n. 4.

the effect enunciated in the interpretation,[25] so that, regarding the events of the past which are governed by the original law, such interpretation is in its effect retroactive unto the original disposition to the extent that it is one with the former. What is declared "today" is as if it had been stated "then": "Quod hodie declaratur, tamquam tunc fuisset dictum".[26] Therefore, the interpreting agent must be considered, inasmuch as its legal effects are concerned, as if it had been promulgated with the original enactment.[27] And therefore Fagnanus declares (distinguishing between new law and what is called a mere *declaratio*) as being the common teaching of canonists and doctors and upon the authority of Bartolus that no second formal promulgation is necessary in the case of a declaratory enactment even when, the same jurist adds, the law which is interpreted is entirely obscure and dubious, so that without an interpretation the law would be null; and this enactment, which is merely declaratory, has retroactive effect, because no new legislation is thereby created.[28] It

[25] " . . . lex declaratoria non est regula actionis, sed supponit et interpretatur illam; ergo ante legem declarativam erat lex . . .; ergo lex, quae declarat tale ius, supponit semper habuisse talem effectum nam effectus antiqui iuris non dependet ex declaratione postea futura; unde confirmatur, quia nova declaratio nihil denuo constituit, argumento, lex Haeredes, n. 1, ff, de testament., ibi, 'Nihil nunc dat, sed datum significat'; . . . ergo quantum in se est, aeque comprehendit praeteritum ac futurum."—Suarez, *De Legibus,* III, cap. 14, n. 3.

[26] Paulus de Castro, *Patavinae Praelectiones,* D. (28, 1,) 21 (Titulus: *De testamentis, Haeredes palam,* § *Si quid*); Philippus Decius, *In Decretales Commentaria, De Constitutionibus,* cap. *Quoniam,* n. 45.

[27] ". . . tamquam si nostra lex ab initio cum interpretatione tali promulgata fuisset."—N. (143, 1) (Auth. CXXXII, Coll. IX, tit. 13, *De raptis mulier.*)

[28] "At secus in legis declaratione, ut tradunt hic communiter canonistae . . . quia tum legis declaratio non faciat ius novum sed tantum manifestat quod prius erat . . . Et lex declarata ab initio promulgata fuerit, solemnitas publicationis semel adhibita in principali dispositione, non est ulterius repetenda in illius declaratione. Ita declarat Bart. in l. Haeredes palam, § Si quid . . . Quod procedit etiamsi lex declarata sit prorsus obscura et dubia. Nam nihilominus in illius declaratione publicatio non requiritur ut clare probatur d. l. Haeredes palam, § Quod vero, ubi dispositio erat ambigua ut nisi testator illam declarasset propter incertitudinem fuisset nulla . . . et satis esse ut sol-

simply states what is already in the law from its inception. In this place Fagnanus also indicates that there are some theologians who hold an opposite view in this matter. Canon 17, § 2, of course, solves this controversy [29] and does not allow the interpretation of doubtful law to have retroactive effect, but treats it as new law.

C. *Practical consequences of the retroactivity of declarative authentic interpretation.*

The practical results or conclusions attendant upon the retroactivity of declarative authentic interpretation described above are as follows.

Declarative interpretation in relation to the content and circumstances of the interpreted law. From the fact that a declarative interpretation has retroactive force, being part and parcel of the original legislation itself, the decretalists in their commentaries on "*Quoniam constitutio*" (c. 13, X, I, 2) point to an important conclusion, referring to a text in the Novels of Justinian.[30] Thus Ioannes Andreas states that the declara-

---

emnia praecesserint in dispositione declarata; atque in hunc sensum DD. communiter illum tex. interpretantur . . . Ergo constitutio declaratoria non eget publicatione, quia cum extendatur ad praeterita et pendentia frustra expectaretur lapsus duorum mensium a publicatione."—*Commentaria,* lib. I, tit. II, cap. *Quoniam,* nn. 43-45.

[29] Cf. e. g., Bouix, *De Curia Romana,* p. 297; Cicognani; *Canon Law,* 602-603.

[30] "In tertia vero constitutione de temporibus nihil adiecimus, cum omnibus apertissimum sit ea, quae per interpretationem adiciuntur oportere de illis quoque valere, de quibus legibus interpretatis locus fit."—N. (19, Praefatio) in fine (Coll. III, tit. 6, *De filiis ante dotalia instrumenta natis*). Neither the *authenticum* nor the second Latin version seems overdone in rendering this text clearly. "De illis (quoque) valere" should be the translation of "ep' ekeinon kratein", which could be rendered clearly, it seems: "govern those things", i. e., those circumstances, scil., of person, time, and place. Also "de

tive constitution operates in the same cases and circumstances in which is operative the law which it interprets;[31] the text of the law which is being interpreted is to be considered as repeated, understood, and supposed in the interpreting agent.[32] In other words, the law which is interpreted forms a context or framework into which is fitted, as it were, the interpretation. One may simply envision the case where an interpretation touches upon a certain point in the law and does not mention other circumstances which are also governed by that law. The interpretation must be understood as attached to those circumstances likewise; moreover, it receives all the extensions and limitations of the law which is interpreted.[33] Thus in the example concerning the *privilegium canonis* and the cleric given at the opening of this discussion the interpretation of the Pope is just as applicable to a case where a *monachus* is involved, because he also enjoys the privilege.

Such is precisely the rule where the interpretation is merely declarative.[34] And these remarks are important as an aid to obviate as much as possible the necessity of authentically interpreting the interpretation. Therefore, as Su-

---

quibus", the translation of "eph' hon", could be rendered: "in which". Thus the entire text, which is pertinet: Interpreting laws govern those circumstances in which the interpreted laws are operative (i. e., *locus fit*).

[31] "Constitutio interpretans locum habet in his casibus in quibus ius interpretatum."—*In Sextum Decretalium Librum Commentaria, De Electione,* cap. 4, *Ut circa,* n. 13.

[32] "Nota . . . quod omnia quae habent locum in lege interpretata, intelliguntur repetita in lege interpretante."—Bartolus, *Commentaria Super Authenticis et Institutionibus,* Coll. III, tit. 6. The same rule, which Angelus de Ubaldis (+1412) recites in connection with the interpretation of a dispensation, reads: "Omnia verba quae continentur in litteris dispensatoriis intelliguntur sigillatim apposita in dictis litteris interpretativis . . ."—*Consilia,* Consilium 274, § 1.

[33] "Nota quod constitutio declarans aliam, recipit ampliationes et limitationes constitutionis declaratae."—*Glossa* ad v. *Consuetudine,* (a marginal annotation), c. 7, *de electione et electi potestate,* I, 3, in Clem; see c. 19, *de electione et electi potestate,* I, 6, in VIo, where a similar situation is described.

[34] Felinus Sandaeus, *Commentaria,* lib. I, tit. II, cap. 13, n. 8.

arez declares, it has been received as sound juristic doctrine that the constitution (in the terminology of the Code, the declarative authentic interpretation) which interprets a second receives, concerning those items which it, the interpreting agent, does not express, all the interpretations which are incident to the interpreted constitution.[35]

Declarative interpretation in relation to acquired rights. Toso points out that the declarative interpretation must be applied to,—that is to say, it governs—all the rights which have been acquired under the law which is interpreted *(per legem declaratam antea quaesitis)*.[36] This thought calls to mind the fact that a declarative interpretation can destroy good faith, which is required for prescription.[37] However, once prescription has been properly completed, where there has been good faith, a contrary declarative interpretation, which issues subsequent to the completed prescription, would not, it seems, operate unto the restoration of the acquired right. Of course, good faith would have to be proven in case the legitimacy of the prescription were challenged incident to the appearance of this interpretation, because ignorance or error concerning the law, upon which the good faith may conceivably be based, is not to be presumed.[38]

---

[35] *De Legibus,* VI, cap. 1, n. 3. Thus the interpreting agent is itself governed and to be understood according to the interpreted law and the prior interpretations incident to the latter together with other laws which may have bearing upon the law which is interpreted: ". . . quia si lex est declarativa; tunc ratio et causa talis legis sumitur secundum leges declaratas, ita Bart [olus] . . . Et sic dicimus, quod Lex [i. e., the interpreting agent], vel statutum loquens, puta augens vel minuens legitimam, regulatur, et recipit interpretationem a legibus de legitima disponentibus . . ."—Tuschus, *Practicae Conclusiones,* I, Litt. C, Concl. 146, nn. 1-2.

[36] *Commentaria Minora,* I, 45; Jone, *Gesetzbuch des kanonischen Rechtes,* I, 36.

[37] Cf. can. 1512.

[38] Can. 16, § 2.

Declarative interpretation in relation to cases pending at law. The interpreting law affects not only the past as such but also those matters whose accomplishment has not been reached.[39] An example of such affairs would be cases pending at law, as Bartolus points out, where the judicial sentence has not yet been pronounced.[40] Therefore, the declarative authentic interpretation directly influences the pending decision. The same rule applies to a case which is in the stage of appeal, because the final issue has not yet been reached.[41]

Declarative interpretation in relation to restatement of existing law. By reason of the retroactive force of declarative interpretation to the time of the original enactment, as Ioannes Andreas points out (referring to a concrete example), the series of declarative interpretations made by Pope Boniface [VIII?] and his predecessors concerning the law of tithes (accruing to the Holy See) from benefices obtain in the requisitions published by their successors, provided always that these *capitula* of the successors are a restatement of former law. Thus the former interpretations continue to apply even to subsequent enactments; the interpretations stand or fall with the content of the original law.[42] The basic reasoning

---

39 ". . . quando est constitutio declaratoria iuris antiqui . . . trahitur ad praeterita et ad pendentia."—Henricus Boich, *Commentaria,* lib. I, tit. II, cap. *Quoniam,* n. 2.

40 ". . . immo in casibus pendentibus locum habet [i. e., lex interpretans], sententia vel transactione nondum usque finitis . . ."—*Commentaria Super Authenticis et Institutionibus,* Coll. III, tit. 6.

41 ". . . quia per appellationem sententia suspensa est; tunc enim iuxta veterem legem causa definienda est . . ."—Gonzalez, lib. I, tit. II, cap. II, n. 19. As regards the decision upon appeal and a *restitutio in integrum* in view of a subsequent declarative interpretation cf. cann. 1902-1907.

42 "Et per hoc deciditur quaestio, an declarationes factae super decimis beneficiorum per Bonifatium et praedecessores de quibus scripsi . . . locum habeant in debitis per successores impositis? Et dico quod sic ratione praedicta, et hoc verum quod ad illa capitula quae sunt eadem in litteris successorum quae in litteris Bonifatii. In illis enim capitulis, quae mutata essent, certum est quod deficiente capitulo deficit ipsius declaratio . . ."—*In Sextum Decre-*

which underlies this rule is, as Ioannes Andreas points out, the fact that a declarative interpretation, being operative even as regards the past (and which is consequently part of the existing original enactment of which the future law is merely a restatement), has greater scope than a statute, ordinance or prorogation, which has respect only to the future.[43] Declarative interpretation operates in the past and in the future, as Baldus declares; thus it has a greater scope of operation than a new law.[44] Accordingly, particular law, e. g., a Diocesan statute, which merely restates the common or universal law of the Code must be understood in the light of the declarative authentic interpretations which attach to the universal law.[45] In other words, under the present supposition, the particular law has already been authentically interpreted. Thus the declarative interpretation extends to the future not only *per se,* as would any law, but also in view of future enactments which are a replica of the original law still extant.

In passing, it is worth noting that the text of Ioannes Andreas quoted above illustrates clearly the unity, permanence, and function of the juridic personality which is present in the individual persons of the legislator and authentic interpreter regarding matters which concern the administration of law.

---

talium Librum Novella Commentaria, de verborum significatione, cap. 5, *Sicut Nobis,* n. 9.

43 "Et in hoc plus habet declaratio, scilicet quo ad praeterita, quam ordinatio, statutum, vel prorogatio, quae proprie respicit futura . . ."—*Ibid.*

44 "Quod quando lex procedit interpretando vel declarando porrigitur non solum ad futura, sed etiam ad praeterita, unde dicit Ioannes Andreas quod in plus se habet declaratio quam constitutio, quia respicit praeterita, sed constitutio solum respicit futura."—*Commentaria,* C. (1, 14) 5 (Titulus: *de legibus et constitutionibus.*), n. 2.

45 "Statutum disponens super eo quod disponit ius commune interpretatur secundum ius commune, ad hoc communiter."—*Superscriptio,* C. (3, 41) 2.

CHAPTER VII.

Explanatory, Restrictive, Extensive Authentic Interpretation.[1]

When the authentic interpretation, given in the form of law, explains a law which is doubtful, or when it restricts or extends the existing law, the authentic interpretation is not retroactive, and it must be promulgated.[2]

ARTICLE I. *Explanatory Authentic Interpretation.*

A. *Nature and function of explanatory interpretation.*

The nature and function of explanatory authentic interpretation in the Code of Canon Law (can. 17, §2) may be presented from the viewpoint of pre-Code jurisprudence as it appears in the following description. The differences between the concepts of the past and of the present will be noted.

The interpretation which is known in the Code as explanatory or explicative: "Interpretatio authentica . . . si legem . . . dubiam explicet . . .", was known among the decretal-

---

[1] The order in which these species of interpretation are presented in the Code has been reversed somewhat in this chapter. The reason for this procedure is the relation between explanatory interpretation as it is known in the Code and declarative interpretation in pre-Code jurisprudence, as outlined in Chapter V.

[2] Can. 17, § 2.

ists and civilists as *interpretatio declarativa* or *declaratio*.[3] This fact appears from a study of texts cited in Philippus Decius (+1536).[4] In this behalf he cites [5] Paulus de Castro (+1441) from the latter's treatise on *"Haeredes palam"* (a law of the Digest which will again be referred to hereinafter), and Abbas Panormitanus (+1435), where Decius identifies *declaratio* with the function of the *princeps* acting in the capacity of authentic interpreter when, in the case of serious doubt, his declaration in virtue of the basic principle of authentic interpretation begets general law. It will here be noted that the interpreter acts exactly as in the capacity of a legislator. Decius states that such is the supposition and import of the language in the jurisprudence of Roman and Canon law when is enunciated this principle: "Eius est interpretari cuius est condere".[6] Again, in favor of this identity he cites Baldus de Ubaldis (+1400), Angelus de Ubaldis (+1417), and Alexander Tartagnus (+1477), where Decius states and in passing at once distinguishes that *interpretatio* sometimes means *correctio*.[7] In the present text this jurist is explaining

---

[3] Cf. Fagnanus, *Commentaria*, lib. I, tit. II, cap. *Quoniam*, nn. 14-45; Chapter V, Art. I, *Nomenclature*. Later jurisprudence indicates the same concept and terminology.—Santi, *Praelectiones Iuris Canonici*, (Romae, 1886), I, p. 17. But cf. Sanguineti, *Iuris Canonici Privati Institutiones*, (Romae, 1844), nn. 113, nota 1, 116, who indicates a trend toward the concept of merely declarative interpretation as it is known in the Code.

[4] *In Decretales Commentaria, De Rescriptis*, cap, *Ex tenore*, n. 24.

[5] *Op. cit.*, *De Iudiciis*, cap. *Cum venissent*, n. 10.

[6] "Prima est interpretatio principis . . . Et talis interpretatio dicitur generalis et necessaria quia facit legem quae debet ab omnibus observari . . . Et de tali interpretatione loquuntur iura, quae dicunt quod eius est interpretari cuius est condere, dicta lege finali [C. (1, 14) 12] et in cap., Inter alia, cum scilicet declarando, ut dixi in cap. Cum venissent, de iudiciis . . . illa interpretatio principis facit legem generalem . . . Et ista interpretatio principis habet locum quando est magna dubitatio, quae per inferiorem declarari non potest, ut notat Abbas in cap. final. columna 2, de constitutionibus . . ."—*Op. cit.*, *De Postulatione Praelatorum*, cap. *Ad haec in beato*, nn. 61-65.

[7] "Nam interpretatio quandoque pro correctione accipitur . . . Et hac

in the name of the juristic thought of the past the nature and function of declarative interpretation given by the Supreme Pontiff, the authentic interpreter of all ecclesiastical law. When recourse is had to the Pope for an interpretation of his law, his declaration is final and must be obeyed, even if this response does not represent his original intent. To illustrate and develop this thought more amply as to its practical import Decius uses the commentary of Paulus de Castro on "*Haeredes palam*". Here, as an example, the Pope is said to issue many declarations concerning papal privileges. The interpretations are retroactive to the extent of being prejudicial to supposedly acquired rights, as though the declarations had been at hand from the beginning; they add nothing new. Such, he concludes, is the nature and function of the declaration properly so called, even where it concerns itself with some doubt of law. It must here be observed that the law "*Haeredes palam*" [8] represents a case of interpreting a legal document, a testament, whose wording is objectively doubtful, a *dubium in se;* it is this law to which the jurists cited here refer as a classical example to explain the declarative interpretation of law. And, as Decius points out, his interpretation does not necessarily depend upon what the legislator-interpreter had in mind at one time or another.[9]

---

ratione statuta invalida confirmata a summo pontifice, quia ab inferioribus tolli non possunt, a summo pontifice interpretari debent, ut notat Baldus et Angelus . . . *declarando* (italics inserted), ut prosequitur . . . Alexander . . ." —*Op. cit., De Iudiciis,* cap. *Cum venissent,* nn. 9-10. Vide etiam, Iason Maynus, *Commentaria,* C. (1, 14) 5 (Titulus: *De Legibus,* l. *Non dubium*), n. 10; *idem, Commentaria,* D. (41, 3) 15 (Titulus: *De* [usurpationibus et] *usucapionibus,* 1. *Si is qui pro emptore*), n. 153.

[8] D. (28, 1) 21.

[9] "Et quando ad papam recurritur, ut dictum est, declarationi et interpretationi eius omnino standum est, dato quod haec sua intentio a principio non fuisset . . . Et hoc idem tradit Paulus de Castro in l. haeredes palam, §. Si quod post, de testam., ubi inquit quod papa saepenumero multas facit declarationes circa gratias factas per eum, et praeiudicat illis quibus erat ius quaesitum . . . quasi illud quod declaratur a principio dictum fuisset, quo casu non

Indeed, the point of Decius is well taken; for what the legislator has in mind or will only is not positive law. Law is the legislator's mind published to his subjects. It is essentially a social institution and consequently must be external and revealed to the community as such.[10] Briefly, what the authentic interpreter in the case of a dubious enactment declares to be the law, that is the law; according to the present concept his interpretation is considered as having been present in the law from the beginning; nothing new is added or produced. And as accessory follows principal, so must the interpretation be external. In the present doctrine therefore the interpretation holds forth the legal signification which has already been posited in the law, as it were, in a container; the signification is already external.[11] The declarative interpre-

---

videtur alteri esse ius quaesitum. Et dicit hoc procedere in propria declaratione, quae consistit circa aliquod verbum dubium."—*Op. cit., De Iudiciis,* cap. *Cum venissent,* n. 10; vide etiam, *op. cit., De Constitutionibus,* cap. *Quoniam,* n. 46, with the *Additio* of Sylvester Aldobrandinus, s. v. *Dubium.*

[10] ". . . non quaevis legislatoris voluntas vel decretum in mente eius existens dicitur proprie dicta lex . . . Consulto autem dicimus, illam promulgationem [i. e., legis] fieri debere communitati . . ., quadusque proinde communitati facta non est promulgatio quamvis unus aut alter privatus notitiam habuerit, lex non obligat; . . ."—De Angelis, *Praelectiones Iuris Canonici,* (Romae, 1877), lib. I, tit. II, n. 10.

[11] Thus Fagnanus uses the simile: " . . . similitudines quibus inter alias utuntur iurisconsulti in exprimenda declarationis natura . . . lex cum explicatur, eius perplexitas et dubietas instar nucis frangitur, enucleari dicitur . . . ita et declaratio cum ex visceribus legis educitur nihil est aliud quam ipsa lex . . . Declarare autem nihil est aliud quam aperire seu manifestare super aliqua lege seu Constitutione intellectum sive sensum, quem habuit Princeps tempore editionis legis, quando scilicet lex est obscura, vel erratur in eius intellectu . . . Similiter resolvere nihil aliud est quam nodum ambiguitatis explicare seu enodare c. inter alia, de sent. excom. l. fin. C. de leg. unde legis obscuritas appellatur nodosa . . . Ea quae veniunt per modum declarationis vere et proprie inesse dicuntur. Qui enim explicat nil novi facit, sed discooperit . . . Haec enim est mera declaratio . . . liqueat sacrae Congregationis declarationes editas Apostolica auctoritate nihil aliud esse essentialiter, quam decreta ipsa Concilii ex se obscura ac dubia seu . . . male ab aliquibus intellecta, explicatione dilucidata et clarificata."—*Commentaria,* lib. I, tit. II, cap. *Quoniam,* nn. 15-21.

tation is an implement of positive law, and the meaning which it conveys is law-extant. Consequently according to this doctrine, this interpretation operates retroactively even in the case of a doubtful legal text. A later canonist, a certain Hieronymus Gigantius, in his remarks to the treatise of Philippus Decius indicates that Cardinal de Zabarella (Franciscus de Zabarella, or de Zabarellis, +1417) propounds the same doctrine.[12]

Finally, Ioannes Andreas (+1348) sees the same identity in *declaratio* and *interpretatio declarativa* where he speaks of the function of a declarative constitution; it issues for the interpretation, the exposition of a doubtful and obscure law,[13] and although the enactment was ambiguous, the interpretation has *per se* retroactive force.[14] Thus according to the decretalists in their commentaries to the law *"Quoniam constitutio"* (c. 13, X, I, 2) and elsewhere and the civilists mentioned the concept of explanatory interpretation as found in the Code, inasmuch as it is the solution of a *dubium iuris,* is known as *lex declaratoria, constitutio declaratoria.*

This declarative interpretation differs from the notion of explanatory interpretation of the Code in two obvious particulars, on the matter of retroactivity and the necessity of promulgation. However, before instituting a full comparison regarding these two ideas of interpretation it will be of interest to note that the same concepts as just portrayed are operative and the same effects produced when an authorized

12 *In Decretales Commentaria, De Rescriptis,* cap. *Ex tenore,* n. 24, *Additiones* s. v. *Declarativa.*

13 "Sed ista [constitutio] dici non potest illius interpretans; nil enim declaratur in illa dubium vel obscurum."—*In Sextum Decretalium Librum Commentaria, De Electione,* cap. 4, *Ut circa,* n. 13; vide etiam, *Clementis Papae Quinti Constitutiones, glossa* in Prooemium.

14 Ioannes Andreas, *Novella Commentaria,* lib. I, tit. II, cap. *Quoniam,* n. 6. Bartolus teaches the same doctrine.—*Commentaria,* D. (49, 1) 4 (Titulus: *de appellationibus et relationibus*), n. 7.

delegate of the legislator performs the office of authentic interpreter. The following description is rendered by Prosper Cardinal Fagnanus (+1678). The Cardinal is outlining the power which resides in the Sacred Congregation of the Council to establish authentic interpretation which has the force of universal law.

Fagnanus testifies to the concept in the field of both Roman and Canon law, using the names of the eminent jurists cited in the foregoing and others, concerning interpretation as applied to the act of an authorized delegate of the *princeps*, the author of the law, which interpretation is the explanation of a doubtful piece of legislation. This interpretation he calls *declaratio*. It does not differ essentially from the law which it interprets; it has the same force as the law itself and simply discovers what lay hidden prior to the time of the interpretation, when the enactment was first established, according to the doctrine of "*Haeredes palam*".[15] Even if the law in question is entirely obscure and doubtful and would be null without this act of the superior because of uncertainty, nevertheless the interpretation of the Sacred Congregation, which issues with supreme apostolic authority, which is necessary in such a case to put an end to controversy and to establish law and order, needs no new promulgation and is retroactive.[16]

---

[15] "Quod vero quis obscurius in testamento vel nuncupat vel scribit, an post sollemnia explanare possit, quaeritur; ut puta Stichum legaverat, cum plures haberet, nec declaravit de quo sentiret: Titio legavit cum multos Titios amicos haberet . . . et puto posse: nihil enim nunc dat, sed datum significat."—D. (28, 1) 21, 1.

[16] ". . . declaratio legis ab eo facta qui a Principe, seu legis conditore ius habet legem interpretandi, essentialiter non differt a lege declarata . . . Ergo eandem authoritatem et obligandi vim habet quam ipsa lex. Nam qui declarat, novum ius non inducit, sed tantum detegit quod prius latebat. l. Haeredes palam, §. Quod vero . . . De testam . . . atque ibi esse casum ad litteram . . . Ideo talis dicitur propria declaratio . . . Declarare autem nihil est aliud quam

It is apparent from the words of the Cardinal that the Sacred Congregation is here acting as an agent of the supreme legislator in the capacity of authentic interpreter according to the basic principle of authentic interpretation in Roman and Canon law: "Eius est interpretari cuius est condere".[17] In a word, it establishes law on a point of law which is doubtful *in se;* it solves a *dubium iuris.*

From the foregoing presentation it is clear that this description of *declaratio* or *interpretatio declarativa* fits to a certain extent that of the declarative authentic interpretation of the Code, if one confines the concept purely to the manner in which this interpretation operates: it explains what is already present; it needs no promulgation; it is retroactive, leaving aside the material object of its activity. But even in the manner in which it functions there is a discrepancy, for it does not explain more clearly, but dispels a real doubt. The Code understands this species of interpretation only of law which is already clear in itself and which could have been known before the interpretation appeared; not so, the jurisprudence of the past. There are, however, important points

---

aperire seu manifestare super aliqua lege seu constitutione intellectum sive sensum quem habuit Princeps tempore editionis legis, quando scilicet lex est obscura vel erratur in eius intellectu . . . nam cum lex declaratur, quasi certum a dubio secernitur et obscurum succiditur . . . Necessaria est superioris authoritas ut tollat ambigua, lites auferat, altercationes dirimat . . . solemnitas publicationis . . . non est repetenda in illius declaratione . . . Quod procedit etiamsi lex declarata sit prorsus obscura et dubia . . . Haeredes palam . . . ubi dispositio erat ambigua, ut nisi testator illam declarasset propter incertitudinem fuisset nulla . . ."—*Commentaria,* lib. I, tit. II, cap. *Quoniam,* nn. 14-43.

[17] ". . . quod Sacrae Congregationis rescripta appellari consueverunt declarationes, resolutiones . . . resolvere nihil aliud est quam nodum ambiguitatis explicare seu enodare, c. Inter alia, de sent. excom. l. fin. C. de leg . . . Ex quibus rescribendi formulis cum similiter satis liqueat sacrae Congregationis declarationes editas apostolica authoritate nihil aliud esse essentialiter, quam decreta ipsa Concilii ex se obscura ac dubia . . . explicatione . . . clarificata: hinc necessario sequitur ut obligandi vim habeant perinde ac decreta ipsa declarata."—*Ibid.,* nn. 16-21.

in the *interpretatio declarativa,* taken in its total comprehension, and in the explanatory authentic interpretation of the Code which are identical.

Imperium. Aside from the material function of the *declaratio* as the great pre-Code jurists conceived it, one will not fail to recognize first of all the element of *imperium* (command) which marks the interpretation in this doctrine, together with its cognate characteristic of positive law. These two elements go hand in hand in the formulation and interpretation of purely positive law, as is expressly set down in a principle of Roman law.[18] As regards the former characteristic of authoritative will, Suarez is explicit where he discusses the difference in approach between interpreting natural law and human positive law. Even the *princeps* interpreting the former concomitantly with his positive law—the positive law in the present supposition being merely a restatement of natural law—must proceed from the common principles of natural reason; not so, in relation to his own purely positive law. Here his authority and will take precedence; he simply gives a certain definite meaning to his law, even though his interpretation may seem less in keeping with, or seem to effect a change in, the law.[19]

---

18 "Quod principi placuit, legis habet vigorem; . . ."—D. (1, 4) 1.

19 Suarez is developing his topic, declarative interpretation by judicial sentence. However, the principle involved is well applicable to interpretation of any kind in the domain of purely positive law: ". . . iudicium cadens in praeteritum ordinarie est declarativum potius quam constitutivum iuris . . .; saepe enim contingere potest ut princeps per talem sententiam non interpretatur ius humanum, sed naturale . . . princeps non habet maiorem potestatem interpretandi ius naturale quam ratio eius probaverit; quia in hoc magnum est discrimen inter interpretationem legis naturalis et civilis; nam interpretatio legis civilis procedit non solum ex scientia, sed etiam ex potestate et voluntate, quae facit esse certam interpretationem, etiam si minus consentanea sit prioribus verbis, vel tantam mutationem facere ut ius antiquum mutare videatur."—*De Legibus,* III, cap. 15, n. 16.

The point of discussion here is that the authentic interpreter can give to his law whatever signification he may will. Canon 17 clearly embodies the idea of *imperium*. The authentic interpretation has the force of law:

> Interpretatio authentica, per modum legis exhibita, eandem vim habet ac lex ipsa.

This statement conveys the thought that in the case of a dubious legal text this interpretation puts an end to any further controversy which a doubtful law may have involved. The material content of the interpretative pronouncement issuing from the superior is established as law by reason of the *imperium*. Moreover, it matters little whether or not the interpretation proceeds from the legislator or from his delegate. As in the case of the S. Congregation of the Council so does the interpretation produced by the Pontifical Commission upon a point of law which represents a *dubium iuris* beget law. In other words, the interpretation of the Commission proceeds from a legislative faculty or power. This point is especially clear under the jurisprudence of the Code, where the solution of a doubt of law is to be considered for all legal purposes as new law.[20] It may also be pointed out that canon 17 makes no distinction between the legal value, the legal essence, of the interpretation which proceeds from the legislator himself and that which issues from his delegate; the interpretation of either has the force of law. Law appertains to the human reason;[21] by its instrumentality the legislator binds the intellect of the subjects of the law to prospective action.[22] Now the authentic interpreter in solving a doubt of

---

[20] Cf. Chapter III, Art. IV.

[21] "Sed imperare est rationis . . . Ergo lex est aliquid rationis."—S. Thomas, *Summa Theologica*, I, IIae, q. 90, Art. I, in corp.

[22] "Dicitur lex a ligando, quia obligat ad agendum."—*Ibid;* ". . . . lex est in aliquo non solum sicut in regulante, sed etiam sicut in regulato . . . inquantum participat ordinem alicuius regulantis."—*Op. cit.,* Art. III, ad primum; ". . . lex imponitur aliis per modum regulae et mensurae. Regula autem et

law performs the very same operation; he commands and obliges, he binds, the subjects to receive the law in this meaning and in no other. In other words, he establishes law,[23] imposing a rule of action; he performs the function of a legislator. Of course, his office must be considered as subsidiary to the office of legislator properly so called.

The legislative intent. It must be observed also that, in connection with what has just been said in the previous paragraph, the legislative content, the meaning of the law, which is conveyed by the *imperium* does not necessarily represent the personal intent of the individual legislator, so that what the original legislator may have had in mind when he issued the law which is doubtful plays no necessary part in the interpretation of this enactment. On the contrary, that meaning or sense content shall be considered the solution of the doubt whichever meaning the authentic interpreter shall set down in clear language, regardless of what the original legislator had in mind. This proposition holds true whether the interpreter in a given instance is the legislator himself or his agent-in-kind, the delegated authentic interpreter. This meaning may be termed the legislative intent, because it is the meaning which must appear in the wording of the law that makes law, not the meaning which remains purely in the mind of the legislator. The thought advanced here is especially borne out in the instance where a doubtful law of a predecessor is authentically interpreted during the tenure of his successor.

---

mensura imponitur per hoc quod applicatur . . . Talis autem applicatio fit per hoc quod in notitiam eorum deducitur ex ipsa promulgatione."—*Op. cit.*, Art. IV, in corp.

23 "Unde ad hoc quod lex virtutem obligandi obtineat, *quod est proprium legis* (italics inserted), oportet quod applicetur hominibus . . ."—*Op. cit.*, Art. IV, in corp.

Solution of a dubium iuris. The *interpretatio declarativa* agrees with the concept of explanatory interpretation therein that it solves a real *dubium iuris;* it saves the law, as Fagnanus expressly points out, from utter nullity. Such is precisely the function of explanatory interpretation, as is evident from the text of canon 17, §2. According to the jurisprudence of the Code such interpretation encounters a law which is null, a law which conveys no obligation,[24] whose meaning for all legal purposes is absent. At this point of contact with the law, however, there is a discrepancy between the concepts of the two eras of jurisprudence as to the manner, so to say, in which the interpretation performs its function. In the pre-Code jurisprudence, outlined in the foregoing, the interpretation finds what is already present from the beginning, but is hidden, obscured from view. It offers nothing new. It must here be remarked that this concept is absent in Wernz, whose language seems to reveal a jurisprudence quite identical with that of the Code,[25] according to which explanatory interpretation does not find what is already present from the beginning. Rather, this interpretation is one which deals with a law doubtful in itself, and the ensuing interpretation is to be conceived as creating a new, clear law. The legislator has chosen to call this result interpretation. The Code clearly warrants this concept of explanatory authentic interpretation. The subject matter is a law which is objectively dubious, or doubtful *in se.* This fact appears from a comparison of the function of declarative with that of explanatory interpretation. The former renders more clear a law which is *in se certa.* The latter explains a law which is *dubia,* that is to say, objectively dubious or uncertain *in se;*[26]

---

[24] Can. 15.

[25] *Ius Decretalium,* (2. ed., Romae, 1905), I, n. 127.

[26] Toso, *Commentaria, Minora,* I, 46.

for if the law is not in itself uncertain, it is the object of merely declarative interpretation.[27]

Secondly, a doubtful law is no law for all practical purposes, because it does not produce an obligation.[28] The subjects of the legislator, being in invincible doubt, are inculpably ignorant of its provisions; doubt is reducible to ignorance.[29] Thus the Code in the matter of a *dubium iuris* gives a well defined recognition to the principle advanced in the gloss to the law *"Cognoscentes"* of the Decretals: *"Nota quod decretum non ligat ignorantes"*, meaning those who are invincibly ignorant.[30] About the question of ignorance more will appear in the following number.

The creation of new law. The explanatory interpretation represents new law.[31] This statement derives from the fact

---

[27] Therefore, in the Vidal edition of Wernz, *Ius Decretalium,* there would appear to be the following contradiction in view of the principles in can. 17, § 2: "Quare cum agitur de lege irritante qui contra legem agit in dubio iuris, actum validum ponit, qui validus manet, tametsi deinde accedat authentica declaratio qua illum actum sub lege comprehendi edicatur; . . ."—*Ius Canonicum,* I, n. 189. Declarative interpretation implies by the rule of positive law that the law which it interprets is clear in itself, so that if a subsequent declarative interpretation appears, the law must be considered to have been present from the beginning with the consequences established in can. 17, § 2. To postulate a *dubium iuris,* as is done in this quotation, eliminates on principle the idea of a declarative interpretation. There appears to be in the above quotation an application of the principles of pre-Code jurisprudence concerning the operation of the *interpretatio declarativa* as it is being here outlined, and as it will further appear in the following number (B), where it is shown when this *declaratio* is not retroactive.

[28] Can. 15; S. Thomas, *Summa Theologica,* I, IIae, q. 90, Art. IV, in corp.

[29] "Dubius ab ignorante non distat . . . imo comparantur . . ."—Barbosa, *De Axiomatibus Iuris usufrequentioribus,* (in *Tractatus Varii*), Axioma LXXVIII, n. 4; "Dubius seu dubitans non dicitur certus; ideo is qui dubitat, non videtur scire . . ."—Tuschus, *Practicae Conclusiones,* II, Litt. D, Concl. 800, n. 2.

[30] *Glossa* ad *Casus,* c. 2, X, *de constitutionibus,* I, 2.

[31] Maroto, *Institutiones,* n. 238, b; Wernz-Vidal, *Ius Canonicum,* I, n.

that this species of interpretation is not retroactive, and that it must be promulgated. It must be promulgated, that is, it must be formally instituted as law, or, to render the thought perhaps more precisely, the doubtful law must be rehabilitated and re-instituted as new law, as though it had never been set down previously in a legal proposition. There is present a new act of the will on the part of the legislator which he alone can posit.[32] Like any new law the norm of action thus established enjoys the *vacatio legis*.[33] Though the pre-Code jurisprudence, as outlined above, does not agree with this last point, yet it does agree that the doubtful law is null. This fact Fagnanus clearly points out.[34] Like the *declaratio,* the explanatory interpretation issues in cases of insoluble doubt, when the law is uncertain *in se,* and where, as Panormitanus says, recourse must be had to the *princeps,* who alone in this instance can enact clear law.[35]

By demanding a new formal promulgation of the solution of a doubt of law the Code decides the question concerning the necessity of such promulgation.[36]

B. *Criteria of the doubtful law.*

The question here is, when is the law doubtful; for the

173, II; Jone, *Gesetzbuch des kanonischen Rechtes,* I, 37; Van Hove, *De Legibus Ecclesiasticis,* n. 244.

32 Chelodi, *Ius de Personis,* n. 67.

33 Cann. 17, § 2; 8, § 1; 9.

34 ". . . dispositio erat ambigua . . . propter incertitudinem fuisset nulla . . ."—*Commentaria,* lib. I, tit. II, cap. *Quoniam,* n. 43.

35 "Quaedam [i. e., interpretatio] consistit in obscuritate sensus, seu dubietate verborum ut quando quis interpretatur verba alicuius constitutionis, et de ista dicimus quod est eius interpretari cuius est condere, ut in c. inter alia, de sen. exc."—*Commentaria,* lib. I, tit. XXIX (Titulus: *de officio et potestate iudicis delegati.*), cap. XXVII, n. 8; Michiels, *Normae Generales,* I, 373.

36 Cf. Toso, *Commentaria Minora,* I, 48.

concept of explanatory interpretation remains incomplete without a consideration of the hallmarks of a *dubium iuris.* At the outset it may be stated again that a doubtful law is not easily admissible. This statement seems apparent from the fact that ignorance of the law is generally not presumed.[37] Indirectly the legislator implies in this norm of law that his enactment is clear, for the norm at the same time conveys the direct implication that the subjects of the law in question can have due knowledge of the law, the absence of which is ignorance. Hence Maroto remarks that in the external forum, at law, the doubt of law must be proven if it is not otherwise sufficiently established.[38]

A doubt is described as a suspension of judgment, a vacillation between two termini, so to say, of contradictory propositions to neither of which there is assent with moral certitude.[39] The mind is poised in equilibrium between the two termini. It is negative or positive doubt according as there are absent or present reasons or motives on either side, whereon the doubt is based. Again, the doubt is probable, when there is solid, prudent foundation (not merely doubtfully probable) for assent to the one proposition, which assent, however, is coupled with reasonable fear of error if the proposition is fully assented to. Miaskiewicz renders the thought well when he declares that the mind ". . . rests in suspense under the reciprocal pressure of serious motives, or also when it chooses an opinion in virtue of serious motives without having to search out whether the contradictory opinion is more, or less, or equally, probable".[40] The latter state-

---

37 Can. 16, § 2.

38 *Institutiones*, n. 230.

39 "Dubitare est ad neutrum animum applicare."—Tuschus, *Practicae Conclusiones*, II, Litt. D, Concl. 800, n. 1.

40 *Supplied Jurisdiction According to Canon 209*, (The Catholic University of America, Canon Law Studies, n. 122, The Catholic University of America Press: Washington, D. C., 1940), p. 181.

ment of this author represents doubt in the wide sense. On the other hand, when there is no such basis, the doubt is said to be improbable and is negligible. Finally, the doubt is objective, when it is warranted by a reason or reasons external to the mind; or it is merely subjective, when it has no such external basis. Negative, subjective, and doubt which is improbable, being tenuous and inconsequential, is to be cast aside; it is equivalent to ignorance. The subject matter of a doubt of law is the law or legal text as such. The doubt may concern itself severally with the meaning and scope of the law, with its existence and cessation, with its mode of operation under given circumstances. Hence a doubt of law is present when after diligent investigation based upon juristic scientific grounds no certainty is attainable concerning the subject matter of the doubt, as just described. Such an investigation requires the disquisition of experts, by whose thorough inquiry solid external probability is established, that is, the probability which is founded on authority.[41] Therefore in a doubt of law the basis or reason for the doubt is in the law itself; the law is dubious. This thought is contained directly in canon 17, §2, for according to its text a doubtful

---

[41] Cf. Van Hove, *De Legibus Ecclesiasticis*, nn. 228-230; Cicognani, *Commentaria ad I Librum Codicis*, p. 106-107; Wernz-Vidal, *Ius Canonicum*, I, n. 189; Toso, *Commentaria Minora*, I, 35-36, 37; Coronata, *Institutiones*, I, n. 17. Such is traditionally the accepted concept of doubt: "Dubium secundum Isid. in li. Etymol. est motus indifferens in utraque parte contradictionis. Vel dic, secundum Philosophum et mentem S. Th. in 3. dist. 17 quod est contrariarum rationum aequalitas, unde proprie homo dubitat de aliquo, vel circa aliquid quando habet rationes ad utramque partem aequaliter, aut quasi aequaliter moventes, ita quod non inclinatur ad hoc magis quam ad illud notabiliter . . . Dubium est duplex, scilicet probabile, cum scilicet rationes probabiles ad utranque partem sunt quasi aequales; et scrupulosum, quando quis, scilicet ex levi suspicione timet alicubi esse peccatum. Scrupulosum dubium ad consilium boni viri [i. e., periti et conscientiati] est deponendum, secundum omnes Doctores et idem est si dubitatur an dubium sit scrupulosum, necne."—Sylvester Prierias, *Summae Sylvestrinae*, s. v. *Dubium*, nn. 1, 4. Thus there is the practical result: ". . . quia dubia res dicitur et redditur, quae multipliciter intelligi potest."—Tuschus, *Practicae Conclusiones*, II, Litt. D, Concl. 802, n. 9.

law is one which is not certain. It is this objective uncertainty in the law which explanatory authentic interpretation seeks to dispel, rendering the enactment certain and clear.

It will be observed here that the doubt of law appears only after diligent investigation. It is then morally and prudently considered to be insoluble at the hands of those who do not enjoy the necessary juridic authority. Under such conditions it has always been the rule of canonical tradition that the solution be sought from the authentic interpreter, as Honorius II (+1130) testifies. Such instances he terms *causae maiores*, cases of graver moment.[42] Clement III (+1191), as appears in the law *"In his"*, places those questions of law ". . . quae in se ambiguitatem continent . . ." among the *maiores quaestiones* which must be terminated by the Holy See.[43] Briefly, it has been the rule in the Church from time immemorial that in perplexing questions of law the decision must rest with the Roman Pontiff, the supreme ruler. A similar norm obtained in Roman law.[44]

More particularly, upon what standard are the questions to be judged as being of graver moment? Ioannes Andreas states that to this category pertain those questions concerning which doctors and laws are in conflict.[45] Plainly, this jurist is referring to matters of law which are involved in insoluble doubt. It may here be pointed out that the concept of the

---

[42] C. 1., X, *de iuramento calumniae*, II, 7; cf. etiam, c. 2, X, *de translatione episcopi*, I, 7.

[43] C. 15, X, *de verborum significatione*, V, 40. The clause here quoted is found in the text of Gonzalez-Tellez (+1649); the editions of the Decretals omit *"in se"*; the edition of Richter-Friedberg includes this in a footnote with the annotation that it is found in the *Compilatio* II. In these editions the above rule is attributed to Celestine III (+1198).

[44] C. (1, 14) 9; 12.

[45] *Novella Commentaria*, lib. II, tit. VII (*De iuramento calumniae*), cap. 1, *Inhaerentes*, n. 3.

dubium iuris embraced a wide scope according to Panormitanus, including, it seems, even such doubt which is subjective or at least attributable to want of acquaintance with legal matters. This decretalist distinguishes a law which is *"multum dubia"*, which cannot be urged at law—the solution of which evidently belongs exclusively to the province of the authentic interpreter—and a doubt of law which can be dispelled by expert advice.[46] The former "species" of a doubt of law would be present in a law which has many significations and comes within the *lex dubia* of canon 17. It is interesting to note in this connection that a popular practice established upon such a law impeded from its retroactive effect a subsequent *interpretatio declarativa* (discussed in the previous number, A) which ran counter to the meaning of the law as represented by the popular practice.[47]

The further question then is who decides whether a law has a multiple meaning, or in general, contains a doubt of law. This question may be studied from the doctrine of Felinus Sandaeus (+1503). The determinant of the doubt of law, which is the subject of discussion, is found in Sandaeus' doctrine on the nonretroactivity of a declarative interpretation when it encounters a contrary popular practice, which practice is based on probable error. The teaching of this jurist is representative of the legal thought of the past concerning this point. The probable error lies in the fact that, until

[46] "Unum tamen scias quod ubi lex est multum dubia excusatur quis a iuris ignorantia . . . Non intelligas indistincte ut pro quolibet dubio iuris sit recurrendum ad principem. Nam et Doctoribus datur potestas interpretandi iura . . ."—*Commentaria,* lib. I, tit. II, cap. 13, *Quoniam,* nn. 2, 5; A similar concept is found in Fagnanus, *Commentaria,* lib. I, tit. II, cap. *Quoniam,* n. 49.

[47] "Unde dicerem quod . . . consuetudo contraria est dubia quia ius contrarium erat multipliciter intelligibile, et tunc posset procedere dictum Dom. Antonii [i. e., constitutio declaratoria extenditur ad praeterita nisi reperiat consuetudinem esse in contrarium]."—Panormitanus, *Commentaria,* lib. I, tit. II, cap. *Quoniam,* n. 13; Felinus Sandaeus, *Commentaria,* lib. I, tit. II, cap. *Quoniam,* n. 6

the declaratory interpretation appeared, according to the opinion of the doctors in the law, there was probable doubt of law. And hence, Felinus Sandaeus teaches in accord with other jurists, whom he cites, that the acts performed under the contrary popular practice are sustained by reason of this juristic opinion, which opinion established a probable doubt of law.[48] It seems therefore that the present situation answers the description of Ioannes Andreas concerning the *causae maiores,* namely a condition of law regarding which the experts are at odds. Thus Tuschus (+1621) lays down the rule that their discordant opinions will render a law doubtful.[49] The opinion of jurists had great weight in determining the status of the law; for Sandaeus further declares in the present context that if the practice in question is deemed unreasonable by a body of legal experts the declarative interpretation is retroactive. A similar exposition on this subject is afforded by Philippus Decius (+circa 1536).[50] Therefore, it is the opinion of jurists which is the determinant of the existence of a doubt of law.

The approach of Suarez (+1617) to the present subject is somewhat different from the foregoing. This jurist speaks concerning the same subject matter and refers to the same example as that to which, among other laws, both Panormitanus and Felinus Sandaeus have reference; namely, a law in the *Liber Sextus,* "*Perpetuo*"[51], which is an interpretation of a previous law. Suarez addresses the situation from

---

48 ". . . quia ille prababilis error sustentabit gesta in praeteritum . . . Sed dicas . . . prius facta cassari non debent, quia pro praeterita consuetudine erat probabile dubium, propter opiniones Doctorum . . . ex quibus rationabiliter excusantur prius gesta . . . etiamsi lex declaret veterem consuetudinem non fuisse rationabilem . . ."—*Commentaria,* lib. I, tit. II, cap. 13, *Quoniam,* n. 6.

49 " . . . opiniones Doctorum discordes reddunt conclusiones iuris dubias."—*Practicae Conclusiones,* II, Litt. D, Concl. 802, n. 7.

50 *In Decretales Commentaria, De Constitutionibus,* cap. *Quoniam,* n. 50.

51 C. un., *de postulatione praelatorum,* I, 5, in VIo.

both a moral and a legal aspect, pointing out that *per se* the declarative interpretation is retroactive. *Per accidens*, however, the retroactive effect is impeded either because of popular practice based on ignorance, or because the law, though it existed under the terms of the interpretation, was not so understood even among the learned.[52] In a word, Suarez reduces to invincible ignorance, existing even on the part of legal experts, what the jurists whose doctrine is presented in the foregoing characterized a *dubium iuris*. It is true that a doubt of law is reducible to ignorance, because in this case one encounters an insurmountable obstacle to certainty, which obstacle is due to the lack of the sources of further knowledge which will solve the doubt, and to this extent one can be said to be ignorant. Under the jurisprudence of the Code, however, this state of mind is more correctly called nescience, because ignorance is properly called the want of *due* knowledge, knowledge which should be present,[53] a *debitum* which must be rendered. Under the Code a law which contains a *dubium iuris* has no legal meaning, that is, no meaning which begets an obligation; the meaning is legally absent. Hence, knowledge thereof is out of question for practical purposes, and is therefore not required as a *debitum legale*. The discussion of Suarez envisions contingencies in which the law is unclear, because he is speaking of the retroactive function of declarative interpretation in terms of the doctrine based on "*Haeredes palam*", which hc cities;[54] he has reference to enactments the meaning of which cannot be discerned even by

---

[52] "Per accidens autem potuit hic effectus impediri, quia fortasse ante illam declarationem ius ignorabatur, vel non ita intelligebatur etiam a viris doctis, quamvis revera existeret . . . ut postea sit culpa, quae antea excusabatur per ignorantiam . . . Et hic videtur fuisse casus in d. c. unic. ut Glossa ibi sentit . . . nam ratione ignorantiae fieri potest, ut effectus poenae non extendatur ad praeteritos actus, etiamsi lex sit declarativa quoad ipsam poenam."—*De Legibus*, III, cap. 14, nn. 5, 6.

[53] Cf. Cicognani, *Canon Law*, p. 590.

[54] *Op. cit.*, n. 3. This doctrine is presented in the previous number, A.

legal experts. Suarez insists, of course, that the law has been present under the meaning revealed in the interpretation, but he also indicates that the determinant of its obscurity is expert legal opinion, which opinion he attributes ultimately to ignorance, albeit inculpable. In this logical progression to the ultimate basis of obscurity Suarez discloses in passing an appreciation of the positive aspect upon which the ignorance or want of knowledge rests: ". . . non ita intelligebatur etiam a viris doctis". This positive aspect is revealed by the glossator in his comment on the law *"Perpetuo"* under the word *"De caetero"*.

The Sovereign Pontiff in the law *"Perpetuo"* prohibits for the future (de caetero), as having been invalid, the use of certain formulas employed in the procedure of elections and postulations. The glossator declares that the constitution is an interpretation of existing law. In spite of the fact that the present constitution is declaratory, the passed elections and postulations are not invalid because in his word *"de caetero"* is discernible a recognition on the part of Boniface VIII of the weight of common juristic opinion to the contrary; one should not be held accountable for having followed the guidance of older and wiser men *(maiorum secutus errorem)*.[55] Hence a marginal gloss puts the question whether such an interpretation is retroactive if custom and the common opinion of prudent men, of those qualified in matters of law *(communis opinio prudentium)*, had held the contrary. Panormitanus says that the situation to which the glossator refers is one in which the law was very doubtful, being subject to a multi-

[55] "Licet ista constitutio sit veteris iuris declaratoria, puto tamen per hoc verbum Papam praecedentes electiones sic factas noluisse comprehendere. Et potuit esse ratio: quia omni communi iudicio ante istam decretalem haec forma bona esse putabatur. Unde iniiceretur laqueus ei qui communi iudicio non peccavit."—*Glossa* ad v. *De caetero,* c. un., *de postulatione praelatorum,* I, 5, in VIo.

plicity of significations,[56] indicating at the same time that the opinion of those skilled in the law has great weight in determining its meaning.[57] This appreciation of expert opinion is born out by the great canonist and Pope, Benedict XIV (Prosper Lambertini, +1758), who in the most laudatory language commends the opinions of the doctors in the law, especially their concordant teaching.[58] By the same token their discordant view would lend great weight as a determinant of a *dubium iuris*, as the present discussion attempts to show. It is common knowledge what great authority the Roman jurists enjoyed.[59] Thus Bartholomaeus a Saliceto (+1412) points out where the jurists are the determinants of doubts concerning the law.[60] The Code canonizes the teaching of the approved authors,[61] and the common and constant teaching of the doctors is a supplementary source of law;[61a] their unanimous and enduring consent can be a manifestation of the law.[62] Consequently, their discordant opinions will also be indicative of a *dubium iuris*, so that Van Hove asserts that in the domain of external authority the opinion of five or six authors of good repute will constitute probability, provided that these have individually examined the question; that even the opinion of one expert could under given circumstances constitute probability.—Therefore the weight of opinion is not necessarily a question of numbers.—However, he im-

[56] ". . . . ubi lex est multum dubia excusatur quis a iuris ignorantia, ut est . . . glo. in c. unico de post. praela. li. 6. verb. de caetero . . . consuetudo contraria est dubia quia ius contrarium erat multipliciter intelligibile . . . Et sic intelligitur gl. in d. c. 1. de post. praelat."—*Commentaria*, lib. I, tit. II, cap. 13. *Quoniam*, nn. 2, 13.

[57] "Aut apud viros doctos illa consuetudo erat irrationabilis et tunc licet forte liberet a poena non tamen validat actum."—*Ibid.*, n. 13.

[58] *Fontes*, n. 350, § 8. Quoted on page 131.

[59] Cf. D. (1, 2); Van Hove, *Prolegomena*, n. 149.

[60] "Secundo movet quaedam dubia, auget dubitationes ex opinionibus veterum."—*Superscriptio*, C. (1, 2) 22.

[61] Can. 6, 20.

[61a] Can. 20.

[62] Van Hove, *Prolegomena*, n. 51.

mediately warns that for a specialist in the field of law serious extrinsic probability must rest at once on the authority of authors and on their intrinsic reasons.[63]

Therefore, it is the prudent, solid probability of professional opinion which is the external manifestation, the determinant, of the doubt of law.

The discussion just presented began on the lines of a psychological definition or description concerning the doubt of law and proceeded to find a basis for the mental state which probable doubt creates. It was found that this basis, as a rule, is the weight of external authority, and at the conclusion it is indicated that at the bottom of external authority is the all important substratum of intrinsic reasons which support a probable doubt.

Since a doubtful law has juridic effects therein that it does not oblige the subjects of the legislator, the question arises according to what rules does the professional expert, or for that matter, anyone, arrive at the conclusion that a doubt of law is present in a piece of legislation. What is the measure of a diligent investigation upon juristic scientific grounds whereby the law is pronounced objectively dubious?

The Code seems to have established a positive juridic measure according to which a law is to be considered as certain or doubtful when it gives the norms for the investigation into the meaning of a law. This question was discussed in connection with the criteria of a law *in se certa*.[64] Therefore it is here submitted as an opinion in view of what was stated in the previous discussion that the juridic determinant of a clear or doubtful law is to be sought in the principles of interpretation set down in canons 18 and 19. Hence a prag-

---

[63] *De Legibus Ecclesiasticis*, n. 228.

[64] Cf. Chapter V, especially *Conclusion*.

matic legal definition of a doubtful law would be, that such a law is one whose text cannot be rendered clear and certain by the norms prescribed in these canons. If the legal text does not respond to the investigation employed according to the principles embodied in these canons, the law is to be pronounced doubtful *in se*. Such seems to be, according to the mind of the Code, the procedure in this matter, which may be termed the juridic approach to the question or problem of the *dubium iuris*.

Van Hove declares that the legislator of the Code has chosen certain norms for the proper understanding of his law.[65] As merely indicated in the previous discussion, referred to above, these norms of canons 18 and 19 themselves embody many individual rules of interpretation—with which the works of pre-Code jurisprudence abound. No pretense was there made of discussing fully their species and application. Is it to be implied that all possible rules of interpretation are to be engaged in the effort (if an enactment should require such effort) to render a law clear, beyond those implied in canons 18 and 19? And if so, upon what authority? It seems that these canons are by positive legislation the measure of application necessary in discerning the meaning of a law. In fact, canon 18 seems to suggest this conclusion. After determining the primary norm, it continues with the words: ". . . quae si dubia et obscura manserit . . .", giving subsidiary norms to furnish clarity to the legal text. And if after these means have been resorted to, the text still ". . . dubia et obscura manserit . . .", what then? Then there is by positive law a *dubium iuris*.

It is not to be hastily and rashly entertained, De Becker correctly states, that a law is doubtful. It was difficult, he continues, and fairly impossible prior to the Code to control conflicting opinions for want of a clear text of positive law.

---

[65] *De Legibus Ecclesiasticis*, n. 248.

This fact, of course, is generally appreciated.[66] Yet, this state of affairs ceased with the advent of the Code, so that at present the contrary is true; the existing law of the Code enjoys a high degree of presumption that it is clear.[67] Upon this hypothesis divergent views of juristic opinion, save for exceptional instances, would point rather to the fact that a law is not correctly understood than that it is objectively doubtful.[68] Such, it seems, was actually proven [69] to be the case in the very important question regarding *ab acatholicis nati* and their exemption from the canonical form of matrimony. These matters have already been dealt with.[70] But in connection with the present subject notice may again be drawn to the fact that Maroto's report (on the extent to which that question concerning canon 1099, § 2 was examined by contemporary authors upon scientific grounds) seems to indicate a lack of sufficient investigation, recognition and appreciation of the matter on the part of juristic thought as a whole, so far as could be ascertained from publications. This incident as understood and outlined here prompts the following concluding general observation based on a comparison of the jurisprudence under pre-Code legislation and that revealed in the Code concerning the matter of the interpretation of law.

It would seem that canonical jurisprudence, as disclosed in the text of canon 17, § 2, and in the mutual relation

66 Cf. Gasparri's preface to the Code.

67 "Intolerabile esset si—implicite etiam—poneretur legislatio Codicis tanquam generaliter incerta vel non clara. Recordemur nos non esse legislatores sed modestos interpretes alicuius legis quae in suum favorem magnam habet praesumptionem claritatis."—"De Recta Methodo Interpretandi Codicem,"—*ETL,* II (1925), 245.

68 "Contingere potest—quis hoc disputat—ut, aliquando et rarius verum exsurgat et remaneat dubium, etiam adhibitis mediis a Codice indicatis ad solvendum illud: . . . At cordatus Iuris cuiusque interpres limitare et minuere dubia conabitur potius quam ea multiplicare."—De Becker, *ETL*, II (1925), 245.

69 Cf. *AAS,* XXI (1929), 573; XXIII (1931), 388.

70 Cf. Chapter V, Art. II, *Examples,* and the references cited.

between this canon and canons 18-19, does not allow the question of the clarity and obscurity, or in general, of the status of the law to depend as freely upon what is commonly called and accepted as the weight of expert opinion, as appears certainly to have been the case under pre-Code legislation.[71] This freedom under the former law was apparent in the previous pages and will again appear in the following presentation on the legal obligation of a doubtful law. Under the Code the ultimate criterion of the status of the law is the authentic interpreter, who will at the same time be the referee, implicitly deciding whether or not the rules of doctrinal interpretation have been fully and properly applied.[72]

C. *Legal obligation of doubtful law.*

It will not be out of place here as supplementary to the previous discussions to say a word concerning the legal obligation of a doubtful law.

The glossator's comment to the word *"probabiliter"* in the constitution *"Perpetuo"* of Boniface VIII speaks about doubts of fact, e. g., as to a person's age, in view of which certain actions are not imputable at law. He has in mind the rule of law: "Ignorantia facti, non iuris excusat".[73] This

---

71 Therefore, Maroto (*Institutiones,* n. 230) correctly gives the warning where there is question of a doubt of law: "Dispensatio, in foro externo saltem (Pro foro interno, Moralistarum probabiles sententias sequi possumus.—nota, 1.), necessaria est pro casibus in quibus theologi moralistae non conveniunt an lex obliget, et vel ad cautelam datur vel saltem ne opiniones Moralistarum praeiudicentur." Cf. also, Cicognani, *Canon Law,* p. 587-588.

72 The tenor of the Motu proprio, *"Cum iuris canonici"* (prin), seems to contain this thought. The Code Commission was instituted ". . . ne . . . incertis privatorum hominum de germano canonum sensu opinionibus et coniecturis, . . . tanti operis [i. e., Codicis] stabilitas in discrimen aliquando vocetur".

73 Reg. 13, R. J., in VIo.

thought he compares with a doubt arising from ignorance of the law, which ignorance, he declares, is imputable. It does not excuse, because there is present the obligation of seeking competent legal advice; ignorance of the law is neither probable nor excusable.[74]

'To doubt in ignorance of law' is not clear. "*Ignorantia probabilis*" (probable ignorance) is defined by Sylvester Prierias (+1523) as ignorance of something which is improbable, such as that of which everyone or the majority of people is ignorant.[75] There is question here of doubt arising because of ignorance of the law. Doubt and ignorance are very closely akin in this respect. Decianus posits a situation in which a piece of writing may be interpreted variously. If the language has a multiple meaning, there is doubt and consequently, ignorance of the true signification. Ignorance begets doubt in this instance.[76] He calls upon Bartolus and Baldus de Ubaldis for confirmation of this view. Thus to doubt in ignorance of law signifies to doubt about the meaning of the law, because one is ignorant of its true meaning, just as in the case of any other written or spoken word. Such doubt of law, the glossator declares, is not excusable, because it is not probable; it is vincible by competent advice. The advice, the glossator points out, must be sought, according to the law of the Digest, of which the rule of law mentioned above is a re-

---

74 "Et quod hic dicit intelligo si dubitetur in facto. Si autem dubitaretur ignorantia iuris, hic secus credo, tum quia peritiores consulere debuerunt, quia iuris ignorantia nec est probabilis nec excusat."—*Glossa* ad v. *Probabiliter,* c. un., *de postulatione praelatorum,* I, 5, in VIo.

75 "Quaedam vero est probabilis, qua scilicet quis ignorat improbabile, ut est illud quod omnes vel maior pars ignorat."—*Summae Sylvestrinae,* s. v. *Ignorantia,* n. 4.

76 "Verba in epistola contenta . . . Certum est ea esse in eo in quo multipliciter possunt intelligi, dubia, quia eius quod multipliciter exponi pŏtest veritas ignoratur, ut dicit Baldus . . . Ignorare enim dicimur ea de quibus dubitamus . . ."—*Responsorum Volumen Primum,* (Venetiis, 1579), Responsum VIII, nn. 34-36.

statement. The text of this Justinian law, *"Regula est"*, recites that ignorance of the law is of no avail where competent direction is at hand.[77]

The gloss to the present law subjoins the corollary to this rule, that when direction is not available, no imputability arises.[78] In other words, the effect of the law, which is to direct authoritatively, to command obedience, is not legally operative. The conclusion from this law and its gloss is that when the source of information is itself in doubt concerning the meaning of the law, such doubt, which is directly reducible to ignorance of the legal content, will render a person excusable from the effect of the law. This ignorance is called probable, as appears from the glossary comment to this law of the Digest, which defines probable ignorance (of a fact, a thing) as ignorance of that which is commonly not known.[79] Certainly, if jurisconsults doubt as to the meaning of the legal content, it is fair to say that there is general ignorance as to what the legislator had in mind and what he wanted to say when he laid down his law. It seems that this doubt of law, namely, as to the meaning of the legal text, is ultimately reducible to a doubt of fact; to wit: What did the legislator have in mind? However, there is an essential distinction between the law, the legal text, and the mind of the legislator. Hence it cannot be said that a doubt of law is *directly* reducible to a doubt of fact, so that a doubt of law can not be solved by a private individual who happens to know what the

---

[77] "Sed iuris ignorantia non prodesse Labeo ita accipiendum existimat, si iuris consulti copiam haberet, vel sua prudentia instructus sit, ut, cui facile sit scire, ei detrimentum sit iuris ignorantia."—D. (22, 6) 9, 3.

[78] "An potuit consulere peritos, ut tunc ei noceat, i. e., non prosit [i. e., ignorantia iuris]; an non, ut tunc non noceat . . ."—*Glossa* ad v. *Regula est,* D. (22, 6) 9, 3.

[79] "Facti autem ignorantia est probabilis, ut in facto alieno."—*Glossa* ad v. *Regula est,* D. (22, 6) 9, 3.

legislator originally meant to say but did actually not express himself with sufficient clarity when he enacted the law. The reason is that law has respect directly or immediately to the community as such and only through this medium does it touch the individual.[80]

Thus the Code demands that the solution of a doubt of law be formally promulgated. 'To doubt in ignorance of the law' where this ignorance is probable would mean, under the definition of probable ignorance given by Sylvester Prierias, such doubt which is had by a majority of people concerning the law because they are ignorant of its true meaning, and would directly imply that the law is unclear. Consequently, such a law does not oblige; for it cannot coerce the mind of the subjects.[81] This thought receives confirmation from Decianus, who cites Bartolus. Similar to language in general, a law which is dubious, admitting of diverse signification, is without foundation and cannot be alleged.[82] If such a law has no foundation and cannot be alleged in prosecution or defense, necessarily it cannot produce a legal obligation. Bartolus is very brief. Laws with variant readings are useful only if they can be sustained by other laws or by legal deductions.[83] One would be inclined to think that Rule 57 of the *Regulae Juris*

---

80 De Angelis, *Praelectiones Iuris Canonici,* lib. I, tit. II, n. 10.

81 ". . . quomodo enim adstringere potest lex, nisi eius habeatur cognitio"—De Angelis, *loc. cit.*

82 "In verbis enim quae dubium habent sensum nullum potest fieri fundamentum. Et ideo videmus quod imo lex ipsa si plures patitur intellectus, allegari non potest, tanquam ea super qua fundamentum nullum fieri debet, ut per Bartolum . . ."—*Responsorum Volumen Primum,* Responsum VIII, nn. 40-41; Alexander Tartagnus (+1477) makes a similar statement.—*Commentaria,* D. (1, 22) (Titulus: *De officio assessorum*), n. 12.

83 ". . . quando habemus leges ponentes plures lecturas dicimus utraque lectura potest esse bona, concedo si probatur per alias leges vel rationes aliarum legum."—*Commentaria,* D. (34, 5), 3 (Titulus: *De rebus dubiis*), n. 1.

in the *Liber Sextus* could be used as a principle relative to the present discussion:

> Contra eum qui legem dicere potuit apertius est interpretatio facienda.[84]

The gloss to this rule, the author of which is Ioannes Andreas, does not admit its use for interpreting law.[85]

Henricus Boich (+1350) approaches the present question from the viewpoint of promulgation. Given the condition in which probable ignorance is sustained by the common opinion of experts found to be in opposition to a subsequent declaratory interpretation, the law does not exert its force. The common opinion, which is in opposition to other doctrinal views, produces probable ignorance of the law. In consequence, the law, which is unclear, must be considered as if it had not been promulgated.[86]

This conclusion of Boich is strikingly in accord with the mind of the Code concerning the status of a law which contains a *dubium iuris*. For such a law certainly is like an unpromulgated enactment; it has no force. On the other hand, however, there is no place in the Code which demands that a doubt of law be proclaimed by juristic opinion in order to effect freedom from further legal responsibility. The Code views the *lex dubia* as external. It projects the source of

---

[84] I. e., interpretation of the law which could have been set down more clearly is to be rendered prejudicial to its author.

[85] Sylvester Prierias agrees; for in case of a doubt of law recourse must be had to its author—*Summae Sylvestrinae*, s. v. *Dubium*, nn. 8-9.

[86] ". . . Est constitutio . . . declaratoria opinionum doctorum . . . quando est declaratoria aliarum oppositionum distingue. Nam aut approbat illam oppositionem quae communiter tenebatur aut alia. In primo casu trahitur et extenditur ad praeterita et pendentia. In secundo casu non; argumentum rationis capitulum cognoscentes, quia partes habent probabilem ignorantiam et sic notat Cardinalis, G, et Ioannes Andreas in de postula. praela., c. unico super verbo carere lib. 6."—*Commentaria*, lib. I, tit. II, *Quoniam*, n. 2.

doubt, which is the law itself, entirely into objectivity, whereas the pre-Code jurisprudence declared that, though the law was doubtful, the meaning was still objective and present, but hidden, like a kernel in a nutshell. However, the words of Bartolus, *plures lecturas*, indicating the capability of variant readings, corresponds to the *lex dubia* of the Code. Canon 17, §2, simply calls the law itself doubtful: ". . . si legem . . . dubiam explicet . . .". The enactment is ambiguous, has diverse significations. The same thought is engendered by the terminology of canon 18, in which the legislator refers to the signification as dubious: ". . . verborum significationem . . . quae si dubia et obscura manserit . . .". This approach to the *dubium iuris* is entirely in harmony with the general concept of the essential status of law; a law, which is an imperative proposition, the *sign* of an idea, is necessarily objective. In other words, the *lex dubia* is already there as such, to be discovered and manifested; legally it contains no meaning. Does the law thereupon legally cease to exist, to exert its force? The answer is that legally it is already non-operative; the *dubium iuris* functions automatically. "It is therefore", says Schaaf correctly, "not the declaration of the Pontifical Commission . . . but the reflex principle of canon 15 that presents the key to the solution of such cases", [i. e., involving a *dubium iuris*].[87] Therefore, it is neither the discovery of the doubt nor the explanatory authentic interpretation which releases the legal obligation; that obligation is and remains non-extant *ipso facto* and concomitantly in point of time with the uncertainty in the law. And the obligation does not revive with the explanatory interpretation and become thereby retroactive.

On the contrary, the *interpretatio declarativa*, as explained in the previous discussions in this chapter, revived

---

87 *AER*, LXXXIII (1931), 493.

the obligation and made it retroactive, not however, as here pointed out,[88] where custom or juristic opinion was to the contrary. It seems that the authentic interpreter deferred to this opinion.[89] And under this circumstance the law is looked upon as unpromulgated.

Boich argues by deducing a parallel from the law *"Cognoscentes"*, which has to do with promulgation of law to the effect that ignorance of a prohibition prior to its establishment as law should not incur legal sanction.[90] He makes no pretense at denying that the law which he postulates has been promulgated; it is considered as existing. Rather, he argues that the doctrinal interpretation sustained by the common opinion, which has solid probability, results in a state of ignorance which is parallel or equivalent to ignorance of the provisions of an unpromulgated law. Thus the ignorance resulting from the common opinion of experts in the question of a doubt concerning the meaning of a law he calls *ignorantia probabilis*. This situation presents the external elements characteristic of what is known today as *dubium iuris probabile*. In behalf of this stand Boich cites Ioannes Andreas and two other canonists. Apparently, the opposing opinion, according to the explanation of Boich is to be considered as devoid of solid probability. The whole force of his argument aims at establishing that the law as subsequently declared had not been obligatory. Consequently, Boich here sets down a rule that ignorance which is founded upon the common opinion of jurists is *probabilis ignorantia* concerning a doubtful law and certainly divests the law of its obligatory force. As mentioned

---

88 See also above, B.

89 It must be taken into account, however, that this *interpretatio declarativa* embraced the entire field of interpretation to the exclusion only of extensive and restrictive interpretation.

90 "Rem quae culpa caret in damnum vocari non convenit . . . ne detrimentum ante prohibitionem possint ignorantes incurrere, quod eos postmodum dignum est vetitos sustinere."—c. 2, X, *de constitutionibus*, I, 2.

above, Boich cites Ioannes Andreas' commentary to the word *"carere"*. The latter's argument appears in that context, at the word *"dubitatur"*. This jurist declares that probable doubt and probable ignorance effect a release from obligation and refers also to the law *"Cognoscentes"* for confirmation of this teaching.[91]

Baldus de Ubaldis considers from a practical point of view the nugatory existence of a doubtful law, that is, of a piece of legislation as to the meaning of which there exists probable doubt. With Bartolus he insists that a law must be certain and free from ambiguity, otherwise it has no probative value at law.[92] The legal reasoning is conclusive. For if an enactment cannot be urged at law, it has no force. Accordingly, no one can be legally bound to follow its provisions. Hence Cardinal Tuschus (+1621) over two centuries later sets an obscure law, one with many significations, at naught, as legally inoperative: "Obscurum nihil operatur".[93]

Panormitanus, who was a contemporary of Baldus de Ubaldis, is clear that a doubtful law is not obligatory. He views the question, like Decianus and Boich, psychologically and by deduction. A law which is dubious cannot be binding because the doubt is reducible to ignorance. This canonist rests his claim upon the gloss to the law of the Digest, *"Regula est"*, and the gloss to the word *"de caetero"* of the constitution *"Perpetuo"* of Boniface VIII,[94] both of which were considered

---

91 "Excusat probabilis dubitatio sicut probabilis ignorantia, supra cap. in de constitutionibus, cap. 2."—*In Sextum Decretalium Librum Commentaria, De postulatione praelatorum*, cap. un., n. 1.

92 "Ulterius nota quod lex debet esse certa et non ambigua, nam statutum, quod est ambiguum non meretur in causis allegari, secundum Bartolum . . . statutum de cuius intellectu probabiliter dubitatur . . ."—*Commentaria*, lib. I, tit. II, cap. 13, *Quoniam*, nn. 13-14.

93 *Practicae Conclusiones*, V, Litt. L, Concl. 273, Tit: *Lex dubia non operatur effectus legis, ideo ut lex allegari non potest.*

94 D. (22, 6) 9, 3; c. un., *de postulatione praelatorum*, I, 5, in VIo.

at the opening of this discussion. According to him the law must be *"multum dubia"*, appreciably doubtful, enough to create ignorance.[95] It is here apparent that the basis of ignorance is considered as objective.

Felinus Sandaeus demands clarity as an essential element in a legislative enactment. He reviews the doctrine of the past in a litany of condemnation of the doubtful law. Explicitly he teaches that ignorance which is due to obscurity in the legal text, because it cannot be understood, is not imputable.[96]

The review of the past which Passerini (+1677) presents concerning *"lex dubia"* is interesting. He states as most certain that there can be *ignorantia probabilis* in positive law. The reason is that there are very many controversies and contrary opinions extant among the doctors as to the existence and obligation of many laws. From Passerini's account it seems evident that as a matter of fact for all practical purposes the question of a doubt of law was placed squarely upon the opinions of the experts in the law. Indeed, under the prevailing state of the law this procedure was the best for expediting the ever present legal problems and difficulties. However, at the same time Passerini postulates that in some quarter *per se* there was error but no formal guilt because of good faith and applied diligence in an effort to know the law. And it is from these premises of legal opinion in the presence of the general unfavorable status of the law, coupled with good faith

---

95 "Unum tamen scias quod ubi lex est multum dubia excusatur quis a iuris ignorantia . . ."—*Commentaria,* lib. I, tit. II, cap. 13, *Quoniam,* n. 2.

96 "Et hinc est quod de essentia legis est, quod sit clara . . . Ideo statutum ambiguum non meretur allegari, nec est nulla sententia contra ipsum lata, secundum Baldum . . . Et idem de lege ambigua, ut non possit allegari ad decisionem causae, dixit notanter Baldus . . . et plene post alios Imola et Romanus . . . Et ideo ignorantia iuris obscuri excusat, per Dominum Cardinalem, [de Zabarella] . . .Et propterea exceptio obscura habetur pro non exceptione, secundum Bartolum . . . Et obscurum est quod intelligi non potest."—*Commentaria in Decretalium,* lib. I, Prooemium, n. 2.

and solicitude in ascertaining its direction, albeit in vain, that proceeds, according to this decretalist, the generally accepted juristic axiom that there can be probable and inculpable ignorance of dubious or controverted law.[97]

The preceding account places ultimately upon a moral basis the freedom from legal responsibility incident to divergent legal opinion. Possibly there was recognizable no general, precise, and exclusive legal determinant of the *dubium iuris* (such as is maintained in this study to be present under the provisions of canons 18 and 19 of the Code) with its correlative legal exemption from obligation, which is present in canon 15. Under the conditions of law established by the Code the fact of a controversy among canonists concerning its provisions will *per se* not form the basis of a *dubium iuris* to function forthwith according to the terms of canon 15. The point is that if and when the authentic interpreter by an explanatory interpretation concurs with juristic opinion, *de iure* he does so not because of the opinion but because the law in question cannot be clarified by the application of canons 18 and 19.

ARTICLE II. *Restrictive and Extensive Authentic Interpretation.*

The object of the present article is to present the nature, function, and effects of restrictive and extensive interpre-

[97] "Indubitatum est . . . legis positivae dari posse ignorantiam probabilem. Hoc enim manifestum est experientia. Nam de legum multarum existentia et obligatione quamplurimae in DD sunt controversiae et opiniones oppositae, quarum sine dubio una est vera, et opposita falsa, et tamen qui illam sequuntur, non peccant, quia bona fide si procedant et diligentiam adhibeant ut veritatem cognoscant, aeternae legi satisfaciunt iuxta id quod verius esse et rationabilius inveniunt. Hinc est axioma commune Iuristarum, quod iuris

tation as these proceed by the authority of the legislator according to the provisions of canon 17, § 2. In order to learn the meaning of the terminology, "*coarctet*" and "*extendat*", as it is used in this canon, it will be necessary to consider the facts as they appear in the history of juristic thought on the present question. For the purpose of comparison declarative interpretation will be mentioned from time to time.

A. *Nature and function of restrictive and extensive interpretation.*

1. Preliminary Observations.

Before describing the notion of restrictive and extensive authentic interpretation as it is found in the Code, it will be useful to make brief mention of the concepts embraced by the terms, *interpretatio restrictiva, extensiva*, in the works of the later decretalists.

Zallinger (+1813) sums up quite well in a brief general survey how restrictive and extensive interpretation was considered and employed. These species of interpretation were used in doctrinal and judicial interpretation in extending the law to similar cases, because of similar reasons; in restricting it, because its purpose had ceased to exist according to the principle: "Ubi cessat ratio, cessat legis dispositio", or because its provisions were modified by another law in accord with the rule of law: "Generi per speciem derogatur",[98] or in

dubii, seu controversi dari potest ignorantia probabilis et excusans."—*Commentaria in Primum Librum Sexti Decretalium*, (Venetiis, 1698, *De Constitutionibus*, cap. II, quaest. 1, art. 12, n. 244.

[98] Reg. 34, R. J., in VIo. Thus, Schmier, *Iurisprudentia Canonico-Civilis*, I, *Tractatus Praeambulus*, Cap. III, n. 64.

restricting the meaning of a law according to the rule: "Odiosa sunt restringenda",[99] and: "In poenis benignior est interpretatio facienda",[100] together with similar rules of interpretation to the same end. Restrictive interpretation also included the use of *epikia,* that is, the withdrawal of a particular case from the provisions of the law because of extraordinary circumstances.[101] A more or less ample treatment of similar concepts considered under the same connotations will be found in other decretalists of the later age.[102] In a word, the restrictive and extensive interpretation was considered by these canonists as represented in the employment of the various rules of law and of interpretation as these were known and used from time immemorial for the application of law. Some of these rules are represented in canons 18, 19, and 20 of the Code.

Considering the meaning in which *interpretatio restrictiva* was used by these decretalists, one has, possibly, reason to conjecture why the legislator in canon 17, § 2, employed the word *"coarctet"* and not *restringat,* which could be taken to refer to the concept of *interpretatio restrictiva* of the decretalists, whose doctrine, according to canon 6, 2°, is to be

---

99 Cf. Reg. 15, R. J., in VIo.

100 Reg. 49, R. J., in VIo; "Doctrinalis interpretatio fit a iudicibus et Iurisconsultis declarando legem obscuram, extendendo ad casus similes, ob rationes similes, restringendo ob cessantem vel contrariam rationem aliave iuris principia: unde dicitur interpretatio comprehensiva, extensiva, restrictiva."—Zallinger, *Institutiones Iuris Ecclesiastici Privati,* (Romae, 1823), lib. I, tit. II, §§ 193-200.

101 Schmalzgrueber, lib. I, tit. II, n. 42; Schmier, *op. cit., Tractatus Praeambulus,* Cap. III, n. 86.

102 Pirhing (+1679), lib. I, tit. II, nn. CXI-CXV; Reiffenstuel (+1703), lib. I, tit. II, nn. 369-371; Schmalzgrueber (+1735), lib. I, tit. II, n. 42; Pichler (+1736), lib. I, tit. II, nn. 72-76; Grandclaude (+1900), *Ius Canonicum,* (Parisiis, 1882), I, 144-145. A particularly good survey is rendered by Schmier (+1728), *Iurisprudentia Canonico-Civilis,* I, *Tractatus Praeambulus,* Cap, III, nn. 59-86.

followed when the law of the Code restates pre-Code legislation. In other words, canon 17, § 2, is not speaking about this manner of "restrictive" interpretation. Regarding this species of interpretation, there is in Reiffenstuel a twofold concept of what he calls *interpretatio restrictiva.* One is the same as explained above, where, e. g., the principle: "Odiosa sunt restringenda", is applied.[103] A second kind of restrictive interpretation is that which he recognizes in the treatise of Fagnanus (+1678), whom he cites in the context, which will be fully dealt with in the following. This interpretation, he says, together with *mere extensiva interpretatio*, is extrinsic to the law and not properly part thereof.[104] This restrictive interpretation is the subject matter of canon 17, § 2. Also, it seems plain in the quotation from Reiffenstuel that he has the concept of the extensive interpretation of the same canon, which he calls *mere extensiva* or *proprie dicta*[105] and yet seems to inject the element of doctrinal interpretation with the phrase, ". . . non contra mentem ipsius". In a certain sense the phrase is noncommittal, especially since Reiffenstuel's example in the context envisions the act of the legislator himself, who "Suadente aequitatis similitudine . . ." extends the law. Hence Schmier says correctly that ". . . ad interpretationem extensivam (quam alii vocant pure extensivam) descendendo, mire variant authores in illius explicatione, reprobatione vel admissione".[106]

---

[103] *Ius Canonicum Universum,* lib. I, tit. II, n. 369.

[104] "Secus dicendum de Interpretatione proprie dicta extrinseca et accidentalis legis: ut est correctiva, restrictiva et mere extensiva, qualis non ita legi inest . . . eo quod sit separabilis a lege et huic intrinsece non insit."—*Op. cit.,* n. 376.

[105] ". . . est illa per quam cuiuspiam legis decisio transfertur ad alium casum vel personas tam ultra verba legis, quam ultra mentem legislatoris, quamvis, non contra mentem ipsius."—*Op. cit.,* n. 371.

[106] *Iurisprudentia Canonico-Civilis,* I, *Tractatus Praeambulus,* Cap. III, n. 67.

2. Notion of Restrictive and Extensive Interpretation.

The notion of restrictive, extensive interpretation as contained in canon 17, § 2, is to be found in the treatise of Cardinal Fagnanus (+1678), who summarizes the entire doctrine on this particular question and derives it from the teaching of the civilists, notably from the glosses to the laws *"Facturus"* and *"Qui operas"*,[107] which together with other examples will now be considered.

In the Digest of Justinian there is a text, *"Facturus"*, borrowed from Gaius. Accordingly, Justinian advises that he is about to undertake the *interpretation* of ancient law.[108] The gloss to this passage gives in a general way two definitions of *interpretatio*. In its proper sense this term seeks to render manifest the meaning of a word.[109] But, the commentator adds, in the text under consideration the term (which describes the act of the supreme legislator) has a much wider connotation. It is received in the meaning of correction, restriction, and extension.[110]

In order to demonstrate his meaning the glossator makes reference to a place in the Digest, *"Qui operas"*. This law speaks of the exclusion of children from their maternal inheritance when they shall have sold their services in the degrading occupation of combat with beasts or have been sentenced to capital punishment,[111] and adds that this legal

107 Respectively, D. (2, 1); (37, 17) 1, 6.

108 "Facturus legum vestustarum interpretationem . . ."—D. (2, 1).

109 "Verbum interpretationis in proprio sensu denotat vocabuli apertam significationem."

110 "Hic tamen largius ponitur pro correctione, arctione, et prorogatione, ut infra, ad Tertyllianum, lex 1, § qui operas."

111 "Qui operas suas ut cum bestiis pugnaret locavit, quive rei capitalis

provision has been rescinded by "humane" interpretation. Such subsidiary changes in the law on individual points are simply a manifestation of good government, which, as do Reiffenstuel's words quoted above, demonstrates the employment of equity in the interests of the common weal.[112] The glossary comment characterizes the present act of *interpretatio* as a correction of the law,[113] and adverts to other meanings of interpretation: to express a word more clearly, an example of which is contemplated by the law of the Justinian Code which enunciates the principle of authentic interpretation;[114] to add, extend, as envisioned in the wording of *"Facturus"*; or to correct, in the sense of making an addition.[115]

Thus far one is to understand that the meaning of *interpretatio* or *interpretor* may be manifold. In its various significations it represents an action upon the law to be "interpreted" as performed by an agency whereby some substantial element is added to or taken from the existing law. In either case there is a correction of the law, with one exception; namely, where *interpretatio* signifies a clear exposition of the legal text, such as that furnished by legitimate authority. In the instance of extension there supersedes an entirely new element. This correction takes place by means of subsequent, general law; it cannot be performed by a private individual, but by the authority which originally gave the law. The selfsame obtains for the act of restrictive inter-

damnatus, neque restitutus est, ex SC. Orphitiano ad matris hereditatem non admittebatur; sed humana interpretatione placuit eum admitti."—D. (37, 17) 1, 6.

112 ". . . oportet . . . imperatoria interpretatione . . . duritiamque legum nostrae humanitati incongruam emendari."—C. (1, 14) 9.

113 "Interpretor, id est corrigo, ut hic."—*Glossa* ad v. *Interpretatione,* D. (37, 17) 1, 6.

114 "Item verbum apertius exprimo, ut C. de legib. et con., lex final."

115 "Item arrogo. Item prorogo, ut supra, de origine iuris, lex 1. Sed econtra, corrigo, id est, addo . . ."

pretation.[116] In a word, according to the glosses mentioned above, as Fagnanus points out, citing Cardinal de Zabarella (+1417) and authorities in the field of Roman law, the term *interpretatio* may be taken to mean any correction or modification, abrogation, extension, restriction of the law, as, for example, in the case of the enactment on bestial combat and capital punishment, where the law is by *interpretatio* corrected, apparently restricted. This manner of interpretation, which is called *argumentalis et extrinseca,* is considered as not being part of the original law to which it is applied.[117] This interpretation is differentiated from another *interpretatio* taken in its proper signification, as indicated in the foregoing, which denotes a suitable declaration, exposition of a dubious passage in the law, and which is named *intrinseca et*

---

116 "Ego . . . talem trado doctrinam, quia interpretatio sumitur quandoque . . . pro additione seu ad novum casum extensione . . . Aut quis interpretari vult statutum esse correctum per legem generalem supervenientem . . . aut quis vult istam correctionem facere ex seipso, et privatus non potest, sed ille qui legem tulit potest . . . Secundo quaero, an statuta recipiant interpretationem arctivam seu restrictivam . . . Dic, aut statutum plura capita habet et tu vis unum detrahere, et dic idem quod supra circa correctionem dictum est. Tertio quaero an statuta recipiant interpretationem declarativam seu expositivam? Et videtur quod non, quia ubi sunt verba legis obscura, recurrendum est ad legislatorem, si praesens est . . ."—Bartolus, *Commentaria,* D. (1, 1) 9 (Titulus: *De iustitia et iure*), nn. 53-56.

117 "Quaedam vero est interpretatio quae non fit per translationem unius idiomatis ad aliud, sed circa idem idioma. Et haec rursus subdividitur: alia enim interpretatio est argumentalis et extrinseca, quae proprio non inest legi, ut inquit Bald., in c. 1, n. 52, De Constit. Et hanc dicit triplicem esse Cardinalis, abrogativam, extensivam et restrictivam. Quae divisio colligitur ex gloss., 2, in lege 1, ff. de orig. iur., dum dicit interpretationem largius poni pro correctione, pro arctatione, et prorogatione. Ad idem est gl., in lege 1, §. Qui operas, in ver., Interpretatione, ff. ad Tertill. Et notat Paul. de Castr., cons. 338, Quia exceptiones, num. 2, lib. 1, dicens interpretationem sumi posse etiam pro omnimoda correctione et pro modificatione, quae in argumento [augmento?] vel diminutione consistit."—*Commentaria,* lib. II, tit. I, cap. *Cum venissent,* n. 4.

substantialis et inseparabilis a lege because it is essential to the law.[118]

The material relation of this *declaratio* or *interpretatio* to the declarative and explanatory interpretation of canon 17, § 2, has been clearly outlined in the first article of this chapter and in the two previous chapters. Therefore it becomes apparent that the restrictive and extensive interpretation as presented thus far has its counterpart in the terms of canon 17, § 2: ". . . si legem coarctet vel extendat . . .", as will be explained clearly hereinafter. The immediate concern at present is to show that restrictive and extensive interpretation is the product of legislative power. For it is clear at this point of the discussion that the restrictive, extensive interpretation is a construction upon a piece of legislation, calculated to be a general norm of action. This same fact appears from the obvious wording of canon 17, § 2: "Interpretatio authentica, per modum legis exhibita, eandem vim habet ac lex ipsa . . .". The basis, or *terminus a quo,* upon which this subsequent construction of the law is made, which basis is also the point of comparison between the restrictive, extensive interpretation as described heretofore and that of the Code, will be considered later.

It is the public authority, as Bartolus in the previous quotation points out, which makes the change in the law, be it by restriction or extension. Canon 17, § 1 makes the same statement in view of its second paragraph. And this canon makes no distinction between the legislator-successor and the

118 "Alia vero interpretatio, ut idem Bald., ait in d. cap. I, n. 52, est substantialis et intrinseca et inseparabilis a lege. Et hoc modo accipitur interpretatio proprie pro congrua verbi dubii declaratione, secundum Paul. de Castr. Ubi supra de qua scripserunt Bartol. in l. omnes populi, in 3 quaest., sextae quaestionis principalis, num. 56, ff. de iust. et iur., et al. . . . quia legum interpretatio naturaliter necessaria est, ut est tex. in l. 2, §, His legibus, ff. de orig, iur . . . iusta interpretatio bene debet et potest fieri."—*Op. cit.*, nn. 4, 96-97.

authorized delegate with the purpose of restricting the latter's jurisdiction to the province of declarative or explanatory interpretation. On the contrary, the canon very deftly names all the actions described in its second paragraph authentic interpretation, which is to be the product of the "*authentice interpretatur*" of the first paragraph, no matter who wields the "*potestas interpretandi*". The obvious conclusion aimed at is that the delegate has *per se,* in virtue of this canon, the power of rendering restrictive and extensive interpretation, and that this power resides in a legislative faculty.[119]

The genuine concept of the restrictive authentic interpretation of canon 17 in pre-Code law is contained in the notion of *derogatio,* whereby a part of the law is suppressed and certain special cases are withdrawn from its provision by the legislator.[120] Regarding this very act of the legislator, Clement V (+1314) enunciates the principle: ". . . quod lex superioris per inferiorem tolli non potest . . .", declaring that the College of Cardinals can in no way *sede vacante* modify, correct, change, suppress or add to the papal constitution concerning the election of the Sovereign Pontiff.[121] The concept of *derogatio* as an act of interpretation is furnished in the law of the Decretals "*Super quaestionum*" in conjunction with its gloss. Pope Innocent III (+1216) replies to the Archbishop of Canterbury that his constitution in no way suppresses *(nullatenus derogatur)* any item of a certain consultation of Pope Alexander, but rather explains and supplements it.[122] Accordingly,

---

119 Cf. Chapter III, Art. IV, C and D.

120 "Derogatio legis, econtra est cum lex ex parte tollitur, quatenus Legislator unum vel alterum legis articulum mutat, aut a generali constitutione certos casus speciales excipit."—Reiffenstuel, lib. I, tit. II, n. 484. *Item,* Lega, *De Iudiciis Ecclesiasticis,* nn. 161-162, 289. The terminology and concept derive their origin from the legislation of republican Rome.—Cf. Zallinger, *Institutiones,* lib. I, tit. II, § 186.

121 C. 2, *de electione et electi potestate,* I, 3, in Clem.

122 "Super quaestionum articulis, de quibus nos consulere voluisti, taliter

in the wording of this decretal there are contemplated at least two species of interpretation, declarative and restrictive. The glossator singles out the word *"derogatur"* and conceives correction, which actually did not take place in the present instance, as an act of restrictive interpretation exemplified in the fragment of the Digest *"Qui operas"*.[123]

Boniface VIII (+1303) observes that Innocent II (+1143) had granted in favor of the clerical state the *privilegium canonis* to clerics who contracted marriage, provided that certain conditions are fulfilled. The Pope thereupon grants the privilege of clerical immunity from trial and condemnation in secular court to clerics contemplated in the act of Innocent II. These enactments represent a restriction in favor of the clerical order upon the law which deprives married clerics of the privileges of their state, as is implied by the glossary comment on the ruling of Boniface VIII.[124]

A situation can arise in which a doubt as to the law is solved together with the issuance of an extensive interpretation. According to a law in the Decretals of Gregory IX (+1241), Honorius II (+1130) gives his decision concerning what appeared to be a conflict of laws. Under the prescript of a certain ancient law *(canones Patrum)* clerics were forbidden to take an oath. A second law demanded an oath of

---

respondemus: quod per constitutionem nostram consultationi Alexandri Papae nullatenus derogatur, sed illa per istam exponitur; immo in ista verius, quae in illa fuerant praetermissa, supplentur."—c. 27, X, *de officio et potestate iudicis delegati,* I, 29.

123 "Immo corrigit qui interpretatur, ff. ad Ter., lex 1, § qui operas." Hostiensis in his commentary to the present law makes the identical remark. Philippus Decius also points to this gloss to confirm his statement that correction of a law is sometimes called interpretation: "Nam interpretatio quandoque pro correctione accipitur . . . Et idem gl. in c. super quaestionum, in princ. de of. dele . . ."—*Commentaria,* lib. II, tit. I, *Cum venissent,* n. 9.

124 ". . . quaeritur, utrum amittat privilegia clericalia? Respondet quod sic, exceptis duobus . . ."—*Glossa* ad *Casus,* c. 1, *de clericis coniugatis,* III, 2, in VIo.

good faith *(iuramentum calumniae)* from the principals at the beginning of an ecclesiastical trial. It appeared, furthermore, that the ancient law prohibiting an oath to clerics had been restated by a certain Marcus [Marcianus?] Augustus Constantinus, prefect of the praetorium, and was believed to be obligatory only for the clerics of Constantinople. This circumstance, therefore, occasioned an added doubt. The question was whether the prohibitive law is universal, and if so, which of the two enactments are clerics obliged to follow. Pope Honorius, adverting to the fact that in accord with tradition questions of graver moment are decided by the Supreme Pontiff, gives a decision in the matter, which is to be final.[125] He approaches the solution from the viewpoint of an interpretation, which is to become universal law. In order to set aside all doubt, the Pontiff decrees that the constitution of Marcus Augustus must be interpreted as extending to all clerics generally and as an immunity from the *iuramentum calumniae.*[126] Wernz (+1914), who on the present question proposes in effect the same doctrine as Fagnanus and the other jurists cited in this discussion, offers these laws as examples of restrictive and extensive interpretation, respectively,[127] as do other contemporary authors.[128] Suarez, referring to the law *"Quantae"*, whereby the Sovereign Pontiff by interpretation extends *(interpretans)* the sanction of excommunication

---

125 "Inhaerentes vestigiis praedecessorum nostrorum dicentium graviores quaestiones per Summum Pontificem terminari . . . huius causae speciem irrefragabiliter . . . decidimus."—c. 1, X, *de iuramento calumniae*, II, 7.

126 "Ut ergo dubietas ista omnibus penitus auferatur . . . divi Marci constitutionem ita interpretari debere decernimus, ut ad omnes ecclesiarum clericos generaliter pertinere iudicetur . . . dignum est, ut totus clericalis ordo a iuramento calumniae praestando sit immunis."—*loc. cit.*

127 *Ius Decretalium,* I, n. 128, II.

128 Toso, *Commentaria Minora,* I, 45; Cicognani, *Canon Law,* p. 602.

incident to the *privilegium canonis,*[129] declares that an extensive interpretation is a product of legislative power.[130]

As mentioned above, there remains to be considered the basis, or the *terminus a quo,* from which restrictive and extensive interpretation proceeds. This point of departure, as it were, of the interpretation will at once serve as the medium of comparison between the species of interpretation described thus far and those mentioned in the Code. Thus it will immediately appear that the interpretation outlined in the foregoing has its counterpart in canon 17, § 2. It is evident, of course, that in speaking of extension or restriction it is necessary to know whence commences the addition or suppression in the law. For upon this criterion one will be able to judge whether an interpretation represents merely an explanatory, a declarative interpretation, or a substantial change in the law.

The Code of Canon Law declares that laws are to be understood in their proper signification.[131] It follows necessarily, then, that the authentic interpreter in extending or restricting the law will proceed from the proper signification of the legal text as a basis. Reiffenstuel declares: ". . . passim variae a Doctoribus adducuntur Regulae . . .", which rules, based upon texts of Roman and Canon law, are used to interpret legislation. Among these doctrinal norms he includes a rule: "Verba sunt intelligenda secundum propriam significationem . . .", as received by doctrinal jurisprudence.[132] He adds at great

---

[129] C. 47, X, *de sententia excommunicationis,* V, 39.

[130] "Oportet autem advertere, aliquando non esse legem pure declarativam, sed habere aliquid admixtum legis constitutivae ex potestate legislatoris declarantis. Et tunc quantum ad id, quod addit praeter nudam declarationem . . . Exemplum est in cap. Quantae, de sentent. excomm., ubi per verbum *interpretamur* declarat Pontifex . . . quae declaratio non est pura, sed per potestatem condendi legem potius quam per interpretationem facta."—*De Legibus,* III, cap. 14, n. 4.

[131] Can. 18. How this proper signification is to be understood has been the subject of a discussion which is sufficiently ample for the purposes of this study and serves as a background. Cf. Chapter V, Art. I, A.

[132] *Ius Canonicum Universum,* lib. I, tit. II, nn. 383, 390.

length, however, citing glosses and other authorities in the field of Roman and Canon law, as the common teaching, that in any event and if at all possible the law must be made operative; if necessary the legal terminology must be taken in an improper signification *(verba sunt improprianda)*. Therefore, as a rule the legal terminology must be understood in its proper sense; the rule admits of exceptions in order to save the law.[133] This is the principle of saving the law at any cost, even by imputing to the text an improper signification. The Code knows of no such principle,[134] because canon 18 directs only that the proper signification shall be employed in interpreting the law and makes neither exceptions nor provisions as to the use of an improper meaning with a view to interpreting a legislative enactment.[135] Therefore the restrictive or extensive interpretation envisioned by the Code proceeds upon the basis of the words [136] taken in their proper meaning.[137]

It must also be noted that even according to the doctrine of Reiffenstuel as a rule the proper signification must be taken as the basis in interpreting law, because the legislator on his

---

133 ". . . ut res de qua agitur, potius valeat quam pereat . . . Quinimo ad sustinendum actum admittitur omnis interpretatio . . . Et ista quae fit pro validitate actus, est regina aliarum interpretationum."—*Op. cit.*, nn. 392-398.

134 Though apparently it is still repeated by some modern writers; ". . . ut salvetur mens legislatoris verba improprianda sunt . . . ita ut . . . verba vel extendenda sint ultra proprietatem verborum vel e contra restringenda citra verborum proprietatem"—Maroto, *Institutiones*, n. 236; Michiels (*Normae Generales*, I, 378, nota 3.) therefore concludes that the *terminus a quo* is the *mens legislatoris* ". . . licet forsan protrahatur [sensus a legislatore intentus] ultra vel restringatur infra proprium verborum sensum".

135 The fact that such interpretation was admissible in pre-Code jurisprudence is no guarantee that the Code does or must admit it. Cf. Can. 6, 2-3°.

136 Cicognani, *Commentarium in Lib. I Codicis*, p. 117; Maroto, *Institutiones*, n. 236.

137 Suarez, *De Legibus*, VI, cap. 1, n. 3; Wernz, *Ius Decretalium*, (3. ed., Prati, 1913), I, n. 128, II, and n. 144, IV; Sägmüller, *Lehrbuch des Katholischen Kirchenrechts*, p. 161; Van Hove, *De Legibus Ecclesiasticis*, n. 241; Vermeersch-Creusen, *Epitome*, I, n. 120.

part must express himself clearly, and hence he must use words in their proper signification.[138] As a matter of fact the exposition of Bartolus relative to the law of the Digest *"Haec verba"* [139] concerning the function of extensive authentic interpretation of penal law expressly names the proper signification of the legal terminology as the point of departure.[140] The meaning which is added to the law is done so by the *interpretatio* of the legislator in contradistinction to the wording of the law [141] taken, as Panormitanus says (he follows the teaching of Bartolus), in its proper signification.[142] The *inter-*

---

138 ". . . alioquin nihil firmum stabiliretur, sed omnia forent plena cavillationibus."—*Ius Canonicum Universum*, lib. I, tit. II, n. 390; Van Hove (*De Leg. Eccl.*, n. 241) declares that the doctrine of restrictive and extensive interpretation as related to the proper signification has been more commonly received ". . . et magis concordat cum definitione can. 17, § 2, qui extensivam et restrictivam vocat omnem interpretationem quae non est mera declaratio vel explicatio legis dubiae et proinde etiam eam quae fit infra vel ultra sensum proprium verborum".

139 "Haec verba legis 'ne quis posthac stuprum, adulterium facito sciens dolo malo', et ad eum qui suasit, et ad eum qui stuprum vel adulterium intulit, pertinet."—D. (48, 5) 13 (12).

140 "Nota quod hic dicit litera, haec verba pertinent ad eum qui suasit et sic innuit quod ille quis suasit vel mandavit et fieri facit, tenetur ex propria verborum significatione non ex interpretatione. Quandoque verba legis sunt scripta in rem, tunc per propriam significationem comprehendunt etiam eum qui fecit fieri [v. g., mandans] . . . Quandoque verba legis sunt scripta in personam, v. g., si quis vim fecerit, tunc ille, qui vim fieri fecit, non proprie facit, sed ex interpretatione, lex 1, §, deiecisse, supra de vi et vi armata. Ubi dicitur quod ex interpretatione tenetur ille qui fieri fecit."—*Commentaria*, D. (48, 5) 13 (12) (Titulus: *Ad legem Iuliam de adult. coercendis*); Cf. etiam *Glossa* ad v. *Videor*, D. (43, 16) 1, 12.

141 ". . . dicitur hic, ita interpretandum. Contra, quia illud comprehenditur ex verbis legis, non ergo est necessaria interpretatio. Solum hic sumitur interpretatio i. e., declaratio."—Bartolus, *Commentaria*, D. (28, 2) 29, 13 (Titulus: *De liberis posthumis*, § *Etiamsi parente*).

142 ". . . nam c. si quis suadente, concipit verba in personam propriam . . . Tamen interpretative mandans incidit in illam poenam. Sed an hoc casu mandans includatur ex interpretatione, an autem ex proprio intellectu verborum notat Bartolus in lege, haec verba . . . verba sunt scripta in rem, tunc mandans includitur . . . et hoc casu includitur ex propria significatione verborum. Aut verba sunt scripta in personam . . . mandator comprehenditur non ex propria significatione verborum, sed ex interpretatione iuris, quia ius interpre-

pretatio is therefore to be considered as something superadded to the law, to the proper signification of the wording, which previously was not embraced in the legal text. This interpretation is known as *interpretatio extranea;* such, namely, which transcends the limits set by the wording of the law. Such interpretation is not permissible, Baldis de Ubaldis remarks, speaking in general about private or doctrinal interpretation. One must follow, as it were, in the footsteps which have been marked out by the law and not digress from the text.[143] There is another interpretation which is called *interpretatio intrinseca et substantialis.* This interpretation is equivalent to, and inseparably part of, the statute; it is the sum and substance of the law as distinguishable from the *interpretatio extrinseca, argumentalis,* which is not contained in, or part of, the statute.[144]

It must here be pointed out that Baldus is speaking of the interpretation of municipal statutes *(statuta municipalia).* Yet even in this quotation the expression *"nec ullum interpretabile"* could be understood, it seems, as referable also to *leges.* However, elsewhere he gives what appears to be a general rule which includes every kind of law. The rule appears to be the same as that given above for municipal statutes; namely, statutes and constitutions may not receive the *interpretatio ex-*

---

tatur eum facere licet vere non faciat . . . quia vere non facit, sed ficte et interpretative, ut dixi."—*Commentaria,* lib. V, tit. XXXIX, cap. VI, *Mulieres,* nn. 4-12.

143 "Ultimo scias quod statuta non recipiunt interpretationem extraneam, vel cervotiam, vel transgredientem terminos suos, sicut nec instrumenta, nec testes, nec ullum interpretabile . . . Et ideo ubi statutum figit pedes, ibi nos figere debemus . . . Ita tamen inferamus quod a verbis non prorsus recedamus . . ."—*Commentaria,* lib. I, tit. II, cap. primum, *Canonum,* n. 50.

144 "Quaero utrum interpretatio statuti dicatur statutum? Respon., sic si est intrinseca et substantialis et inseparabilis a statuto . . . Sed si est argumentalis et extrinseca, tunc non est statutum."—*Ibid.,* n. 52.

trinseca except from the lawgiver, but only the *intrinseca*.[145] This quotation, it must be noted, is a commentary to the decretal law *"Quoniam"*.[146] In other words, Baldus, who is both a decretalist and a civilist, is giving a rule regarding ecclesiastical law.

Bartolus seems to give a similar rule, applicable to the interpretation of law in general. The point here, as in the foregoing, is that restrictive and extensive interpretation proceeds from the proper signification. This jurist, after conceding that interpretation is also understood in the sense of correction, restriction, addition or extension—in the sense illustrated above—none of which a private individual may undertake, declares as the common teaching that *statuta,* when there is doubt, may receive declarative or expositive doctrinal interpretation just as in the case of *leges,* which interpretation consists in a *congrua expositio,* for the execution of which Bartolus then proceeds to give some practical rules. Of particular bearing upon the present discussion is the rule that when there is a choice between the proper and the improper signification of a term, the proper signification, according to the laws of the Digest *"Non aliter"* [147] and *"Utilitatem"* in the fragment *"Si is qui navem"*,[148] must prevail unless the mind of the lawgiver appears to the contrary; for example, when the proper signification bears out an absurdity or an injustice.[149] The rule of

[145] "Ulterius nota quod statuta et constitutiones non recipiunt interpretationem extrinsecam, sed intrinsecam sic, nisi ab earum conditore, etiam loquendo de interpretatione declarativa. Quod verum est generaliter in omnibus causis."—*Commentaria,* lib. I, tit. II, cap. XIII, *Quoniam,* n. 15.

[146] C. 13, X, *de constitutionibus,* I, 2.

[147] "Non aliter a significatione verborum recedi oportet, quam cum manifestum est aliud sensisse testatorem."—D. (32, 69).

[148] "In re igitur dubia melius est verbis edicti servire et neque scientiam solam et nudam patris dominive in navibus onerare neque in peculiaribus mercibus voluntatem extendere ad solidi obligationem."—D. (14, 1) 1, 20. (N. B. This rule is in the following fragment, 20, scil., *"Licet autem"*.)

[149] "Tertio quaero an statuta recipiant interpretationem declarativam seu

saving the law by imputing an improper signification seems to be referable, according to Bartolus, to the law *"In ambigua"*.[150]

Bartolus then proceeds to give rules how the proper signification is to be found, which rules seem to be entirely the same as those used for interpreting any body of laws. He derives them from the Digest. The very point here is that the rule of the use of the proper signification in the doctrinal interpretation of *statuta* seems to be the same as that for the doctrinal interpretation of *leges;* for Bartolus says that the former may be interpreted just as in the case of laws: "E contra quod sic quia sic fit in legibus"; namely, by a *congrua expositio,* which as a rule seeks the proper signification of the terminology when the law is doubtful. This statement regarding the similarity of procedure is especially suggested by the fact that Bartolus points out that when a statute forbids the interpretation, the glossating, or the *extraneus intellectus* of statutes, this prohibition has little effect *(nihil aut modicum operari)* and refers only to what he calls a frivolous interpre-

expositivam? Et videtur quod non quia ubi sunt verba obscura, recurrendum est ad legislatorem, si praesens est . . . E contra quod sic quia sic fit in legibus . . . et istud est verum secundum . . . omnes, dum tamen dicta expositio, seu declaratio sit consona iuri. Ubi vero statutum est adeo obscurum, quod non potest haberi congrua expositio, tunc fateor quod recurritur ad statuentes . . . Ut igitur videamus quid sit illa congrua expositio, aliqua perstringamus . . . quando habet [i. e., verbum in statuto] unam propriam, aliam impropriam [i. e., significationem], regula est quod debet assumi propria, et omitti impropria, ut l. non aliter, infra de lega. 3. et infra de exer. l. 1, §. Si is qui navem, ver. in re igitur dubia. Fallit si de mente disponentis aliud apparet. d. l. non aliter. De mente autem dico apparere si intelligendo secundum propriam significationem continet iniquitatem, seu absurditatem, et tunc assumemus impropriam, ut. l. in ambigua, infra titu. 2 . . . Quarto quaero utrum statuta recipiant interpretationem extensivam? Et videtur quod non: nam non est nostrum legem extendere . . ."—*Commentaria,* D. (1, 1) 9 (Titulus: *de iustitia et iure*), nn. 56-60.

[150] "In ambigua voce legis ea potius accipienda est significatio, quae vitio caret, praesertim cum etiam voluntas legis ex hoc colligi possit."—D. (1, 3) 19.

tation *(solum frivola interpretatio videtur remota)*.[151] It seems that the only difficulty and doubt which Bartolus raises concerning the interpretation of statutes is in the application of the rule: "Indefinita aequipollet universali" to these enactments, as appears in his present context. If therefore the proper signification is the rule, then restrictive and extensive authentic interpretation takes its rise from the proper signification.

In concluding the present discussion, it seems therefore, considering especially the doctrine of Fagnanus recited above on restrictive and extensive interpretation, which he derives from Roman law, that the legislator of the Code reached back of the later decretalists and derived his idea of these species of interpretation from the sources mentioned.

It is necessary to distinguish restrictive and extensive interpretation from strict and wide or broad interpretation. According to the Code, restrictive and extensive interpretation rests exclusively within the province of the authentic interpreter of the law as such, that is to say, of the law in the abstract, whose interpretation issues *per modum legis*. This interpretation represents an act of the legislative will. This fact appears from what has already been said as also from the following number. The latter kind of interpretation pertains primarily to the province of doctrinal interpretation. Strict and broad *(stricta, lata)* interpretation are as species to the genus, "proper signification"; frequently, words have a strict and a broad meaning within their proper signification. This interpretation is found in its pure state in declarative doctrinal interpretation produced according to the prescripts of canons

[151] *Op. cit.*, n. 65. Fagnanus (*Commentaria*, lib. II, tit, I, cap. *Cum venissent*, n. 97) adopts this rule for the interpretation of ecclesiastical law; namely, a prohibition to interpret the law has respect only to the *interpretatio extrinseca*.

18 and 19,[152] and it never transcends the boundaries of the proper signification,[153] because the law must always be understood in the proper signification of its terminology, whence restrictive and extensive interpretation takes its rise. Thus it is clear how these two genera of interpretation differ. Michiels says correctly that the terminology in a given law has only one signification, strict or broad; the legislator cannot mean to signify two different matters at once.[154]

B. Effects of restrictive and extensive interpretation.

From the previous discussion it is already clear that the restrictive, extensive authentic interpretation produces something new regarding the law upon which it operates.[155] Such is plainly the import of canon 17, § 2, relative to canon 8, § 1, when it declares that these species of interpretation must be promulgated and do not have retroactive force. Therefore, *in effect,* but not in name, new law is created,[156] a product which represents a new act of the will on the part of the legislator which is proper to him exclusively.[157] The act of making

152 Michiels, *Normae Generales,* I, 381; Maroto, *Institutiones,* n. 236; Van Hove, *De Legibus Ecclesiasticis,* n. 242.

153 Beste, *Introductio in Codicem,* p. 76.

154 *Normae Generales,* I, 380-381; cf. Vermeersch-Creusen, *Epitome,* I, n. 120. The words, *stricta* and *restrictiva* were used interchangeably in pre-Code doctrinal interpretation.—Reiffenstuel, lib. I, tit. II, n. 369; Schmier, *Iurisprudentia Canonico-Civilis,* I, *Tractatus Praeambulus,* Cap. III, n. 80.

155 Sägmüller, *Lehrbuch des Katholischen Kirchenrechts,* p. 161.

156 Vermeersch-Creusen, *Epitome,* I, n. 120; Van Hove, *De Legibus Ecclesiasticis,* n. 244; "Item qui interpretatur, addit vel minuit. Sed qui hoc facit, novum ius facit . . ."—Baldus de Ubaldis, *Commentaria,* lib. I, tit. II, cap. primum, *Canonum,* n. 38.

157 "Si autem interpretatio legem . . . coarctat aut protrahit, evidenter habetur novus actus voluntatis legislatoris (ideoque ab eo tantum huiusmodi admittitur)."—Chelodi, *Ius de Personis,* n. 67.

an addition to a law is called an interpretation by Azo (+circa 1230).[158] This point is well taken. By addition, or by any change in the law, some new juridic meaning is given to the enactment, which may therefore well be called an interpretation, which meaning becomes forthwith the new juridic, proper signification.

Restrictive, extensive interpretation approaches the existing law as an extraneous element whereby the scope of the law becomes restricted, embracing fewer objects; or its obligatory force becomes amplified by the inclusion of items which were previously not governed by the law.[159] Thus in a real sense this interpretation is accidental[160] or accessory to the law. Hence Justinian observes that no law is adequately fashioned from its inception to govern all things; for in the course of time it becomes deficient and needs correction because of the vicissitudes of human nature.[161] Therefore it happens not infrequently that for the common good the law undergoes some change whereby the authentic interpreter adds or suppresses something in the law, all of which falls within his power to perform, as Suarez points out, who considers the interpretation as a law given in interpretation of a law.[162]

---

158 "Id est, adiicimus et interpretamur. Azo."—*Glossa* ad v. *Corrigimus,* N. (74, pr.), cited below. Azo was a great scholar in Roman law at Bologna.

159 Toso, *Commentaria Minora,* I, 45; Michiels, *Normae Generales,* I, 384; Cicognani, *Canon Law,* pp. 599, 602; Wernz-Vidal, *Ius Canonicum;* I, n. 171, II.

160 Reiffenstuel, lib. I, tit. II, n. 376.

161 "Recte dictum est . . . neque legem ullam neque senatusconsultum rei publicae Romanae latum videri ad omnia sufficienter ab initio sancitum, verum multiplici indigere emendatione, ut ad varietatem naturae eiusque inventa sufficiat . . . quoniam autem ex iis quae in diem a natura struuntur deesse aliquid legibus iam sancitis deprehendimus, hoc in praesentia emendamus [Authenticum: *"corrigimus"*]."—N. (74, pr.), (Authen. Coll. VI, tit. I, *Quib. modis nat. filii efficiantur legitimi*).

162 "Unde etiam intelligitur frequenter contingere, ut haec interpretatio non sit nuda declaratio sensus prioris legis, sed mutatio etiam aliqua, vel addendo vel minuendo, quia totum hoc cadit sub potestatem eius cuius auctoritate fit talis interpretatio, et potest esse ad commune bonum necessarium.

Thus it appears that restrictive and extensive interpretation seeks to govern the community in such a way as to provide for its current needs.

Since, however, something new has been introduced, the interpretation must be promulgated[163] and does not have retroactive force[164] unless it explicitly takes cognizance of the past.[165] Therefore the *vacatio legis* usually intervenes.[166]

Felinus Sandaeus makes a very useful observation concerning an addition made to a law. The addition must be understood in the meaning of the statute to which it is joined, because it becomes part of the enactment; the mere presence of an addition or supplement may not be taken as a correction of the existing law.[167] Therefore in case of a restrictive interpretation it is necessary to have an eye to canon 23.

Unde lice contingat, interpretationem non videri omnino adaequatam proprietati verborum legis, non est dubitandum de auctoritate et efficacia interpretationis, quia cum auctor possit aliquam mutationem facere, saepe, illam miscet sub eodem interpretationis nomine illam comprehendendo fortasse per modestiam et comitatem, ut videre licet in cap. 1, de iuram. calum. et cap. unic. de Cleri, coniug. in VIo . . . Denique observare oportet haec omnia intelligenda esse de lege, quae directe fit ad interpretandum priorem."—*De Legibus,* VI, cap. 1, n. 3; VI, cap. 17, n. 3.

163 Can. 8, § 1; Reiffenstuel, lib. I, tit. II, n. 376.

164 Can. 17, § 2.

165 Can. 10; Chelodi, *Ius de Personis,* n. 67.

166 Can. 9. In can. 2226 there is an exception to this rule.

167 "Primo nota quod ubi alicui statuto vel dispositioni fit aliqua additio, in illa censentur repetita omnia quae erant in statuto, etiamsi non dicatur in additione . . . quia illud quod fit per modum additionis, fit pars illius cui additur . . . Secundo nota quod addere vel supplere non est contradicere."—*Commentaria,* lib. I. tit. XXIX, cap. *Super quaestio.,* n. 2.

CHAPTER VIII.

Authentic Interpretation by Judicial Sentence and Rescript.

Introduction.

The Code of Canon Law declares in canon 17, § 3, that an authentic interpretation of law rendered in the form of a judicial sentence or rescript concerning a particular affair does not have the force of law; that the interpretation is obligatory only upon the persons and dispositive regarding only those matters for which it is given.

The subject of authentic interpretation by judicial sentence and rescript is not infrequently treated jointly in the sources referred to in this study. Accordingly, it is not surprising that the Code deals with these items in a single paragraph. In fact, Lega, speaking about the administrative duties of the S. Congregations, states that judicial and administrative powers are closely connected, being parts of executive power.[1] In the present study the subject matter will be reduced into two parts, the first (A) treating on judicial interpretation, the second (B), on interpretation by rescript.

The difference between the settlement of a conflict of rights or of any question in general by judicial sentence or rescript consists for the most part, it seems, in the solemnities

---

[1] *De Iudiciis Ecclesiasticis,* II, n. 20.

or formalities attendant upon judicial procedure, which the importance or the difficulty of the issue demands. Hence the subject matter as such will have some moment in deciding which of the two procedures will be followed. The essential or substantial approach to the solution does not seem to differ greatly in either case, except that in the extra-judicial solution of the case the element of good faith occupies the foreground, and the question is often solved according to the dictates of equity *(ex bono et aequo)*.[2] It seems that the distinction between the two species of jurisdiction is not easily definable,[3] so that the assignment of causes to either a judicial procedure or an administrative procedure would depend partly on the nature of the subject matter, partly on the disposition made by the law itself, and partly on the judgment of the respective ecclesiastical superior.[4]

This study does not deal with the rules of judicial procedure. Further, what will be said in the first part of this chapter regarding the judicial interpretation obtains for the authentic interpretation by rescript which issues concerning a particular matter. In the second part of the chapter this rescript will be dealt with specifically.

---

[2] After the "*Sapienti Consilio*" of Pius X and before the promulgation of the Code there is in evidence a division of opinion as to the formal difference between judicial and extra-judicial procedure.—Cf. Monin, *De Curia Romana*, p. 176-185.

[3] "In praxi tamen Sacrae Congregationes plures controversias decidunt via disciplinari, quae per se essent deferendae ad tribunalia; quod multo magis accidit post Codicem, in quo maior rigor divisionis potestatis administrativae a iudiciali per Pium X sancitus non leviter est attenuatus."—Wernz-Vidal, *Ius Canonicum*, (2. ed., Romae: apud Aedes Universitatis Gregorianae, 1928), II, n. 484, III; Chelodi, *Ius de Personis*, n. 161, nota 1.

[4] Coronata, *Institutiones*, I, n. 333.

A. Authentic Interpretation by Judicial Sentence.

ARTICLE I. *Nature of the Judicial Office.*

The legislator of the Code states in effect in canon 17, § 3, that the judge is an authentic interpreter of the law. A judge does not merely apply the law. The application of law demands and presupposes that its meaning be understood. Thus the *Decretum* of Gratian remarks that the ecclesiastical judge interprets legislation; he is the administrator of the law.[5]

That the judge is an authentic interpreter is clearly indicated by the word *"data"* of the present canon, which term indirectly links the judge with canon 17, § 1, and enumerates him as one of those "... cui potestas interpretandi fuerit ab eisdem commissa". Here also is applied the rule of law: That which one can do himself, he can perform by the agency of another; and the complementary rule: Who performs an act by the agency of another is considered to have performed the act himself.[6] Therefore under the Code the judge acts in the capacity of a public minister of the law,[7] for as Pope John XXII says in commissioning certain judges: "... parum esset iura condere, nisi qui ea tueatur existat".[8] Accordingly, canon 1904, §2, prescribes that a *res iudicata,* a matter irrevocably adjudicated, begets law as between the parties to the cause. The law of the Code does not introduce anything new in nam-

[5] "Iudex etiam interpretatur legem . . . ecclesiasticarum legum ecclesiasticus iudex est administrator,"—c. 30, C. XI, q. 1; Reiffenstuel, (lib. I, tit. II, n. 362) says: "Interpretatio necessaria particularis, seu non generalis, est ea, quae fit per iudicem . . . potest Iudex etiam interpretari Leges quoad causas dicendas per eum . . .".

[6] Resp., Reg. 68, 72, R. J., in VIo. Cf. Chapter III, at the beginning.

[7] Chelodi, *Ius de Personis,* n. 67.

[8] C. un., *de iudiciis,* II, 1, in Extravag. com.

ing the judge an authentic interpreter. This fact is already clear from the first and second chapters of this study.

The principle of judicial interpretation as being authentic is enunciated in the law of the Justinian Code *"Cum de novo"*,[9] which contemplates a doubt concerning a new law the meaning of which has not been determined by custom. This law declares that the decision *(suggestio)* of the judge is binding *(necessaria est)* as between the litigants. That the decision is binding or authoritative is apparent from the words of this law, which makes the judicial sentence just as much of obligation as the *interpretatio* of the emperor; both are *necessaria*.[10] Thus the glossator of the law of the Code of Justinian *"Inter aequitatem"* calls the interpretation of the judge *necessaria*. His meaning is clear from the context. While the interpretation of a private doctor is only *probabilis*, the pronouncement of the judiciary is *necessaria tantum*, that is, it is definitive and binding, but only for the one case,[11] whereas the interpretation of the emperor has universal force *(generalis et necessaria)*.[12]

The very same doctrine concerning the judicial office was received into the law of the Decretals from Roman law by the

---

[9] C. (1, 14) 11.

[10] "Si a primo incipias: haec duo sunt necessaria."—*Glossa* ad v. *Tam*, C. (1, 14) 11.

[11] "Sed . . . interpretatio . . . doctoris autem tantum probabilis . . . Necessaria tantum ut iudicis in una causa, quae etiam in scriptis est redigenda" —*Glossa* ad v. *Et ius*, C. (1, 14) 1. Thus Panormitanus (*Commentaria*, lib. I, tit. II, cap. 13, *Quoniam*, n. 6) speaks about the binding force of general interpretation as *necessaria:* ". . . quo ad interpretationem necessariam quae omnes astringit. Nam interpretatio inferioris *non necessitat*" (italics inserted); "Interpretatio necessaria particularis est ea quae fit per iudicem . . . quia . . . partes litigantes necesse habeant eidem obsequi, nisi malint per legitimam appellationem ad Superiorem provocare . . . ea merito vocatur necessaria, . . ." —Reiffenstuel, lib. I, tit. II, n. 362-363.

[12] *Glossa* ad v. *Solis*, C. (1, 14) 1.

glossators.[13] Thus Panormitanus, citing the great canonist, Innocent IV (Sinibaldus Fliscus, +circa 1254), declares that in accord with their judicial oath judges are the interpreters of the law, concerning cases which are brought before their tribunal.[14] In like manner, the Code of Canon Law in canon 17, § 3, grants to the judge the power to bind the litigants to abide by his decision:

> Data [i. e., interpretatio authentica] autem per modum sententiae iudicialis . . . vim legis non habet et ligat tantum personas . . . pro quibus data est.

There is the added provision, however, concerning the *res iudicata*,[15] which will be considered later.

The judge is vested with a public office; for as the law "*Forus*" of the Decretals points out in the words of St. Isidor of Seville (+636), he is called *iudex* because in judging justly he pronounces law to the people.[16] Whereas any private individual can give an admonition, says St. Thomas of Aquin (+1274), only the community or a person in public office is empowered to inflict punishment, to make laws, or in general, to pronounce a judicial sentence.[17] Hence Justinian decreed, as did later Gregory IX in promulgating his Decretals,[18] that

---

[13] "Alia [i. e., interpretatio] non est generalis, sed necessaria, et in scriptis redigenda: ut iudicis, ff. de leg. l. non possunt, arg. l. nam ut ait."—*Glossa* ad v. *Interpretatus*, c. 1, X, *de postulatione praelatorum*, I, 5.

[14] "Item et iudices possunt interpretari iura in causis vertentibus coram se, ut no. Inno. in c. cum speciali. de appe. Facit quod habetur in Authenticum iusiurandum. Quod praestatur ab his."—*Commentaria*, lib. I, tit. II, cap. 13, *Quoniam*, n. 6; *item*, Sylvester Prierias, *Summae Sylvestrinae*, s. v. *Interpretatio*, nn. 1-2.

[15] Cf. cann. 1902, 1904.

[16] "Iudex dicitur quasi ius dicens populo, sive quod iure disceptet. Iure autem disceptare est iuste iudicare."—c. 10, X, *de verborum significatione*, V, 40; Reiffenstuel, lib. I, tit. XXXII, n. 2.

[17] *Summa Theologica*, I, IIae, quaest. 90, Art. III, ad secundum; II, IIae, quaest. 67, Art. I, in corp.

[18] Bull "*Rex pacificus*", 5 sept. 1234.—cf. *Decretalium D. Gregorii Papae IX Compilatio, Prooemium*.

his new body of laws, the Institutes, Digest, and Code, were to be applied by all judges.[19] It appears therefore that the judge is the instrument of the legislator in the matter of applying the law.

ARTICLE II. *Nature of Judicial Interpretation.*

Canon 17, § 3, declares that the vehicle of judicial interpretation is the sentence of the judge. The sentence is the terminus of the trial in the case of the definitive sentence; for toward it tends the entire judicial process.[20] In order to understand wherein consists the authentic interpretation rendered by this agent of the legislator, it is necessary to present a description of the judicial sentence.

1. *Nature of the judicial sentence.*

The judicial sentence is the legitimate, or legal pronouncement whereby the judge defines the cause submitted by the litigants and dealt with according to the rules of judicial procedure. The sentence is called interlocutory when it defines an issue which is incidental to the principal cause of action, to which it has a nexus; such, namely, that it must usually be settled prior to the definition of the principal cause.[21] The

---

[19] Const. "*Tanta*", *De Confirmatione Digestorum*, n. 23.—third document at the beginning of the Digest, (Mommsen-Krueger, 15. ed., Berolini: apud Weidmannos, 1928); "*Cordi nobis*", *De Emendatione Codicis Iustiniani et Secunda Eius Editione.*—third document at the beginning of the *Codex Iustinianus,* (Krueger, 10. ed., Berolini: apud Weidmannos, 1929).

[20] Noval, *Commentarium Codicis Iuris Canonici,* Lib. IV, *De Processibus,* (Augustae Taurinorum—Romae, 1920), n. 618 (cited, *De Processibus*).

[21] Cf. cann. 1837-1839.

sentence is called definitive when it determines the principal question at issue.[22]

As to the intrinsic nature of the judicial sentence, Noval states that it consists in the pronouncement whereby the judge expresses his conviction with moral certitude in favor of one party to the cause rather than the other.[23] In other words, by his sentence the judge expresses what he *thinks,* as Panormitanus says, and thereby puts an end to the controversy.[24] The sentence is the opinion of the judge, which he must follow, declares Felinus Sandaeus, citing the glossator of Gratian's *Decretum,* not the expression of his will. Or, the sentence is the expression of the will of the judge in accord with, or regulated by, the law. His judgment is not arbitrary.[25] He is not a legislator. This thought is born out by Sylvester Prierias (+1523), who states that there is a *sententia iuris,* which represents a statute given by one who has the requisite authority. Thus this *sententia* is, so to say, the mind of the law. The pronouncement of the judge as between the litigants, he continues, citing Goffredus de Trano (+1245) and Tancredus (+circa 1234), is the expression of the mind of a man,[26]

---

22 Can. 1868, § 1.

23 *De Processibus,* n. 619.

24 "Dicitur autem sententia, quia iudex secundum quod sentit, declarat, diffinit et determinat lites et dubia inter partes."—*Commentaria,* lib. II, tit. XXVII *(De sententia et re iudicata,) Rubrica,* n. 4; *item,* Reiffenstuel, lib. II, tit. XXVII, n. 6.

25 "Et dicit glos. 1. in fi. in c. iudicet 3. q. 7. quod iudex tenetur sequi opinionem suam, sed non voluntatem . . . Non eius voluntati mandatur, sed legis authoritati reservatur . . . sententia iudicis est opinio, non voluntas . . . ratione subiectae materiae potest capi pro voluntate iure regulata, sicut per verbum Volumus promulgatur lex . . . Et in evangelio dicitur, omnia quaecumque vultis ut faciant homines, etc. Quod exponitur, id est, velle debetis per rationem non per liberum appetitum . . ."—*Commentaria,* lib. II, tit. XXVII, *Rubrica,* n. 1.

26 "Quaedam enim est sententia iuris . . . statutum . . . Quaedam est sententia hominis, ut quando iudex iudicat inter partes . . . Sententia autem hominis secundum Gofr. et Tanc. est iudicialis definitio . . ."—*Summae Sylvestrinae,* s v. *Sententia,* n. 1.

albeit of one who is vested with public authority, "... qui iure potest iustam cuique decernere et reddere, arg. d. c. forus".[27] Though his pronouncement is the expression of his clear intent or meaning *(intentio)*,[28] he must set aside any preoccupation of affection or aversion, says Gratian (+before 1179) together with his glossator in the words of St. Ambrose (+397), and render his decision according to the law, the allegations, and the nature of the matter before him.[29] In other words, the judge is moved from without, so that his sentence represents, Hostiensis (+1273) points out, the "... rei aptae ... in dubium versae ... iudicialis et diffinitiva humana veritas declarata"; for he does not inject anything, as it were, of his own initiative, but states that which exists.[30] The decision is received by men as truth, hence the expression, *"humana veritas"*. For as appears from the context, Hostiensis is speaking of the *res iudicata* with the rule of Roman law in mind: "Res iudicata pro veritate accipitur".[31] Briefly, the judge pronounces as he sees the given case,[31a] or a concatenation of events and circumstances in fact and before the law. It appears therefore from the foregoing description that the judicial sentence is the precipitate which results from the merging of

---

[27] *Op. cit.*, s. v. *Iudex* I, in prin.

[28] Petrus de Ancharano (+1416), *Consilia sive Iuris Responsa*, (Venetiis, 1574), Consil. XVI, n. 2.

[29] "... non obediat tunc propriae voluntati; sed secundum leges et sicut audit et natura negotii se habet, decernere debet et iudicare"—*Glossa* ad v. *Iudicet ille*, c. 4, C. III, q. 7; "Non enim secundum conscientiam simpliciter iudicare debet, sed informare eam secundum allegata et probata."—*Glossa* ad v. *Et contra*, c. l, *de sententia et re iudicata*, I, 14, in VIo.

[30] "Declarata, iudex enim nil intelligitur dare, sed quod est declarare."—*Summa Aurea*, lib. II, *De Sententia, Rubrica*, n. 1.

[31] D. (50, 17) 207; cf. can. 1904, § 1.

[31a] "Et ita est causa antequam respondeat pars altera. Est ergo causa res in dicendo posita cum interpositione certarum personarum, scilicet, actoris et rei, iudicis et testis. Et ideo dicitur a casu; quia frequenter casualiter occurrunt praeter voluntatem hominis."—*Glossa* ad v. *Causa a casu*, c. 10, X, *de verborum significatione*, V, 40.

fact and law. Accordingly, the judge does not make legislation as such. He effects an application of law to a particular set of facts, which is received as law for that case.[32]

The details described above from pre-Code jurisprudence are reflected in the law of the Code relative to the judicial sentence, which will now be considered in its external form as a point of departure. In this external form [33] seems more clearly perceptible the formal element of authentic interpretation which the judge contributes at the close of the process when he renders the definitive sentence.

The judicial sentence in its external solemnities includes the invocation of the divine name, the listing of the principals in the case, a brief history thereof together with the claims of the parties. The canon then prescribes that there shall follow the dispositive part of the sentence prefaced by the enumeration both in fact and in law [34] of the motives whereon is based this dispositive part of the sentence. This dispositive portion of the judicial sentence is the nucleus of the first part of this chapter. The sentence closes with the prescribed date, place, and signatures. The present description obtains alike for the definitive and the interlocutory sentence.[35] Here it is applied principally to the definitive sentence.[36]

---

[32] *Summa Theologica,* I, IIae, quaest. 96, Art. I, in corp et ad primum: ". . . Philosophus ponit tres species iuris legalis quod est ius positivum. Sunt enim quaedam quae simpliciter in communi ponuntur; et haec sunt leges communes . . . Dicuntur etiam quaedam legalia, non quia sint leges, sed propter applicationem legum communium ad aliqua particularia facta, sicut sunt sententiae, quae pro iure habentur; et quantum ad hoc subdit: Et sententialia."

[33] Cf. can. 1874.

[34] Can. 1873, 3°.

[35] Can. 1875.

[36] The interlocutory sentence can have definitive force: "Sententia autem interlocutoria habet vim definitivae quando licet directe non definiat meritum causae, tamen praeiudicat causae in merito, ita ut institutum iudicium quodammodo perimat; nec alia sententia in eodem iudicio sperari possit. Ita ex. gr., si iudex sententia sua adprobet exceptionem peremptoriam; . . ."—Santi, *Prae-*

The definitive sentence of the judge must determine, that is, terminate, the principal issue—there may be several [37]—as established between the parties;[38] that is, on the part of the judge this sentence must terminate the controversy [39] in a practical,[40] concrete manner; such, namely, is the function of the judicial power as an essential complement of the legislative authority in a perfect society.[41]

It has been stated that on the part of the judge the sentence must terminate the controversy because, first of all, the sentence must be certain and definite as to its object and absolute, not conditional, otherwise there is actually no sentence;[42] the controversy is not solved by the judge. The sentence therefore (whether definitive or interlocutory) must represent an unqualified, apodictic statement as to its object. The very point in this discussion is that if the sentence is not

---

lectiones Iuris Canonici, lib. II, tit. XXVII, n. 3. The *res iudicata* is a peremptory exception.—cf. can. 1629, § 1.

[37] Cf. can. 1669, § 1.

[38] Cann. 1873, § 1, 1°, 1552, § 1, 1726-1728; "Iudex proinde ad hoc attendere debet, nempe ut controversiam propositam dirimat . . . Ad hoc tendit tota iudicialis procedura ad lites nempe evitandas aut sopiendas determinando iura partium litigantium; . . ."—Coronata, *Institutiones,* III, n. 1403; "Sententia diffinitiva est diffinitio iudicialis, controversiae finem imponens, ex pronuntiatione Iudicis damnationem vel absolutionem continens."—Reiffenstuel, lib. II, tit. XXVII, n. 9.

[39] Santi, *Praelectiones,* lib. II, tit. XXVII, n. 2.

[40] Cf. can. 1873, 2°.

[41] Noval, *De Processibus,* n. 43; Ottaviani, *Institutiones Iuris Publici Ecclesiastici,* I, nn. 46-48.

[42] Cf. Wernz, *Ius Decretalium,* V, n. 668, nota 32; Santi, *Praelectiones,* lib. II, tit. XXVII, n. 10; "Inprimis autem sententia, ut eius sit controversiae finem imponere, generalis et absoluta esse debet . . . nulla adiecta conditione, quae ulteriorem disceptationem postulet; adeoque nullius momenti sententia est, qua iudex pronuntiaret Titium ex. gr., non teneri mutuum restituere, eumque a restitutione absolvere, si probaverit pactum de non petendo intercessisse. Enimvero haec sententia controversiam non dirimit, cum adhuc incertum sit, utrum actori, an reo causa adiudicetur."—Vecchiotti, *Institutiones Canonicae,* (Augustae Taurinorum, 1875), II, 308-309.

properly formulated, there is no authentic interpretation. Secondly, it is only on the part of the judge that the controversy is terminated because there usually remains to the parties the right of appeal.[43]

With these preliminary observations the immediate antecedents of the judicial pronouncement will now be considered in preparation to discerning the formal element of the sentence and consequently of authentic interpretation.

2. *Immediate antecedents of the judicial sentence.*

It is prescribed in canon 1874, § 4, that the dispositive part of the sentence shall be prefaced by the motives (reasons) upon which it is based. These reasons are known as the motives in law and in fact,[44] which will now be considered.

The law of the Code directs that for the pronouncement of any sentence the judge must have moral certitude concerning the matter to be adjudicated and must derive his information from the acts of the process and the proofs.[45] This law is a restatement of decretal legislation, which declares that the judge, weighing all things with an unbiased mind, as Innocent IV demands,[46] must apply his mind to all the proofs and allegations which are brought before him, whereby he shall dispose himself *(formet animi sui motum)*,[47] in order to formulate the sentence.[48] Hence the *terminus a quo* or the source of the judicial sentence are the allegations and proofs, where-

[43] Cf. cann. 1879-1880.

[44] Can. 1873, § 1, 3°.

[45] Can. 1869, §§ 1-2.

[46] ". . . iudices . . . stateram gestent in manibus, lances appendant aequo libramine ut in omnibus quae in causis agenda fuerint, praesertim in concipiendis sententiis et ferendis, prae oculis habeant solum Deum . . ."—c. 1, *de sententia et re iudicata*, II, 14, in VIo.

[47] C. 6, X, *de renunciatione*, I, 9.

[48] "Papa vero . . . dicit quod iudex . . . omnia debet considerare quae

with the judge informs his mind.[49] Hence these allegations and proofs are the source material for his authentic interpretation. He will therefore consider the alleged law or laws,[50] according to which he must judge,[51] not perforce of precedents, as will be seen later. The judge will also weigh the proofs,[52] objectively as they lie before him.[53] For in fashioning a judgment truth is a fundamental requisite.[54] Hence, as Reiffenstuel declares, the approach to the law in the formation of a judicial sentence on the part of an inferior is entirely different from that employed by the legislator in rendering a general interpretation of the law of his predecessor. The latter does not need to seek the original intent of his predecessor as it is revealed in the law; he simply declares in what meaning the law is to be received. The judge and the doctor must endeavor to seek out this original meaning.[55]

---

fiunt in eius praesentia, et ex his informare debet motum animi sui et formare sententiam."—*Glossa* ad *Casus,* c. 6, X, *de renunciatione,* I, 9.

[49] "Non enim secundum conscientiam simpliciter iudicare debet, sed informare debet [iudex] eam secundum allegata et probata."—*Glossa* ad v. *Et contra,* c. 1, *de sententia et re iudicata,* II, 14 in VIo.

[50] Cann. 1873, § 1, 1°, 1708, 1-2°.

[51] "Bonus iudex nichil ex arbitrio suo facit, . . . sed iuxta leges et iura pronunciat, scitis iuris, obtemperat . . . Qui iudicat non voluntati suae obtemperare debet, sed tenere quod legum est."—c. 4, C. III, q. 7 (Ambrosius super *Beati immaculati,* sermo XX, ad vers. "*Miserationes tuae, Domine*".); S. Thomas, *Summa Theologica,* II, IIae, quaest. 67, Art II, in corp; Suarez, *De Legibus,* I, cap. 3, n. 8; Reiffenstuel, lib. I, tit. XXXII, nn. 7, 25, 32-33; Wernz, *Ius Decretalium,* V, n. 666.

[52] Can. 1869, § 3.

[53] "Bonus iudex . . . nichil paratum et meditatum de domo deferat, sed sicut audit, ita iudicat et sicut se habet natura, decernit; obsequitur legibus, non adversatur, examinat causae merita, non mutat."—c. 4, C. III, q. 7 (Ambrosius super *Beati immaculati,* sermo XX, ad vers. "*Miserationes tuae, Domine*"); c. 1, *de sententia et re iudicata,* II, 14, in VIo.

[54] "In iudicando cordi magis est custodia veritatis quam obedientia voluntatis."—c. 4, C. III, q. 7.

[55] *Ius Canonicum Universum,* lib. I, tit. II, n. 382.

It is necessary in the following exposition to make a number of observations regarding each of these immediate objects of the judicial sentence.

A. Motives in law.

This portion of the present discussion is devoted to the motives in law with reference to the pronouncement of the judicial decision; for the judge is not a source of legislation, as appears from the previous consideration of his position with reference to the law. He is the servant of the law inasmuch as he adjudicates to a given party his right, his *ius*, which he determines according to the prescripts of the *lex*.[56] The judge is the living mouthpiece of the law.[57] Consequently, he must be well conversant with its provisions.[58] He must be able to apply the rules of doctrinal interpretation[59] and the rules of the so-called "suppletory law";[60] in difficult situations it is necessary for him to seek expert advice.[61] For the judge may not simply follow what he supposes to be the meaning of the

---

[56] "Iudex ius non creat, sed partibus adiudicat; debet proinde leges et facta perpendere ad cognoscendum utri parti ius lex agnoscat aut concedat."—Coronata, *Institutiones,* III, n. 1396.

[57] Reiffenstuel, lib. I, tit. XXXII, n. 25.

[58] Cann. 1573, § 4, 1574, § 1; Reiffenstuel, lib. I, tit. XXXII, n. 6. This study cannot proceed further into the qualifications of the judge. Also, closely akin to the present study at this point is the question of internal defects in the sentence in the face of clear law, which likewise cannot be treated here. Cf. e. g., Wernz, *Ius Decretalium,* V, n. 666; Santi, *Praelectiones,* lib. II, tit. XXVII, n. 7; Coronata, *Institutiones,* III, nn. 1394, 1403; Wernz-Vidal, *Ius Canonicum,* (Romae: apud Aedes Universitatis Gregorianae, 1927), VI, n. 592. Or, procedural defects. Cf. cann. 1892, 1894.

[59] Cann. 6, 2-3°, 18, 19, 2219; §§ 1, 3; Van Hove, *De Legibus Ecclesiasticis,* n. 241.

[60] Can. 20; Wernz-Vidal, *Ius Canonicum,* VI, n. 590.

[61] Cf. can. 1575; Reiffenstuel, lib. I, tit. XXVII, nn. 6, 59; Wernz, *Ius Decretalium,* V, n. 663.

law, giving it a merely lexicographic interpretation[62] and thus formulate his sentence.[63]

It is apparent that the judge must address the law alleged in court[64] from the viewpoint of its meaning *in se*, or in the abstract. In other words, he approaches the law from the standpoint of doctrinal interpretation,[65] considering, weighing, the meaning of the law,[66] because he must respond to the *allegationes iuris* in his sentence.[67]

In executing this portion of his office, the judge is most certainly not acting as authentic interpreter. Why? Because he is not here pronouncing sentence; canon 17, § 3, reads: "*Data autem per modum sententiae iudicialis* . . .". This discussion has not yet progressed to the formal element of the judicial sentence. It is clear that a given law in the abstract and in its general scope has one, sole, meaning. In order that the judge could interpret authentically this meaning, he would have to be the authentic interpreter of canon 17, § 2, which he is not.

a°. Interpretation in case of doubt.

The question here arises whether the judge may proceed to formulate his decision in view of what is considered a doubt-

62 "Et nemo in actionibus vel iudiciis ecclesiasticis suo sensu sed eorum [canonum statutorum] auctoritate ducatur."—c. 1, X *de constitutionibus*, I, 2.

63 ". . . id est de opinione animae, nemo enim ex suo capite debet formare sententiam, sed secundum quod ius dictat, alioquin non esset minister legis." —Baldus de Ubaldis, *Commentaria*, lib. I, tit. II, cap. primum, *Canonum*, n. 16.

64 Cf. cann. 1708, 2°, 1728. ". . . notandum est, quod per Probationes Iuris intelligantur allegationes textuum Iuris, seu Legum, una cum rationibus, Authorumque citationibus"—Reiffenstuel, lib. I, tit. XXVII, n. 57.

65 Cf. e. g., any Rotal Decision at the place styled *In iure*.

66 C. 1, *de sententia et re iudicata*, II, 14, in VIo; Coronata, *Institutiones*, III, n. 1396.

67 Can. 1873, § 1, 1°, 3°.

ful law; such, namely, about which there is a dispute among the authors.

It may here be stated that there is no authentic norm concerning the existence of a *dubium iuris,* except an authentic pronouncement expressly stating this fact. The disagreement of authors on a point of law does not mean *per se* that they agree that the law is doubtful. Their unanimous agreement on any point concerning the law begets moral certitude; where they disagree, there is probability.[68] Yet even their common opinion does not have the force of law.[69]

Reiffenstuel points out that in ancient times *(antiquitus)* inferior judges, e. g., Bishops, referred to the Pope their doubts of law concerning a pending case by means of the *relatio* or *consultatio,*[70] but that with the development of Roman and Canon law this practice *(usus)* has fallen into desuetude.[71]

---

[68] "Ubi doctores omnes conspirant faciunt moralem certitudinem: ubi discrepant, probabilitatem."—Pichler, lib. I, tit. II, n. 72.

[69] Van Hove, *Prolegomena,* n. 51; Reiffenstuel, lib. I, tit. II, n. 364: "Tandem Interpretatio non necessaria, seu mere probabilis ac doctoralis . . . est illa, quae a Magistris seu Doctoribus dari potest et solet . . . Et haec probabilitatem dumtaxat affert, non autem necessitatem: unde huic necessario inhaerendum non est, nisi concurrat communis Doctorum consensus, aut alia meliora Iuris fundamenta non suppetant. Alioquin attendere oportet ad illud Imperatoris effatum, quo L. 1. §. *Sed neque C. de Veteri iure enucleand.* refertur illis verbis: *Sed neque ex multitudine Authorum, quod melius, et aequius est, iudicatote; cum possit unius forsan, et deterioris sententia et multos et maiores in aliqua parte superare.*"

[70] Cf. c. 68, X, *de appellationibus,* II, 28.

[71] *Ius Canonicum Universum,* lib. I, tit. XXXII, n. 5; Coronata, *Institutiones,* III, n. 1399; Vidal (Wernz-Vidal, *Ius Canonicum,* VI, n. 590), who gives the same information, says also that this procedure of referring to the Roman Pontiff such matters was of obligation on the principle "eius est interpretari cuius est condere" (making reference to C. (1, 14) 12, the principle of authentic interpretation) when the law was actually doubtful, because the judge was considered incapable of proceeding. He seems to have no authority for this statement. Panormitanus (*Commentaria,* lib. II, tit. XXVIII, cap. LXVIII, in prin.), who usually says nearly all that there is to say, knows nothing of such obligation in judicial procedure, though plainly he says that

Justinian commanded the judges never, under any condition, to refer their judicial matters to the Emperor, but to render judgment according to justice and law.[72] He adds that the aggrieved party could thereafter appeal. His purpose was to obviate long litigation. Hence in the law of the Code *"Cum de novo"* [73] the legislator commands that in case of a dubious law the pronouncement of the judge is *necessaria.* Bartolus, citing this law of the Justinian Code, declares that when there appears during a judicial process a doubt of law, the meaning of which has not been firmly established in the past,[74] one proceeds on the principle of similar instances *(de simili ad similia)* where there is an identical reason; otherwise recourse must be had to the legislator.[75] Thus it would appear from Bartolus' citation of the law *"Non possunt"* [76] in conjunction

---

such an appeal can be made if so desired: "Si iudex de iure dubitans *vult* (italics inserted) consulere superiorem . . .", adding that the appeal of the judge will be rejected unless he allows the parties to assist at the concordance of the *dubium* which is submitted. This much is also plain from c. 68, X, *de appellationibus,* II, 28.

[72] "Iubemus . . . nullum iudicum ullo modo aut tempore in causis apud eos propositis ad nostram serenitatem rem deferre, sed perfecte examinare causam et quod sibi iustum atque legitimum visum sit iudicare."—N. (125, 1). The glossator of this novel, of a much later time, of course, allows recourse in case of a doubt of law.

[73] C. (1, 14) 11. Cf. Chapter I, Art. III

[74] "Minime sunt mutanda, quae interpretationem certam semper habuerunt"—D. (1, 3) 23.

[75] "Si aut emergit dubium super legem . . . infra e. l. minime aut apparet una significatio verborum aut certa aut multiplex et incerta . . . Secundo casu aut apparet quod sit benignior intellectus aut non. Primo casu illum sequimur. Secundo casu aut apparet aliquid simile habens identitatem rationis aut non. Primo casu procedimus de simili ad similia ut d. l. non possunt. Secundo casu recurrimus ad Principem ut l. humanum et l. cum de novo. Et ibi no. C. eo. Et hoc obtinet quando emergunt dubietates in iudicio."—*Commentaria,* D. (1, 3) 9 [10] (Titulus: *De legibus et senatus consultis*), n. 5.

[76] "Non possunt omnes articuli singillatim aut legibus aut senatus consultis comprehendi: sed cum in aliqua causa sententia eorum manifesta est, is qui iurisdictioni praeest ad similia procedere atque ita ius dicere debet."—D. (1, 3) 12.

with *"Cum de novo"* that the judge is conceded the power to pronounce judgment in the presence of controverted law. This conclusion seems further borne out by the fact that this jurist allows a matter which is new, a *novum negotium*, and concerning which there is doubt, to be referred, according to the law of the Digest *"Et ideo"*,[77] to the interpretation of the judge, who is to decide whether by custom there exists an interpretation ". . . in simili casu", which similar case has already been established by a certain interpretation in virtue of the law *"Minime"*, which is quoted immediately above in this study.[78] Hence again there is the deduction or procedure by judicial interpretation *de simili ad similia*. Only if such a process cannot be effected is recourse had to the *princeps*.[79]

It appears therefore that the antecedents of the judicial decision are rooted in doctrinal interpretation. Hence the judge must follow canons 18 and 19 and pronounce judgment accordingly when the law is clear, that is, when there is no question that the object or the fact at issue falls under a law interpreted according to their provisions. However, the Code at once provides for the case where the law appears undetermined in the presence of a determined set of facts which are placed before the judge. Thus, canon 20 reads: *"Si certa de re desit expressum praescriptum legis sive generalis sive particularis,"* etc. In this instance there may be a doubt of law, but the judge may proceed in view of canon 20.[80] Certainly,

---

77 "Et ideo de his, quae primo constituuntur, aut interpretatione aut constitutione optimi principis certius statuendum est."—D. (1, 3) 11.

78 D. (1, 3) 23.

79 "Dic aut super negotio novo est varietas, seu dubietas, aut super veteri. Primo casu recurrimus ad iudicis interpretationem ut infra eod. l, et ideo iudex inspiciat, si consuetudo unquam in simili casu sit interpretata, ut infra e. l. minime. Si hoc non appareat ad Principem recurretur, ut hic dicitur, sive sit de propinquo, sive de longinquo."—*Commentaria*, D. (1, 3) 9 [10] (Titulus: *De legibus et senatusconsultis*), n. 5.

80 Wernz-Vidal, *Ius Canonicum*, VI, n. 590. Lega-Bartoccetti, *Commen-*

where there is, perchance, a doubt of law, it can truly be said that there is at hand no express prescript of law. In fact, the judge must proceed to give his interpretation—*norma sumenda est;* and he proceeds as an authentic interpreter in the particular case.[81]

Over and above the fact that canon 20 is to be used where the law appears wanting with reference to a particular, concrete case, Michiels also allows this canon to operate in formally supplying a deficiency in a given law as such, taken in the abstract.[82] Thus canon 20 will supply also the deficiency which is inherent in a doubtful law.[83] However, the norm of Michiels seems to grant to the judge the power of establishing a legal precedent.[84] Van Hove understands Michiels' doctrine in this sense. While Van Hove admits readily that canon 20 will operate directly to supply a formal defect in the law, the norm of canon 20 is and remains for him a medium to be used in expediting individual matters; thus he correctly rejects the doctrine of Michiels to this extent. In other words, supplying a defect in a piece of legislation as far as formulating a general norm is concerned is a matter which rests with the legislator.[85] The present occasion may be taken to point out that

---

iurius in Iudicia Ecclesiastica, (Romae: Anonima Libraria Cattolica Italiana, 1939), II, 936.

81 Michiels, *Normae Generales,* I, 460.

82 ". . . non videmus tamen cur norma suppletiva, per recursum ad media canonis 20 inventa, non haberi possit ut norma, *omnes casus eiusdem speciei* iam in actu primo, ut ita dicam, et in abstracto solvere nata, eodem omnino modo ac ipsa lex formalis expressa deficiens, si adesset."—*Normae Generales,* I, 460.

83 "Deficiente lege clara, nam lex dubia est lex nulla, saepius si agitur de facultate exercenda aut de iuribus mutuis ordinandis, supplendum erit silentio legis."—Van Hove, *De Legibus Ecclesiasticis,* n. 312.

84 Cf. *op. cit.,* 461.

85 ". . . quod norma desumenda est 'a legibus latis in similibus', id est in similibus materiis . . . ex una parte lacuna legis occurens in casu particulari necessario recurrit in omnibus casibus identicis, ex alia parte si res dirimitur

this norm is applicable just as well in administrative jurisdiction.

Neither Canon law nor Roman law knows the doctrine of precedent for inferior judges, as this study reveals. (This question will be taken up in the following and in the last article of this chapter).[85a] This doctrine is expressly excluded in canon 17, § 3: "... ligat *tantum* personas et afficit res pro quibus data est". Canonical tradition has held to the rule that the sentence of an inferior judge is *necessaria tantum,* and not *necessaria et generalis.*

The situation envisioned in canon 20 is not a strange one. The enduring jurisprudence of Roman law appreciated the fact that no legislator can contemplate within the ambit of his law all individual items which conspire to form the woof and warp of human activity.[86] Here must be pointed out clearly what is implied in the foregoing concerning the application of the first portion of canon 20. Namely, that a law may be deficient in two ways: formally and materially. A formal defect is here understood as the absence of that which ought to be present, that is, the absence of clarity, certainty, in the law. A material defect, the absence of a norm which, if present, would determine a given concrete case. Certainly it cannot be said that because a law does not provide for all things it is therefore formally, or internally, deficient. This statement rests on the principle of Roman law just mentioned. In either

---

authentice per sententiam iudiciariam vel per viam administrationis, solutio tantum ligat personas et afficit personas [*sic*] pro quibus data est. Etiamsi Codex contemplaret materiam [i. e., legis], non casum, ex eo deduci non posset ex suppletione legi in casu particulari oriri ius quoddam obligatorie omnibus casibus similibus applicandum, ut vult G. Michiels."—*De Legibus Ecclesiasticis,* n. 312; cf. etiam, n. 314.

[85a] Cf. pp. 244-246; 248-249; 274; 279.

[86] "Neque leges neque senatus consulta ita scribi possunt ut omnes casus qui quandoque inciderint comprehendantur, sed sufficit ea quae plerumque accidunt continere."—D. (1, 3) 10; cf. etiam, D. (1, 3) 12, quoted above.

case of deficiency there is question of the *materia legis* (the subject matter of the law) referred to above in the quotation from Van Hove. The former defect (formal) is an *indigentia;* the latter (material), a *carentia.* Thus the phrase in canon 20: "Si certa de re . . ." has reference to a formal or a material defect in the law.[87] This statement would seem to be confirmed by the use of the word *"desit"* in the present canon, considering the principle, "verba generalia generaliter sunt intelligenda." [88] The judge in virtue of canon 20 has therefore the power to take cognizance of a case whether the law is formally or materially defective.[89]

The legislator of the Code has empowered the judge (and even private interpreters) [90] to invoke for the solution of his case such law as disposes matters which are similar to his case [91] in virtue of a parity of reasoning, so that, as Pichler (+1736) very appropriately says, there is here the application of the juristic axiom: Cases similar to that expressed in the law are not to be considered as having been omitted from

---

[87] Cf. Michiels and Van Hove, quoted above, pp. 239-240.

[88] Hence Van Hove (*De Legib. Eccl.*, n. 312) states: "Controversia orta est circa significationem verborum, 'certa de re', utrum intelligenda sint: in casu particulari, ut vult S. d'Angelo, an in materia determinata, ut vult G. Michiels, eo vel magis quod norma desumenda est 'a legibus latis in similibus', id est in similibus materiis. Opinemur rem esse nullius momenti, quia ex una parte . . ." (cf. context as quoted above).

[89] Van Hove (*op. cit.*, n. 312) advises: "Sunt materiae de quibus legislator positive noluit disponere. Si agitur de obligatione aliquid faciendi aut ab actu abstinendi, frequentius standum erit libertati, cum de existentia praecepti aut prohibitionis non constat". The reader will readily appreciate the fact that it is impossible to digress further into can. 20. For added particulars refer to Van Hove, *De Legibus Ecclesiasticis*, n. 312; Michiels, *Normae Generales*, I, 454; Cicognani, *Canon Law*, p. 620; et al., especially the pre-Code authors referred to below.

[90] Van Hove, *De Legibus Ecclesiasticis*, n. 314.

[91] ". . . norma sumenda est, nisi agatur de poenis applicandis a legibus latis in similibus; . . ."—can. 20.

its provision.[92] Therefore, the judge in formulating his judicial decision authentically extends the law (or restricts it) by interpretation. As Pichler points out, he is proceeding in accord with principles derived from Roman law, as will be more clearly apparent in the following. Thus an aggregate of circumstances such as is envisioned in the law *"Neque leges"* [93] may concur in a particular case and engender doubt concerning the law, though the law as such is not doubtful—apparently a new case.[94] In the present supposition, of course, there is no actual *dubium iuris,* for the law is supposed as clear, taken alone and apart; namely, that it does not have a variant or unclear signification. If a deficiency in cognition is to

[92] "Dico 2 Per interpretationem possunt quidem et debent Iudices in iudicando extendere Legem ad casus similes ubi reperitur par ratio, seu paritas rationis; privatis hominibus id regulariter non licet. Prior pars patet ex l. 1, 10, 12, 13 ff. de LL. Ubi redditur haec ratio; quia non possunt omnes casus et articuli singillatim exprimi in legibus; ergo, cum Iudices debeant omnes casus et causas decidere, debent a casu simili, qui exprimitur in Iure vel a paritate rationis iuvari et extendere Legem posse ad casum, quem prae manibus habent. Concordat c. 3, h. t. Unde natum est hoc axioma; casus similis expresso a Lege non censetur omissus."—*Ius Canonicum,* (Ingolstadii, 1728), lib. I, tit. II, n. 75. This principal is found in the decretal law *"Translato,"* (c. 3, X, *de constitutionibus,* I, 2) in conjunction with its gloss: ". . . quod de uno dicitur: necesse est ut de altero intelligatur." *Glossa* ad v. *Quod de uno:* "Arg. quod ubi est eadem ratio, ibi debet esse idem ius, et quod de similibus idem iudicium est habendum . . . Et quando dicit, quod de uno dicitur, id est, quod de uno constitutum est; et sic facit ad titulum . . ." In canon 20 seems to be represented the "quasi" extensive and restrictive interpretation mentioned in the Preliminary Observations in the previous chapter. Cf. Chapter VII, Art. II, A; Van Hove, *De Legibus Eccl.,* n. 316.

[93] D. (1, 3) 10, quoted above, p. 240.

[94] ". . . nam variae sunt factorum circumstantiae quae rationem legis variant. Ideoque sufficit, si regula plerumque procedat. Quare si novus casus emergat, ad quem lex accommodari ob suam rationem vix potest, Princeps statuet de casu novo. Interdum vero non opus est, ut Princeps consulatur; sed iudex rationem legis restringere vel extendere potest prout materia vel odiosa vel favorabilis est."—Brunnemannus, *Commentarius in Pandectas,* (*Coloniae Allobrogum, 1762*) lib. I, tit. III, *De Legibus, etc., Ad L. neque leges 10 et. seqq. tres,* nn. 1-2. "Dubium potest provenire vel quia lex est obscura, dubia, vel quia lex in se certa, dubitatur utrum rei controversae applicetur."—Lega-Bartoccetti, *Commentarius in Iudicia Ecclesiastica,* II, 936.

be imputed at all, it seems that it would consist *prima facie* in a state of nescience as to the mutual relation between the stipulated group of circumstances and the law, rather than in the ignorance of law or of the facts, for the very reason that the legislator himself admits that no one can foresee all contingencies. Again, the fact that there can be appeal upon appeal is sufficient guarantee to suggest that the adjudication of law and facts combined becomes an intricate matter at times. Hence Baldus de Ubaldis, citing Bartolus, says concerning the adjudication of a judicial case that "interpretatio est dubii casus decisio".[95] In other words, there is here the matter of the *dubium practicum* taken in a legal sense; namely, a doubt which concerns itself with an act or a juridic fact, not in the abstract, but one to be determined and regulated here and now,[96] that is, under these practical circumstances.

Moreover, together with the present rule of canon 20 there are the remaining norms of the canon, which are so many means at the disposal of the judge (or the ecclesiastical superior in administrative jurisdiction) of formulating authentically a decision to terminate the issue.[97] According to the law of the Code, however, this process of authentic interpretation is not permissible in the case of inflicting penalties, and here a benign interpretation must always be followed.[98] However, there is nothing to prevent the creation of a penalty by judicial authority on the basis of canon 2222, § 1.

---

95 *Commentaria,* lib. I, tit. II, cap. primum, *Canonum,* nn. 57-58.

96 Distinguitur dubium speculativum et practicum, prout actionem eiusque liceitatem in genere et in abstracto considerat, aut de actione, sitne hic et nunc ponenda, versatur."—Lehmkuhl, *Theologia Moralis,* (6. ed., Friburgi Brisgoviae, 1890), I, n. 47; E. g., the declaration of a controverted *factum iuridicum* (can. 1552, § 2, 1°), cf. c. 13, X, *de sententia et re iudicata,* II, 27; Coronata, *Institutiones,* III, n. 1089.

97 Van Hove, *De Legibus Ecclesiasticis,* n. 314.

98 Cann. 20, 2219, §§ 1, 3.

From what has been said it appears that under such circumstances as just described or suggested the judge, as Baldus de Baldis states, succeeds to the power and position of the legislator with respect to the case before his tribunal; namely, when the law is not determined with respect to that case.[99] This doctrine is propounded today by Van Hove (not citing Baldus), who appeals to the common opinion of jurists and confirms what was mentioned above; namely, that the judge must proceed (whether the law itself is controverted or the case as such is dubious) to formulate, to invent, a decision according to the norms of canon 20—*regula sumenda est*. Hence he actually constitutes authentically a *ius novum*, but only for the given case.[100]

In this last particular Canon law and Roman (Justinian) law differ from other legal systems.[101] The creation of the

---

99 "Caveant tamen iudices ne eligant opinionem quae minus habet rationis. Iudex succedit loco legis et vocatur princeps et ideo in non determinatis a lege habet arbitrium simile rebus determinatis . . . Excusantur autem si sequuntur opinionem communem, nisi notorie sit irrationabilis, seu falsa secundum Hostiensem quod tene menti."—*Commentaria*, lib. I, tit. II, cap. primum, *Canonum*, nn. 33-34.

100 "Sed cum in omni hypothesi deficiat regula iuris normativa, admittendum videtur iudicem et illum cui agnoscitur potestas authentice in casu particulari rem dirimendi, verum ius novum inducere, sed in casu tantum applicandum . . . Huic doctrinae favere videntur verba Codicis: 'norma sumenda est', et opinio communior iuristarum. Ius imponit iudici obligationem decidendi litem eique potestatem necessariam concedit ad illam finiendam, etiam in silentio legis."—*De Legibus Ecclesiasticis*, n. 314.

101 "A process of judicial lawmaking has always gone on and still goes on in all systems of law . . . the courts, willing or unwilling, must to some extent make the law under the guise of interpretation."—Pound, *The Spirit of the Common Law*, (Boston: Marshall Jones Co., 1931), pp. 172, 174; "Case law in England . . . As Sir Henry Maine has shown, an English judge never admits that he is making law; he is merely applying known rules to different sets of circumstances; but whenever he determines a case to which no existing custom, statute, or precedent applies, he creates a new precedent which, save in the comparatively rare case of reversal on appeal, will be followed by other judges in the like circumstances, and so form new law."—Leage, *Roman Pri-*

judge is *ius novum* because he is dealing with law outside the proper signification of the legal terminology.[102] This consideration serves to suggest why his decision should not be used as a precedent. He is outside the common law. Moreover, as the law of Justinian plainly states, he could have erred in making his decision.[103] There is the further consideration precisely in the domain of ecclesiastical law, namely that ecclesiastical law cannot spring dynamically from the people.[104]

That the ecclesiastical judge lawfully proceeds in the manner indicated and in the presence of situations at law such as are outlined above is sustained by canonical tradition. Furthermore, this tradition at the same time claims for the judge a decision which is *necessaria,* but *necessaria tantum;* that is to say, his decision establishes no binding precedent.

The *glossa ordinaria* of the law of the decretals *"Ad haec in beato"* [105] is the chief place referred to generally by commentators on decretal legislation to demonstrate the existence and extent of the judicial power of one inferior to the *princeps* or the Sovereign Pontiff. As distinguished from the interpretation of the head of society, which is *generalis et necessaria,* there is the interpretation which is not general, but which is *necessaria,* binding, which is that given by the judge.[106] At the same time this gloss describes the material

---

vate Law, (2. ed., C. H. Ziegler, London: MacMillan and Co., Ltd., 1937), p. 29.

[102] Cf. cann. 18, 19.

[103] ". . . non enim, si quid non bene dirimatur, hoc et in aliorum iudicum vitium extendi oportet, cum non exemplis, sed legibus iudicandum est . . ."—C. (7, 45) 13.

[104] Cf. cann. 25, 29.

[105] C. 1, X, *de postulatione praelatorum,* I, 5.

[106] As to the principle in the domain of Roman (Justinian) law, cf. Chapter I, Artt. I, III, IV.

power of the judiciary in terms of the law of the Digest *"Non possunt"* [107] and *"Nam ut ait"*.[108]

It will be remembered from the foregoing that Bartolus (+1357) uses *"Non possunt"* to show that the judge has authority to adjudicate a matter by the process of interpretation, by proceeding *de simili ad similia* as heretofore described. Accordingly, Accursius (+1260) declares concerning the law *"Nam ut ait"* that this procedure by analogy,[109] whereby the deficiency in the law is supplied,[110] is effected by the jurisdiction of the *princeps* and the interpretation of the judge, whether the issue has respect to a new case *(novum negotium)* or directly concerns a point of law *(super lege aliqua)*.[111]

---

107 "Non possunt omnes articuli singillatim aut legibus aut senatus consultis comprehendi: sed cum in aliqua causa sententia eorum manifesta est, is qui iurisdictioni praeest ad similia procedere atque ita ius dicere debet."—D. (1, 3) 12.

108 "Alia [interpretatio] non est generalis, sed necessaria, et in scriptis redigenda: ut iudicis, ff. de leg. l. non possunt, arg. l. nam ut ait."—*Glossa* ad v. *Interpretatus*. "Nam, ut ait Pedius, quotiens lege aliquid unum vel alterum introductum est, bona occasio est cetera, quae tendunt ad eandem utilitatem, vel interpretatione vel certe iurisdictione suppleri."—D. (1, 3) 13.

109 Cf. Van Hove, *De Legibus Ecclesiasticis*, n. 316.

110 "Suppleri. Procedendo de similibus ad similia . . . "—*Glossa* ad v. *Nam ut ait*, D. (1, 3) 13.

111 ". . . in se. [quenti] l. [ege] . . . ut dicas iurisdictione, scilicet principis: ut princeps dicat ius ad hoc porrigendum, vel prorsus novum statuendum . . . Io. [annes] tamen dicit interpretatione scilicet iudicum in iudicio. Haec est vera . . . Et ut haec sint plana, distingue cum dubitatio in iudicio contigit: aut super aliquo novo negotio, aut super lege aliqua. Si super negotio, dominus Imperator est consulendus, si tamen praesens sit, et eius sit copia . . . Si autem non sit eius copia procedam de similibus ad similia: ut hic. Si vero super lege . . . si ex consuetudine expositio non est certificata: recurritur ut dictum est ad principem, si sit eius copia: . . . Alioqui interpretabor in benigniorem partem . . . Tertio procedam de similibus ad similia . . . Accur."—*Glossa* ad v. *Non possunt*, D. (1, 3) 12; cf. etiam *Glossa* ad v. *Cum de novo*, C. (1, 17) 10; *Glossa* ad v. *Scribi possunt*, D. (1, 3) 11 [10]: "Vel melius [dic] econtra "constituuntur" [quotation marks inserted; cf. D. (1, 3) 11, *"Et ideo"*], proprie sumitur cum dubitatur verbis legis. Lex autem sequens, scilicet, non possunt, loquitur cum dubitatur de facto novo, quod non est in

How the glossator of "*Ad haec in beato*" understands the details of the procedure to which he refers in the terms of these two laws of the Digest is not said. It is clear, however, from the apparent wording of these laws and from the words of the glossator that the judge authentically interprets law by analogy in behalf of his case. At all events, Baldus de Ubaldis (+1400) in his treatise on the decretals clearly allows the use of *interpretatio declarativa,* which includes interpretation of doubtful law,[112] and also the *interpretatio extrinseca* of law: to the legislator, of course, in the form of general law; to the judge, for deciding cases brought before him,[113] according to the laws of the Pandects "*Non possunt*" and "*Et ideo,*" [114] the second of which is also used in the doctrine of Bartolus. Consequently, the judiciary has the power of what may here be called restrictive and extensive interpretation [115] in behalf of a given case, besides that of adjudicating a case when the law is dubious. For if, in virtue of canon 20, the judge can establish a "*ius novum*" for a given case, and clearly he can do so, he can likewise adjust a known law to fit his case in virtue of the same canon.

Panormitanus (+1435) declares that judges can undertake to interpret doubtful law incident to the cases to be decided by them. This jurist bases his doctrine upon the gloss

lege. Et quod dicit: aut "interpretatione", scilicet iudicis: ut ita iudex interpretatur legem."

[112] Cf. Chapter V, Art. I, A, 3, *(Nomenclature)*.

[113] "Ulterius nota quod statuta et constitutiones non recipiunt interpretationem extrinsecam, sed intrinsecam sic, nisi ab earum conditore, etiam loquendo de interpretatione declarativa. Quod verum est generaliter in omnibus causis. Sed in causa vertente in iudicio iudex potest interpretari, non quod sit interpretatio generalis, sed inter litigatores tantum, ut ff. de legibus l. non possunt, et l. ideoque [*sic*]."—*Commentaria,* lib. I, tit. II, cap, XIII, *Quoniam,* n. 15.

[114] "Et ideo de his, quae primo constituuntur, aut interpretatione aut constitutione optimi principis certius statuendum est."—D. (1, 3) 11.

[115] Regarding the *interpretatio extrinseca,* cf. Chapter VII, Art. II, A, 2.

of *"Ad haec in beato"* and cites also as his authority Innocent IV (Sinibaldus Fliscus, eminent canonist, +1254).[116] Of particular note in his doctrine is the fact that he indicates what may be termed a discretionary latitude or power inherent in the judicial office, which is also entirely in keeping with the tenor of canon 20. For, "All the above—it is understood—are offered", says Cicognani referring to canon 20, "as norms or rules for supplying law. Hence to apply them properly one must have correct knowledge of the art of what is good and equitable".[117] Namely, the judge binds himself upon oath[118] to decide the case before him according to a good and sound judgment, as he shall find proper, not however, in an arbitrary fashion, but in virtue of a decision which is in accord with the laws. Panormitanus at once expressly teaches upon the basis of the law of the Justinian Code *"Nemo iudex"*[119] that the judicial interpretation does not establish a precedent.[120] The *Summae* of Sylvester Prierias (+1523) repeats the present teaching and likewise uses the *glossa ordinaria* mentioned, referring to the laws *"Non possunt"* and *"Nam ut ait"* of the Digest. This jurist declares furthermore, citing Panormitanus, that when a certain decision cannot be reached because of some difficult law, ". . . aliquid arduum. Quod certus intellectus dari non possit . . .", recourse must be sought at the court of the *princeps* according to the laws

---

[116] *Commentaria,* lib. I, tit. II, cap. XIII, *Quoniam,* nn. 6-7.

[117] *Canon Law,* p. 624; *item,* Jone, *Gesetzbuch des kanonischen Rechtes,* I, 41-42, 43; Michiels, *Normae Generales,* I, 461-462.

[118] Cf. can. 364, § 2.

[119] C. (7, 45) 13, which forbids the establishment of precedent.—cf. Chapter I, Art. IV.

[120] "Nam iudex potest interpretari leges quo ad causas decidendas per eum ut notat Innocentius in c. cum speciali, de app . . . iudex iurat iudicare secundum id quod sibi videbitur, scilicet, non secundum voluntatem sed secundum bonum iudicium informatum a legibus. Et haec interpretatio non est generalis quia alii iudices non tenentur iudicare secundum quod iste iudicavit quum non exemplis, sed legibus iudicandum est, ut in l. nemo C. de sen. et inter."—*Commentaria,* lib. I, tit. V, cap. I, *Ad Haec,* n. 20.

of the Justinian Code *"Cum de novo"* and *"Si Imperialis"*.[121] This statement is in accord with present Canon law inasmuch as anyone of the faithful is privileged to have recourse to the Sovereign Pontiff even during the progress of a proceeding at law.[122] Secondly, it also recalls the fact that a judge, if he cannot arrive at a decision with moral certitude based on the acts and the proofs, must dismiss the case or pronounce judgment in accord with canon 1869, §4. Finally, as to the matter of precedent, Reiffenstuel (+1703) and others of a later period teach the traditional doctrine.[123]

As to the material scope of the interpretative judicial faculty, Reiffenstuel, citing eminent authorities of an earlier age, also reveals the same teaching as heretofore advanced and according to the same laws of the Digest mentioned.[124] From this doctrine he apparently deduces the statement that the judge is the authentic interpreter of the law in doubtful causes pending his judgment, which the parties are obliged to follow, save for their appeal to the superior court.[125] Therefore, considering what has been said throughout this discussion, it is the doctrine commonly received that the judge may pass sentence, thus rendering an authentic judicial interpretation, when the law is obscure, doubtful.[126]

---

121 *Summae Sylvestrinae*, s. v. *Interpretatio*, nn. 1-2; C. (1, 14) 11; 12—cf. Chapter I, Artt. III, IV.

122 Cf. cann. 218, 1569.

123 *Ius Canonicum Universum*, lib. I, tit. II, nn. 362-363; Santi (+1885), *Praelectiones*, lib. II, tit. II, n. 16; Sanguineti (+1893), *Institutiones*, p. 63; Wernz, (+1914), *Ius Decretalium*, (Prati, 1914), V, n. 672.

124 *Ius Canonicum Universum*, lib. I, tit. II, n. 362.

125 "Iudex etenim est Iuris interpres in causa dubia eiusque sententiae, tanquam habenti vim particularis authenticae interpretationis, tenentur partes obsequi nisi ad iudicem superiorem appellaverint . . ."—*Op. cit.*, lib. I, tit. II, n. 362; cf. etiam, *op. cit.*, lib. I, tit. XXXII, nn. 56-58.

126 "Attamen adverti debet, sententiis [iudicialibus] vim inesse interpretandi leges obscuras; . . ."—Lega, *Praelectiones de Iudiciis Ecclesiasticis*, II, n. 288; Vermeersch-Creusen, *Epitome*, I, nn. 120, 122; Van Hove, *De Legibus*

Thus Baldus de Ubaldis already taught that a sentence pronounced contrary to a law as to the meaning of which there exists probable doubt cannot be considered expressly erroneous.[127] Hence one finds a marginal gloss to the law of the Digest *"Cum prolatis"* which affords special emphasis to this conclusion, reporting as the doctrine of Ioannes de Imola (decretalist and civilist, +1436) and Alexander Tartagnus (civilist, +1477) that such a sentence is entirely valid.[128] For, as the glossator declares concerning the domain of law in his annotation to the famous *Lex Barbarius,* which will be dealt with in the following: What is uncertain is to be considered as if it does not exist.[129] This dictum is *per se* juridically sound in the domain of mere human postive law. Hence the ultimate consideration in this particular matter is that a doubtful law, a *dubium iuris,* is not a law; the judge will have to create a rule for his case.[130]

Ecclesiasticis, nn. 241, 3; 312; Wernz-Vidal, *Ius Canonicum,* VI, n. 590; Coronata, *Institutiones,* III, n. 1393.

127 "Unde sententia lata contra statutum de cuius intellectu probabiliter dubitatur, non dicitur continere errorem expressum . . ."—*Commentaria,* lib. I, tit. II, cap. XIII, *Quoniam,* n. 14. The term, "erro'r expressus", is understood here as of a sentence which is expressly contradictory to clear law: "Non valet sententia, quae contra ius est lata (i. e., sententia lata contra leges, i. e., ius constitutionis . . . nulla est ipso iure.—*Glossa* ad v. *Contra legés,* c. 1, X, *de sententia et re iudicata,* II, 27.) expresso errore in sententia, ita summat dom. Ant . . . hoc summarium est in se verum . . . Abb."—Summarium, *Glossa* ad v. *Sententia,* c. 1, X, *de sententia et re iudicata,* II, 27.

100 ". . . et ista lex secundum Ioan. de Imola et Alexan. hic est singulare ad hoc, quod sententia lata contra tenorem alicuius legis dubiae quae habet plures et varios intellectus et sic quae est super ambiguo iure lata, illa talis sententia valet et non est omnino nulla."—*Glossa marginalis,* ad v. *Cum prolatis,* D. (42, 1) 32.

129 ". . . nam cum incertum est aliquid, perinde est ac si nec illud sit . . ." —*Glossa* ad v. *Functus sit,* D. (1, 14) 3.

130 ". . . ubi ius est vere dubium, et secundum diversas probabiles Doctorum opiniones intelligibile, non est maior ratio cur quis unam potius, quam aliam opinionem sequi teneatur; cum ignoret, quaenam earum revera Iuri sit conformis. Quin imo talis ignorantia proprie non est ignorantia iuris; cum de ratione iuris, seu legis sit esse manifestum. Can. Erit autem lex, dist. 4."—Reiffenstuel, lib. II, tit. XXVI, n. 77.

Therefore, the conclusion is here offered that the judge not only interprets authentically in virtue of his sentence when he decides causes according to strict and clear law, following the norms of canons 18 and 19, but also that he does so according to canon 20, when he pronounces sentence in causes in which the law is doubtful, or when it seems doubtful in view of the circumstances of his case. Likewise, that by judicial interpretation according to canon 20 he restricts or extends law, whether the deficiency of the law is formal or material, or forms a new rule when the proper solution of the case so demands, but without establishing a precedent. This latter conclusion will receive corroboration in the following.

b°. Interpretation in the case of *lex in se certa.*

Here there is no intention to outline the rules of doctrinal interpretation for the members of the judiciary department. The purpose of this title is to determine the effect of the declarative authentic interpretation of canon 17, §2, upon a judicial sentence. It is here understood, of course, that the sentence is definitive and that it has passed into a *res iudicata.*[131]

It will be noted from the words of Panormitanus quoted above that in the last analysis the sentence of the judge represents ". . . quod sibi videbitur . . . secundum bonum iudicium informatum a legibus". The question therefore simply is, what becomes of the judicial sentence in the event of a subsequent declarative authentic interpretation which certainly appears to be contrary to the judicial decision?

It is clear from canon 1869, which deals with the formulation of the sentence, that the law throws the whole burden

[131] Cf. cann. 1902-1904.

upon the judge. The law penetrates to the mind of the minister of justice and declares that he must have moral certitude concerning the matter to be defined by him,[132] and that this moral certitude is to be derived directly from the acts and proofs yielded by the judicial procedure[133] and not from elsewhere; for the juristic axiom is certain: "Quod non est in actis, non est in mundo".[134]

The material object of the present discussion is the activity of the judge as directed to the question of the justice of either the legal or the jural claims made by the parties,[135] or its counterpart, the justice of his sentence as the public minister of the law in the presence of the divine law of justice and of a just ecclesiastical law.[136] Here, if anywhere, at the tribunal of justice one must distinguish between the *ius* and the *lex*. This fact is clear from canon 1667, which guarantees: "Quodlibet *ius* . . . actione munitur . . .". Therefore the office of the ecclesiastical judge goes beyond the *lex*, the *ius scriptum*, and protects the right in natural law and in equity; in fact, any right receives his protection.[137] This fact is also apparent from a consideration of canon 20 and the discussion immediately preceding. Therefore the judicial interpretation (and that in administrative procedure contemplated in canon 17, §3) is commensurate with *ius*.[138] Hence

---

132 "Ad pronuntiationem cuiuslibet sententiae requiritur in iudicis animo moralis certitudo circa rem sententia definiendam."—Can. 1869, § 1.

133 Can. 1869, § 2.

134 Cf. Lemieux, *The Sentence in Ecclesiastical Procedure*, (The Catholic University of America, Canon Law Studies, n. 87: Washington, D. C., 1934), p. 39-42; Noval, *De Processibus*, nn. 621-622.

135 Cf. can. 1708, 2°, note: "Indicare . . . quo *iure* innitatur actor . . ."

136 Thus Noval defines "circa rem sententia definiendam", which is the object of the sentence: ". . . circa iustitiam suae publicae vel iudicialis sententiae, id est, circa suae definitionis conformitatem cum lege divina iustitae, et cum lege ecclesiastica iusta . . ."—*De Processibus*, n. 621.

137 Noval, *De Processibus*, n. 294.

138 The definition of the great Roman jurist, Aurelius Cornelius Celsus: "Ius est ars boni et aequi".—D. (1, 1) 1; cf. Cicognani, *Canon Law*, p. 10-14.

Cardinal Hostiensis (+1273) says most correctly that the judge must proceed according to the conscience of the *ius*,[139] citing Gratian's "*Iudicet ille*",[140] where in the words of St. Ambrose (+397) the latter distinguishes between *ius* and *lex*, and Justinian's "*Nemo iudex*", which bears out the same thought.[141] The latter is the law which rules out precedent. (Hence it is clear why the Church in canon 17, §3, excludes precedent; each case is juridically unique, alone and apart.)

It must, however, at once be stated here that the judge *per se* is not outside the law. This fact has already been established above. Rather, the point here is precisely that the present considerations give ample evidence of the fact that while the declarative authentic interpretation of canon 17, §2, confines itself to law *(lex)* only, the judicial interpretation as such embraces not only law but *ius* and concrete facts. This thought is confirmed by the words of Pope Innocent IV, who admonishes ecclesiastical judges to weigh all things in the balance before God and to judge according to His authority, never failing against justice.[142] One may therefore well ask first of all whether in a given instance a judicial sentence is really in conflict with an authentic interpretation of one individual law considered in the abstract, divorced from the concrete, individualizing facts and circumstances which, themselves governed by law universal or particular, all together form a case, which represents an inter-relation of laws whose

139 "Debet ergo iudex secundum iuris conscientiam iudicare. Et sic intellige iii q. vii iudicet . . . et C. de sent. et interlo om. iud. nemo."—*Commentaria*, lib. I, tit. II, cap. I, *Canonum*, n. 12.

140 "Bonus iudex . . . iuxta leges et iura pronunciat, scitis iuris obtemperat . . ."—c. 4, C. III, q. 7.

141 ". . . sed omnes iudices nostros veritatem et legum et iustitiae sequi vestigia sancimus."—C. (7, 45) 13.

142 C. 1, *de sententia et re iudicata*, II, 14, in VIo.—Gasparri's footnote to can. 1874, § 1.

individual claims mutually limit each other. Secondly, at the same time, since a cause represents a controversy, there are conflicting claims *(iura)* which it is the native right and duty of the judge to adjudicate according to his discernment, in which matter he is sustained by an irrebutable presumption of law.[143] Finally, there is also the question of legal custom, which may have to be considered, which itself is an authentic interpreter of law,[144] and which, unless it is notorious (can. 1747), must be proven at law.[145]

Baldus de Ubaldis declares that ". . . ratione casuum emergentium . . ." [146] judges may exceed the bounds of the *leges* and pronounce sentence as in their good judgment appears just and equitable.[147] Such, it will be recalled, is also the teaching of Panormitanus. However, Baldus immediately adds on the authority of Innocent IV that this procedure is

---

143 Can. 1904. § 1; "Siquidem circa casus particulares, cum sint infiniti, habet iudex vi sui officii facultatem arbitrandi, atque diiudicandi, cuius partis iura sunt potiora: unde propter hanc auctoritatem iudiciariam praesumunter omnia legitime facta . . . et quidem praesumptione iuris et de iure."—Reiffenstuel, lib. II, tit. XXVII, n. 76.

144 Cf. cann. 25-30; ". . . dicendum est multum valere interpretationem ex usu desumptam ad legis obligationem praescribendam, et interdum talem esse posse ut authentica sit et pro lege habenda. Haec assertio communis doctorum est . . . quatenus . . . dicitur consuetudinem esse optimam legum interpretem."—Suarez, *De Legibus*, VI, cap. 1, n. 4.

145 Van Hove, *Commentarium Lovaniense in Codicem Iuris Canonici*, III, *De Consuetudine et Temporis Supputatione*, (Mechliniae-Romae: H. Dessain, 1933), n. 268.

146 Can one render this phrase with "in cases of emergency"? Certainly, from the context it is clear that this jurist has reference to cases out of the ordinary. Thus his thought would agree with the general principle of legislating; namely, that the legislator contemplates only the usual course of events in making his law.

147 ". . . utrum . . . possint iudices ordinarii licite leges transgredi? Et videtur quod possint sequi iudicium animi sui quia iurant iudicare quod sibi aequum ac iustum videbitur . . ."—*Commentaria*, lib. I, tit. II, cap. primum, *Canonum*, n. 17.

not the ordinary one, ". . . quia aequitas non scripta non habet vim legis ubi rigor scriptus est in contrarium".[148]

Here it is evident that when the case is taken care of by clear law, the judge must follow its prescripts and render his interpretation accordingly. But the fact is at once nevertheless true from the nature of things that this very question rests with him. This statement is borne out by the law of the Pandects *"Cum prolatis"*, which states that if a judge considers certain laws as nonmaterial to the cause at issue and hence pronounces contrary to their provisions, his sentence is not deemed as *"contra constitutiones"*, that is, it is valid and must be appealed to avoid a *res iudicata*.[149] It would appear from this law that there is no question of a *dubium iuris* or of a controverted law, because neither the law itself nor its gloss envisions this contingency, but rather that the judge erred[150] in his interpretation of the law ". . . eo quod non existimat causam de qua iudicat per eas [i. e., constitutiones] iuvari . . .".[151] In other words, he elected to adjudicate the case according to a norm which was not the correct one. Yet his sentence is sustained when it becomes a matter irrevocably adjudged. Hence one finds the teaching that a sentence is by law null[152] and as such, *"contra constitutiones"*, only when[153] it is expressly erroneous *(utpote expressum errorem continens)* contrary to indubitably clear law *(sententia lata*

---

148 *Op. cit.*, n. 18; cf. Reiffenstuel, lib. I, tit. XXXII, nn. 58-59; *idem*, lib. I, tit. II, nn. 415-418.

149 D. (42, 1) 32.

150 "Sententia lata contra tenorem constitutionis, si non fuit error expressus valet mero iure. Pau [lus de Castro]"—*Superscriptio*, D. (42, 1) 32.

151 ". . . allegavi legem scriptam in corpore iuris . . . iudex credens quod haec lex nihil faceret ad quaestionem iudicavit contra me."—*Glossa* ad *Casus*, D. (42, 1) 32.

152 C. 1, X, *de sententia et re iudicata*, II, 27.

153 Schmier, *Iurisprudentia Canonico-Civilis*, lib. II, Tractatus III, cap. XII, n. 50.

contra ius scriptum clarum et indubitatum) [154] and custom.[155] This principle does not obtain when the law is controverted [156] or represented as obscure because of divergent opinions of authors. Under such circumstances the sentence in default of appeal becomes, according to the common opinion, a matter irrevocably adjudicated.[157]

Accordingly, let it be supposed that a question of law concerning which there is a difference of opinion among authors is decided by the general declarative authentic interpretation of canon 17, §2, contrary to a previous sentence which has become a *res iudicata.*[158] The question is whether the supposed case is to be subjected to revision in other judicial procedures.

In any event, before proceeding further in the present discussion two items must be pointed out. There can be no question of conflict or nullity of the sentence unless it is first established that the authentic interpretation is actually declarative, a circumstance which, unless it is expressly stated in the document of the Pontifical Commission, does not, as a matter of fact, appear *per se* and *prima facie.* Secondly, as regards the supposed case, it would have to be shown that the authentic interpretation is the reverse interpretation of the law which formed the keystone of the case, that is, of the law which was of decisive moment in the sentence. Therefore, let these two items be answered in the affirmative. It is

---

154 Reiffenstuel, lib. II, tit. XXVII, nn. 70-76; cf. etiam, Coronata, *Institutiones,* III, n. 1403, citing this passage of Reiffenstuel.

155 Wernz, *Ius Decretalium,* V, n. 666; Vecchiotti, *Institutiones,* II, 309; Wernz-Vidal, *Ius Canonicum,* VI, n. 592.

156 Santi, *Praelectiones,* lib. II, tit. XXVII, n. 7

157 "Secus tamen dicendum est de sententia lata contra Ius obscurum, sive dubium; hoc est, de cuius vero intellectu variae sunt Doctorum sententiae: nam sententia contra istud lata valet ac transit in rem iudicatem, nisi intra decem dies ab ea fuerit appellatum. Ita Abbas . . . atque allegens communem." —Reiffenstuel, lib. II, tit. XXVII, n. 74.

158 Cf. Coronata, *Institutiones,* III, n. 1423.

supposed, then, that the case involved only the operation of *leges in se clarae,* and that the tribunals of both first and second instance erred in their interpretation of the law upon which the case turned, inasmuch as they followed a doctrinal opinion implicitly rejected by the subsequent authentic interpretation.

To state that the sentence is a *res iudicata* appears to beg the question. As far as the scope of this study is concerned, the only condition under which there would be no *res iudicata* is that the sentence represented a judicial interpretation which is expressly contrary to indubitably clear law and which is therefore *ipso iure* null, as appears in the citations adduced in the foregoing. For such a sentence is rather a correction,[159] a condemnation of the law, not its application by the judge, who cannot arbitrarily establish legislation[160]—a clear and evident error of law.[161] In other words, this sentence represents a direct contravention against legitimately constituted authority, an act which is ultimately against natural law. No inferior can set aside the law of his superior.[162]

It is apparent that both tribunals erred in the supposed case. However, it cannot be said that the sentence is expressly contrary to indubitably clear law; an opinion was followed which later proved to be erroneous. Consequently, as pointed out above, the sentence was valid and therefore became a mat-

159 Schmier, *Iurisprudentia Canonico-Civilis,* lib. I, *Tractatus Praembulus,* III, cap. XII, n. 50.

160 Santi, *Praelectiones,* lib. II, tit. XXVII, n. 7: "Hinc si iudex decernat, electionem factam ab electoribus suspensis esse validam eius sententa nulla est."

161 Coronata, *Institutiones,* III, n. 1403, citing Reiffenstuel, lib. II, tit. XXVII, nn. 70-74.

162 Reiffenstuel, lib. I, tit. II, n. 75. Whether or not the act is subjectively culpable is, of course, outside the question. Nor do the authorities above cited make such a distinction. The present matter has to do entirely with the external forum, and with the judge, who is a public personality, a representative of the legislator.

ter irrevocably adjudged, creating law as between the parties, affording at the same time an exception which prevents further judicial revision,[163] which exception is peremptory [164] and is by nature perpetual.[165] There is here an instance of an error on the part of the tribunals concerning the interpretation of law, which, as Baldus de Ubaldis points out on the authority of Bartolus, is exemplified in the law of the Digest *"Cum prolatis"* (treated above, p. 255) and does not invalidate the judicial sentence, which is precisely a *dubii casus decisio.*[166]

Plainly, the courts are functioning exactly within the purpose for which they exist, to adjudicate civil and criminal controversy. As will appear later, the error is simply an accident; there cannot always be perfect justice here. On the other hand, however, the authentic interpretation is retroactive and affects acts of the past,[167] for the law should have been understood and put into practice in the sense conveyed by the authentic declaration. Does it undo what the courts have decreed? The answer is that there is here an evident exception to the rule of the retroactivity of declarative authentic interpretation, and the principle is applicable: "Generi per speciem derogatur".[168] There can be no conflict of laws, namely, the law of the *res iudicata* as against the law of retroactivity: "Romanus Pontifex iura omnia in scrinio pectoris sui censetur habere". There must be either a reconciliation of apparently conflicting laws or an abrogation of one of them.[169]

---

[163] Cann. 17, § 3, 1902, 1904, § 2. An exception to this rule is in can. 1905.

[164] Can. 1629, § 1.

[165] Can. 1667.

[166] "Item dicit [Bartolus] quod interpretatio est dubii casus decisio, ut C. de leg. l. fi. Et si iudex erret contra textum legis, sententia non valet expresso errore. Secus si erret contra interpretationem legis, ff. de re iu. Cum prolatis."—*Commentaria,* lib. I, tit. II, cap. primum, *Canonum,* n. 58.

[167] Can. 17, § 2.

[168] Reg. 34, R. J., in VIo.

[169] Cf. c. 1, *de constitutionibus,* I, 2, in VIo, and its gloss.

This very exception to the principle of the retroactivity of a declarative authentic interpretation [170] was clearly maintained by the jurists of the classical period of Canon law.

In the commentary of Ioannes Andreas (+1348) to the law of the Decretals of Gregory IX *"Quoniam"* this canonist immediately deduces a practical inference from the rule of retroactivity. Must the judicial sentence pronounced contrary to an authentic interpretation be rescinded? He answers in the negative and bases his claim upon a law in the Digest, *"Barbarius"*. According to this law a certain Barbarius Philippus, a slave incognito, obtained the praetorship and exercised that office. *Per se* he had no juridic capacity as a slave, and his legal acts in the light of *ius strictum* ought to have been void. Ulpian is reported as solving the problem, with the authority of Pomponius, by declaring that the acts are valid because of the common good.[171] The glossator develops the juristic thought behind this solution. As noted previously, he declares that in the field of law what is uncertain is non-extant and continues with the statement that common error (on the part of the community at large) creates law.[172] In effect,

[170] This term is here understood as referring to the solution of any doubt concerning the law.—cf. Chapter V, Art. I, A, 3.

[171] ". . . quid dicemus? Quae edixit, quae decrevit, nullius fere momenti? An fore propter utilitatem eorum, qui apud eum egerunt vel lege vel 'quo alio iure' [fuerit legitimo iudicio—Gradenwitz]? Et verum puto nihil eorum reprobari; 'hoc enim humanius est'; . . ."—D. (1, 14) 3.—*Corpus Iuris Civilis, Iustiniani Digesta,* 15. ed., stereotypa, Mommsen-Krueger, (Berolini, 1928).

[172] "Et sic fuit praetor; nam cum incertum est aliquid, perinde est ac si nec illud sit . . . Hic autem est . . . communis error, qui facit ius."—*Glossa* ad v. *Functus sit,* D. (1, 14) 3. Certainly, it can be said that the law can be to a degree unclear or obscure to one who investigates its meaning, though *in se* it is clear. Hence there can be probable error of law.—cf. Miaskiewicz, *Supplied Jurisdiction According to Canon 209,* p. 163-167; Vermeersch-Creusen, *Epitome,* I, n. 322: "Error iuris . . . probabilis . . . i. e., iis rationibus innixus quae virum prudentem et honestum movere possunt." That the law can appear obscure in the course of investigation is clearly supposed by the legislator in canon 18. There is subjective obscurity.

it creates for all practical legal purposes a certainty for that which is *in se* not certain. This approach to the problem of judicial controversy is juridically sound. The clause "hoc enim humanius est", whereby the solution is characterized in the text of Justinian's law,[173] sustains this view; namely, that the solution is more in conformity with the dictates of human reason. Thus the doctrine of Ioannes Andreas is that a declarative law has retroactive force except where a judicial sentence has been pronounced. He has in mind, of course, a judicial matter which has become a *res iudicata*. If the authentic interpretation of the law at issue occurs when the case is in the court of appeal, it affects the sentence given in the court of first instance.[174] Such is precisely the rule of canon 17, §2, for in the stage of appeal the sentence is not a matter irrevocably adjudged, and consequently it does not as yet produce law for the parties.[175] Hence in behalf of the common good, as the glossator also maintains,[176] it is the teaching to Ioannes Andreas that the sentence should remain intact even if in a given case the wrong opinion was followed, for what was well done, says the commentator to *"Barbarius"*, must not be revived because of another supervening event.[177] Justinian had decreed that the cause acquitted by judicial sentence and according to law shall enjoy complete security for the future:

> ". . . si et iudex pronuntiaverit et debitor persolverit sequitur huiusmodi causam plenissima securitas, ut nemo

---

[173] The clause is probably an interpolation; *vide*, *Iustiniani Digesta*, Mommsen-Krueger, (Berolini, 1928), *loc. cit.*

[174] "Numquid ergo sententia data per priorem intellectum debuit revocari . . . Credo quod sententiata non sunt revocanda, argumentum, ff. de officio praetorum, Barbarius . . . Et hoc nisi esset appellatum a sententia et declaratio fieret in causa appellationis."—Ioannes Andreas, *Novella Commentaria*, lib. I, tit. II, cap. *Quoniam*, n. 11.

[175] Cf. can. 1902.

[176] "Et breviter hoc intendit propter publicam utilitatem . . ."—*Superscriptio*, D. (1, 14) 3.

[177] *Glossa* ad v. *Reprobari*, D. (1, 14) 3.

in posterum inquietetur: non enim debet, quod rite et secundum leges ab initio actum est, ex alio eventu resuscitari.[178]

The same thought as contained in *Lex Barbarius* of protecting the common good, regardless of the error of the courts, is advanced by a Rotal Decision with reference to canon 1904, which declares that the judges of both first and second instance may err. Yet the sentence, though actually false and unjust, nevertheless creates law as between the litigants, because the common good demands rather that there be an end to controversy than that individual rights be in each case and above all safeguarded according to justice and truth.[179] The very fact that the legislator in canon 1904 *presumes* (a *probabilis coniectura)* that the sentence is true (according to the facts as proven) and just (according to the *ius)* gives ample evidence that there is room for error on the part of the tribunal concerning either the *ius* or the factual proofs, or regarding both. Consequently, it can err in its interpretation of law and still the sentence, the judicial interpretation, will be valid and will constitute law according to canons 1902 and 1904. For a presumption is: "Rei incertae probabilis coniectura". For all practical purposes, therefore, there is declared in behalf of the judicial interpretation a certainty concerning a matter (the sentence) which is *in se* uncertain.[180]

---

178 C. (5, 37) 25, cited by the glossator of "*Reprobari*" (quoted immediately above) in confirmation of his principle.

179 S. R. R., *Nullitas Matrimonii,* 20 iun. 1922, *coram R. P. D. Ioanne Prior, Decano,* dec. XIX.—*Decisiones,* (Romae: Typis Polyglottis Vaticanis, 1930) XIV (1922), 191-192, citing Pichler, lib. II, tit. 27, n. 20: "Sententiae (uti et praescriptionis) firmitas et auctoritas non fundatur in veritate huius praesumptionis, sed in ordinatione legali et in bono publico cum publice magis expediat res iudicatas esse firmas, quam esse iustas".

180 Cf. Reiffenstuel, lib. II, tit. XXVII, n. 106. The very fact that by law itself there is granted an appeal directly suggests the possibility of error.

The incident described in the *Lex Barbarius,* mentioned in the foregoing,[181] seems to represent a case of common error which was basically popular error concerning a juridic matter. According to the juristic doctrine developed from this incident, such common error concerning the law will sustain the validity of a judicial sentence which is contrary to a subsequent declarative interpretation. In virtue of a further development of this idea concerning the effect of error, by the same token the influence of probable juristic opinion concerning a given law is also considered as contributory toward impeding in behalf of the judicial sentence the retroactivity of a subsequent contrary declarative interpretation, except when the sentence is still in the stage of appeal. Matrimonial causes, of course, are also explicitly excepted. Such was definitely the commonly received doctrine of canonists according to the report of Felinus Sandaeus (+1503), which doctrine is based precisely on the *Lex Barbarius.* Here therefore there is question of a probable error on the part of jurists concerning the law, which error the tribunal supposedly followed. Accordingly, it is considered by the jurists sufficient to establish on a firm basis the judicial interpretation if the judge in pronouncing sentence has followed a probable juristic opinion, even if this probable opinion is contradicted by an authentic interpretation subsequent to the *res iudicata.* And even where this opinion merits reproof by the interpretation of the superior, it is nevertheless maintained by the decretalists that the sentence still prevails.[182]

---

[181] Cf. p. 259, sqq.

[182] "Tertio limita hanc fallentiam [i. e., constitutio nova trahitur ad praeterita] nisi secundum opinionem Doctorum praecedentem lata fuisset aliqua sententia, quia licet constitutio nova declaret errorem illius opinionis tamen sententia non revocabitur secundum Vincen. hic late, quem sequuntur Ioan. And., do. Anto. [de Butrio] et Imol. hic et Domi [nicum] in d. c. ex antiquis. Moventur per l. Barbarius. ff. de offic. praeto. et per not. per Innocent. in c. nihil, de elect. et quia iudex debet iudicare secundum ll. scriptas et non scriptas . . . Et ideo satis videtur quod iudex iudicet secundum intellectum qui

In effect, Baldus de Ubaldis (+1400), following the civilist and glossator Iacobus de Buttrigarius (+1342), taught the same doctrine. Namely, that the tribunal may follow a probable [183] opinion (one of opposing opinions in the *Glossa*) [184] which in its good judgment is preferable.[185] As a matter of fact, that this doctrine was the common teaching of civilists and canonists is confirmed by the statement of Iason de Mayno (+circa 1507), who sets down what has been outlined in the foregoing from the report of Felinus Sandaeus.[186]

---

tunc servabatur. Facit quod notat Domi [nicus] . . . ubi dicit quod non imputatur ei qui tenuit opinionem probabilem, licet supervenerit lex illam declarans et reprobans. Facit quod notat Innoc . . . Excipiuntur ab ista limitatione tres casus. Primus est, quando a sententia esset appellatum: quia si pendente appell. superveniat lex declaratoria illa sequenda est secundum Vincen. et praedictos hic . . . secundus est in sacramentalibus . . . propter periculum animarum . . . tertius casus est in sententia lata pro matrimonio."—*Commentaria*, lib. I, tit. II, cap. 13, *Quoniam*, n. 7.

[183] Hence the opinion of Noval (*De Processibus*, n 621) has great merit: "Et quidem requiritur et sufficit certitudo moralis lata vel imperfecta, seu probabilis; nam, ut docet S. Thomas (II-II, q. LXX, a. 2, et I-II, q. XCVI, a. 1, ad 3), 'in actibus humanis . . . sufficit probabilis certitudo quae in pluribus veritatem attingat, etsi in paucioribus a veritate deficiat', et proinde tollat non omnem sed dumtaxat prudentem dubitationem seu gravem erroris formidinem . . .", speaking of the certainty required to form a judicial opinion. Hence also the *glossa* says: "Respondeo . . . ad opinionem iudicis referatur, quid dicatur probabile, ut per hoc possit et debeat appellationi deferri . . ."—*Glossa* ad v. *Non quae iudici*, c. 24, X, *de verborum significatione*, V, 40.

[184] Cf. *Introduction*, in fine.

[185] ". . . tamen caveant iudices ne eligant opinionem, quae minus habet rationis . . . Excusantur autem si sequuntur opinionem communem, nisi notorie sit irrationabilis, seu falso secundum Hostiensem quod tene menti . . . Dicit Iac. But. . . . Ubi vero essent glo. contrariae, teneat [iudex] illam opinionem, cui magis ratio intellectus sui consentit, nec propterea facit litem suam, quia habet necesse eligere, unde necessitas officii eum excusat . . ."—*Commentaria*, lib. I, tit. II, cap. primum, *Canonum*, nn. 33-35.

[186] It is worthy of note that in this particular the civilists seem to have been the teachers of the canonists. At least, the present authority observes that canonists do not have a legal text to offer as a basis for the development of this principle of jurisprudence: "Et credo quod non sit textus notus

Hence it may here be pointed out again that the question of judicial sentence or interpretation rests ultimately upon the opinion of the judge, upon the "ratio intellectus sui", as Baldus says. Thus Hostiensis (+1272) declares that the tribunal is not bound always to follow the opinion of others. A common opinion must be followed always unless it is notoriously in error or can be gainsaid on the strength of valid reasons, all of which is a matter for the judge to determine.[187]

These considerations directly suggest the explicit prescript of canon 1869, §1, concerning the "in iudicis animo moralis certitudo" relative to the judicial interpretation. Moreover, they also point directly to the use of canon 20, which basically is involved in the tribunal's procedure under the circumstances which are at present supposed, a controversy concerning the meaning of a law which here and now the tribunal must invoke. There is plainly no "expressum legis praescriptum". Otherwise one cannot reasonably conceive that there will be ordinarily a serious division of opinion.[188]

Can [onistis] [Canonum?] Unde Dominicus [dicit] . . . quod non est imputandum Doctori qui secutus est opinionem probabilem dato quod illa postea sit expresse reprobata per legem vel statutum."—Iason Maynus, *In Codicem Commentaria,* (Venetiis, 1589), C. (1, 14) 5 (Titulus: *De Legibus, l. Non dubium*), n. 14. Iason, however, does not cite the *Lex Barbarius* in this context.

187 "Sed nec tenetur [iudex] semper sequi alios . . . Communis opinio semper sequenda est, nisi notorie male dicat, vel rationabiliter convincatur. Et hoc bonus iudex, et acutissimi ingenii aestimabit."—*Commentaria,* lib. I, tit. II. cap. I, *Canonum,* nn. 13-14.

188 There is here every intention to stress the word *"expressum"* in can. 20. This canon does not necessarily suppose that there is *no* prescript of law *at all* either implicitly or explicitly contained in the body of the law in order that its provisions may be applied (cf. can. 6, 6°). The canon reads *express* prescript of law. If the legislator meant a complete absence, it seems that he would not have had to use the word *"expressum"*. Hence, Sägmüller (*Lehrbuch des Katholischen Kirchenrechts,* 4. ed., [Frieburg im Breisgau: Herder & Co., G. M. B. H. Verlagsbuchhandlung, 1926], I, Zweiter Teil, 187) says: "Fehlt in bestimmtem Falle ein *ausdrückliches* Gesetz . . ."; Leitner, *Handbuch des katolischen Kirchenrechts,* In Einzellieferungen, 2. ed., [Regensburg: Verlag Jos. Kösel & Friedrich Pustet, 1921], Erste Lieferung, p. 40) declares: "Fehlt über

Whence, then, is the "norma sumenda"? Here there is question (supposing that the other rules of can. 20 are of no aid) of following the "communis et constans opinio doctorum" [189] which is not at hand. Therefore, in the presence of controversy, says Reiffenstuel, the judge must make his own sober choice and interpretation, having diligently reviewed everything.[190]

B. Motives in fact.

The present section of this discussion need not be protracted, because it is evident that the judge must have a proper appreciation of the facts in order to declare whether they are in conformity with or contrary to the *ius*. However, this step in forming the judicial sentence has great importance; it is an essential part of judicial interpretation. In fact,

---

einen Gegenstand der *klare* Ausspruch eines . . . Gesetzes . . ." and especially Falco, (*Introduzione Allo Studio del "Codex Iuris Canonici"*, [Torino: Fratelli Bocca, Editori, 1925], p. 105) points out: "Il canone non può quindi intendersi se non come disposizione espressa di ricorrere per colmare le lacune delle leggi alla analogia ed ai principi generali del diritto, e come ammonimento, che abbraccia anche un campo piú vasto di quello delle lacune in senso tecnico [e. g., *dubia iuris*], *di decidere i casi non preveduti o controversi tenendo conto* della giurisprudenza della Curia romana e *della commune opinione degli scrittori*". (Italics inserted).

[189] According to the *regula antiqua*, a common opinion is that which is maintained by six doctors of importance *(graves)* who treat the question *ex professo*.—Van Hove, *De Legibus Ecclesiasticis*, n. 330, citing D'Annibale.

[190] "Iudex, postquam cuncta rimari, ac sedulo discutere studuit, debet ex opinionibus disceptantibus eam eligere, cui magis ratio intellectus sui consentit. Ita Glossa in c. Cum olim, 24. V. Non quae iudici. de Verb. signif."—*Ius Canonicum Universum*, lib. I, tit. XXXII, n. 58. The reference reads: "Immo iudex secundum motum animi sui et secundum sensum iudicare tenetur. . . et secundum quod sibi videtur. . . dum tamen secundum leges et canones. . ." —*Glossa* ad v. *Non quae iudici*, c. 24, X, *de verborum significatione*, V, 40; cf. etiam, Wernz-Vidal, *Ius Canonicum*, VI, n. 590.

the application of law to the facts is the very reason of existence for the judicial sentence. Here there is question of interpreting the facts, and the judge must render an account in the text of his pronouncement as to the reasons in fact which led him to his decision.[191]

After the meaning of the law, the yardstick of human activity in society, has been established, the judge weighs the proofs either in his own conscientious opinion *(ex sua conscientia)* or according to their legal evaluation.[192] At this stage of the proceeding the tribunal brings the facts into contact with the law, showing how the *ius* is applicable to the question at issue; it applies the jural criterion of right and wrong. This demonstration constitutes the formulation of the *motiva in facto.*[193] Hence it appears that the facts must be understood properly by the judge. It is significant to note that all the proofs must be considered and interpreted together upon the background of the circumstances.[194] Hence there is the dictum received through decretal law: "Iudex usque ad prolationem sententiae debet universa rimari";[195] the judge must pry into all the angles of his case and consider, not only one fact, but all the facts presented to him, in order therefrom to fashion the disposition of mind[196] neces-

---

[191] Can. 1873, § 1, 3°.

[192] Cf. Can. 1869, § 3.

[193] Coronata, *Institutiones,* III, nn. 1393, 1403.

[194] Thus Vecchiotti points out the rule in the Theodosian Code (published A. D. 438): "Hinc Lex 1. Cod. Theod. de offic. Iudicis in causis cognoscendis haec habet: 'Iudex cum causam audire coeperit. . . tandiu actio ventiletur, quousque rei veritas perveniatur, frequenter interrogari oportet, ne aliquid praetermissum fortasse maneat; quia apud ipsum finienda causa est, totum debet agnoscere.' "—*Institutiones,* II, 306; cf. C. Th. (2, 18) 1, *Interpretatio.*

[195] C. 10, X, *de fide instrumentorum,* II, 22; "Iudicantem oportet cuncta rimari et ordinem rerum plena inquisitione discutere, interrogandi ac proponendi adiciendique patientia praebita ab eo. . ."—C. Th. (2, 18) 1.

[196] "Licet igitur iudex non semper ad unam speciem probationis applicet mentem suam sed ex confessionibus et depositionibus, allegationibus et aliis,

sary to pronounce sentence. Indeed, as the glossator says, the truth becomes clearer after one has rehearsed the facts several times.[197]

However, there can be error not only as to the existence or status of an alleged fact *in se,* because of false representation, but on the part of the judge, who has apprehended a fact wrongly. The result is an interpretation *contra ius litigatoris.* Thus the Sovereign Pontiff, Innocent III (+1216), reviewing a case found that the document upon which the issue turned was incorrectly evaluated by the court of first and second instance; the interpretation was *contra ius litigatoris* but not expressly *contra ius constitutionis.* However, no appeal was taken, with the result:

> Quamvis forte dicto instrumento donationis non sit plurimum innitendum . . . attendentes tamen quod quantum ad litigantes ipsos, ius ex sententia factum fuit, postquam in rem transiit iudicatam, etiam si contra ius litigatoris lata fuisset, cum contra ius constitutionis expresse lata non fuerit . . . diffinimus . . .

that the case was dismissed because ". . . cum nulla fuerit appellatione suspensa [i. e., sententia] in rem transiit iudicatam".[198] Hence the judicial interpretation nevertheless established law as between the litigants, but without prejudice to others,[199] in spite of the incorrect apprehension of fact, consequent false motivation *in facto,* and the final result of an unjust sentence. Error can especially occur when there is al-

---

quae in eius praesentia proponuntur, formet animi sui motum. . ."—c. 6, X, *de renunciatione,* I, 9.

[197] "Quia veritas saepius examinata magis splendescit in lucem."—*Glossa* ad v. *Postquam,* c. 10, X, *de fide instrumentorum,* II, 22.

[198] C. 13, X, *de sententia et re iudicata,* II, 27.

[199] *Glossa* ad v. *Ad litigantes*: "secus quod ad alios."—*loc. cit.*

leged a juridic fact, which itself involves questions of law.[200] Thus in the present case, as will be noted below, juridic facts are alleged, *donatio, confirmatio, privilegium.*[201]

It may hardly be considered a digression to point out how clearly is emphasized in this case the force of the *res iudicata*, which is the sentence, or in other words, the judicial interpretation, precisely from the viewpoint of motives in fact. Though the Pope himself declares that the facts were wrongly apprehended by the inferior courts, he decrees that the sentence is presumed as true and correctly executed, namely, as being in accord with the facts, which at the same time admittedly it is not.[202] The *glossa ordinaria*, which is that of Bernardus Parmensis de Botone (+1263),[203] explains that the sentence here is called *veritas* (the truth). The things which were done under the aegis of judicial authority are presumed as true and correct, and legitimately per-

---

200 ". . . facta vero iuridica sunt praeter contractus omnia negotia iuridica quibus aliquod ius gignitur aut extinguitur."—Coronata, *Institutiones*, III, n. 1089; "Facta iuridica illa sunt ex quibus dependet habilitas ad iura acquirenda vel exercenda aut ipsorum iurium acquisitio, mutatio vel amissio, v. g., aetas maior, status matrimonii, qualitas haeredis, legitimitas natalium etc."—Wernz-Vidal, *Ius Canonicum*, VI, n. 11.

201 Regarding papal privileges there is the principle laid down by Innocent III in the law *"Cum venissent"*: "Cum super privilegiis sedis Apostolicae causa versatur, Nolumus de ipsis per alios iudicari"—c. 12, X, *de iudiciis*, II, 1. Not that the judge cannot take cognizance of this juridic fact in any event, says the glossator; he cannot do so when its terminology is doubtful (cf. cann. 67-68): "Sed nunquid incidenter [cf. cann. 1837-1841] potest alius cognoscere quam Papa; Videtur quod sic . . . inspiciendo privilegium . . . Dicas quod hoc locum habet, cum verba obscura sunt et ambigua, quia tunc eius est interpretari cuius est condere; ubi vero aperta sunt et clara, potest iudex decre. [*sic;* decernere?] obstat privilegium vel non obstat. Bernard."—*Glossa* ad v. *Iudicari. loc. cit.*

202 "Quamvis forte dicto instrumento donationis non sit plurimum innitendum, nec confirmationibus vel privilegiis [the facts] . . . veritate gestorum sermonibus praevalente, quae praesumitur rite per omnia celebrata: diffinimus . . ."—c. 13, X, *de sententia et re iudicata*, II, 27.

203 Cf. Van Hove, *Prolegomena*, n. 273.

formed, although the allegations in fact upon which the sentence is based are actually worthless.[204]

Such is clearly the import of canon 1904, § 1. The law here *presumes* that the sentence of the judge—who is the representative of the legislator in his act of judicial interpretation (the sentence), because in pronouncing sentence he is an authentic interpreter [205]—reflects the correct evaluation of the facts placed before him as judge, and hence that the sentence is the expression of the true relation between the facts and the *ius*.[206] Therefore, as Devoti (+1820) says, the *res iudicata* is accepted in the place of truth;[207] consequently, an error in fact on the part of the judge does not *(per se)* vitiate the sentence.[208] Hence Gonzalez (+1649) in his brilliant commentary on the *res iudicata*, citing Felinus Sandaeus (+1503), Philippus Decius (+1536), and Andreas Alciatus (+1540), teaches that the word *"rite"* used by Innocent III [209] implies that the sentence (and therefore, the judicial

---

204 "Sensus huius litterae talis est: sententia hic appellatur veritas gestorum: quia res iudicata pro veritate accipitur, ff. de sta. ho. ingenuum, sermones hic appellat alia quae allegabantur s. donationes, privilegia, confirmationes super donatione quae nihil valebant: et ita veritas gestorum i. sententia, quae lata fuit auctoritate gestorum, quae in prima causa probata fuerunt, quae praesumuntur legitime acta, praevalent sermonibus, praedictis donationibus et confirmationibus nihil valentibus: . . . Ber."—*Glossa* ad v. *Sermonibus praevalente*, c. 13, X, *de sententia et re iudicata*, II, 27.

205 Can. 17, §§ 1, 3.

206 ". . . iudex censetur tum subiective tum obiective veritatem iuris definivisse"—Vermeersch-Creusen, *Epitome*, (5. ed., Mechliniae-Romae: H. Dessain, 1936), III, n. 245, 3.

207 "Proprie res iudicata, non sententia, controversiae finem imponit . . . veritatis loco habetur."—*Institutionum Canonicarum Libri IV*, (Leodii, 1860), II, 118.

208 "Pariter nulla non est sententia in qua laesum est ius litigantis vel quia immerito exclusa est probatio caeteroquin efficax, vel quia factum non est rite receptum a iudice et inspectum prout oportet."—Santi, *Praelectiones*, lib. II, tit. XXVII, n. 7; Vecchiotti, *Institutiones*, II, 309. Cf. Coronata, *Institutiones*, III, n. 1403.

209 Cf. p. 268.

interpretation) in its status of *res iudicata,* because of the judicial authority,[210] is presumed to have been rendered well not only regarding the justice and merits of the cause, but in its relation to the entire process.[211] Thus the judicial interpretation is the crystallization of the whole procedure. His statement concerning the authority of the tribunal agrees admirably with the provisions of canon 17, § 3. It is therefore easily understandable why Reiffenstuel says that the sentence as a matter irrecovably adjudicated is accepted as truth (*adeo ut pro veritate accipiatur*—as the statement of objective reality, as it were), and is of such authority that existence ceases, what is false becomes true, and black becomes white.[212] These considerations aptly form the transition to the discussion concerning the essence of the judicial sentence.

ARTICLE III. *Essence of the Judicial Sentence.*

Considering the words of Gonzalez together with the thought advanced by Reiffenstuel, referred to immediately above, one comes to the conclusion that the judicial sentence *(res iudicata)* is materially nothing more than the opinion [213] of the judge as regards the true conformity of human

---

[210] Cf. Vermeersch-Creusen, *Epitome,* III, 245, 3.

[211] "Ergo sententia postquam in rem iudicatam transivit, praesumitur bene prolata quoad iustitiam et merita causae. . . Nec solum haec praesumptio datur quoad iustitiam causae, verum etiam quoad processum, modum, et ordinem procedendi, quod importat in praesenti dictio illa *rite* . . . Resolvunt in praesenti Felinus n. 31, Decius n. 32 . . . Alciatus de praesumpt. p. 3 praesumpt. 9 et 10. Et suadetur, quoniam auctoritas iudicialis facit, ut non solum pro sententia, verum et pro processu praesumantur. . ."—*Commentaria,* lib. II, tit. XXVII, cap. XIII, n. 3; cf. c. 6, X, *de renunciatione,* I, 9.

[212] *Ius Canonicum Universum,* lib. II, tit. XXVII, n. 106.

[213] Thus the glossator speaks of the sentence: "Et hoc est ideo quia iudi-

acts with the *ius*. Accordingly, his judgment is characterized by the gloss of the *Decretum* of Gratian as the expression of his sincere belief or conviction, his opinion, which he is obliged to follow.[214]

This opinion of the tribunal the legislator vests at once with a formal authoritative element of positive law with respect to the cause which is decided.[215] St. Thomas calls the sentence of the judge a kind of particular law *(quasi quaedam particularis lex)* concerning a particular fact.[216] Citing Aristotle, from whom he derives a classical definition of positive law, he enumerates the sentence together with common law and privilege among the three species of positive law. Like the subject matter of purely positive law, he contemplates the subject matter of the judicial decision as something which is in itself, so to say, "at large" and not ruled by law. Hence it is apposite matter to receive the disposition of judicial authority, whereby common law is applied to this particular matter, which disposition is thenceforward received as law.[217]

---

cium Dei innititur veritati, quae nec fallit nec fallitur, iudicium hominis opinioni, quae fallit et fallitur."—*Glossa* ad v. *Condemnat*, c. 1, *de sententia et re iudicata*, II, 14, in VIo.

214 "Sed nonne iudex potest iudicare secundum quod sibi iustum videtur? Et ex sententia sui animi aestimabit quid aut credat aut parum esse probatum videatur. . . Sed dico quod tenetur sequi opinionem suam, sed non voluntatem."—*Glossa* ad v. *Voluntatis*, c. 4, C. III, q. 7. Cf. Wernz-Vidal, *Ius Canonicum*, VI, n. 590.

215 Cann. 17, § 3, 1904, § 2; Koeniger, *Katholisches Kirchenrecht*, p. 87.

216 *Summa Theologica*, II, IIae, quaest. 67, Art. I, in corp.

217 "Ad primum ergo dicendum, quod Philosophus ponit tres species iuris legalis, quod est ius positivum. . .dicit quod 'legale est quod ex principio quidem nihil differt sic vel aliter; quando autem ponitur differt'. . . Dicuntur etiam quaedam legalia, non quia sint leges, sed propter applicationem legum communium ad aliqua particularia facta, sicut sunt sententiae, quae pro iure ha-

The judicial pronouncement is the external manifestation of the disposition of mind induced, as it were, by all that the judge has gathered from the procedure.[218] This expression of his mind is precisely his judicial interpretation, his conclusive decision, the resultant of the application of the law to a concrete case.[219] The pronouncement of what the tribunal thinks *(sententia)* ought to and shall in law and justice obtain concerning the disposition of the cause is the essence of the judicial sentence. This thought is rendered by Justinian in one of his Novels, where the emperor commands judges not to refer causes to him:

> . . . sed perfecte examinare causam et quod sibi iustum atque legitimum visum sit iudicare.[220]

The motives which induced the tribunal to this conclusion are not of the essence of the sentence as such. In fact, it is the Code which first introduced into the common law of the Church the rule of procedure whereby the motives in fact and in law, the reasons for the decision, are to be added to the dispositive part of the sentence.[221] Hence a Rotal Decision, citing a Decision of the Supreme Signatura Apostolica, points out as a fact beyond question that only the dispositive portion of the

---

bentur; et quantum ad hoc subdit: 'Et sententialia'."—*Op. cit.*, I, IIae, quaest. 96, Art. I, ad primum.

218 "Papa vero . . . dicit quod iudex . . . omnia debet considerare quae fiunt in eius praesentia, et ex his informare debet motum animi sui et formare sententiam . . . Bern."—*Glossa* ad *Casus, c. 6, X, de renuntiatione,* I, 9.

219 Cf., Boudinhon, *LeCC*, XL (1917), 397.

220 N. (125, 1).

221 Lega-Bartoccetti, *Commentarius in Iudicia Ecclesiastica,* II, 958; Wernz, *Ius Decretalium*, V, n. 669. The addition of the motives was strongly urged by Santi as an aid to the parties concerning the advisability of taking an appeal. He also points out that according to decretal law ". . . praesumitur iudex semper legitime sententiam proferre . . ."—*Praelectiones,* lib. II, tit. XXVII, n. 11.

sentence actually constitutes the *res iudicata,*[222] and not the reasons from which it is derived.[223]

The truth of this statement appears exemplified in the case reviewed by Pope Innocent III reported in the preceding article. There the law is shown to have made a practical disposition of a particular right and in a particular case in a very positive fashion, a disposition which but for the error of the court, could have been correctly made. However, the disposition stands as posited. Here is tangibly perceptible the element of authentic interpretation in the judicial sentence inasmuch as it decrees authoritatively how the law is to be observed in a particular case.

ARTICLE IV. *Effect of Judicial Interpretation.*

The effect produced by the judicial sentence will here be considered from the vantage point of canon 17, § 3. Hence the question to be discussed is the juridic scope of judicial interpretation.

The present section of canon 17 states that the authentic

222 ". . . et notissimum est in re iudicata determinanda, attendendas esse tantummodo partes dispositivas sententiarum, non autem rationes a iudice datas (Decis. Signaturae typis ed. II ser. an. 1845-1854, decis. 14, p. 20)."—S. R. R. *Molinen. Iurium,* 17 Iunii 1920, *coram R. P. D. Ioanne Prior, Decano,* dec. XVII—*Decisiones,* (Romae: Typis Polyglottis Vaticanis, 1927), XII (1920), 156.

223 ". . .cum canones pro re iudicata habenda, non rationes in sententiis expensas, sed decisiones inde captas attendant . . ."—S. R. R. *Rottemburgen, Nullitatis Matrimonii,* 13 augusti 1924, *coram R. P. D. Francisco Parrillo,* dec. XL—*Decisiones,* (Romae: Typis Polyglottis Vaticanis, 1934), XVI (1924), 366; Coronata, *Institutiones,* III, n. 1404. Hence Coronata (*op. cit.,* n. 1400) says concerning the collegiate tribunal (cf. can. 1871): "Dummodo iudices concordent in ipsa sententia nihil refert quod in eius motivatione dissentiant", citing Roberti, *De Processibus,* II, 451.

interpretation of law rendered in the form of a judicial sentence (or of a rescript concerning a particular matter) does not have the force of law, and that it is obligatory only as regards the persons and affects those affairs for which it is given. This discussion necessarily implies that the sentence has become a *res iudicata*, according to canon 1904, § 2. It has already been shown in the second article of this chapter that the sentence of an inferior judge does not constitute a judicial precedent.[223a]

1. *Vim legis non habet.*

The glossator of the law *"Forus"* in the Decretals of Gregory IX conceives very ingeniously the *lex* as a status of *ius*. By means of the judicial sentence the *ius* is not constituted, but rather the status of the *ius* is declared.[224] In other words the gloss envisions the judicial sentence as representing a *lex*, a declaration of the *ius*. St. Thomas, as mentioned in the previous article, considered the sentence as a certain species of *lex*. It seems certain that the glossator has the same fundamental idea, and also the further concept that the judicial sentence is the interpretation *(declaratio)* of the *ius* respecting a particular case.The result of this interpretation, being a positive disposition (such is also the concept of St. Thomas), can well be called a *lex*. Thus the concept of the effect of a judicial sentence, being a positive disposition of the *ius*, would agree with that propounded by St. Thomas; namely, the effect is a *lex* "quae pro iure accipitur" for a particular case.

The Code in the present section of canon 17 evidently

223a Cf., pp. 240; 244-246; 248-249.

224 "Lex enim dicitur status iuris et vere, quia per sententiam ius non constituitur, sed status iuris declaratur."—*Glossa* ad v. *Iuris status*, c. 10, X, *de verborum significatione*, V, 40.

conceives *lex* as a general, abstract precept, since it denies that the judicial interpretation has the force of a *lex*; rather, judicial interpretation is confined to the particular. Hence according to the Code *lex* must be referable to the general. The legislator is here speaking in terms of "vim legis" *communis*. Therefore the judicial interpretation in the jurisprudence of the Code cannot be conceived as in any sense constituting *per se* general law. However, though the Code does not place the same meaning in the legal terminology, "*lex*", as that contained in this term as used by the glossator, nevertheless the same concept (as contained in the gloss and in the doctrine of St. Thomas) of the functional effect of the judicial sentence, which is the declaration of the conformity or disagreement of a certain set of facts (a case) in relation to the *ius*, is certainly embodied in the Code's concept of judicial interpretation. This fact has been established throughout the previous articles of this chapter. In particular, this concept is revealed in canon 1904, where the legislator declares that the sentence is presumed "*iusta*" and "Facit *ius* inter partes". In other words, the sentence is the interpretation of the demands of justice for the particular case. The doctrine of Suarez reveals the self same concept as that presented in the foregoing.[225] Hence it may here be pointed out again that there is an essential difference between the *lex*, which is written law, and which is, as the gloss quoted above plainly indicates, a derivative of the *ius* (the *ars boni et aequi*), and the *ius* itself. Now, the province of the judiciary as such is not confined to the *lex*.[226] In other words, the law itself allows that the judiciary has a wider range than is marked by the confines of the written law.

---

225 "Nam hinc actus iudicis solet nomine iuris appellari, vel quia secundum leges fieri debet, vel quia interdum videtur quasi legem constituere, et sic dictur iudex, cum munus suum exercet, ius dicere; . . ."—*De Legibus*, I, cap. 2, n. 8.

226 Cf. can. 20.

Therefore a rule cannot be set up that its interpretation is synonymous with the meaning of the *lex*; in fact, the tribunal does not render in its sentence the abstract meaning of the law or laws taken singly and apart.[227] If the judicial interpretation be conceived as formulating general law, the subsequent effect is a general obligation unto the subjects to conform their respective acts not to the law *(leges)* but to the adjudicated case. At best the practical question would always remain: Was the case correctly adjudicated?

2. *Ligat tantum personas atque afficit res pro quibus data est.*

In the previous number it was shown that the legislator of the Code denies the power of general authentic interpretation to the judicial sentence. Here the positive feature of the sentence is considered. The authentic interpretation given by judicial sentence (or rescript in a particular matter or affair) is binding only upon the persons and affects the matters for which it is given. Its authenticity is confined to the particular case exclusively.[228]

---

227 Cf. Toso, *Commentaria Minora*, I, 47-48; Michiels, *Normae Generales*, I, 387, 397; Jone, *Gesetzbuch des kanonischen Rechtes*, I, 37.

228 It is outside the pale of this study to dwell on the question regarding the persons who are admissible as parties to the cause before an ecclesiastical tribunal. It may be pointed out that the term *persona* has a juridic signification; by Baptism a man is constituted in the Church of Christ as a person. From this juridic fact definite rights and duties proceed.—cf. can. 87. Also, it may be mentioned that in ecclesiastical law there is the distincton between moral and physical personality.—cann. 99-100. In particular, moral persons have in law the status of minors, who themselves must be represented by others in judicial proceedings, except in certain cases.—cf. cann. 100, § 3; 88, § 1; 1648; 1649. The subject matter referable to the ecclesiastical tribunal is described in canons 1552-1554.

The principle of law here under discussion is enunciated in the decretal law "*Quamvis*" by Gregory IX (+1241):

> Quamvis regulariter aliis non noceat res inter alios iudicata . . .,[229*]

derived, as noted from the testimony of Gonzalez, from Roman law. Hence the juristic axiom: "Res inter alios acta nec nocet nec prodest".[230] What the tribunal has decided concerning the rights of the litigants does not redound to the benefit or detriment of others. For, as Santi says, the judicial process, representing a special case involved as it is in concrete circumstances, is a matter between private individuals.[231] Indeed, the jurisprudence in this matter is very reasonable and just. If the plaintiff or defendant or even the judge has played ill his part in judgment, why should others suffer thereby? As Reiffenstuel says, the judicial interpretation is particular in two ways; it neither prejudices the right of others, nor does it dictate the decision of judges in similar cases.[232] Considered from any angle, each sentence represents a single case adjudicated.[233] The sentence of the Supreme Pontiff *per se*, that is, unless it is promulgated as universal law, is binding only upon the parties to the cause.[234] The rights of others could be

---

229 C. 17, 25*, X, *de sententia et re iudicata*, II, 27; c. 6, X, *de fide instrumentorum*, II, 22; cf. cann. 1898-1901. Gonzalez (*Commentaria*, lib. II, tit. XXVII, cap. XXV, *Notae*) states of Gregory IX: "Qui a nemine consultus, sed proprio motu praesentem edidit constitutionem depromptam ex principiis iuris civilis. . ."; cf. C. (7, 56) 1-4.

230 Gonzalez, *Commentaria*, lib. II, tit. XXVII, cap. XXV, n. 1.

231 "Nam iudicium negotium est privatorum. Hinc sententia nihil adiud est quam applicatio iuris casui speciali prout resultat ex circumstantiis expositis et probatis a partibus collitigantibus. Quare in iudicio ius pronunciatur coarctatum ad personas, quae partem in causa habuerunt."—*Praelectiones*, lib. II, tit. XXVII, n. 16.

232 *Ius Canonicum Universum*, lib. I, tit. II, n. 362.

233 Cf. Van Hove, *De Legibus Ecclesiasticis*, n. 246.

234 Wernz, *Ius Decretalium*, V, n. 672.

prejudiced if third parties have an independent interest in a given case; likewise, if judges were constrained to follow the decision of another tribunal.

Therefore, regarding the independent right of others, it follows that an *exceptio rei iudicatae* is peremptory for judge and the second party only when it is certain that in the action at law a) the same subject matter is at issue, b) between the same parties juridically considered, and c) in virtue of the same cause of action.[235] The "same person" juridically would be, e. g., the legal successor to an inheritance, or an heir, or children whose parents according to canon 1648 sustained litigation for them when they were minors.[236] An "other person" is properly, and hence juridically, one who has an equal right, not a right merely dependent upon the right of another.[237] The point here, of course, is to determine who are the "tantum personas" of canon 17, § 3. The phrase "tantum personas" therefore excludes from the effect of a *res iudicata*, from the

---

[235] "Ut autem exceptio rei iudicatae actionem impediat, de tribus constare debet: nimirum, in actione intenta 1° eamdem esse rem petitam, 2°. easdem esse personas iuridice consideratas, et 3°. eamdem esse causam petendi. Cfr. Lega, De Iudiciis, vol. I, p. 642."—S. R. R., *Societatis Quaestionum Incidentalium de Exceptione Rei Iudicatae*. 18 martii 1922, *coram R. P. D. Ioanne Prior, Decano*, dec. VII—*Decisiones*, (Romae: Typis Polyglottis Vaticanis, 1930), XIV (1922), 67-68.

[236] Gonzalez, *Commentaria*, lib. II, tit. XXVII, n. 3: ". . . quia nemo potest plus iuris in alium transferre quam ipse habet"; *idem*, lib. II, tit. XXV, cap. XIII, n. 8: "Sane eaedem personae dicuntur non solum quae principale fuerunt in lite, sed earum successores, tam universales, quam singulares. . . Et parentes, si ex personis filiorum conveniantur. . . Aliis autem res iudicata nec nocet nec prodest, ut latius dicemus in cap. penult. de re iudic."; *idem*, lib. II, tit. XXVII, n. 3: "Etiam quandoque una eademque causa ad plures spectat; ad unum primo et principaliter; ad alios dependenter a iure ipsius: quo casu cum iura non sint dissimilia, alii dici non possunt, atque res iudicata contra unum nocet aliis. . ."

[237] "Proprie igitur alius in proposito dicitur ille, qui aeque princpale ius habet nec dependens a iure victi. . Secundo sciendum est, sententiam regulariter non nocere aliis qui diversum et par ius habent. . ."—*Idem*, lib. II, tit. XXVII, nn. 3-4.

judicial interpretation, one who has an equal right to file suit concerning the same thing, not one who enjoys a right merely dependent upon the right of another. The latter therefore is not a third party; he is included in the "tantum personas."

It has already been shown in the second article of this chapter (Cf. p. 240) that judicial interpretation is particular in the sense that other judges are not bound thereby. Here, for the sake of completeness a further word will be said.

In similar or even identical cases judges are not constrained by a previous decision. Hence *per se* no judge is bound to follow a decision of the Roman Rota or even of the Supreme Signatura Apostolica,[238] though their pronouncements have admittedly considerable and in certain instances great juristic value for inferior judges.[239]

ARTICLE V. *Interpretation of the Judicial Sentence.*

The sentence is executed by public authority.[240] However, whether there is an execution of the sentence or not, there can arise the question of interpreting the judicial pronounce-

---

238 Cf. *Fontes*, n. 2079; Wernz, *Ius Decretalium*, (3. ed., Prati, 1913), I, n. 253. Justinian decreed that judges were free in this matter. They were not obliged to follow a decision, even that of the *praefectus praetorio*, if they did not agree with its disposition: ". . . (non enim si quid non bene dirimatur, hoc et in aliorum iudicum vitium extendi oportet, cum non exemplis, sed legibus iudicandum est), nec si cognitionaliter sint amplissimae praefecturae. . .".—C. (7, 45) 13. Regarding the eminent position of the *praefectus praetorio*, Kuebler (*Geschichte des Römischen Rechts*, [Leipzig-Erlangen: A. Deichertsche Verlagsbuchhandlung Dr. Werner Scholl, 1925], p. 312-313) declares: ". . . mit Recht nennt man wohl den *Praefectus praetorio* das *alter ego* des Kaisers (nota 1.—z. B., Seeck, Gesch. de. Unterg. II², 63)."

239 Michiels, *Normae Generales*, I, 397-398; Van Hove, *De Legibus Ecclesiasticis*, n. 246.

240 Can. 1918.

ment. Canon 1921, § 1, declares that the executor shall perform his office in accord with the obvious sense of the decision. If doubt regarding its tenor arises, can the tribunal proceed to interpret the sentence? Doubt could also appear at the instance of the *oppositio tertii.*[241] After the definitive sentence has been passed, the minister of justice ceases in his capacity of judge. He has fulfilled his charge and cannot withdraw his decision, provided it be considered valid.[242]

The Code does not seem to have a general express prescript on this question; consequently, one will follow the rules of canon 20. Hence if the tenor of the sentence is such that it does actually not determine or define the question[243] in the sense that its language is ambiguous, it follows necessarily that it is null. That is, there is no sentence; just as a doubtful law is no law. Consequently, the judge will follow canon 1897, § 2, and correct the fault.[244] On the other hand, there can be mere subjective doubt concerning the meaning of the sentence. Or, the decision may be unclear as to its practical execution.

There is a constant juristic teaching on the power of the judge to interpret his sentence, as is revealed by Reiffenstuel (+1703), who teaches explicity that the judge is the authentic interpreter of his sentence.[245] It becomes evident from the investigation of the sources which he cites that the doctrine

---

[241] Cf. can. 1898.

[242] Wernz, *Ius Decretalium*, V, n. 670, Santi, *Praelectiones*, lib. II, tit. XXVII, n. 2.

[243] Cf. can. 1873, § 1, 1°-2°.

[244] "Quodsi sententia fuerit invalida, iudex ordinarius illam revocare atque corrigere potest. . ."—Wernz, *Ius Decretalium*, V, n. 670.

[245] "Interpretatio necessaria particularis, seu non generalis, est ea quae fit per iudicem. Nam Iudex imprimis potest interpretari sententiam suam, arg. l. Paulus, ff. de re iudicat. Et l. In ambiguis, [*sic*] ff. de Praetoriis stipulationibus. Ac notat Glossa cit. cap. vers. Interpretatus, de Postulat. praelat." —*Ius Canonicum Universum*, lib. I, tit. II, n. 362; Vecchiotti, *Institutiones*, II, 308. (N. B. There is no *"In ambiguis"* in the title cited by Reiffenstuel; the law is *"In praetoriis"*.)

on this head is constant and undeviating. It is derived from Roman law.

The *glossa* to the law of the Decretals *"Ad haec in beato"*, which Reiffenstuel cites, is similarly clear on this principle. It explains that the tribunal can interpret its sentence by reason of the fact that according to the law *"Paulus"* of the Digest, the praetor must supply what is deficient in his sentence concerning the practical results consequent upon his pronouncement, though he cannot withdraw it.[246] Hence, the gloss continues, like the praetor, who can interpret according to the explicit law of the Digest *"In praetoriis"* [247] if there should occur any ambiguity, so the judge can similarly function in the capacity of an authentic interpreter.[248] The same principle is enunciated in the gloss of the law of the Digest *"Ab executore"*.[249] It may be mentioned that a marginal gloss to the law *"In praetoriis"* sees in this interpretation of the sentence an application of the fundamental principle of authentic interpretation.[250]

Briefly, the present doctrine is sustained by Hostiensis,[251] Boich,[252] Bartolus,[253] to whom Panormitanus

246 ". . . reliqua autem, quae ad consequentiam quidem iam statutorum pertinent, priori tamen sententiae desunt, circa condemnandum reum vel absolvendum debere supplere, scilicet eodem die."—D. (42, 1) 42.

247 D. (46, 5) 9.

248 "Alia . . . [interpretatio] . . . necessaria . . . ut iudicis . . . Quod possit iudex interpretari sententiam suam est arg. ff. de iudi. l. Paulus. Ubi potest supplere quae desunt sententiae, sic et interpretari sicut praetor potest, ff. de praeto. stipu. l. in praetoriis."—*Glossa* ad v. *Interpretatus*, c. 1, X, *de postulatione praelatorum*, I, 5.

249 *Glossa* ad v. *Interpretari*, D. (49, 1) 4, citing a concordance of laws in the Decretals of Gregory IX.

250 "Nota quod illius est interpretari cuius est constituere vel condere."—*Glossa marginalis*, ad. v. *Interpretatio*, D. (46, 5) 9.

251 *Commentaria*, lib. V, tit. XL, cap. XV, *In his*.

252 *Commentaria*, lib. V, tit. XL, cap. *Olim*, n. 7.

253 *Commentaria*, D. (49, 1) 4 (Titulus: *De Appellationibus et Relationibus*, lex *Ab executore*), n. 7.

makes reference for confirmation of the same teaching,[254] and finally by Sylvester Prierias.[255] Therefore it is the clear and correct teaching in Reiffenstuel that the judge is the authentic interpreter of his decision.

In conclusion, it may be remarked that the successor of the judge can interpret the sentence, because, as Noval correctly says, the same tribunal continues to exist regardless of the individual persons; the judge is a public personality, not a private individual.[256] Moreover, if his services are found necessary in this respect,[257] the residential Bishop himself, after he has consulted the acts of the case, can authentically interpret the sentence, even though he did not preside at the hearings.[258]

ARTICLE VI. *The Doctrine of Judicial Precedent in Canonical Jurisprudence.*

In the foregoing (Cf. p. 240) it was shown that the decision of inferior judges does not constitute a precedent for similar cases, and that it never had this juridic force. The subject of this presentation is the juridic scope of the judicial decisions of the superior tribunals of the Holy See which, until the constitution of Pius X, *"Sapienti Consilio"*, June 29, 1908,

---

[254] "An autem iudex possit interpretari suam sententiam postquam eam tulit, si de novo circa eam oriatur aliquod dubium? Glossa ista arguit quod sic et tene menti in hac glossa. Sed vide latius per doctores in c. ex par. 3. de ver. sig. plenius per Bar. in l. ab executore, ff. de ap."—*Commentaria,* lib. I, tit. V, cap. I, *Ad haec,* n. 22; *idem,* lib. V, tit. XL, cap. XV, *In his,* n. 3.

[255] *Summae Sylvestrinae,* s. v., *Interpretatio,* n. 1.

[256] *De Processibus,* nn. 622, 660, 662; Vermeersch-Creusen, *Epitome,* III, n. 229; ". . . Iudex publica authoritate fungitur et ex ea iudicat. l. Barbarius ff. de offic. praetor . . ."—Reiffenstuel, lib. I, tit. XXXII, n. 41. Note his very remarkable citation of the *Lex Barbarius,* D. (1, 14) 3.

[257] Ordinarily the Bishop should not handle judicial matters.—can. 1578.

[258] Cf. cann. 1572, § 1; 1573, § 2.

were represented by the several Sacred Congregations.[259] Likewise, a brief sketch of the jurisprudence regarding the decision of the Supreme Pontiff himself will be presented.

The *"Sapienti Consilio"* solved for the future in a practical way the controversy whether the decisions of the S. Congregations have universal force. Judicial matters were withdrawn from their competence. The Code in canon 17, § 3, solves the same question in regard to any judicial decision, even that of the Supreme Pontiff. Wernz (+1914), contrary to the common opinion, already taught that his decision does not *per se*, that is, without promulgation to the Church at large, have the force of universal law but is binding only upon the parties.[260]

Speaking about the judicial sentence, Santi (+1885) declares that since the S. Congregations constitute the tribunal of the Roman Pontiff, their decrees emanate *ad instar legis* (after the manner of law); they perform the function of a legislator in contradistinction to the office of an inferior judge.[261] Lega inclines strongly to the same opinion. His reason is that the S. Congregations have the authority of *authentically*[262] interpreting law as opposed to mere judicial interpretation. His only hesitancy lies in the question whether the S. Congregations intend to impose a universal obligation in giving their judicial decisions. The whole question has respect, of course, only to the law as it stands, not to any sub-

---

[259] *Fontes*, n. 682, § II, 2. Thereafter judicial matters were to be referred to the S. Roman Rota, which was always a superior tribunal of the Holy See. Its decisions were considered as binding only for the given case.—Reiffenstuel, *Prooemium*. n. 140.

[260] *Ius Decretalium*, V, n. 672.

[261] *Praelectiones*, lib. II, tit. XXVII, n. 11.

[262] He uses this term in connotation of the force of universal law.—*De Iudiciis Ecclesiasticis*, II, 359.

stantial change in its original provisions.[263] Bouix (+1870) declares absolutely concerning the decisions of the S. Congregation of the Council that they have the force of universal law. He cites many eminent canonists in support of his view, among them Benedict XIV (+1758), and compiles a brief list of moral theologians, such as Bonacina, Layman, Sanchez, who oppose his view and maintain that these decisions have only doctrinal value for the faithful at large.[264] Reiffenstuel (+1703) citing Barbosa (+1649) and others, anticipates Bouix.[265] Lastly, Fagnanus (+1678) emphatically teaches in his very extensive treatise on the law of the Decretals *"Quoniam"* in conjunction with the law *"Cum venissent"* that the decisions of the S. Congregation of the Council, and it is around this Congregation that the question largely centers, have universal force.[266] As Bouix very correctly points out,[267] the basis of the controversy is chiefly the question of the necessity of promulgating an interpretation of a law which is doubtful. The division of opinion is between canonists on the one side and moralists on the other, as appears from the report of Bouix. Wernz (+1914), citing St. Alphonsus, D'Annibale, Aichner, Zallinger and others, was the first, it seems, who taught clearly and without reserve what is contained in canon 17, § 3.[268]

Whatever may be the correct solution of this question,

---

[263] *De Iudiciis Ecclesiasticis,* II, 352-353, 359. On p. 359 he seems to answer his doubt in the affirmative and without reservation.

[264] *De Curia Romana,* pp. 302, 304, 329.

[265] *Ius Canonicum Universum, Prooemium,* nn. 124-132. Bouix does not lay much stress, if any, on the necessity on the part of the S. Congregation of consulting the Supreme Pontiff prior to the issuance of a decision, contrary to the common opinion, as appears from Reiffenstuel, *loc. cit.*

[266] *Commentaria,* lib. I, tit. II, cap. *Quoniam, per totum*; lib. II, tit. I, cap. *Cum venissent,* nn. 16-17.

[267] *De Curia Romana,* p. 307.

[268] *Ius Decretalium,* (2. ed., Romae, 1905), I, n. 146: *Op. cit.,* V, (Prati, 1913), n. 672; Oietti, *De Romana Curia,* (Romae, 1910), p. 11.

it is not surprising that a great deal of power should have been attributed to the S. Congregations because of their immediate connection with the Supreme Pontiff. That the force of universal law attached to his judicial decision is a principle of long standing.

Accordingly, as to the interpretation by judicial sentence, the *Decretum* of Gratian reports the decision of a case by Pope Gelasius I (+496). The Sovereign Pontiff declares that the decision given by him in this case is to be followed in subsequent cases.[269] The glossator sees in this case the principle that what is enjoined upon certain persons or determined regarding a certain matter, is to be extended to others or to similar matters; he recites the law of Innocent III (+1216) in the Decretals of Gregory IX, which establishes the same principle.[270] The law of the Decretals reads as follows:

> In causis quae summi Pontificis iudicio deciduntur et ordo iuris et vigor aequitatis est subtiliter observandus, cum in similibus casibus caeteri teneantur similiter iudicare; nisi forte cum aliquid (causa necessitatis et utilitatis inspecta) dispensative duxerit statuendum.[271]

To wit: The procedure of law and the force of equity must be carefully observed in causes which are decided in the tribunal of the Sovereign Pontiff, because in similar cases others are held to pronounce similar judgment, except where he should decide—by reason of necessity or utility—to ordain otherwise by way of dispensation. The gloss states that inferior judges

---

269 ". . .ea quae inter fratrem et coepiscopum nostrum Constantinum Camiscanae ecclesiae sacerdotem et directos ab Anconitano pontifice decrevimus . . . tunc formam in ceteris cognitionibus, quae sit sequenda perscripsimus."—*Decretum Magistri Gratiani,* (2. ed., Richter-Friedberg, Lipsiae, 1879), c. 5, C. XVI, q. 3.

270 "Argumentum quod certis personis mandatur ad alios extendi; et quod in uno negotio statuitur, ad similia extendi."—*Glossa* ad v. *Formam,* c. 5, C. XVI, q. 3.

271 C. 19, X, *de sententia et re iudicata,* II, 27.

are bound by the decision pronounced by the Pope between certain litigants; his sentence is law for all; in similar cases the same judgment must issue.[272] The gloss remarks, moreover, that a dispensation granted in this matter does not constitute a precedent.[273] Thus the glossator accepts as clear law that the definitive sentence of the "princeps" constitutes a precedent; not so the interlocutory sentence unless it is inserted into the *Corpus Iuris*. Concluding, the gloss cites the parallel law in the Code of Justinian *"Si Imperialis"*, which contains the same rule of precedent,[274] and also the case in Gratian mentioned above.[275] This principle is again recited in connection with the law *"In his"* of the Decretals, where another judicial decision of the Pope is reported.[276]

Hostiensis (+1271), Ioannes Andreas (+1348) citing Innocent IV (+1254),[277] and Henricus Boich (+1350) [278]

---

272 "Inferiores tenentur iudicare secundum quod Papa inter certas personas iudicaverit. . ."—*Summarium* ad v. *In causis*, c. 19, X, *de sententia et re iudicata*, II, 27; ". . . sententia Papae ius facit quo ad omnes . . . et sic in similibus idem iudicium est habendum."—*Glossa* ad *Casus, ibid.*

273 "Item dispensationes non debent trahi ad ius commune."—*Glossa* ad *Casus, ibid.*

274 C. (1, 14) 12; "Sententia definitiva principis lata super causa de qua plene cognovit, et eius declaratio habet vim legis generalis: et eius est interpretari cuius est condere. Sali. [cetus]."—*Superscriptio*, C. (1, 14) 12.

275 "Et sic patet quod diffinitiva sententia principis trahenda est ad consequentiam, ex quo alii similiter iudicare debent. Sed interlocutoria non, C. de legi . . . Si quis [*sic*] Imperialis . . . nisi interlocutoria in corpore iuris claudatur . . . Et est simile huic 16, q. 3, licet."—*Glossa* ad v. *In similibus*, c. 19, X, *de sententia et re iudicata*, II, 27.

276 "Quae interpretatio generalis est et ius facit et ab omnibus servanda est; Inter alia et C. de leg. l. prima."—*Glossa* ad v. *Interpretamur*, c. 15, X, *de verborum significatione*, V, 40. It will be noted that the glossator confirms his annotation by referring to the two laws, the first from Decretal law, the second from Roman law, which contain the principle of authentic interpretation.

277 *Novella Commentaria*, lib. II, tit. XXVII, cap. XIX, *In causis, passim*, where he furnishes a long report on a controversy concerning the force of the definitive and interlocutory sentence.

278 *Commentaria*, lib. II, tit. XXVII, cap. *In causis*, n. 1; he denies this

severally agree that the sentence, definitive or interlocutory, of the "princeps", whether Pope or emperor, according to the law of the Code of Justinian [279] and the canon in Gratian's *Decretum* [280] has the force of general law and is a binding precedent provided he has examined the cause in the presence of the litigants.[281] The doctrine that this definitive sentence creates general law, with certain qualifications expressed by later authors, is constant [283] down to Reiffenstuel (+1703) [284] and Schmalzgrueber (+1735).[285] Suarez (+1617) is also to be included in this tradition.[286] It will be interesting to dwell briefly on his teaching.

Suarez observes that it is the common opinion of civilists and canonists that the sentence of the head of the state consti-

---

prerogative to inferior judges: "Sententia vero alterius non facit ius generale, sed solum inter quos lata est, ut l. nemo [C. (7, 45) 13] . . . idem tenent Innocentius, Hostiensis, et Ioannes Andreas."—*Op. cit.*, n. 4.

279 C. (1, 14) 12.

280 C. 5, C. XVI, q. 3, quoted above.

281 "Est et alia interpretatio quae fit secundum propriam verborum significationem, et haec etiam omnibus praeiudicat et ius facit ex quo fit a Principe sive fiat in iudicio sive extra iudicium."—Hostiensis, *Commentaria*, lib. V, tit. XL, cap. XVI, *Olim*, n. 6; "Dummodo examinatione praecedente causa cognita et partibus praesentibus etiam interpretando vel interloquendo pronunciaverit. C. de legibus, l. fi. unde hoc sumptum est; 16, q. 3."—*Idem*, lib. II, tit. XXVII, cap. XIX, *In causis*, ad v. *teneantur*. Hostiensis remarks that this rule of law is an exception: ". . . non exemplis, sed legibus iudicandum est. Solutio speciale est hoc in sententia Principis, cuius exemplum sequendum est."—*loc. cit.*

283 Cf. Baldus de Ubaldis (+1400), (*Commentaria*, lib. II, tit. XXVII, cap. XIX, *In causis*, n. 2), who demands that the sentence receive some form of publicity in order to be obligatory; it should at least be in writing; Panormitanus (+1435), *Commentaria*, lib. II, tit. XXVII, cap. XIX, *In causis*, n. 4; Felinus Sandaeus (+1503), *Commentaria*, lib. II, tit. XXVII, cap. XIX, *In causis*, nn. 3-8; *idem*, lib. I, tit. II, cap. I, *Canonum*, n. 16; Pirhing (+1617), lib. II, tit. XXVII, n. 19.

284 *Ius Canonicum Universum, Prooemium*, n. 141.

285 *Ius Ecclesiasticum Universum*, lib. II, tit. XXVII, n. 85.

286 *De Legibus*, III, cap. 15, nn. 11-22.

tutes general law; he indicates the sources cited generally from Roman[287] and Canon law.[288] The sentence of the "princeps" is a rule for inferior judges and of such authority as to forbid subjects to depart therefrom; thus it is virtually a precept and as such it has the force of law.[289] The sentence can have two functions; it may be a declaration of prior law, which contingency is perhaps more frequently the case, or the enactment of a new law. Of itself the judicial sentence is not constitutive of law, but declarative, because of its nature it deals with a fact in the past.[290] Suarez demands some adequate publication or promulgation of the sentence since this act is the complementary element of legislating, whereby the sentence, being a rule for deciding similar cases, is constituted in the status of law.[291]

It was clear law, therefore, in the period of decretal legislation and hence clearly taught by the jurists that the sentence of the Supreme Pontiff begets general law binding inferior judges.[292]

However, departing from the interpretation of earlier canonists, canon 17, § 3 makes no distinction. Therefore, the sentence of the legislator, by reason of his own choice, is not a binding precedent.

---

[287] C. (1, 14) 12; D. (1, 4) 1, 1.

[288] C. 19, X, *de sententia et re iudicata,* II, 27.

[289] "Ratio reddi potest quia sententia Principis est veluti regula ad quam omnes inferiores iudices conformari tenentur . . . tantam habere auctoritatem ut subditos obliget ne in simili causa ab illa discrepent et quoad hoc virtuale praeceptum obtinere et ita habere vim legis."—*De Legibus,* III, cap. 15, n. 11.

[290] Suarez, *op. cit.,* n. 16, where he adds that the will to legislate must appear in the sentence, the tenor of which must not evidence merely a prudent opinion, as is always true in the case of inferior judges.

[291] *Op. cit.,* n. 17.

[292] Cf., however the teaching of Wernz, p. 283.

B. Authentic Interpretation by Rescript.

ARTICLE I. *General Notion of Rescript.*

This brief discussion has reference to the rescript which is contemplated in canon 17, § 3, and will serve as an introduction to what must be said concerning the rescript of that canon.

An introductory gloss in the *Decretum* of Gratian [293] defines "decretal letter" and canon. The former is one which issues from the Pope, either alone or at the advice of his Cardinals, upon the consultation of someone *(ad consultationem alicuius)*; [294] a canon is established in a general council. Therefore, the notion of rescript as such is generic, a written reply from the Sovereign Pontiff *(quod ab Apostolico rescribitur)* to a consultation, report, announcement, complaint, petition, etc.[295] In its strict acceptation, however, the rescript includes all written responses for the observance of the law, as when the legislator commits a cause for decision. These are termed "literae ad lites" (instruments of action at law).[296] This notion of rescript, as differentiated from other species of rescript, is constant down to later canonical jurisprudence [297] and to

---

[293] C. 1, D. III.

[294] Hostiensis, *Summa Aurea, Prooemium*, n. 4.

[295] Hostiensis, *Summa Aurea*, Liber Primus, *De Rescriptis*, n. 1.

[296] "Tunc dic clarius . . . alia rescripta, quae emanant ad iuris observantiam . . . tractatur de literis ad lites . . . stricte rescriptum . . . proprie est id quod Princeps scribit ad iuris observantiam, ut quando committit causam decidendam inter aliquos."—Panormitanus, *Commentaria*, lib. I, tit. III, *Rubrica*.

[297] Cf. Reiffenstuel, lib. I, tit. III, nn. 1-32.

the present time,[298] and consequently it has its counterpart in present canonical legislation.

This species of rescript has special interest here. It is that instrument which is given for the observance of the law, and which must, incidentally, be interpreted according to the law as a natural consequence.[299] This last remark has been brought in to bear out the fact that in interpreting the rescript cognizance must be taken of the previous general authentic interpretations which may have issued concerning the law or laws to which the rescript has reference.

Bernard of Pavia (+1216) declares that a rescript often has the force of a constitution, a general law. A rescript given in accord with the law *(secundum ius)* is a decretal letter with authority in the adjudication of judicial causes.[300]

It will be noted that the rescript as just described is said to have the force of a general law. For the present it will suffice to know that this document has been employed as a vehicle to expedite matters according to the prescripts of law *(secundum ius)*. In other words, it was given in interpretation of law, leaving aside for the present the juridic scope which

---

298 Van Hove, *Commentarium Lovaniense in Codicem Iuris Canonici,* (Mechliniae-Romae: H. Dessain, 1936), IV, *De Rescriptis,* nn. 7, 91, 225-226.

299 "Accipiendo Rescriptum stricte, . . . Rescriptum proprie est id, quod Princeps scribit ad iuris observantiam . . . Et ideo verba Rescriptorum interpretationem recipiunt a Iure communi . . . Rescripta iustitiae, sive ad lites; sunt illa . . . ut si Papa causae ad se devolutae Iudicem delegatum constituat; vel quando de iure partium obscuro consultus interpretatur illud, et quid Iudex in iudicando sequi debet, declarat."—Reiffenstuel, lib. I, tit. III, nn. 16, 28.

300 ". . . saepe rescriptum vim habet constitutionis . . . Rescriptum . . . quod ab Apostolico rescribitur ad consultationem. Ut autem melius sciatis quas vires in causis habeat notandum quod rescriptum aliud secundum ius . . . Quod est secundum ius habet vim constitutionis et tale namque est epistola decretalis et habet auctoritatem in causis diffiniendis, ut D. XIX, c. 1, c. XXV, qu. 1, *Omnia.*"—*Summa Decretalium,* (ed. E. A. Th. Laspeyres, Ratisbonae, 1860), I, tit. II, nn. 2-3.

it enjoyed at various times. Lega, speaking of interpretation by rescript, declares that this document was called forth with a view of interpreting law in a particular instance.[301]

From what has been outlined it will appear that the rescript considered in canon 17, § 3, is in the panorama of canonical history just one species of rescript.

ARTICLE II. *Nature and Force of Rescript.*

1. *Nature of Rescript.*

Canon 17, § 3 declares that an authentic interpretation given in the form of a rescript in a particular affair, like the judicial sentence, begets law only for the parties and affects the things for which it is given.

First of all, as Toso correctly remarks,[302] the rescript contemplated in this paragraph of the present canon is a *rescriptum iustitiae*, not *gratiae*; it is one given in justice, not one which conveys a favor. This document is therefore a *rescriptum secundum ius*. This fact is apparent because this rescript has respect to the interpretation of law. Here will be considered the conditions which the interpretation by rescript implies and under which the rescript is given, in order to derive therefrom a pragmatic notion of the rescript.

It will be noted in the present section of canon 17, that the interpretation by rescript in a particular matter is, in a

---

[301] "Etenim rescripta, utpote quae respondent consultationi alicuius nata sunt ius facere particulare, et hoc exploratissimi iuris est."—*De Iudiciis Ecclesiasticis*, II, 351.

[302] *Commentaria Minora*, I, 46.

certain sense, counterposed to the notion of interpretation by means of a judicial sentence. Now, the specific difference is not in the phrase "in re peculiari", which is, indeed, a qualification of the rescript here mentioned, for it must also be remembered that an interpretation of law purely in the abstract can be and is given by rescript. The judicial sentence is most certainly given in view of a particular juridic matter. Rather, by exclusion, the difference lies clearly in the procedure which produced either the sentence or the rescript, as the case may be. Consequently, interpretation by rescript implies the absence of judicial procedure. Hence the procedure previous to the issuance of a rescript supposes what is known as *de plano cognoscere,*[303] as distinguished from judicial procedure. Thus Devoti draws a distinction between the judicial procedure and the present method of expediting a particular matter. *De plano* simply means that the public authority has stepped down from his exalted position on the dias of the tribunal to the level of the petitioner.[304] The description is classical of the extrajudicial procedure in solving a controversial subject. It plainly signifies that the approach to the solution of the controverted matter at hand, albeit legal, is characterized by the employment of equity *(ex bono et aequo)*; the sentence that is pronounced is in *linea disciplinari* as distinguished from the judicial sentence.[305] The whole procedure, in a word, is marked by an attitude of good faith and compatibility.

---

303 Toso, *Commentaria Minora,* I, 46.

304 ". . . ideo legum auctores saepe magistratum designant iis verbis, *qui tribunali praeest, qui pro tribunali cognoscit.* Cui loco a Latinis opponitur *locus planus.* Unde de plano cognoscere, videlicet ex aequo loco cognoscere, non ex superiore, neque pro tribunali, sed in via, in transitu, cum vel lavandi, vel gestandi, vel ludorum gratia magistratus prodierit."—*Institutiones,* II, 112.

305 Cf. Van Hove, *De Legibus Ecclesiasticis,* n. 245; Wernz, *Ius Decretalium,* I, n. 146, I. Thus, speaking of the office of the SS. Congregations, Monin (*De Curia Romana,* pp. 200-201) explains: "Quid ergo intelligitur per proceduram *in linea disciplinari?* . . . Primo quidem abstinet a contestatione litigiosa partium et a iuris solemnitatibus determinatis. Secundo, aliquantum de

The present procedure lies in the province of the Sacred Congregations, from whose competence judicial matters are excluded.[306]

It must be pointed out, therefore, that the rescript is truly *in re peculiari,* not one which deals purely with an abstract point of law, but, as Blat aptly says, one which has respect to a *negotium singulare,* an affair peculiar to itself.[307] Like the subject matter of the judicial sentence, this rescript supposes a case of concrete circumstances, otherwise the phrase "in re peculiari" is nugatory. Hence the matters negotiated by this document are considered in the classical sense *peculiaria,* proper to time, place, circumstance.[308]

The same general principle of approach and procedure is opportunely applicable in expediting, e. g., in the Diocesan Curia questions referable to purely Diocesan statute, because the present canon speaks of ecclesiastical law in general, not only of the *ius commune* of the Code.

As to the subject matter, there is here an evident parallel between this rescript and the judicial sentence, the difference being, as already noted, a question of procedure and the negotiating of an equitable settlement of difficulties where this is

---

rigoroso iure remittens, ex aequo et bono ea statuit, quae, omnibus perpensis, expedire videntur. Minus ius strictum reddit . . . Unde saeplus recurrit ad media conciliationis, amicabiles compositiones; quandoque etiam negotium grave et arduum prudentibus ordinationibus terminat."

306 Can. 259; *Fontes,* n. 682; Van Hove, *De Legibus Ecclesiasticis,* n. 245; Blat, *Commentarium Textus Codicis Iuris Canonici,* (Romae: Ex Typographia Pontificia in Instituto Pii IX, 1921), I, 98.

307 *Commentarium,* I, 98.

308 Thus Perathoner (*Das Kirchliche Gesetzbuch,* [3. ed., Brixen: A. Weger's Buchhandlung, 1923], p. 40) speaks of this rescript as given ". . . in einer besondern Angelegenheit (interpretatio forensis) . . ."; *item,* Bernhardt, *Die normae generales des Codex Iuris Canonici,* p. 31.

opportune.[309] At the same time the affairs which are expedited in the present way clearly imply a petition made to the proper ecclesiastical superior for the settlement of a matter which involves the operation of law. Therefore, the rescript is truly *secundum ius*. This instrument has its counterpart in the most ancient legal practice of the Church.

The nature of the decretal letters, or rescripts, appears from the *Decretum* of Gratian. There the text of Pope Gelasius (+496), quoted in part by Pope Nicholas (+867), speaks of responses which the Popes at different times had issued upon the inquiry of the various Bishops *(Patrum)* [310] regarding ecclesiastical discipline and orders,[311] to the inclusion, it seems of judicial matters.[312] The gloss to the present canon of Gratian's *Decretum* sets forth a classification of the decretals which casts them into three species: general, which are directed to all; special, issued to individuals, but bearing general import; special, not exceeding the limits of the particular case as to time, place, and purpose.[313] This triple division of documents representing decrees interpretative of law and issuing from the Holy See endured to our own times.[314] The purpose of these documents will appear more clearly in the discussion on the force of rescript, which follows immediately.

---

[309] Wernz, *Ius Decretalium,* I, 146, I.

[310] "Decretales epistolae quas beatissimi Papae diversis temporibus . . . pro diversorum Patrum consultatione dederunt . . ."—c. 1, D. XIX. This canon in Gratian is known as *"Si Romanorum"*.

[311] ". . . decretalia constituta . . . quae de ecclesiasticis ordinibus et canonum promulgata sunt disciplinis . . ."—c. 1, D. XIX, *Palea.*

[312] "Etiam illa tempora vir sanctus [Gelasius] comprehendit, quae crebrescentibus paganorum persecutionibus ad sedem Apostolicam deferri causas Episcoporum difficillime permittebant."—c. 1, D. XIX.

[313] *Glossa* ad v. *De Epistolis,* c. 1, D. XIX.

[314] Cf. Bouix, *De Curia Romana,* p. 358; Wernz, *Ius Decretalium,* I, nn. 144-145; Monin, *De Curia Romana,* p. 216-220; Chelodi, *Ius de Personis,* n. 67.

2. *Force of rescript.*

Like the judicial sentence, so the rescript of canon 17, §3, does not extend beyond the persons and the subject matter to which it is applicable. Wernz (+1914) taught clearly that responses of the Sacred Congregations which issue in virtue of their administrative and executive powers and in view of special circumstances of the case or the application of equity neither constitute general law nor grant permission or impose the obligation to employ them in similar cases.[315] The same principle he taught concerning any *decretum particulare* containing an interpretation of law which is doubtful and given to individuals.[316] His doctrine engenders an immediate deduction. How could one ascertain whether or not a given particular response is rendered in equity or according to strict law?[317] Therefore canon 17, §3, very wisely confines to the parties involved and to the matters at issue the solution given in a particular case. The sense in which this solution is confined to the parties has been outlined in connection with the effect of the judicial decision. Such, however, was not always by any means the case in canonical jurisprudence. The Code in this paragraph settles the uncertainty and the long dispute concerning this very matter, namely, the juridic scope of the rescript, as Van Hove correctly points out.[318] However, before recounting this period of uncertainty, it will be of interest to know that a doctrine of precedent similar to that con-

[315] *Ius Decretalium,* I, n. 146, I.

[316] *Ius Decretalium,* I, n. 146, IV. Monin calls such decrees *novae leges,* according to the more common opinion, as he says; they require, therefore, a proper *(rite)* promulgation in order to create general law.—*De Curia Romana,* p. 219.

[317] The same thought is suggested by the treatise of Monin, *De Curia Romana,* p. 219.

[318] *De Legibus Ecclesiasticis,* n. 244.

cerning the judicial sentence is clearly perceptible in the history of Canon law regarding the juridic scope of the rescript.

The canon of the *Decretum* of Gratian *"Si Romanorum"* referred to above [319] is a letter of Pope Nicholas (+867) in which the Sovereign Pontiff, citing the authority of Popes Leo I (+461) and Gelasius (+496), insists that all decretal letters, even those not contained in the collection of canons *(etiamsi non sint codici canonum compaginatae)*, continue to have the force of law.[320] The nature of the decretal letter has already been described. Thus in the time of Pope Nicholas the existing law is that all of these documents have the force of general law. Such was the doctrine of Gratian and the gloss; decretal epistles have the force and authority of *canones*—universal effect.[321] The glossator points out that whether the decretals are general, directed to all, or special, directed to individuals, if something is defined therein, the decretal must be considered as general law, as in the case where the Sovereign Pontiff pronounces a judicial sentence, unless the decretal is issued in view of a certain time, place, and purpose.[322] Such was the doctrine of Bernard of Pavia, as aforementioned (p. 290), who distinguishes the juridic scope of the interpretation contained in a constitution or a rescript from that given by a judge; the former constitutes

---

319 Cf., p. 294.

320 C. 1, D. XIX.

321 "De epistolis vero decretalibus quaeritur, an vim auctoritatis obtineant, cum in corpore canonum non inveniantur."—*Superscriptio*, c. 1, D. XIX; "Decretales sunt duplices . . . generales et speciales. [Gratianus] ostendit quod decretales epistolae eandem vim habent et auctoritatem quam canones." —*Glossa* ad v. *De Epistolis*, c. 1, D. XIX.

322 ". . . sive generalis sive sit specialis; dummodo aliquid definiatur per eam pro iure generali habenda est ut 16, q. 3, licet [c. 5, C. XVI, q. 3], extra de sent. et re iudic. in causis, [c. 19, X, *de sententia et re iudicata*, II, 27], nisi sit tradita ex tempore, ex loco, et ex causa, ut 29 distin. [c. 1, D. XXIX]."—*Glossa* ad v. *De Epistolis*, c. 1, D. XIX.

general law.[323] The principle that a response to a consultation begets general law is clearly enunciated by Pope Innocent III (+1216).[324] That the decretal letter is the vehicle of interpretation of law in the form of a response to a consultation[325] is evidenced by Pope Gregory IX (+1241), who declares that his decretal letters have dispelled certain doubts concerning previous papal constitutions.[326] It is therefore clear law according to the Decretals that a response to a consultation is a vehicle of general legislation, as appears from the law *"Ex multa"* of Innocent III just quoted.

Cardinal Hostiensis (+1271) is explicit in maintaining that a consultation begets general law *(ius, scilicet, generale)*, obliging everyone after the manner of a papal constitution[327] when the rescript contains the element of common law; when it is in keeping with law and equity; especially, when it bears out equitable and general determinations concerning the law —what is just and canonical and ordinarily to be observed.[328]

---

323 "De interpretationibus vero sciendum est quod interpretatio constitutionis vel rescripti . . . generalis necessaria ut principis . . . alia necessaria et non generalis, ut iudicis . . ."—*Summa Decretalium,* I, tit. II, n. 4.

324 ". . . utrum quod in ea . . . consultatione . . . dicitur, . . . ius constituat generale . . . solicite requisisti. Ad hoc igitur inquisitioni tuae breviter respondemus, quod in consultatione nostra ius commune editur . . ." —c. 9, X, *de voto et voti redemptione,* III, 34. Note: Quotation is taken from *Corp. Iur. Can.,* Richter-Friedberg, Editio Lipsiensis Secunda, 1881. Editions with the glossary omit the word "commune" after "nostra ius". The word "generale" is supplied by the glossator. "Quia cum respondetur consultationi, ius commune ostenditur per responsionem. Argumentum infra de vo. et vo. redem. ex multa."—*Glossa* ad v. *Consultationem,* c. 9, X, *de filiis presbyterorum,* I, 17.

325 "Decretalis est quando respondet . . . princeps . . . ad consultationem."—*Glossa* ad v. *Constitutiones, Decretalium D. Gregorii Papae IX Compilatio, Prooemium.*

326 *Decretalium D. Gregorii Papae IX Compilatio, Prooemium.*

327 *Commentaria,* lib. III, tit. XXXIV cap. IX, *Ex multa.*

328 "Quod continet ius commune. Illud quod consonat iuri et aequitati, maxime quando continet in se iuris determinationes aequaliter . . . quod iustum

In passing it is worthy of note that this rule, it seems, may now stand in good stead for the *doctrinal application* of the rescripts of the Sacred Congregations published in the *Acta Apostolicae Sedis*.

Decretal letters were agencies of interpretation *(iuris determinationes)* of law, so that even special rescripts given *secundum ius* were to be extended to other matters and persons, e. g., those rescripts given with regard to judicial matters; they applied generally wherever circumstances permitted.[329] Hence there is applied the principle: "De similibus simile debet esse iudicium". The decretal letter given in a particular case was to be used as the basis of solving similar cases,[330] according to the law of the Digest *"Non possunt"* [331] and the same principle contained in Decretal law,[332] to which Hostiensis refers, stating that the presumption of the general applicability of the rescript prevails in case of doubt.[333]

This doctrine of Hostiensis on the application of a decretal epistle to similar causes in judicial matters is endorsed by Ioannes Andreas (+1348),[334] who declares that this document has the force of a constitution.[335] Likewise, Panormitanus (+1435) teaches explicitly that the papal rescript stands as a precedent, upon the principle of the Decretals

---

vel quod canonicum et ceteras consimiles . . . quae aequalitas servanda est regulariter."—*Summa Aurea*, Liber Primus, *De Rescriptis*, n. 9.

329 Hostiensis, *Summa Aurea*, Liber Primus, *De Rescriptis*, n. 19. Here may be recalled the dictum of this jurist, that the interpretation of the "princeps" begets general law whether given in court or outside of court.—*Commentaria*, lib. V, tit: XL, cap. XVI, *Olim*, n. 6; cf. *idem*, *Summa Aurea*, Liber Primus, *De Rescriptis*, § *Quas vires habeat*.

330 Hostiensis, *Commentaria*, lib. II, tit. I, cap. XI, *Quia V.*, n. 3.

331 D. (1, 3) 12.

332 "Et idem in similibus observandum est."—c. 4, X, *de rescriptis*, I, 3.

333 It must be proven that the rescript is confined to a single case.—*Summa Aurea*, Liber Primus, *De Rescriptis*, n. 9.

334 *Novella Commentaria*, lib. II, tit. I, cap. XI, *Quia V.*, n. 13.

335 *Novella Commentaria*, lib. I, *In Prologum Gregorii*, ad v. *Rex*, n. 23.

enunciated in the law *"In causis"*, which, it will be recalled, lays down the rule of judicial precedent.[336]

This principle, however, did not remain unchallenged. Henricus Boich (+1350) quotes Hostiensis [337] as maintaining the doctrine outlined above, even if the rescript is not inserted in the *Corpus Iuris*. Boich holds a contrary view *(videtur verius de iure)*, citing in his favor the gloss of Accursius (+1260) [338] and decretalists, among them Vincentius Hispanus, the teacher of Bernardus Parmensis de Botone (+1263).[339]

On the other hand, Felinus Sandaeus (+1503) manifestly holds to the traditional doctrine with Archidiaconus (+1313), Dominicus de Sancto Geminiano (+ante 1436), and Ioannes Andreas (+1348), citing Ludovicus Romanus (+1439) to the effect that an interpretation given by rescript upon the request of an individual concerning the meaning of the law or of a rule of the Apostolic Chancery *(regula Apostolica)* is general law for everyone, according to the law of Justinian *"Si Imperialis"* [340] and of the Decretals of Gregory IX, *"In causis"*.[341] And it is explicitly manifest that he

336 "Nam sicut Papa diffinit et praecipit in casu dubio procedendum, ita et nos diffinire debemus, de re iudic. c. in causis."—*Commentaria*, lib. II, tit. I, cap. XI, *Quia V.*, n. 5.

337 Hostiensis, *Commentaria*, lib. I, tit. III, cap. V, *Si quando*, where Hostiensis takes issue on this head with Bernardus Parmensis de Botone (+1263), who wrote the *glossa ordinaria* of the Decretals of Gregory IX.

338 *Glossa* ad C. (7, 45) 13, where the following of precedent is forbidden in Roman law to inferior judges.

339 *Commentaria*, lib. II, tit. XXVII, cap. *In causis*, n. 4. Philippus Decius (+1536) manifests hesitancy in accepting the traditional doctrine, citing in his favor Paulus de Castro (+1443). Cf. Philippus Decius, *In Decretales Commentaria*, lib. I, tit. III, *Rubrica*, n. 6. Decius seeks some note of promulgation to justify the general obligation.

340 C. (1, 14) 12.

341 Cf. c. 19, X, *de sententia et re iudicata*, II, 27; "Et dicit Ludovicus Romanus, consilium 260 . . . quod interpretatio facta per rescriptum ad

demands no insertion into the *Corpus Iuris* in order to produce this effect.[342] The doctrine of Sylvester Prierias (+1523) is substantially a brief repetition of the teaching of Hostiensis.[343]

Suarez (+1617) sums up the entire doctrine on this question, referring to sources which appear in the foregoing.[344] As to papal rescript he declares that there is a controversy among canonists. Suarez clearly outlines the issue. The question is: Are papal rescripts a vehicle for introducing Canon law? In other words, does a rescript which is admittedly a response to a special consultation or inquiry *(speciales interrogationes, consultationes)* constitute a precedent? This jurist points to a group of canonists who reply in the negative because the document represents only a response to a private consultation. The contrary opinion, however, according to Suarez is accepted by canonists and civilists as certain. The reason is that the Supreme Pontiff can and actually did by positive law set down that a rescript, whether placed in the body of the law or not, constitutes a precedent.[345]

---

postulationem unius concessum super iuris vel Apostolicae regulae intellectu, facit ius generale quo ad omnes per l. finalem, C. de legib., et per notam in c. causis, de re iud."—*Commentaria*, lib. I, tit. III, *Rubrica*, n. 1; *idem, Commentaria*, lib. II, tit. XXVII, cap. XIX, *In causis*, n. 3: "Et quod responsio facta per Papam ad interpretationem alicuius constitutionis facit ius generale . . ."; Again, citing other eminent decretalists he says: ". . . quoties Papa respondet ad consultationem alicuius, quamvis dirigat verba ad casum consulentis, tamen censetur condere ius commune, secundum gl. fi. in c. consultationi, de tempo. ord. et glos. in c. ex tua, de fi. presby . . ."—*Commentaria*, lib. I, tit. II, cap. I, *Canonum*, n. 17.

342 *Commentaria*, lib. I, tit. III, *Rubrica*, n. 1.

343 *Summae Sylvestrinae*, s. v. *Rescriptum*.

344 *De Legibus*, III, cap. 15, n. 22; *op. cit.*, IV, cap. 14, n. 3.

345 "Canonistae enim interdum indicant haec responsa Pontificum non introducere legem . . . quia solum continet responsum ad privatam consultationem . . . Contraria vero sententia vera est . . . et inter Iurisperitos communis . . . hoc non solum esse verum de Epistol. in iure canonico insertis, sed etiam de omnibus aliis, quia Pontifices habent auctoritatem ad ferendas leges hoc modo, et ipsimet declararunt hoc sensu, et hac potestate esse scriptas

Therefore, as indicated in the foregoing, the rescript *per se* was a piece of positive legislation, and its use as such had been established by positive law. However, Barbosa (+1649) seems to be the last of the line of canonists in whose teaching the traditional doctrine is apparent. He still holds the common opinion.[346] Thereafter a definite uncertainty appears as to the use of the rescript in the interpretation of law. This matter will be presented in the following article.

ARTICLE III. *Use of Rescript in Interpreting Law.*

It will be shown in this article that the rescript as a vehicle of law is called seriously into question. The demand for an adequate promulgation comes to the front. Consequently this discussion seeks to outline briefly a more recent trend of thought as to the use of a rescript for the interpretation of law.

The canonists whose views have been presented in a foregoing article, concerning judicial precedent, could well be translated to the present article. The division of views is the

huiusmodi Epistolas, vel responsa."—*De Legibus,* IV, cap. 14, nn. 3-4. In this context Suarez explains that the controversy has respect to a response on a matrimonial question; an individual case. Bartolus a Saxoferrato (+1357) (*Commentaria,* C. (1, 14) 2, [Titulus: *De legibus et constitutionibus principum*]) denies that the rescript of the emperor has universal force, but explicitly grants this juridic scope to the rescript of the Pope: "Rescriptum Principis non facit ius generale . . . Papa de suis epistolis statuit quod esset ius generale. Imperator contrarium statuit in suis legibus. Unum, aliud in epistolis Papae: aliud in epistolis principis", pointing out that the Sovereign Pontiff has expressly legislated on this question. Therefore the juridic scope of the rescript is a matter of positive law.

346 *Augustini Barbosa Lusitani Collectanea Doctorum tam Veterum quam Recentiorum in Ius Pontificium Universum,* (Lugduni, 1656), lib. I, tit. XVII, cap. *Ex tua,* IX, citing Sanchez, *De Matrim.* lib. II, disp. 31, n. 6; Barbosa, lib. II, tit. I, cap. *Quia V.* XI.

same on the question of the juridic extent of the rescript. However, since the question of promulgation is strongly accentuated in the works of the canonists who are presented in the following, their opinions are here set forth.

Gonzalez (+1649), who was incidentally a contemporary of Barbosa (+1649), declares that rescripts given at the petition of individuals *(privatorum)* are not general law unless they are intended to be perpetual or have issued for the interpretation of law, or are placed in the *Corpus Iuris*. Like Philippus Decius (+1536), he views the general juridic force of a rescript as the exception and not the rule.[347] Gonzalez states that since these documents are generally not promulgated, they do not create law, save for the exceptions mentioned.[348] Accordingly, a judicial decision running counter is reprehensible but not void.[349] Thus Gonzalez indirectly points out two important items. Namely, the difficulties incident to knowing the status of the law, since rescripts were usually not promulgated; and the resultant effect by way of controversy which this situation can occasion in regard to judicial matters.

A view quite to the contrary is held by Cardinal Fagnanus (+1678), who teaches that an interpretation rendered by the Supreme Pontiff or his authorized delegate (note that this author is here introducing the S. Congregation of the Council) produces general law even if it was not issued generally and in the manner of law, but only in a particular case upon consultation. This jurist bases his position squarely on the law of Justinian *"Si Imperialis"*.[350] Hence any response,

---

[347] Cf. Philippus Decius, *In Decretales Commentaria,* lib. I, tit. III, *Rubrica,* n. 6.

[348] ". . . alias rescripta cum generaliter non promulgentur, ius non faciunt."—*Commentaria,* lib. II, tit. XXVII, cap. I, n. 13.

[349] *Ibid.*, where he cites Pinellus as in cap. 19, n. 16, [*sic*].

[350] Cf. C. (1, 14) 12; "Porro interpretatio quam facit Papa vel generalem authoritatem habens ab ipso, habet vim generalis constitutionis et facit ius quoad omnes, etiam si non generaliter et per modum legis sed in aliquo

judicial or otherwise, has the force of general law. Fagnanus maintained that the solution of a doubt of law given in a rescript or decision does not need promulgation because it merely declares what is already *in the law*.[351]

These two canonists actually represent the issue. The doctrine of the moralists referred to in the article on judicial precedent would take sides with Gonzalez. The canonists whose doctrine is presented in the following seem in the last analysis more or less undetermined or at least mention their view with hesitancy.

Pirhing (+1679) declares that *per se* the rescript is particular law. Nevertheless, he continues, where a definitive sentence is passed in a certain cause by the head of society *(princeps)*, or where an interpretation of law is given by rescript, the result is precedent, which all judges must follow; the interpretation is law.[352] Wernz (+1914) later followed in the path of Pirhing, stating that a rescript *can* be a general norm according to the law of the Decretals on judicial precedent,[353] but ordinarily and *per se* it is not general law.[354] It may here be pointed out that Wernz uses the principle of judicial precedent in connection with the status of rescript. This procedure gives additional proof of the fact that the jurisprudence concerning rescript and the judicial sentence ran parallel, a phenomenon which may be noticed in other citations in thc foregoing. It is evidenced in Reiffenstuel (+1703). This jurist at first lays great stress on the fact that rescriptis are *ius inter partes* only, and not general law be-

speciali casu et ad consultationem alicuius edita fuerit. Hic est textus in l. fin., in princ., C. de leg., cuius haec sunt verba: 'Si imperialis . . .' "—*Commentaria*, lib. II, tit. I, cap. *Cum venissent*, n. 16.

[351] *Commentaria*, lib. I, tit. II, cap. *Quoniam*, *passim*.

[352] *Ius Canonicum in V. Libros Decretalium*, lib. I, tit. III, *Prooemium*.

[353] C. 19, X, *de sententia et re iudicata*, II, 27.

[354] *Ius Decretalium*, (Prati, 1913), I, n. 149, II.

cause there is no promulgation, which is required for the status of law.[355] Yet in the same context the author is manifestly pressed by the law of Justinian *"Si Imperialis"*.[356] Thus, if the "princeps" in a private response gives his interpretation to a doubtful law, the rescript becomes by deduction *(in consequentiam)* a piece of general legislation. The reason is that the interpretation is considered as inherent in the law from the beginning (the idea of Fagnanus) and that, according to the law of Justinian just mentioned, every act of interpretation given by the Emperor or any supreme head of society is never to be gainsaid or questioned.[357] Manifestly, then, it must obtain in other instances by deduction *(in consequentiam)*. He is likewise urged by the traditional principle, which he quotes from Decretal law: "In similibus casibus ceteri teneantur similiter iudicare".[358] It is evident that Reiffenstuel is driven between the necessity of promulgation and the principles of jurisprudence in Roman and Canon law. Caietanus (+1713) seems to have much the same difficulty. Hence again it is asserted that by deduction *(in consequentiam)* rescripts in a particular case establish common law because the head of the State has manifested his will and has given a rule of action for the community, a norm to be followed in similar circumstances.[359] His doctrine is based on the canon of Gratian which reports the command of Pope Nicholas (+867), *"Si Romanorum"*, mentioned in the foregoing,

[355] *Ius Canonicum Universum,* lib. I, tit. III, nn. 9-11.

[356] C. (1, 14) 12; *op. cit.*, n. 13.

[357] Reiffenstuel, *loc. cit.*, n. 13.

[358] Reiffenstuel, *loc. cit.*, n. 14.

[359] "Ratio est quia huiusmodi rescripta seu responsa ad casus particulares sunt ordinativa communitatis et ut directiva eiusdem emanant a Principe; sunt enim haec rescripta veluti regulae quas principes volunt servari in talibus casibus cum iisdem circumstantiis; . . ."—*Iuris Canonici Universi Commentarius Paratitlaris,* (Monachii, 1703) lib. I, tit. III, n. 12. Suarez' doctrine is quite similar: the rescript was for him a rule for understanding the law: " . . . proponere regulam ad intelligendum quid decernat."—*De Legibus,* IV, cap. XIV, n. 6.

where the Pontiff enjoins that all decretal epistles shall have the force of law,[360] and upon the law of the Digest: "Quod principi placuit legis habet vigorem".[361] Peculiar to this jurist is the thought that the solution of a particular case bears out a pattern of action, a universal idea, applicable to the entire community.[362] This thought is classical of the doctrine of precedent. The author senses great difficulty on the question of promulgation. His difficulty lies in showing how the rescripts become public. They do not have to be included in the *Corpus Iuris;* it is sufficient if they are set before the public *(publice exposita)*, and that it is established in their wording that they are intended to be observed. Since these two items are certain, the conclusion is that they are law.[363]

Finally, Schmalzgrueber (+1735) deals with the present question very much after the manner of Gonzalez. Particular rescripts do not extend to others unless they have been given with the intention that they shall be permanent, or by way of interpretation of law, or have been placed in the *Corpus Iuris*.[364]

The Code in canon 17, §3, put an end to this question by assigning to rescript the function of establishing law only for the particular case.

ARTICLE IV. *Effect of a Rescript in Interpreting Law.*

What has been said previously concerning the effect of a judicial sentence together with the reasons adduced obtains

360 C. 1, D. XIX.

361 D. (1, 4) 1.

362 ". . . quia ita sunt [rescripta] pro casu ut contineant rationem universalem, seque extendant ad totam communitatem."—*Ibid.*

363 Caietanus, *op. cit.*, n. 14. He does not explain how this certainty is established.

364 *Ius Ecclesiasticum Universum*, lib. IV, tit. XXVII, n. 48.

for the effect of a rescript given in a particular matter. The juridic force of this rescript does not reach beyond the subjects of the law for whose benefit the document was issued, nor does it embrace other matters except precisely those for which it was given.

The nature of the rescript of canon 17, §3, does not allow of further juridic extension. Therefore, as in the case of the judicial sentence the same principle is applicable: "Res inter alios acta neque nocet neque prodest". Such is the clear language of the present law. This portion of canon 17 represents new law, a piece of legislation contrary to decretal law, as explained in the articles immediately preceding. Therefore it is to be interpreted from the tenor of its own wording.[365]

Accordingly, the present canon first of all denies the force of law to the authentic interpretation of law given in the form of a rescript concerning a particular matter peculiar to itself. As for the positive aspect of this document, its juridic effect is circumscribed in the manner just stated. This rule of canon 17 obtains for any body of ecclestiastical laws *(leges)* concerning which a response is given by the proper ecclesiastical superior. The reason for this statement is that canon 17 has reference to all laws *(leges)*, not only to the canons of the Code.

The publication of these rescripts in the *Acta Apostolicae Sedis* does not convert them into authentic interpretations of law conveying a general obligation.[366] The reason is that the interpretation which the S. Congregations issue in this re-

---

[365] Cf. can. 6, 3°.

[366] Van Hove, *De Legibus Ecclesiasticis*, n. 246; Michiels, *Normae Generales*, I, 397-398; Wernz-Vidal, *Ius Canonicum*, I, n. 173, II; Beste, *Introductio in Codicem*, p. 77-78; Jone, *Gesetzbuch des kanonischen Rechtes*, I, 37. A contrary opinion is maintained by Coronata, *Institutiones*, I, n. 23, 2°; Vermeersch-Creusen, *Epitome*, I, n. 122, 2°, who propound it with hesitancy, referring to Van Hove in the passage cited above.

script is not an interpretation of laws as such, in the abstract, but only as referable to the particular case.[367] It is opportune here to remark that in the publication of rescripts in the *Acta Apost. Sedis* the Holy See is simply executing the purpose for which this Official Commentary was created by Pius X in his constitution *"Promulgandi"* 29 sept. 1908. For besides being the ordinary means of promulgating law, it also serves to acquaint the Church with such acts as it will be useful to know. Hence some of the rescripts are made public.[368] These instruments proceed from the executive power of the Congregations to apply the law in particular cases;[369] for the rest they have betimes great doctrinal value.[370] In fact, as regards the canons of the Code, the S. Congregations do not have the faculty to interpret these laws as such.[371]

FINIS

---

367 Says Mothon: ". . . les rescrits du Saint-Siège, addressés pour des cas particuliers, ne constituent pas une interprétation authentique des lois générales de l'Eglise, mais seulement une interprétation jurisprudentielle, n'atteignant que les personnes ou les choses pour lesquelles ces rescrits ont été donés", citing canon 17, § 3—*Institutions Canoniques,* (Paris: Société Saint-Augustin, Desclée, de Brouwer et Cie, 1922), I, Art. 37; "Quoad vero Codicis interpretationem, non reliquitur Congregationibus, nisi facultas resolutiones edendi, quibus canones utique interpretantur, sed in quantum ad casus particulares referuntur, ita ut resolutiones inter partes tantummodo ius faciant nisi iteratae in stylum Curiae transierint."—Toso, *Commentaria Minora,* (Romae: Ephemeridis Ius Pontificium, 1923), II, 51.

368 *Fontes,* n. 684, in fine.

369 Blat, *Commentarium,* I, 98.

370 "Nec demum omittat bonus interpres legum nostrarum serio attendere non tantum ad responsa doctrinalia SS. Congregationum . . ."—De Becker, "De Recta Methodo Interpretandi Codicem", *ETL,* II (1925), 246.

371 Motu proprio, *"Cum Iuris Canonici",* I,—*AAS,* IX (1917), 483.

CONCLUSIONS

The following opinions are offered as conclusions resulting from the present study:

1. The faculty of authentic interpretation represents a legislative power.

2. In substance, the principle of authentic interpretation: "Eius est interpretari, cuius est condere", implied in canon 17, §1, was in operation as a juridic norm long before the scientific development of Canon law at Bologna. The application of this principle, therefore, is rooted in the tradition of the Church. With the scientific development of Canon law this principle received its formal terminology and emphasis together with its parallel principle in Roman law.

3. The doctrine is constant throughout the centuries of juristic thought that the successor in office in the capacity of authentic interpreter is identical with the original lawgiver.

4. The identity of juridic personality mentioned in n. 3 is to be understood also of the delegated authentic interpreter.

5. The interpretative power of the Pontifical Commission for the authentic interpretation of the canons of the Code of Canon Law, considering the sources available, embraces all the species of authentic interpretation mentioned in canon 17, §2.

6. The interpretative power of the Sacred Congregations with respect to the Code is limited to the application of the law (the *ius*) to individual cases under the provisions of canon 17, §3. In other respects, regarding law outside the Code, the Sacred Congregations retain their pre-Code jurisdiction in the field of authentic interpretation.

7. Departing from the pre-Code jurisprudence, today neither the Instructions nor the Decrees of the Sacred Congregations represent strictly authentic interpretations of the canons of the Code. These documents belong to the field of administrative jurisdiction as distinguished from legislative power.

8. In pre-Code jurisprudence *interpretatio declarativa* was used with reference to any doubt of law, subjective or objective.

9. To the time of Wernz the *interpretatio declarativa* by a majority opinion of canonists was considered as retroactive, according to the doctrine expressed in the law "*Haeredes palam*" of the Digest.

10. Canon 17, §2, decides in the negative the controversy whether authentic interpretation of doubtful law has retroactive force.

11. It is highly probable that the juridic measure of the *lex in se certa* (and therefore also, of the *dubium iuris*) with reference to canon 17, §2, is coextensive with the means of discovering the signification of a given law outlined in canons 18 and 19. In other words, if a law is not clear after the application of the norms prescribed in these canons, there is present a *dubium iuris*. The subsequent authentic interpretation to such a law is not retroactive.

12. The tenor of a given authentic interpretation must be understood in the light of the context of the law of which the interpretation forms a part; also, in view of parallel passages in the body of law which may have bearing on the point of law which is interpreted.

13. The *terminus a quo*, or the point of departure, of restrictive or extensive authentic interpretation is the proper signification of the legal terminology of the law thus inter-

preted. This proper signification is established according to the prescripts of canons 18 and 19.

14. Authentic interpretation rendered by the medium of the judicial sentence or the rescript of canon 17, §3, does not reflect the meaning of law in the abstract, that is to say, of law in its comprehensive meaning alone and apart from the concrete circumstances of a given case. These vehicles of authentic interpretation declare whether or not a given case is in accord with the prescripts of law and justice.

15. The jurisdiction implied in canon 17, §3, may reach beyond the confines of the *lex scripta* and with the aid of supplementary law administer justice in keeping with the exigencies of the concrete case.

16. Canon 17, §3, represents a change in the jurisprudence in decretal law. Formerly, the judicial sentence or rescript of the supreme legislator was a binding precedent; today this is not indicated in canon 17, §3.

BIBLIOGRAPHY

SOURCES

Acta Apostolicae Sedis, Commentarium Officiale, Romae, 1909—

Codex Iuris Canonici, Pii X Pontificis Maximi iussu digestus Benedicti Papae XV auctoritate promulgatus, ed. Petri Card. Gasparri, Civitate Vaticana: Typis Polyglottis Vaticanis, 1934.

Codicis Iuris Canonici Fontes cura Emi Petri Card. Gasparri editi, 9 voll., Romae [later, Civitate Vaticana]: Typis Polyglottis Vaticanis, 1923-1939. (Voll. VII, VIII, IX, *ed. cura et studio Emi Justiniani Card. Seredi*).

Collectio Librorum Iuris Anteiustiniani in Usum Scholarum, Krueger-Mommsen-Studemund, Berolini: apud Weidmannos, 1923.

Corpus Iuris Canonici, Editio Lipsiensis, 2 voll., Richter-Friedberg, Lipsiae, 1879-1881:
Pars Prior, *Decretum Magistri Gratiani*,
Pars Secunda, *Decretalium Collectiones*.

Corpus Iuris Civilis, 3 voll., Berolini: apud Weidmannos, 1928-1929:
Vol. I ed. stereotypa quinta decima, *Institutiones*,—Paul Krueger; *Digesta*,—Theodorus Mommsen, retractavit Paulus Krueger.
Vol. II ed. stereot. decima, *Codex Iustinianus*,—P. Krueger.
Vol. III ed. stereot. quinta, *Novellae*,—Rudolphus Schoell; opus Schoellii morte interceptum absolvit Guilelmus Kroll.

Corpus Iuris Civilis, 5 voll., Lugduni, 1553-1557.

Decretales D. Gregorii Papae IX suae integritati una cum glossis restitutae, cum privilegio Gregorii XIII, Pont. Max., et aliorum Principum, Romae, 1582.

Decretum Gratiani emendatum et notationibus illustratum una cum glossis, Gregorii XIII, Pont. Max., iussu editum, 2 voll., Romae, 1582.

Fontes Iuris Romani Anteiustiniani in Usum Scholarum, Riccobono-Baviera-Ferrini, Florentiae, 1909.

Liber Sextus Decretalium D. Bonifatii Papae VIII, suae integritati una cum Clementinis et Extravagantibus, earumque Glossis restitutus, Cum privilegio Gregorii XIII, Pont. Max., et aliorum Principum, Romae, 1582.

AUTHORS

Alexander Tartagnus, *In Digestum Commentaria*, 4 voll., Venetiis, 1570.

Angelus de Ubaldis, *Consilia*, Lugduni, 1571.

Baldus de Ubaldis, *In Decretalium Volumen Commentaria*, Venetiis, 1580.

Baldus de Ubaldis, *Commentaria in Digestum,* 3 voll. Venetiis, 1572.

Baldus de Ubaldis, *Commentaria in XI Codicis Libros,* 3 voll., Venetiis, 1572.

Barbosa, Augustinus, *Collectanea Doctorum tam Veterum quam Recentiorum in Ius Pontificium Universum,* 4 voll., Lugduni, 1656.

Barbosa, Augustinus, *Tractatus Varii,* Lugduni, 1660.

Bareille, Georges, *Code du Droit Canonique,* nouvelle ed., Montrejeau: Cardeilhac-Soubirou, 1929.

Bartolus a Saxoferrato, *In Digestum Commentaria,* 6 voll., Venetiis, 1585.

Bartolus a Saxoferrato, *In Codicem Iustiniani Commentaria,* 2 voll., Venetiis, 1585.

Bartoli a Saxoferrato, *Omnia Quae Extant Opera,* 10 voll., Sexta Editio Iuntarum, Venetiis, 1590.

Bartolus a Saxoferrato, *Gemma Legalis,* Venetiis, 1595.

Bernhardt, Erich, *Die normae generales des codex iuris canonici,* Marburg. [ ], 1927.

Bernardus Papiensis, *Summa Decretalium,* ed. E. A. Th. Laspeyres, Ratisbonae, 1860.

Beseler, Gerhard von, *Beiträge zur Kritik der Römischen Rechtsquellen,* 4 Hefte, Tübingen: Verlag von J. C. B. Mohr (Paul Siebeck) 1910-1920; 5tes Heft, Universitätsverlag von Robert Noske in Leipzig, 1931.

Beste, Udalricus, *Introductio in Codicem,* Collegeville: St. John's Abbey Press, 1938

Blat, Albertus, *Commentarium Textus Codicis Iuris Canonici,* 6 voll., 1921-1927.

Boich, Henricus, *In Quinque Decretalium Libros Commentaria,* Venetiis, 1576.

Bouix, D., *Tractatus de Curia Romana,* Parisiis, 1859.

Bouscaren T. Lincoln, *Canon Law Digest, Officially Published Documents Affecting the Code of Canon Law,* 2 vols., and supplement, Milwaukee: The Bruce Publishing Company, 1934-1938.

Brunnemannus, Johannes, *Commentarius in Codicem Iustinianeum,* 2 voll., Coloniae Allobrogum, 1771.

Buckland, W. W., *A Text-Book of Roman Law from Augustus to Justinian,* 2. ed., London: Cambridge University Press, 1932.

Caietanus, Felix Veranus, *Iuris Canonici Universi Commentarius Paratitlaris,* 3 voll., Monachii, 1703-1705.

Cappello, Felix, *Summa Iuris Canonici,* 2 voll., 2. ed., Romae: apud Aedes Universitatis Gregorianae, 1932.

Cappello, Felix, *De Curia Romana,* 2 voll., Romae, 1911-1912.

Chelodi, Ioannes, *Ius de Personis,* Tridenti: Libr. Edit., Tridentum, 1922.

Choupin, Lucien, *Valeur des Décision Doctrinales et Disciplinaires du Saint-Siège,* Paris, 1907; 3. ed., Paris: Gabriel Beauchesne, 1928.

Cicero, M. Tullius, *Scripta Quae Manserunt Omnia,* 5 voll., C. F. W. Mueller, Gulielmus Friedrich, Lipsiae: B. G. Teubner, 1893-1905.

Cicognani, Hamletus J., *Commentarium ad Librum I Codicis,* Romae: ex Schola Typographica "Pio X", 1925.

Cicognani, Amleto G., ***Canon Law***, authorized English translation, 2. ed., revised, Philadelphia: The Dolphin Press, 1935.

Coronata, Mattheus, Conte a, ***Institutiones Iuris Canonici***, 5 voll., [Vol. I, II, 2. ed.], Taurini: Ex offina Marietti, 1933-1939.

Crome, Carl, *Grundzüge des Römischen Privatrechts*, Bonn: A. Marcus & E. Webers Verlag, 1922.

Cuq, Edouard, *Les Institutions Juridiques des Romains*, 2 voll., Paris, 1891-1902.

Decianus, Tiberius, ***Responsa***, 3 voll., Venetiis, 1579.

Decius, Philippus, *In Decretales Commentaria*, Lugduni, 1576.

DeMeester, *Iuris Canonici et Iuris Canonico-Civilis Compendium*, nova ed., 4 voll., Brugis: Desclee, De Brouwer et Si, 1921-1928.

Devoti, Ioannes, *Institutionum Canonicarum Libri IV*, Vol. II, Leodii, 1860.

Fagnanus, Prosper, *Commentaria Super Quinque Libros Decretalium*, 5 voll., Romae, 1661.

Felinus Sandaeus, *Commentaria in V. Libros Decretalium*, 3 voll., Pars Prima, Tertia, Venetiis, 1570; *Felini Volumen Secundum*, [ ].

Gai Institutionum Commentarii Quattuor; 6. ed.,—B. Kuebler, Lipsiae: in Aedibus B. G. Teubneri, 1928.

Geny, Francois, *Méthode d'Interprétation et Sources en Droit Privé Positif*, 2 voll., 2. ed., Paris: Librairie Générale de Droit et de Jurisprudence, 1932.

Giacchi, Orio, *Formazione e Sviluppa della Dottrina della Interpretazione Autentica in Diritto Canonico*, Milano: Società Editrice "Vita e Pensiero", 1935.

Gonzalez-Tellez, Emanuel, *Commentaria Perpetua in Quinque Libros Decretalium*, 4 voll., Venetiis, 1766.

Haring, Johann B., *Grundzüge des Katolischen Kirchenrechtes*, 3te Aufl., Graz: Verlag von Ulrich Mosers Buchhandlung (J. Meyerhoff), 1924.

Hergenröther, Philipp, *Lehrbuch des Katolischen Kirchenrechts*, 2te Auflage von Dr. Joseph Hollweck, Freiburg i. Breisgau, 1905.

Hostiensis (Henricus de Segusio), *In Decretalium Commentaria*, 3 voll., Venetiis, 1581.

Hostiensis, *Summa Aurea*, Venetiis, 1570.

Iason Maynus, *In Digestum Commentaria*, 5 voll., Venetiis, 1589.

Iason Maynus, *In Codicem Commentaria*, 2 voll., Venetiis, 1589.

Ioannes Andreas, *In VI Libros Decretalium Novella Commentaria*, 5 voll., Venetiis, 1581.

Jaffé, Ph., *Regesta Romanorum Pontificum ab condita Ecclesia ad annum post Christum natum MCXCVIII*, Berolini, 1851.

Jolowicz, H. F., *Historical Introduction to the Study of Roman Law*, London: Cambridge University Press, 1932.

Jone, *Gesetzbuch des kanonischen Rechtes*, 2 voll., Paderborn: Ferdinand Schöningh, 1939-1940, (Vol. II: Kan. 726-Kan. 1551; Vol. III not published).

Jörs, Paul, *Geschichte und System des Römischen Privatrechts,* Berlin: Verlag von Julius Springer, 1927.

Karlowa, Otto, *Römische Rechtsgeschichte,* 2 voll., Leipzig, 1885-1901.

Keller, Paul, *Die "Normae Generales" des Codex iuris canonici,* Calw: A. Oelschlager'sche Buchdruckerei, 1923.

Kipp, Theodor, *Geschichte der Quellen des Römischen Rechts,* 4te Aufl., Leipzig-Erlangen: A. Deichert'sche Verlags-Buchhandlung, Dr. Werner Scholl, 1919.

Koeniger, Albert M., *Katholisches Kirchenrecht,* Freiburg im Breisgau: Herder & Co., 1926.

Krueger, Paul, *Histoire des Sources du Droit Romain,* Manuel des Antiquités Romaines, Mommsen-Marquardt-Krueger, Tome 16iéme, Paris, 1894.

Kuebler, Bernhard, *Geschichte des Römischen Rechts,* Leipzig-Erlangen. Deichert'sche Verlagsbuchhandlung, Dr. Werner Scholl, 1925.

Leage, R. W., *Roman Private Law founded on the 'Institutes' of Gaius and Justinian,* 2 ed., C. H. Ziegler, London: MacMillan and Co., Ltd., 1937.

Lega, Michael, *Praelectiones in Textum Iuris Canonici, De Iudiciis Ecclesiasticis,* Lib. I, Vol. II, Romae, 1898.

Lega-Bartoccetti, *Commentarius in Iudicia Ecclesiastica iuxta Codicem Iuris Canonici,* auctore Michaele Card. Lega, curante Vitorio Bartoccetti, 2 voll., Romae: Anonima Libraria Cattolica Italiana, 1938-1939.

Lemieux, Delisle A., *The Sentence in Ecclesiastical Procedure,* The Catholic University of America, Canon Law Studies, n. 87, New York: The Paulist Press, 1934.

Lobingier, Charles Sumner, *The Evolution of the Roman Law,* 2. ed., Published by the author, 1932.

Mareto, Philippus, *Institutiones Iuris Canonici ad Normam Novi Codicis,* 3. ed., Vol. I, Romae: apud Commentarium pro Relgiosis, 1921.

Maupied, Franciscus, *Iuris Canonici Universi Compendium,* 2 voll., Parisiis, 1863.

Mayr, Robert von, *Römische Rechtsgeschichte,* Sammlung Göschen, 4 voll., Leipzig, 1912-1913.

Michiels, Gommarus, *Normae Generales Iuris Canonici,* 2 voll., Lublin, Polonia: Universitas Catholica, 1929.

Mitteis, Ludwig, *Römisches Privatrecht,* Leipzig, 1908.

Mitteis-Levy-Rabel, *Index Interpollationum Quae in Iustiniani Digestis inesse dicuntur,* 3 voll., Weimar: Hermann Böhlaus Nachfolger, 1929-1935.

Monin, Arthur, *De Curia Romana, iuxta Reformationem a Pio X Inductam,* Lovanii, 1912.

Mothon, Joseph Pie, *Institutions Canoniques,* 3 voll., Paris: Desclée, de Brouwer & Cie, 1922-1924.

Muirhead, James, *Historical Introduction to the Private Law of Rome,* 3. ed., London, 1916.

Müller, Alphons Victor, *Papst und Kurie,* Gotha: Friedrich Andreas Perthes, A.-G., 1921.

Neuberger, Nicholas J., *Canon 6, or The Relation of the Codex Iuris Canonici to Preceding Legislation,* The Catholic University of America, Canon Law Studies, n. 44, Washington: The Catholic University of America, 1927.

Noval, Josephus P., *Commentarium Iuris Canonici, De Processibus,* 2 voll., Romae, 1920.

Ojetti, B., *De Romana Curia,* Romae, 1910.

Ottaviani, Alaphridus, *Institutiones Iuris Publici Ecclesiastici,* 2 voll., Typis Polyglottis Vaticanis, 1935-1936.

Panormitanus, Abbas (Nicolaus de Tudeschis), *Omnia Quae Extant Commentaria in Decretales,* 6 voll., Venetiis, 1588.

Passerini, Petrus Maria, *Commentaria in Sextum Librum Decretalium,* 2 voll., Venetiis, 1698.

Paulus Castrensis (de Castro), *In Digestum Patavinae Praelectiones,* 5 voll., Lugduni, 1553.

Perathoner, Anton, *Das Kirchliche Gesetzbuch,* 3. ed., Brixen, A. Weger's Buchhandlung, 1923.

Pichler, Vitus, *Ius Canonicum secundum Quinque Decretalium Titulos Explicatum,* 2 voll., Ravennae, 1741.

Pirhing, Ernricus, *Ius Canonicum in V Libris Decretalium,* 4 voll., Dilingae, 1722.

Prierias, Sylvester (Muzolinus Sabaudus), *Summae Sylvestrinae,* 2 voll., Venetiis, 1601.

Puchta, G. F., *Cursus der Institutionen,* 4te Aufl. 3 voll., Dr. A. Rudorff, Leipzig, 1853.

Reiffenstuel, Anacletus, *Ius Canonicum Universum,* ed., novissima, 5 voll., Romae, 1831-1833.

Reiffenstuel, Anacletus, *Tractatus de Regulis Iuris,* Romae, 1834.

Sägmüller, Johannes Baptist, *Lehrbuch des Katholischen Kirchenrechts,* 4te Aufl., Vol. I, 4 Hefte, Freiburg i. Breisgau: Herder & Co., 1925-1935.

Sanguineti, Sebastiano, *Iuris Ecclesiastici Privati Institutiones,* Romae, 1884

Santi, Franciscus, *Praelectiones Iuris Canonici,* 2 voll., Romae, 1886.

Sartori, Cosmas, *Enchiridion Canonicum, seu Sanctae Sedis Responsiones post editum Codicem I. C. datae iuxta Canonum Codicis ordinem digestae notulisque ornatae,* 6. ed., (1917-1938), Vicetiae: ex Typographia Commerciali, 1938.

Schmalzgrueber, Franciscus, *Ius Ecclesiasticum Universum,* 12 voll., Romae, 1834-1845.

Schmier, Franciscus, *Jurisprudentia Canonico-Civilis seu Ius Canonicum Universum,* 2 voll., Venetiis, 1754.

Sebastianelli, Guilelmo, *Praelectiones Iuris Canonici,* 2. ed., 3 voll. Romae, 1905-1906.

Sherman, Charles Phineas, *Roman Law in the Modern World,* 2. ed., 3 vols., New York: Baker, Voorhis, & Co., 1924.

Sipos, Stephanus, *Enchiridion Iuris Canonici,* Pécs: ex Typographia "Haladás R. T.", 1926.

Sohm, *The Institutes, A Textbook of the History and System of Roman Private Law,* transl., by J. C. Ledlie, Oxford: Clarendon Press, 1926.

Sohm-Mitteis-Wenger, *Institutionen, Geschichte und System des Römischen Privatrechts,* München-Leipzig: Verlag von Duncker & Humbolt, 1930.

Suarez, Franciscus, *Tractatus de Legibus et Legislatore Deo* Voll., V. VI, Parisiis, 1856.

Toso, Albertus, *Ad Codicem Iuris Canonici Commentaria Minora,* 2 voll., Tiferni Tiberini: ex Offic. Typogr. Vinciana, 1921.

Tuschus, Dominicus, *Practicae Conclusiones Iuris in omni foro frequentiores,* 8 voll., Lugduni, 1634; *Additiones,* Vol. IX, Lugduni, 1670.

Van Hove, A., *Commentarium Lovaniense in Codicem Iuris Canonici,* Vol. I, *Prolegomena,* Mechliniae: H. Dessain, 1928; Vol. II, *De Legibus Ecclesiasticis,* Mechliniae: H. Dessain, 1930; Vol. IV, *De Rescriptis,* Mechliniae: H. Dessain, 1936.

Vecchiotti, Septimius M., *Institutiones Canonicae,* 3 voll., Augustae Taurinorum, 1875.

Vermeersch, A.,-Creusen, J., *Epitome Iuris Canonici,* 3 voll., Mechliniae: H. Dessain, Vol. I, 3. ed., 1927, 6. ed., 1937; Vol. II, 5. ed., 1934; Vol. III, 5. ed., 1936.

Wernz, F. X., *Ius Decretalium,* Vol. I, 2. ed., Romae, 1905, 3. ed., Prati, 1913; Vol. V, Prati, 1914.

Wernz, F. X.,-Vidal, Petrus, *Ius Canonicum,* 8 voll., Romae: apud Aedes Universitatis Gregorianae, 1927-1938.

Zallinger, Iac. Ant., *Institutiones Iuris Ecclesiastici,* 3 voll., Romae, 1823.

Articles

Boudinhon, A., "La Commission Pour L'Interprétation Officielle du Code"—*Le Canoniste Contemporain,* XL (1917), 397-399.

Brems, A., "De Interpretatione Authentica Codicis I. C. Per Pont. Commissionem,"—*Ius Pontificium,* XV (1935), 161-190; 298-313; XVI (1936), 78-105; 217-256.

Hilling, N., "Gesetzgeberische Tätigkeit Benedikts XV seit der Promulgation des CIC,"—*Archiv für Katholisches Kirchenrecht,* CIII (1923), 9.

Hilling, N., "Zum zehnjährigen Jubiläum des CIC,"—*Archiv für Katholisches Kirchenrecht,* CVIII (1928), 392.

Hilling, N., "Zur Promulgation des Codex iuris canonici,"—*Archiv für Katholisches Kirchenrecht,* XIIC (1918), 82.

Maroto, Ph, "Adnotationes," (Ad *Motum proprium, "Cum iuris canonici"*), —*Commentarium pro Religiosis,* I (1920), 34-45.

Periodicals

Apollinaris, Romae, 1928—

Archiv für Katholisches Kirchenrecht, Innsburck, 1857-1861; Mainz, 1862—

Australasian Catholic Record, The, Manly, 1923—
Canoniste Contemporain, Le, Paris, 1878—
Clergy Review, The, London, 1931—
Collationes Brugenses, Bruges, 1895—
Commentarium pro Religiosis (later *Commentarium pro Religiosis et Missionariis*), Romae, 1920—
Ecclesiastical Review, The (originally *The American Ecclesiastical Review*), Philadelphia, 1889—
Ephemerides Theologicae Lovanienses, Lovanii, 1924—
Homiletic and Pastoral Review, The, New York, 1900—
Irish Ecclesiastical Record, The, Dublin, 1864—
Ius Pontificium, Romae, 1921—
Jurist, The, Washington, D. C., 1941—
Periodica de Re Canonica et Morali utili Praesertim Religiosis et Missionariis, Bruges, 1905—
Theologische Quartalschrift, Tübingen, 1819—
Theologisch-Praktische Quartalschrift, Linz, 1832—
Zeitschrift der Savigny-Stiftung für Rechtsgeschichte, Kanonistische, Abteilung, Weimar, 1911—

BIOGRAPHICAL NOTE

John Rogg Schmidt was born on November 1, 1908, in Freiburg im Breisgau, province of Baden, Germany. His primary education was received in St. Nicholas Parochial School, Wilkes-Barre, Pennsylvania. In September of 1922 he was admitted to the Pontifical College Josephinum, at that time located in Columbus, Ohio, where he began his preparatory studies for the priesthood. In June, 1928, he received the Degree of Bachelor of Arts in the classical languages of Latin and Greek. The following September he entered the Seminary department of the same institution, where he completed his ecclesiastical studies and was ordained to the priesthood on May 26, 1934. Hereupon he took his departure for the service of the Diocese of Amarillo, Texas, into which he had been incardinated. In September of 1938, he was admitted to graduate studies in the School of Canon Law of the Catholic University of America, Washington, D. C. He received the Baccalaureate in Canon Law in June, 1939, and the Licentiate in Canon Law in June, 1940.

ALPHABETICAL INDEX

CANON LAW STUDIES

1. Freriks, Rev. Celestine A., C.PP.S., J.C.D., Religious Congregations in Their External Relations, 121 pp., 1916.
2. Galliher, Rev. Daniel M., O.P., J.C.D., Canonical Elections, 117 pp., 1917.
3. Borkowski, Rev. Aurelius L., O.F.M., J.C.D., De Confraternitatibus Ecclesiasticis, 136 pp., 1918.
4. Castillo, Rev. Cayo, J.C.D., Disertacion Historico-Canonica sobre la Potestad del Cabildo en Sede Vacante o Impedida del Vicario Capitular, 99 pp., 1919 (1918).
5. Kubelbeck, Rev. William J., S.T.B., J.C.D., The Sacred Pentitentiaria and Its Relations to Faculties of Ordinaries and Priests, 129 pp., 1918.
6. Petrovits, Rev. Joseph, J.C., S.T.D., J.C.D., The New Church Law On Matrimony, X-461 pp., 1919.
7. Hickey, Rev. John J., S.T.B., J.C.D., Irregularities and Simple Impediments in the New Code of Canon Law, 100 pp., 1920.
8. Klekotka, Rev. Peter J., S.T.B., J.C.D., Diocesan Consultors, 179 pp., 1920.
9. Wanenmacher, Rev. Francis, J.C.D., The Evidence in Ecclesiastical Procedure Affecting the Marriage Bond, 1920 (Printed 1935).
10. Golden, Rev. Henry Francis, J.C.D., Parochial Benefices in the New Code, IV-119 pp., 1921 (Printed 1925).
11. Koudelka, Rev. Charles J., J.C.D., Pastors, Their Rights and Duties According to the New Code of Canon Law, 211 pp., 1921.
12. Melo, Rev. Antonius, O.F.M., J.C.D., De Exemptione Regularium, X-188 pp., 1921.
13. Schaaf, Rev. Valentine Theodore, O.F.M., S.T.B., J.C.D., The Cloister, X-180 pp., 1921.
14. Burke, Rev. Thomas Joseph, S.T.D., J.C.D., Competence in Ecclesiastical Tribunals, IV-117 pp., 1922.
15. Leech, Rev. George Leo, J.C.D., A Comparative Study of the Constitution, "Apostolicae Sedis" and the "Codex Juris Canonici," 179 pp., 1922.
16. Motry, Rev. Hubert Louis, S.T.D., J.C.D., Diocesan Faculties According to the Code of Canon Law, II-167 pp., 1922.
17. Murphy, Rev. George Lawrence, J.C.D., Delinquencies and Penalties in the Administration and Reception of the Sacraments, IV-121 pp., 1923.

18. O'Reilly, Rev. John Anthony, S.T.B., J.C.D., Ecclesiastical Sepulture in the New Code of Canon Law, II-129 pp., 1923.
19. Michalicka, Rev. Wenceslas Cyrill, O.S.B., J.C.D., Judicial Procedure in Dismissal of Clerical Exempt Religious, 107 pp., 1923.
20. Dargin, Rev. Edward Vincent, S.T.B., J.C.D., Reserved Cases According to the Code of Canon Law, IV-103, pp., 1924.
21. Godfrey, Rev. John A., S.T.B., J.C.D., The Right of Patronage According to the Code of Canon Law, 153 pp., 1924.
22. Hagedorn, Rev. Francis Edward, J.C.D., General Legislation on Indulgences, II-154 pp., 1924.
23. King, Rev. James Ignatius, J.C.D., The Administration of the Sacraments to Dying Non-Catholics, V-141 pp., 1924.
24. Winslow, Rev. Francis Joseph, A.F.M., J.C.D., Vicars and Prefects Apostolic, IV-149 pp., 1924.
25. Correa, Rev. Jose Servelion, S.T.L., J.C.D., La Potestad Legislativa de la Iglesia Catolica, IV-127 pp., 1925.
26. Dugan, Rev. Henry Francis, A.M., J.C.D., The Judiciary Department of the Diocesan Curia, 87 pp., 1925.
27. Keller, Rev. Charles Frederick, S.T.B., J.C.D., Mass Stipends, 167 pp., 1925.
28. Paschang, Rev. John Linus, J.C.D., The Sacramentals According to the Code of Canon Law, 129 pp., 1925.
29. Pointek, Rev. Cyrillus, O.F.M., S.T.B., J.C.D., De Indulto Exclaustrationis necnon Saecularizationis, XIII-289 pp., 1925.
30. Kearney, Rev. Richard Joseph, S.T.B., J.C.D., Sponsors at Baptism According to the Code of Canon Law, IV-127 pp., 1925.
31. Bartlett, Rev. Chester Joseph, A.M., LL.B., J.C.D., The Tenure of Parochial Property in the United States of America, V-108 pp., 1926.
32. Kilker, Rev. Adrian Jerome, J.C.D., Extreme Unction, V-425 pp., 1926.
33. McCormick, Rev. Robert Emmett, J.C.D., Confessors of Religious, VIII-266 pp., 1926.
34. Miller, Rev. Newton Thomas, J.C.D., Founded Masses According to the Code of Canon Law, VII-93 pp., 1926.
35. Roelker, Rev. Edward G., S.T.D., J.C.D., Principles of Privilege According to the Code of Canon Law, XI-166 pp., 1926.
36. Bakalarczyk, Rev. Richardus, M.I.C., J.U.D., De Novitiatu, VIII-208 pp., 1927.
37. Pizzuti, Rev. Lawrence, O.F.M., J.U.L., De Parochis Religiosis, 1927. (Not printed).
38. Bliley, Rev. Nicholas Martin, O.S.B., J.C.D., Altars According to the Code of Canon Law, XIX-132 pp., 1927.
39. Brown, Mr. Brendan Francis, A.B. LL.M., J.U.D., The Canonical Juristic Personality with Special Reference to Its Status in the United States of America, V-212 pp., 1927.

40. Cavanaugh, Rev. William Thomas, C.P., J.U.D., The Reservation of the Blessed Sacrament, VIII-101 pp., 1927.
41. Doheny, Rev. William J., C.S.C., A.B., J.U.D., Church Property: Modes of Acquisition, X-118 pp., 1927.
42. Feldhaus, Rev. Aloysius H., C.PP.S., J.C.D., Oratories, IX-141 pp., 1927.
43. Kelly, Rev. James Patrick, A.B., J.C.D., The Jurisdiction of the Simple Confessor, X-208 pp., 1927.
44. Neuberger, Rev. Nicholas J., J.C.D., Canon 6 or the Relation of the Codex Juris Canonici to the Preceding Legislation, V-95 pp., 1927.
45. O'Keefe, Rev. Gerald Michael, J.C.D., Matrimonial Dispensations, Powers of Bishops, Priests and Confessors, VIII-232 pp., 1927.
46. Quigley, Rev. Joseph, A.M., A.B., J.C.D., Condemned Societies, 139 pp., 1927.
47. Zaplotnik, Rev. Johannes Leo, J.C.D., De Vicariis Foraneis, X-142 pp., 1927.
48. Duskie, Rev. John Aloysius, A.B., J.C.D., The Canonical Status of the Orientials in the United States, VIII-196 pp., 1928.
49. Hyland, Rev. Francis Edward, J.C.D., Excommunication, Its Nature, Historical Development and Effects, VIII-181 pp., 1928.
50. Reinmann, Rev. Gerald Joseph, O.M.C., J.C.D., The Third Order Secular of Saint Francis, 201 pp., 1928.
51. Schenk, Rev. Francis J., J.C.D., The Matrimonial Impediments of Mixed Religion and Disparity of Cult, XVI-318 pp., 1929.
52. Coady, Rev. John Joseph, S.T.D., J.U.D., A.M., The Appointment of Pastors, VIII-150 pp., 1929.
53. Kay, Rev. Thomas Henry, J.C.D., Competence in Matrimonial Procedure, VIII-164 pp., 1929.
54. Turner, Rev. Sidney Joseph, C.P., J.U.D., The Vow of Poverty, XLIX-217 pp., 1929.
55. Kearney, Rev. Raymond, A., A.B., S.T.D., J.C.D., The Principles of Delegation, VII-149 pp., 1929.
56. Conran, Rev. Edward James, A.B., J.C.D., The Interdict, V-163 pp., 1930.
57. O'Neil, Rev. William H., J.C.D., Papal Rescripts of Favor, VII-218 pp., 1930.
58. Bastnagel, Rev. Clement Vincent, J.U.D., The Appointment of Parochial Adjutants and Assistants, XV-257 pp., 1930.
59. Ferry, Rev. William A., A.B., J.C.D., Stole Fees, V-135 pp., 1930.
60. Costello, Rev. John Michael, A.B., J.C.D., Domicile and Quasidomicile, VII-201 pp., 1930.
61. Kremer, Rev. Michael Nicholas, A.B., S.T.B., J.C.D., Church Support in the United States, VI-1930.
62. Angulo, Rev. Luis, C.M., J.C.D., Legislation de la Iglesia sobre la intencion en la application de la Santa Misa, VII-104 pp., 1931.
63. Frey, Rev. Wolfgang Norbert, O.S.B., A.B., J.C.D., The Act of Religious Profession, VIII-174 pp., 1931.

64. Roberts, Rev. James Brendan, A.B., J.C.D., The Banns of Marriage, XIV-140 pp., 1931.
65. Ryder, Rev. Raymond Aloysius, A.B., J.C.D., Simony, IX-151 pp., 1931.
66. Campagna, Rev. Angelo, Ph.D., J.U.D., Il Vicario Generale del Vescovo, VII-205 pp., 1931.
67. Cox, Rev. Joseph Godfrey, A.B., J.C.D., The Administration of Seminaries, VI-124 pp., 1931.
68. Gregory, Rev. Donald J., J.U.D., The Pauline Privilege, XV-165 pp., 1931.
69. Donohue, Rev. John F., J.C.D., The Impediment of Crime, VII-110 pp., 1931.
70. Dooley, Rev. Eugene A., O.M.I., J.C.D., Church Law On Sacred Relics, IX-143 pp., 1931.
71. Orth, Rev. Raymond Clement, O.M.C., J.C.D., The Approbation of Religious Institutes, 171 pp., 1931.
72. Pernicone, Rev. Joseph M., A.B., J.C.D., The Ecclesiastical Prohibition of Books, XII-267 pp., 1932.
73. Clinton, Rev. Connell, A.B., J.C.D., The Paschal Precept, IX-108 pp., 1932.
74. Donnelly, Rev. Francis B., A.M., S.T.L., J.C.D., The Diocesan Synod, VIII-125 pp., 1932.
75. Torrente, Rev. Camilo, C.M.F., J.C.D., Las Procesiones Sagradas, V-145 pp., 1932.
76. Murphy, Rev. Edwin J., C.PP.S., J.C.D., Suspension Ex Informata Conscientia, XI-122, pp., 1932.
77. Mackenzie, Rev. Eric F., A.M., S.T.L., J.C.D., The Delict of Heresy in its Commission, Penalization, Absolution, VII-124 pp., 1932.
78. Lyons Rev. Avitus E., S.T.B., J.C.D., The Collegiate Tribunal of First Instance, XI-147 pp., 1932.
79. Connolly, Rev. Thomas A., J.C.D., Appeals, XI-195 pp., 1932.
80. Sangmeister, Rev. Joseph V., A.B., J.C.D., Force and Fear as Precluding Matrimonial Consent, V-211 pp., 1932.
81. Jaeger, Rev. Leo A., A.B., J.C.D., The Administration of Vacant and Quasi-vacant Episcopal Sees in the United States, IX-119 pp., 1932.
82. Rimlinger, Rev. Herbert T., J.C.D., Error Invalidating Matrimonial Consent, VII-79 pp., 1932.
83. Barrett, Rev. John D. M., S.S., J.C.D., A Comparative Study of the Third Plenary Council of Baltimore and the Code, IX-221 pp., 1932.
84. Carberry, Rev. John J., Ph.D., S.T.D., J.C.D., The Juridical Form of Marriage, X-177 pp., 1934.
85. Dolan, Rev. John L., A.B., J.C.D., The Defensor Vinculi, XII-157 pp., 1934.
86. Hannan, Rev. Jerome D., A.M., S.T.D., LL.B., J.C.D., The Canon Law of Wills, IX-517 pp., 1934.

87. Lemieux, Rev. Delisle A., A.M., J.C.D., The Sentence in Ecclesiastical Procedure, IX-131 pp., 1934.
88. O'Rourke, Rev. James J., A.B., J.C.D., Parish Registers, VII-109 pp., 1934.
89. Timlin, Rev. Bartholomew, O.F.M., A.M., J.C.D., Conditional Matrimonial Consent, X-381 pp., 1934.
90. Wahl, Rev. Francis X., A.B., J.C.D., The Matrimonial Impediments of Consanguinity and Affinity, VI-125 pp., 1934.
91. White, Rev. Robert J., A.B., LL.B., S.T.B., J.C.D., Canonical Ante-Nuptial Promises and the Civil Law, VI-152 pp., 1934.
92. Herrera, Rev. Antonio Parra, O.C.D., J.C.D., Legislation Ecclesiastica sobra el Ayuno y la Abstinencia, XI-191 pp., 1935.
93. Kennedy, Rev. Edwin J., J.C.D., The Special Matrimonial Process in Cases of Evident Nullity, X-165 pp., 1935.
94. Manning, Rev. John J., A.B., J.C.D., Presumption of Law in Matrimonial Procedure, XI-111 pp., 1935.
95. Moeder, Rev. John M., J.C.D., The Proper Bishop for Ordination and Dismissorial Letters, VII-135 pp., 1935.
96. O'Mara, Rev. William A., A.B., J.C.D., Canonical Causes for Matrimonial Dispensations, IX-155 pp. 1935.
97. Reilly, Rev. Peter, J.C.D., Residence of Pastors, IX-81 pp., 1935.
98. Smith, Rev. Mariner T., O.P., S.T.L., J.C.D., The Penal Law For Religious, VII-169 pp., 1935.
99. Whalen, Rev. Donald W., A.M., J.C.D., The Value of Testimonial Evidence in Matrimonial Procedure, XIII-297 pp., 1935.
100. Cleary, Rev. Joseph F., J.C.D., Canonical Limitations on the Alienation of Church Property, VIII-141 pp., 1936.
101. Glynn, Rev. John C., J.C.D., The Promoter of Justice, XX-337 pp., 1936.
102. Brennan, Rev. James H., S.S., A.M., S.T.B., J.C.D., The Simple Convalidation of Marriage, VI-125 pp., 1937.
103. Brunini, Rev. Joseph Bernard, J.C.D., The Clerical Obligations of Canons, 139 and 142, X-121 pp., 1937.
104. Connor, Rev. Maurice, A.B., J.C.D., The Administrative Removal of Pastors, VIII-159 pp., 1937.
105. Guilfoyle, Rev. Merlin Joseph, J.C.D., Custom, XI-144 pp., 1937.
106. Hughes, Rev. James Austin, A.B., A.M., J.C.D., Witnesses in Criminal Trials of Clerics, IX-140 pp., 1937.
107. Jansen, Rev. Raymond J., A.B., S.T.L., J.C.D., Canonical Provisions for Catechetical Instruction, VII-153 pp., 1937.
108. Kealy, Rev. John James, A.B., J.C.D., The Introductory Libellus in Church Court Procedure, XI-121 pp., 1937.
109. McManus, Rev. James Edward, C.SS.R., J.C.D., The Administration of Temporal Goods in Religious Institutes, XVI-196 pp., 1937.
110. Moriarity, Rev. Eugene James, J.C.D., Oaths in Ecclesiastical Courts, X-115 pp., 1937.

111. Rainer, Rev. Eligius George C.SS.R., J.C.D., Suspension of Clerics, XVII-249 pp., 1937.
112. Reilly, Rev. Thomas F., C.SS.R., J.C.D., Visitation of Religious, VI-195 pp., 1938.
113. Moriarty, Rev. Francis E., C.SS.R., J.C.D., The Extraordinary Absolution from Censures, XV-334 pp., 1938.
114. Connolly, Rev. Nicholas P., J.C.D., The Canonical Erection of Parishes, X-132 pp., 1938.
115. Donovan, Rev. James Joseph, J.C.D., The Pastor's Obligation in Prenuptial Investigation, XII-322 pp., 1938.
116. Harrigan, Rev, Robert J., M.A., S.T.B., J.C.D., The Radical Sanation of Invalid Marriages, VIII-208 pp., 1938.
117. Boffa, Rev. Conrad Humbert, J.C.D., Canonical Provisions for Catholic Schools, X-211 pp. 1939.
118. Parsons, Rev. Anscar John, O.M. Cap., J.C.D., Canonical Elections, XII-236 pp., 1939.
119. Reilly, Rev. Edward Michael, A.B., J.C.D., The General Norms of Dispensation, X-156 pp., 1939.
120. Ryan, Rev. Gerald Aloysius, A.B., J.C.D., Principles of Episcopal Jurisdiction, XII-172 pp., 1939.
121. Burton, Rev. Francis James, C.S.C., A.B., J.C.D., A Commentary on Canon 1125, X-222 pp., 1940.
122. Miaskiewicz, Rev. Francis Sigismund, J.C.D., Supplied Jurisdiction According to Canon 209, XII-340 pp., 1940.
123. Rice, Rev. Patrick William, A.B., J.C.D., Proof of Death in Prenuptial Investigation, VIII-156 pp., 1940.
124. Anglin, Rev. Thomas Francis, M.S., J.C.L., The Eucharistic Fast.
125. Coleman, Rev. John Jerome, J.C.L., The Minister of Confirmation.
126. Downs, Rev. John Emmanuel, A.B., J.C.L., The Concept of Clerical Immunity.
127. Esswein, Rev. Anthony Albert, J.C.L., Extrajudicial Penal Powers of Ecclesiastical Superiors.
128. Farrell, Rev. Benjamin Francis, M.A., S.T.L., J.C.L., The Rights and Duties of the Local Ordinary Regarding Congregations of Women Religious of Pontifical Approval.
129. Feeney, Rev. Thomas John, A.B., S.T.L., J.C.L., Restitutio in Integrum,
130. Findley, Rev. Stephen William, O.S.B., A.B., J.C.L., Canonical Norms Governing the Deposition and Degradation of Clerics.
131. Goodwine, Rev. John, A.B., S.T.L., J.C.L., The Right of the Church to Acquire Property.
132. Heston, Rev. Edward Louis, C.S.C., Ph.D., S.T.D., J.C.L., The Alienation of Church Property in the United States.
133. Hogan, Rev. James John., S.T.L., J.C.L., Judicial Advocates and Procurators

134. Kealy, Rev. Thomas M., A.B., Litt.B., J.C.L., Dowry of Women Religious.
135. Keene, Rev. Michael James, O.S.B., J.C.L., Religious Ordinaries and Canon 198.
136. Kerin, Rev. Charles A., S.S., M.A., S.T.B., J.C.L., The Privation of Christian Burial.
137. Louis, Rev. William Francis, M.A., J.C.L., Diocesan Archives.
138. McDevitt, Rev. Gilbert Joseph, A.B., J.C.L., Legitimacy and Legitimation.
139. McDonough, Rev. Thomas Joseph, A.B., J.C.L., Apostolic Administrators.
140. Meier, Rev. Carl Anthony, A.B., J.C.L., Penal Administrative Procedure Against Negligent Pastors.
141. Schmidt, Rev. John Rogg, A.B., J.C.L., The Principles of Authentic Interpretation in Canon 17 of the Code of Canon Law.
142. Slafkosky, Rev. Andrew Leonard, A.B., J.C.L., The Canonical Episcopal Visitation of the Diocese.
143. Swoboda, Rev. Innocent Robert, O.F.M., J.C.L., Ignorance in Relation to the Imputability of Delicts.
144. Dubé, Rev. Arthur Joseph, A.B., J.C.L., The General Principles for the Reckoning of Time in Canon Law.
145. McBride, Rev. James T., A.B., J.C.L., Incardination and Excardination of Seculars.

www.ingramcontent.com/pod-product-compliance
Lightning Source LLC
LaVergne TN
LVHW050258080826
844660LV00012B/656

* 9 7 8 0 8 1 3 2 2 3 3 0 8 *